THE EDUCATOR'S GUIDE TO TEXAS SCHOOL LAW

EIGHTH EDITION

The Educator's Guide to Texas School Law

EIGHTH EDITION

by Jim Walsh,
 Frank Kemerer, and
 Laurie Maniotis

 University of Texas Press, Austin

Requests for permission to reproduce material from this work
should be sent to:
    Permissions
    University of Texas Press
    P.O. Box 7819
    Austin, TX 78713-7819
    http://utpress.utexas.edu/index.php/rp-form

♾ The paper used in this book meets the minimum requirements
of ANSI/NISO Z39.48-1992 (R1997) (Permanence of Paper).

Library of Congress Cataloging-in-Publication Data

Walsh, Jim, 1950– author.
    The educator's guide to Texas school law / by Jim Walsh, Frank
Kemerer, and Laurie Maniotis. — Eighth Edition.
        pages   cm
    Includes bibliographical references and index.
    ISBN 978-0-292-76084-4 (pbk. : alk. paper)
    1. Educational law and legislation—Texas.   2. Educators—
Legal status, laws, etc.—Texas.   I. Kemerer, Frank R., author.
II. Maniotis, Laurie, author.   III. Title.
    KFT1590.K45   2014
    344.764'07—dc23
                                                    2014012272

doi:10.7560/760837

To Caroline, Melody, Elise, Claire, Carly, Sander, and Lyla

Contents

Appendixes

Index of Cases

Index of Topics

Tables

Figures

Preface

ONCE AGAIN, the ever-changing nature of the laws affecting public school districts has necessitated a new edition of *The Educator's Guide to Texas School Law*. In this Eighth Edition we have attempted to cull through and eliminate older case law in an effort to provide you the latest and most up-to-date information from the federal and state courts. This edition also highlights significant revisions of the Texas Education Code brought about by the last several sessions of the Texas Legislature, including major changes to the laws pertaining to student assessment and school district accountability. The new laws reflect the efforts of the state to reduce the standardized testing required for graduation while still complying with the mandates of the No Child Left Behind Act, which at the time of this writing is up for reauthorization. The state legislature also substantially revised the laws concerning the granting and revocation of charters.

The book begins with a discussion of the legal structure of the Texas school system and describes the relationships among federal and state constitutional, statutory, administrative, and judicial law. A basic understanding of this legal framework is helpful to the reader before moving on to the other sections. The book then goes on to discuss several major topics affecting public school districts, including religion in the schools, freedom of speech, employment issues, student discipline, special education, and privacy concerns related to both students and employees. The book illustrates the challenge that modern technology presents in many of these areas, such as the extent to which a school district can take action pertaining to an employee or student's electronic communications. The Eighth Edition also adds a new section on bullying, which has come to the forefront in public education as a result of tragic, high-profile cases. The book ends with a discussion of liability concerns for school districts and educators.

This book is intended for all Texas school personnel, school board members, attorneys, parents, and taxpayers. Our goal is to explain in lay language what the law is and what the implications are for effective school operations. We aim to help professional educators avoid expensive and time-consuming lawsuits by taking effective preventive action. We believe this book is an especially valuable resource for school law courses and staff development sessions.

Statute and case references are kept as simple as possible, but a complete index of case citations is included for those readers who wish to consult the cases themselves. The appendices describe how case law is reported, provide a glossary of legal terms, and list other sources on Texas school law, including online resources.

Please note that this book is intended to furnish accurate information regarding the subject matter covered. It is published with the understanding that neither the authors nor the publisher is rendering legal advice. If specific legal advice or assistance is required, the services of a competent professional should be sought.

In closing, the authors would like to thank the staff at the University of Texas Press for the continued support of this project ever since Frank Kemerer initially presented the idea and authored the First Edition in 1986. The authors also are grateful to Scott Stalnaker, paralegal at Walsh, Anderson, Gallegos, Green and Trevino, P.C., for his invaluable assistance in updating the Index of Cases. Finally, the authors would like to thank their families and colleagues for their endless patience, encouragement, and support throughout the drafting and preparation of the Eighth Edition.

Both the University of Texas Press and we as authors are gratified by the wide acceptance accorded *The Educator's Guide* through the years as an authoritative and comprehensive source on Texas school law. We hope the education community will find this new Eighth Edition a valuable professional resource.

JIM WALSH
FRANK KEMERER
LAURIE MANIOTIS

EDUCATOR'S GUIDE TO TEXAS SCHOOL LAW

EIGHTH EDITION

ONE

An Overview of Education Law, Texas Schools, and Parent Rights

IN THIS CHAPTER, we examine the basic legal framework of school law in Texas. We begin by discussing the sources of school law and then describe the roles of the state and federal governments in the establishment and operation of the Texas school system. We examine the functioning of the State Board of Education, the Texas Education Agency, local school districts, private schools, and charter schools. And we discuss the responsibilities of school administrators and the functioning of site-based management. Later sections look at important federal laws affecting the operation of Texas schools and review the long-running controversy over the financing of Texas schools. The chapter ends by examining parent rights in the context of public schools, private schools, and home schooling.

SOURCES OF LAW

Constitutional Law

Since power over education is not specifically delegated to the federal government by the U.S. Constitution, it is a state function. The Tenth Amendment to the Constitution declares that all powers not delegated to the federal government are reserved to the states. This amendment gives state governments their traditional power over schools. Viewing the school as an important socialization device, states gradually expanded public education in the nineteenth century. By 1918 all states had compulsory school laws.

When a state decides to provide public education, as all the states have done, it has established an important benefit, which, as we will see later, it cannot take away from students without following due process procedures. Consistent with the Tenth Amendment, the Texas Constitution of 1876 established the legal basis for a public school system in the state. Section I of Article VII reads: "A general diffusion of knowledge being essential to the preservation of the liberties and rights of the people, it shall be the duty of the legislature of the State to establish and make suitable provision for the support and maintenance of an efficient system of free public schools." The Texas school finance litigation centers on whether a finance system resulting in substantial interdistrict disparities is "efficient" within the meaning of this constitutional provision.

Since the mid-1960s, the Bill of Rights and the Fourteenth Amendment to the U.S. Constitution also have furnished a basis for litigation against public schools. Claims to freedom of speech, press, religion, and association; due process; and other rights have a constitutional basis, just as the state's power to establish and operate schools stems from the Constitution. The Bill of Rights of the Texas Constitution protects many of these same civil liberties. Constitutional law at both the federal and state levels thus is an important source of education law.

Statutory Law

A *statute* is a law enacted by a legislative body. Most of the statutes passed by the Texas Legislature that directly affect education are grouped together in the Texas Education Code (TEC). The Code is an important source of law because it applies to the daily operation of schools, detailing the responsibilities and duties of the State Board of Education (SBOE), the Texas Education Agency (TEA), school boards, charter schools, and school personnel.

Beginning in the early 1980s, the Texas Legislature began taking an increasing interest in improving an educational system that it regarded as deficient. The result has been a plethora of reform laws, which initially were top-down in nature. By the late 1980s, the legislature began shifting authority and responsibility back to school districts and district personnel in the face of evidence that top-down mandates were having only marginal, if not negative, effects on increasing educational quality. In 1995 the legislature embarked on a complete reworking of the Texas Education Code—the first major overhaul since 1949. Not only did the legislature produce a more systematic, readable code, it took the opportunity to change, and in some cases streamline, many features of the Texas schooling system. The legislature significantly downsized TEA, gave local districts and school personnel more independence, and provided parents with more authority over the education of their children. It also expanded parent options through the establishment of charter schools.

Many other state statutes besides the Texas Education Code affect the activities of local schools, and we will discuss them in the succeeding chapters. One point worth emphasizing now is that, despite their essentially local character, public school districts are governed by the state. The present system of some 1,200 Texas school districts and over 9,000 individual school campuses could be changed should the legislature desire, given the latter's authority over public education under the Texas Constitution.

Federal statutes also have significant influence over the operation of public schools in the state. Some of the more important are described later in this chapter. Since the power to establish and operate schools is not one that the U.S. Constitution delegates to the federal government, most federal laws affecting education are passed pursuant to the Congress's power to collect taxes and spend for the general welfare. As the late Supreme Court Justice William O. Douglas noted in a famous case, *Lau v. Nichols* (1974), "the Federal Government has power to fix the terms on which its money allotments . . . shall be disbursed" (p. 569). Thus, these laws contain the "strings" the federal government attaches to the use of its money. Schools receiving direct or indirect federal assistance must comply with the conditions the government attaches. Good examples are Section 504 of the Rehabilitation Act of 1973, which prevents discrimination on the basis of disability in any program "receiving federal financial assistance," and the Individuals with Disabilities Education Act (IDEA), which ensures a free, appropriate education to students with disabilities.

Administrative Law

A third, often overlooked, source of law is administrative law, which consists of the rules, regulations, and decisions that are issued by administrative bodies to implement state and federal statutory laws. Special education personnel, for example, are familiar with the extensive "regs" accompanying the Individuals with Disabilities Education Act, as developed by the Department of Education. These regulations are designed by the implementing agency to apply the law to the realities of day-to-day schooling and of necessity must be quite detailed in order to eliminate as much ambiguity as possible. The length of a statute's regulations often exceeds that of the statute itself.

Administrative law also includes the rules and regulations that state agencies establish to carry out their responsibilities. When promulgating rules, administrative agencies are said to be acting in a quasi-legislative capacity. In the education context, this responsibility lies with the State Board of Education and the Texas Commissioner of Education. The rules that they enact are grouped together in volume 19 of the Texas Administrative Code (TAC).

The policy manuals and handbooks developed by local school districts are excellent close-to-home examples of administrative law. TEC §11.151(d) provides that school trustees "may adopt rules and bylaws necessary to carry out [their] powers and duties." Board policies and administrative directives represent the law of the district, and all personnel must observe them as a condition of employment.

Administrative law also has a quasi-judicial character. State law provides an appeal to the commissioner of education for anyone aggrieved by the school laws of the state, defined as Titles I and II of the Education Code and the rules adopted thereunder, or by actions or decisions of any school district board of trustees that violate the school laws of the state or that violate a provision of a written employment contract, causing possible monetary harm to the employee (TEC §7.057). In recent years, the commissioner has defined his jurisdiction narrowly under the terms of §7.057. For example, the commissioner has no jurisdiction to hear complaints involving:

- Code of ethics violations (*Hernandez v. La Joya I.S.D.*, 2011);
- Violations of school board policies (*Williams v. Port Arthur I.S.D.*, 2003);
- Violations of the student code of conduct (*Child b/n/f Parents v. Iowa Park C.I.S.D.*, 2011);
- Violations of constitutional rights (*Student v. Kingsville I.S.D.*, 2012);
- Violations of other state and federal statutes, e.g., the Texas Election Code (*Roma I.S.D. v. Guillen*, 2013) and the anti-discrimination laws (*Port Arthur I.S.D. v. Edwards*, 2012);
- Teacher certification issues (*McCandless v. Pasadena I.S.D.*, 2010);
- Alleged board member misconduct (*Parents v. Galveston I.S.D.*, 2013); and
- Disputes over student grades, class rank, graduation honors, or transfer requests (*Tidmore v. Mineral Wells I.S.D.*, 2001; *Charles B.S. v. Elysian Fields I.S.D.*, 2002; and *Michael S. v. Northeast I.S.D. Board of Trustees*, 2002).

As presently worded, §7.057 applies neither to student disciplinary actions nor to the termination or nonrenewal of professional employee contracts, since those matters have their own appeal procedures, as noted in Chapters 8 and 4, respectively.

Before appealing to the commissioner, the complainant first must exhaust administrative remedies within the school district. As the courts and the commissioner have noted on numerous occasions, this includes seeking redress before the school board within 45 days after the decision complained of was first communicated to the parent (*Child v. Killeen I.S.D.*, 2013), and filing grievances, where appropriate (see Chapter 5).

When the commissioner hears an appeal against an action or decision by a school district, the commissioner most often reviews the written record of the school district hearing to determine if there was substantial evidence to support the board's decision. In such case, the commissioner has 240 days to issue a decision, but the parties can agree in writing to extend the deadline by not more than 60 days. In some instances, the commissioner conducts an evidentiary hearing and has much the same authority as a state district judge to issue subpoenas, take depositions, and order production of documents in an effort to determine the facts. However, unlike those of a judge, the powers of the commissioner are limited to directing districts to comply with state law. The commissioner cannot issue restraining orders, assess fines, or order contested items removed from a personnel file. Also, unlike a judge, the commissioner does not hear the cases personally. Rather, licensed attorneys acting as TEA hearing officers conduct the hearings and draft decisions for the commissioner to review and sign. The commissioner has 180 days to hold a hearing and issue a decision after an appeal is filed (TEC §7.057).

The commissioner has developed rules governing hearings and appeals, found in Texas Administrative Code, Title 19, Part II, Chapter 157, in the interest of efficiency and fairness. Both the rules and the hearing decisions from the local board on up are classified as administrative law. Figure 1 illustrates the overall structure of Texas administrative law. School districts, like other governmental entities in the state, also have the option under state law of seeking to resolve disputes through what is called "alternative dispute resolution" (ADR). This process involves a trained impartial third party who works with the parties in conflict to reach agreement short of litigation. The details are spelled out in Chapter 2009 of the Texas Government Code.

Judicial Law

A fourth source of law is composed of state and federal court decisions. When disputes arise under constitutions, statutes, and administrative law, some authority must have final say. The courts serve this function. With certain exceptions, as previously noted, when a person wants to contest a school board decision that violates the school laws of the state or the terms of a written employment contract, the person has a statutory right of appeal to the commissioner. If, after appeal to the commissioner, the matter still is not resolved to the appellant's satisfaction, that person may appeal to a district court in Travis County, Texas (TEC §7.057(d)).

Courts generally refuse to become involved until all administrative remedies are exhausted. The reason for the exhaustion requirement is obvious. Administrative agencies are staffed by persons familiar with the educational setting and, theoretically, are more qualified than judges to arrive at satisfactory and workable solutions to disputes that arise within that setting. In fact, judges are not educators and, generally, will be the first to admit that the resolution of educational disputes is

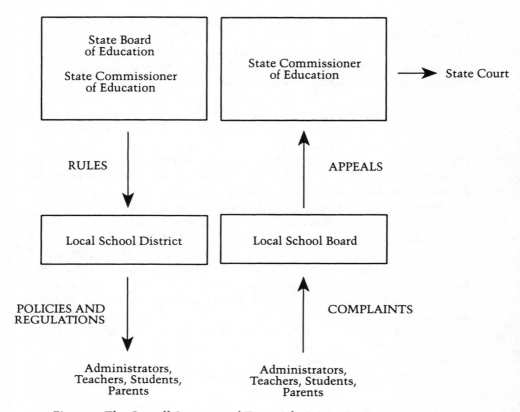

Figure 1. The Overall Structure of Texas Administrative Law

best left to educational professionals. Further, the exhaustion requirement has the effect of channeling and resolving most conflicts before they reach the judiciary.

Regardless of whether litigation is filed initially in a state district court or as an appeal from a decision of the commissioner, the state court system plays an important role in the resolution of educational disputes. Therefore, it is important to review the composition of the Texas judiciary. District courts are the major trial courts in the state judicial system, having jurisdiction over major criminal and civil matters. From a district court, an appeal goes to one of the fourteen courts of appeals located throughout the state and, finally, to the Texas Supreme Court. An appeal from a Travis County district court goes to the Third Court of Appeals in Austin. The Third Court, by virtue of its jurisdiction over appeals from the district courts of Travis County, has great influence over the development of educational and other public law matters. Only the Texas Supreme Court, however, can speak for the entire state in civil matters. For criminal matters, the highest court is

the Texas Court of Criminal Appeals. Thus, in Texas, we have two supreme courts, one concerned with civil matters and one with criminal
matters.

Although the Texas judicial system provides a theoretically efficient structure for adjudicating disputes, frivolous lawsuits often arise.
In an effort to deal with this problem, the legislature enacted two statutes holding a person potentially liable for court costs and attorneys'
fees for filing a frivolous lawsuit under state law against a school district
or an officer or employee of the district who is pursuing official duties
(TEC §§11.161, 22.055). State law, however, provides specific protection
for persons who report suspected violations of law. The Texas Whistleblower Act is discussed at some length in Chapter 6.

If the matter in dispute involves a *federal question*, individuals often can avoid administrative law procedures and state courts altogether
and go directly to a federal district court in the state. Federal questions
are those involving some provision of the U.S. Constitution (e.g., freedom of speech), a federal statute, or a federal treaty. Since many disputes involve federal constitutional or statutory rights, the number of
disputes going directly to the district courts in Texas's four federal judicial districts continues to increase. Figure 2 illustrates the geographic
jurisdictions of the four Texas federal judicial districts.

The most important function of federal courts is to adjudicate disputes arising under the Constitution and statutes of the United States.
As a general rule, disputes arising under state law must be tried in state
courts. Decisions of the Texas federal district courts are appealable to
the U.S. Court of Appeals for the Fifth Circuit in New Orleans, one
of thirteen circuit courts in the nation. The present jurisdiction of the
Fifth Circuit encompasses Louisiana, Mississippi, and Texas. On occasion, a decision of the Fifth Circuit will be reviewed by the U.S. Supreme
Court in Washington, D.C., which, of course, has the last word for the
entire country. Unlike most other courts, the U.S. Supreme Court has
the authority to decide which cases it will hear. From as many as ten
thousand cases filed annually for review, the Justices will select only
about seventy-five to eighty for a full hearing. Thus, most federal questions are resolved by the U.S. courts of appeals. For this reason, the
precedents established by the U.S. Court of Appeals for the Fifth Circuit
are particularly important in the context of Texas schooling.

One might assume that state and federal case law has relatively
little impact on Texas public education, compared with state statutes
and administrative rules and regulations. However, since the late 1960s,
courts have been increasingly involved in a maze of litigation involving the day-to-day management of schools. The rulings they hand down
have become an important part of school law and are ignored at one's
peril.

Other sources of law besides the four primary types discussed above

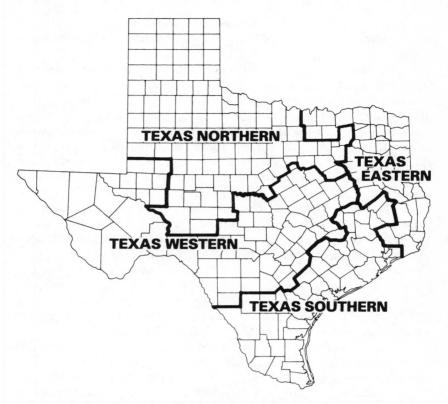

Figure 2. Geographic Jurisdiction of U.S. District Courts in Texas

also have an impact on education law. For example, contract law plays an important role in the context of employment. For our purposes, however, separating school law into the four previously discussed types—constitutional, statutory, administrative, and judicial—will help us understand how the system works. Table 1 provides an outline of the four types, and Table 2 shows how they interrelate.

THE STRUCTURE AND GOVERNANCE OF THE TEXAS SCHOOL SYSTEM

Texas Legislature

The Texas Legislature, acting pursuant to the Tenth Amendment to the U.S. Constitution and Article VII of the Texas Constitution, is responsible for the structure and operation of the Texas public school system. The nearly continuous flow of reform legislation since 1980 makes it

Table 1. Basic Components of Texas Education Law

Types of Law	Source	Impact on Texas Schooling
Constitutional	Tenth Amendment to U.S. Constitution	States that "the powers not delegated to the United States by the Constitution, nor prohibited by it to the States, are reserved to the States respectively. . . ." Since education is not delegated to the federal government, it is a power reserved to the states.
	The Bill of Rights and the Fourteenth Amendment to the U.S. Constitution	Protect certain civil liberties of employees and students in the public schools.
	Texas Constitution of 1876, Art. 7, §1 and Bill of Rights	Authorizes the state legislature to support and maintain an efficient system of public free schools and provides for individual civil liberties.
	Acts of the U.S. Congress	Acts of Congress guarantee various civil rights and establish the conditions upon which states and political subdivisions may receive federal funds.
Statutory	Acts of Texas Legislature; most pertaining to education are found in the Texas Education Code	Set up the State Board of Education and the Texas Education Agency to carry out limited educational functions. Actual operation of schools is left to school districts.

(continued)

Table 1. (continued)

Types of Law	Source	Impact on Texas Schooling
Administrative	Federal administrative regulations	Both TEA and local school districts must comply with the regulations promulgated by federal educational agencies implementing federal statutes.
	Policies and rulings by school boards, Texas Commissioner of Education, and State Board of Education	Boards of trustees develop policies to be utilized in operating their schools. State board and commissioner have the authority to establish rules that govern school district activity in areas designated by the legislature. Any person aggrieved by the school laws of Texas or actions of school districts involving school laws or impairing employment contracts can appeal to the commissioner. Policies, rules, and appeal decisions are classified as administrative law.
Judicial	Decisions of state courts	Any aggrieved person can appeal an adverse administrative ruling from the commissioner into state courts. Highest state court (civil) is the Texas Supreme Court, which has the last word on matters of state law, subject, of course, to the ultimate authority of the U.S. Supreme Court to review questions of state law in light of federal statutes and the U.S. Constitution.
	Decisions of federal courts	Any person alleging state interference with a right granted by the U.S. Constitution or federal law can bring an action in a federal court. The lowest federal court is the district court. There are thirteen intermediate appellate federal courts (ours is the U.S. Court of Appeals for the Fifth Circuit). At the top is the U.S. Supreme Court, which has the last word on matters of federal law. The U.S. Constitution provides that any state action, law, or constitutional provision that conflicts with the Constitution or a federal law is null and void.

Table 2. Relationship of Law to Establishment and Operation of Texas Public Schools

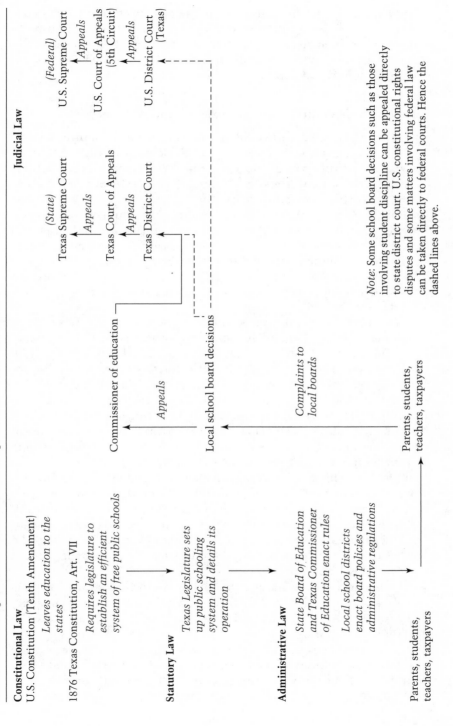

readily apparent that the legislature is the biggest player in Texas education. Thus, those wanting to influence the way Texas education is structured and conducted are well advised to focus their efforts on the Texas Legislature. Both school districts and educators are becoming increasingly sophisticated in this regard.

State Board of Education and the Texas Education Agency

The State Board of Education (SBOE) is an elected body of fifteen members that is limited to performing only those duties assigned to it by the state constitution or by the legislature. While many of its functions have shifted in recent years to the Texas Commissioner of Education, the SBOE is still a powerful entity. Among its designated duties as set forth in TEC §7.102 are establishing a state curriculum and graduation requirements, determining the standard for satisfactory student performance on assessment instruments, adopting and purchasing or licensing instructional materials, and investing the permanent school funds. The SBOE is required to broadcast its open meetings over the Internet and to archive video and audio broadcasts of prior meetings on TEA's website (TEC §7.106).

The Texas Education Agency (TEA) is headed by the Texas Commissioner of Education and supported by agency staff. Like the state board, TEA can perform only those duties specifically assigned to it by the legislature. The legislature's disenchantment with top-down control is clearly evident in the wording of TEC §7.003: "An educational function not specifically delegated to the agency or the board [of education] under this code is reserved to and shall be performed by school districts or open-enrollment charter schools." TEC §7.021 lists fourteen educational functions that TEA is to perform. Among them are monitoring district compliance with federal and state programs, conducting research to improve teaching and learning, developing a teacher recruitment program, and maintaining an electronic information transfer system. TEA also is authorized to enter into agreements with federal agencies regarding such activities as school lunches and school construction. In addition, TEA administers the capital investment fund established by the legislature to provide grants to school districts for improving student achievement (TEC §7.024).

Other than the legislature, the most powerful state-level player is the Texas Commissioner of Education, whom the governor appoints and removes with the advice and consent of the Texas Senate. Like the governor, the commissioner serves a four-year term. The only qualification for serving as commissioner is U.S. citizenship. The legislature designates the commissioner as the educational leader of the state. The commissioner also serves as the executive officer of TEA and executive secretary of the State Board of Education. Among some forty responsibilities the legislature has assigned to the commissioner are adopting an annual budget for the Foundation School Program, reviewing school district waiver requests, adopting rules for optional extended-year programs, performing duties in connection with the public school accountability system, and reviewing school district audit reports (TEC §7.055). Other sections of the Code give the commissioner added responsibilities, e.g., imposing interventions and sanctions for low-performing campuses and school districts (TEC §§39.102–.103). Several of the commissioner's current responsibilities previously belonged to the state board, such as adopting a recommended state appraisal process for teachers and administrators, performing duties associated with the guaranteed bond program, and approving and monitoring charter schools.

Operating under the oversight of the Texas Commissioner of Education, the twenty regional education service centers located throughout the state assist school districts in improving student achievement and increasing the efficiency of school operations (TEC §8.002). Their core services include teacher and program training, assistance to low-performing school districts and campuses, site-based management training, and assistance in complying with state law and administrative rules.

Funding for the service centers is provided by the state through the Foundation School Program and state appropriations. The centers may offer additional services requested and purchased by school districts and may seek grant support for various purposes. Each service center is governed by a seven-member board as established under rules developed by the commissioner of education. The commissioner also approves the selection of service center executive directors and conducts evaluations of service center operations. Regional service centers and employees are subject to or exempt from taxation in the same manner as school districts and school district employees (TEC §8.005). Service center employees and volunteers are entitled to the same immunity protections under state law as are school district professional employees and volunteers (TEC §8.006). School district and employee liability issues are discussed in Chapter 10.

Local School Districts

The governance of schools is left to local boards of trustees. Section 11.151(b) of the Texas Education Code states that "the trustees as a body corporate have the exclusive power and duty to govern and oversee the management of the public schools of the district. All powers and duties not specifically designated by statute to the agency or to the State Board of Education are reserved for the trustees, and the agency may not substitute its judgment for the lawful exercise of those powers and duties by the trustees." Accordingly, the local school board may acquire and hold real and personal property, sue and be sued, receive bequests and donations, and sell real and personal property belonging to the district. In addition to those general powers, the legislature has outlined several specific responsibilities of the board of trustees, including to establish community relationships; adopt a vision statement and comprehensive goals; publish an annual educational performance report; adopt an annual budget and tax rate; monitor finances and publish a yearly financial report; adopt a grievance process for personnel, students, parents, and the community to present complaints to administrators and the board; make contract termination and nonrenewal decisions; issue bonds and collect taxes; enter contracts; adopt an employment policy; and employ and evaluate the superintendent (TEC §§11.051, 11.1511, and 11.1513).

The board by policy must accord the superintendent the sole authority to make recommendations to the board regarding the selection of all personnel other than the superintendent and may delegate final authority for hiring to the superintendent (TEC §11.1513(a)(2)). The board and superintendent shall collaborate together to promote community support for high student achievement; provide educational leadership; and support professional development of principals, teachers, and staff (TEC §11.512).

TEC §11.158 allows school boards to charge fees for a number of activities, such as membership dues in voluntary student organizations, security deposits for return of materials, parking, and transportation for which the district does not otherwise receive funding. The board may not charge fees for instructional materials, school lockers, required field trips, and library books, to name a few such items. However, TEC §31.104 permits a district to fine a student who fails to return in satisfactory condition all instructional materials and technological equipment issued to the student. The student is not eligible for future books or equipment until the fine is paid, but must be permitted to use those items at school. The district may waive the fee for low-income families. A school board may not require an employee acting in good faith to pay for materials or equipment that is damaged or misplaced, unless the employee has agreed in writing to assume that responsibility in exchange for use of the items off campus or for personal business. TEC §11.162 allows school boards to require the wearing of school uniforms, provided that the uniforms are furnished free of cost to the "educationally disadvantaged." See Chapter 9 for a discussion of student dress codes and uniform policies.

The law clarifies that unless so authorized, a trustee may not act individually on behalf of the board (TEC §11.051(a-1)). A trustee may act only by majority vote at a lawful meeting where a quorum of the board is present and voting. As long as a quorum is present, a motion will pass by majority vote, even if a member of the quorum abstains (*Att'y. Gen. Op. GA-0689*, 2009). The board must allow the superintendent to present an oral or written recommendation concerning any item up for a vote at a meeting. See Chapter 9 for a discussion of the Texas Open Meetings Act.

The majority of Texas school districts elect their board members in at-large elections. However, many school districts have replaced the at-large system with single-member districts at the urging of minority voters. In a single-member system, the school district is divided into five or more separate election districts, each with its own trustee position. Thus, each election district will be assured at least one trustee who is from that area and represents the special concerns or needs of that election district. TEC §§11.052–11.053 govern the changing of an at-large system to a single-member system.

In 2013 the Supreme Court struck down as unconstitutional the coverage formulas of the Voting Rights Act of 1965, which have been used since the 1960s in determining whether states require federal supervision prior to making changes in voting laws and procedures, such as a change from an at-large system to single-member districts. The case effectively mooted the requirement to obtain preclearance from the U.S. Justice Department prior to implementing a change until Congress develops updated formulas (*Shelby County v. Holder*). Within hours after the Court's ruling, Texas Attorney General Greg Abbott declared that the state would immediately put into practice a controversial voter identification program that had been put on hold by federal judges. Several legal challenges ensued, including one filed by the Justice Department, seeking to stop implementation of the stricter voter ID provisions. The Justice Department also joined in a challenge to the state's redistricting plan in a federal voting rights case out of San Antonio. Stay tuned for more on this issue.

School board trustees serve without compensation for a term of three or four years (TEC §11.059). Elections for trustees with three-year terms are held annually, with one-third expiring each year. Elections for trustees with four-year terms are held biennially, with one-half expiring each biennium. The staggered terms assure continuity to school board functioning. Trustee elections must be held jointly with either the general election for state and county officers or the election for members of the governing bodies of municipalities, counties, hospital districts, or public junior college districts. A person must be an eligible voter to be qualified for office as a trustee. The SBOE is required to provide a training program for school board members through the regional service centers. Other training programs are offered through professional associations such as the Texas Association of School Boards (TASB). TASB is a comprehensive private organization that provides a host of services to school boards, including model school board policies that most districts have adopted. TASB also is influential in the legislative arena on behalf of its members and provides financial support to districts embroiled in expensive litigation.

Charter Schools

School choice has become one of the most controversial school reform measures in recent years. Driven largely by concerns about the ability of the "one-size-fits-all" public school to provide a high-quality and safe education to all children, the school choice movement has gained steam across the country. The fastest-growing form of school choice is the charter school. A charter school in effect is a newly created public school that operates free of some state regulation. The legislature in 2013 imposed significant reform to the laws regarding charter schools in an effort to ensure high standards. The three basic forms of charter schools are home-rule charters, campus charters, and open-enrollment charters.

Home-rule school district charters allow school districts to free themselves from most state requirements. TEC §12.012 provides that home-rule districts are subject only to those state laws and administrative rules that specifically apply to them. TEC §12.013 sets forth a list of state requirements that must be followed, in addition to the mandates in federal laws on such matters as special education and nondiscrimination. These include the laws pertaining to educator certification, student admissions and attendance, high school graduation requirements, class size restriction for low-performing schools, public school accountability, state purchasing, and accreditation sanctions.

If at least 5 percent of the registered voters of a school district sign a petition or two-thirds of the school board members adopt a resolution, the district is required to appoint a fifteen-member commission to develop a charter. The proposed charter becomes effective if adopted by majority vote in an election where at least 25 percent of the registered voters in the district participate. The 25 percent requirement remains a significant hurdle for many districts to overcome, and to date there are no home-rule district charter schools in Texas.

Under the second charter option, a school district board of trustees or governing body of a home-rule school district may grant a charter to parents and teachers to operate a campus or program free from much regulation, including district instructional and academic requirements, if presented with a petition signed by the majority of parents and teachers at the school (TEC §12.052). The board or governing body must grant or deny the charter by public vote but may not arbitrarily deny a charter, meaning that it can only be rejected for cause.

Campus charter schools and programs remain public and are subject to federal law and to those state statutes that specifically apply to them. Among matters specified by the latter are compliance with the Public Education Information Management System (PEIMS), high school graduation requirements, special education and bilingual education requirements, and provisions regarding prekindergarten programs, extracurricular activities, and health and safety measures (TEC §12.056). But campus charter schools are exempt from most other provisions of the Code. TEC §12.065 provides that geography and residence are to be given first priority in student admissions. Age, grade level, and academic qualifications are secondary considerations. The governing body of the campus or program is subject to the provisions of the Texas Open Meetings and Public Information Acts, which are discussed in Chapter 9. While the campus charter school has a good deal of autonomy within the district, the school board retains legal responsibility for its activities.

Open-enrollment charter schools have been the most popular charter school option. A previously established cap of 215 open-enrollment charter schools will increase gradually to 305 by September 1, 2019 (TEC §12.101). Senate Bill 2, from the 2013 legislative session, established the commissioner of education as the authority over granting, monitoring, and revoking open-enrollment charter schools. The commissioner can grant a charter to a public or private institution of higher education, a tax-exempt organization, or a governmental entity, and the school may operate in the facility of such an eligible entity, a commercial or nonprofit entity, or a school district. The commissioner also can grant a charter to a high-performing out-of-state applicant. Formerly the authority over granting charters, the State Board of Education now has veto power over charter grants (TEC §§12.101, 12.151).

A school district may grant a charter to one or more low-performing campuses serving no more than 15 percent of the district's student enrollment for the preceding school year. The district may operate the campus as a "neighborhood school" (TEC §§12.0522, 12.0532). The board of trustees must enter into a performance contract with the principal or equivalent officer of the campus or program, and the charter expires after ten years unless the goals are substantially met (TEC §12.0531). These district charters, college and university charters, dropout recovery charters under TEC §12.1141(c), and charters designed to serve students with disabilities do not count toward the open-enrollment charter school cap.

The commissioner, in coordination with a member of the State Board of Education, must determine that an applicant can meet certain financial, governing, educational, and operational standards and that the applicant is capable of carrying out the charter's responsibilities and likely to operate a school of high quality. A charter will not be granted to an entity, or any related affiliate, that has had a charter revoked, denied, surrendered, or returned within the preceding ten years. Priority will be given to charters proposed in the attendance zones of schools with unacceptable performance ratings for two years. The SBOE has ninety days to reject a charter proposed by the commissioner (TEC §12.101). The commissioner may not grant more than one charter to any charter holder; however, a high-performing charter holder may be permitted to establish a new campus charter without going through the commissioner-approval process, pursuant to TEC §12.101(b-4).

Like the other two forms of charter school, open-enrollment charters are subject to only those state laws and rules specified in the Education Code. The governing boards of open-enrollment charter schools specifically must comply with the state open meetings and public information laws, local government records laws, public purchasing and contracting laws (unless the charter describes different procedures approved by the commissioner), conflict of interest laws, nepotism laws, and municipal zoning ordinances governing public schools. In addition, the open-enrollment charter school must comply with a list of requirements in TEC §12.104 (similar to the list for the other forms of charters), which includes the accelerated instruction and high school graduation requirements. Open-enrollment charter schools also must offer the state-required curriculum and may receive a "distinction designation" based on student performance, as discussed in Chapter 2.

Open-enrollment charter schools may attract students either from within a school district or across district lines in competition with existing public and private schools. Open-enrollment charter schools may not discriminate in admissions on the basis of sex, national origin, ethnicity, religion, disability, academic or athletic ability, or school district the student would otherwise attend. However, they may reject students who have committed criminal offenses or who have a history of disciplinary problems. Open-enrollment charter schools may not charge tuition and must provide transportation on the same basis as existing school districts. The governing board of an open-enrollment charter school may charge a fee that the board of trustees of a school district would be entitled to charge.

Senate Bill 2 established an initial term of five years for new charters, with a ten-year period for subsequent renewals. A three-tiered renewal process was put in place based on performance in the academic and financial ratings system accountability standards under Chapter 39 of the Education Code: (1) expedited, for charters performing in the top two rating categories for three consecutive years, (2) discretionary, for charters that do not meet the expedited criteria but merit renewal based on growth in academic goals, and (3) expiration, for low-performing charters in academic or financial ratings for the last three of five years. Charter schools must be evaluated annually according to performance frameworks developed by the commissioner. The commissioner may conduct only one financial or administrative audit of a charter school in a fiscal year, absent specific cause to conduct more (TEC §12.1163).

If a charter school does not meet academic and/or financial standards for three consecutive years, the commissioner must either revoke the charter or reconstitute the school's governing body. Probation is no longer an option. A charter also must be revoked for violation of a material charter provision or legal requirement, failure to satisfy fiscal management standards, failure to protect students, and insolvency. A revocation decision is subject to review by the State Office of Administrative Hearings but must be upheld unless found to be arbitrary, capricious, or clearly erroneous.

To relieve concern about liability, an open-enrollment charter school, its employees, and its volunteers are entitled to the same immunity from lawsuits as traditional public schools and their personnel (TEC §12.1056). Texas courts have ruled that an open-enrollment charter school is a "governmental entity" and thus entitled to governmental immunity from suit to the same extent as a school district under Texas law (*LTTS Charter School, Inc. v. C2 Construction, Inc.*, 2011). This immunity also extends to employees of charter holders (i.e., organizations that operate charter schools) where those employees are engaged in "matters related to the operation of an open-enrollment charter school" (*Rosencrans v. Altschuler*, 2004). Board members are immune from liability to the same extent as public school district trustees. Members of the governing body of a charter school or a charter holder must undergo board member training pursuant to 19 TAC §100.1102. Restrictions concerning who may serve on the governing board of a charter school are found in 19 TAC §§100.1101 et seq. Charter schools are required to follow the same guidelines as independent school districts in employing classroom teachers; however, the certification requirements do not apply to charters unless certification is required by federal law, such as in special education.

Given that charter schools have no taxing authority, the legislature has given charter schools the opportunity to issue revenue bonds for the acquisition, construction, repair, or renovation of educational facilities. An open-enrollment charter school also may apply for designation as a charter district that can receive bond guarantees from the permanent school fund (TEC §12.135). A municipality that has a charter school may borrow funds, issue debt, and spend funds to acquire land, construct facilities, or expand or renovate facilities for the charter school (TEC §12.132). Any property purchased or leased with public money is public property. Charter schools also are entitled to receive state funding pursuant to Chapter 42 of the Education Code. Moreover, charter schools have access to the same level of services from regional service centers as school districts and must be represented on service center boards. In addition, the commissioner may permit charter schools to participate in any state program open to traditional public schools, such as a purchasing program, and charter schools are entitled to the instructional materials allotment the same as a school district. In addition, officers and employees of open-enrollment charter schools may participate in state travel service contracts (Gov't Code §2171.055).

The board of trustees of an independent school district that decides to sell or lease facilities must provide open-enrollment charter schools located in the district the right of first refusal; however, the board is under no obligation to accept the charter school's offer (TEC §11.1542). When an existing district campus is converted to a campus charter or campus program charter, the school district may not require the charter school to pay for the facility and may not charge more than the actual cost of any service the district contracts to provide (TEC 11.1543).

Private Schools

In a seminal 1925 decision, the U.S. Supreme Court ruled that the states cannot require all children to attend public schools only (*Pierce v. Society of Sisters*). Such a requirement, the Court held, would deprive private school operators of their constitutionally protected property right to operate a business and would interfere with the rights of parents. In upholding the right of private schools to coexist with public schools, the high court noted that "No question is raised concerning the power of the State reasonably to regulate all schools, to inspect, supervise and examine them, their teachers and pupils; to require that all children of proper age attend some school, that teachers shall be of good moral character and patriotic disposition, that certain studies plainly essential to good citizenship must be taught, and that nothing be taught which is manifestly inimical to the public welfare" (p. 534).

States have relied on this passage for years to set standards for private schools encompassing such matters as compliance with health and safety regulations, length of the school year, and enrollment reporting. Less frequently, states have included certification of teachers and curricular specifications. While there have been challenges to state regulation on the basis of unreasonableness and unconstitutional interference with First Amendment freedoms, especially freedom of religion, states generally prevail.

State regulation of private schools in Texas has not generated very much litigation over the years. The reason is that the Texas Education Agency ceased accrediting private schools in 1989. Instead, the commissioner of education has endorsed the accreditation decisions of a consortium of private school accreditation associations called the Texas Private School Accreditation Commission (TEPSAC), located in San Antonio. The commissioner recognizes the standards for accreditation of private schools by TEPSAC as being comparable to those applied to public schools. Consequently, student credit earned in TEPSAC-accredited schools is transferable to Texas public schools, and teacher service has been recognized for salary increment purposes in public schools. Though not required to do so, many private schools seek TEPSAC accreditation as a means of demonstrating the quality of their programs and facilitating entry of their graduates into Texas public colleges and universities. While private schools are not required to follow the state curriculum and student assessment program or employ certified teachers and administrators, they are not exempt from basic health and safety laws passed by local, state, and federal governments.

Private schools also are subject to selected federal civil rights laws such as Title VII of the 1964 Civil Rights Act, which outlaws discrimination in employment, though exemptions may apply for very small schools and those with religious affiliation. Most private schools are not subject to the federal laws that require receipt of federal funding to be applicable. Statutes falling into this category include the Individuals with Disabilities Education Act, Title IX of the 1972 Education Amendments (forbidding sex discrimination), and the No Child Left Behind Act.

In 1976 the Supreme Court ruled that private schools cannot discriminate in admissions on racial grounds, under another federal statute that we will discuss later in this chapter, 42 U.S.C. §1981 (*Runyon v. McCrary*). This decision had great significance for the so-called freedom schools, or "white academies," established during the desegregation of public schools in the South. A 1983 Supreme Court case upheld the Internal Revenue Service's curtailing tax-exempt status to private religious schools that refused to admit minority children for religious reasons (*Bob Jones University v. United States*). The Court rejected the contention that racial discrimination could be justified by religious doctrine. "The government has a fundamental, overriding interest in eradicating racial discrimination in education. . . . [T]hat governmental interest substantially outweighs whatever burden denial of tax benefits places on petitioners' exercise of their religious beliefs" (p. 604).

School Administrators

The superintendent is the chief operating officer of the public school district, responsible for implementing the policies of the board. TEC §11.201 lists eleven superintendent duties. Among them are responsibility for the operation of the educational programs, services, and facilities; assigning and evaluating personnel; and making personnel recommendations to the school board. The superintendent also is responsible for managing district operations, developing and administering a budget, and organizing the district's central administration (TEC §11.201(d)).

The school principal is the frontline administrator, with statutory responsibility under the direction of the superintendent for administering the day-to-day activities of the school. Principals have seven major functions, as listed in TEC §11.202. Based on criteria developed in consultation with the faculty, they have general approval power for teacher and staff appointments to the campus from a pool of qualified applicants. Principals set campus education objectives, develop budgets, and administer student discipline. They also assign, evaluate, and promote campus personnel, as well as make recommendations regarding suspension, nonrenewal, and termination.

The certification requirements for principals developed by the State Board for Educator Certification (addressed in more detail in Chapter 4) must be sufficiently flexible so that an outstanding teacher may substitute approved experience and professional training for part of the educational requirements (TEC §21.046). Further, qualifications for certification as a superintendent or principal must allow the substitution of management training and experience for part of the educational requirements. The legislature increasingly has emphasized the importance of recruiting and retaining the highest caliber of personnel for the principalship. School boards are required to institute multilevel screening processes, validated comprehensive assessments, and flexible internships with successful mentors to determine whether a candidate for certification as a principal is qualified.

Believing principals to be the persons with the most responsibility for school improvement, the legislature has given them more authority than in the past to operate their schools. At the same time, principals are held more accountable for their work through the appraisal process (TEC §21.354). The appraisal of a school principal must include consideration of the performance of the campus on the student achievement indicators set forth in TEC §39.053 and on the campus objectives established under TEC §11.253. The legislature appears particularly serious about administrator appraisal. School district funds cannot be used to pay an administrator who has not been appraised in the preceding fifteen months. In addition, TEC §39.307 provides that the campus performance report assembled each year by school districts shall be a primary consideration of superintendents in evaluating principals. Likewise, the district performance report is to be a primary consideration of school boards in evaluating school superintendents. These reports will be discussed in more detail in Chapter 2. With increased responsibility also comes increased liability. For example, principals must be familiar with employment law in order to carry out their personnel responsibilities effectively and without legal liability. The general topic of liability is discussed in some depth in Chapter 10.

District- and Campus-Level Decision-Making

Despite the authority given to local school boards, the Texas Legislature since 1990 increasingly has sought to "flatten the decision-making pyramid" by involving others in district and campus governance. Over the years, these requirements have become more complex. TEC §11.251 requires the establishment of committees at the district and campus level to participate in establishing and reviewing educational plans, goals, performance objectives, and major classroom instructional programs. The committees must be composed of professional staff (including a special education teacher, if practicable), parents, community members, and business representatives. The latter need not reside in the district. In partnership with the district-level committee, the board also is required to delineate the roles of those involved in planning, budgeting, curriculum, staffing, staff development, and school organization at both the district and campus level.

TEC §11.251 requires each board to have a procedure for the nomination and election of professional staff representatives to the district-level committee (two-thirds must be classroom teachers; one-third must be other campus- and district-level professional staff) and to establish procedures for selecting the other members and for holding meetings periodically with the board or board designee. The statute stipulates that the committee process is not intended to limit the power of the board to manage and govern the schools and is not to be construed as a sanction for collective bargaining. Nor is the statute intended to restrict the board from conducting meetings with teacher groups or receiving input from students, paraprofessional staff, and others.

A companion statute, TEC §11.253, requires that the school principal regularly involve the campus committee in planning, budgeting, curriculum, staffing, staff development, and school organization. Otherwise advisory, the committee does have approval power over the portion of the improvement plan addressing staff development. The membership of the campus committee and its selection are similar to those of the district-level committee. Like the district-level process, campus-level decision-making is not to be construed as any form of collective bargaining.

Using the deliberative processes set forth in these statutes, school boards and campus administrators are required to engage in an annual planning and improvement process linked to student achievement. Each district's improvement plan is to encompass such matters as a comprehensive needs assessment addressing student performance on the student achievement indicators set forth in TEC §39.053, performance objectives, and strategies for improving student achievement. Among the strategies to be discussed are those relating to the need for special programs, dropout reduction, integration of technology in instructional and administrative programs, discipline management, and staff development (TEC §11.252). Each campus's improvement plan must assess every student's performance using the student achievement indicators, identify how campus goals will be met, determine the resources and staffing needed, set timelines, and establish a periodic assessment process (TEC §11.253). The campus improvement plan also must include goals and methods for preventing and intervening in campus violence, as well as a program for encouraging parental involvement. Every campus-level committee must hold at least one public meeting per year, after receiving the annual campus rating from TEA, to discuss campus performance as well as the campus performance objectives.

HOW THE U.S. CONSTITUTION AND FEDERAL GOVERNMENT AFFECT TEXAS SCHOOLS

Key Provisions of the U.S. Constitution

In the past, the role of Congress and the federal courts in education matters was quite limited. However, the quest for individual rights and greater procedural safeguards triggered by the civil rights movement of the 1960s spilled over into the schools, and a new generation of constitutional rights law evolved. The changes have been significant and are discussed in detail in subsequent chapters, but here we will provide an overview.

We begin with the Bill of Rights of the U.S. Constitution. Most of our basic civil liberties are included among its provisions. The First Amendment is particularly important, for it lists several liberties inherent in a democratic society: the right to be free from governmental control in the exercise of speech, publication, religious preference, and assembly. However, the First Amendment, like the other nine in the Bill of Rights, applies only to the federal government (the first word in the First Amendment is *Congress*).

To determine what U.S. constitutional rights we enjoy in the state setting, we must look to the Fourteenth Amendment. For our purpose, two clauses from the first section of that amendment are important: "nor shall any State deprive any person of life, liberty, or property without due process of law, nor deny to any person within its jurisdiction the equal protection of the laws." These two clauses, the due process clause and the equal protection clause, together with the federal laws that implement them, provide the basis for constitutional rights suits against public educational institutions and personnel.

Congress passed a statute after the Civil War to enforce the Fourteenth Amendment by enabling aggrieved persons to pursue their claims in federal court. That statute, known as 42 U.S.C. §1983, is one of the major sources of litigation against both school districts and school personnel. The statute provides that "Every person who, under color of any statute, ordinance, regulation, custom, or usage, of any State or Territory, subjects, or causes to be subjected, any citizen of the United States or other person within the jurisdiction thereof to the deprivation of any rights, privileges, or immunities secured by the Constitution and laws, shall be liable to the party injured in an action at law, suit in equity, or other proper proceedings for redress [in federal court]." As will be noted often in this book and particularly in the last chapter, on legal liability, the consequences can be severe. At the same time, courts do not look kindly on persons who use this venerable civil rights law to get trivial cases into federal court. A case in point involves the parents of a freshman band student in College Station I.S.D. who had numerous complaints about the high school band director. Among them were allegations that the band director lacked discipline, insisted their son play only the B-flat clarinet, failed to distribute band rules in a timely fashion, yelled at their son, and walked into the girls' locker room. The trial court dismissed the claims, and the U.S. Court of Appeals for the Fifth Circuit affirmed. Wrote the appellate judges in an unsigned opinion, "a constitutional violation does not occur every time someone feels that they have been wronged or treated unfairly." The appellate court viewed the case as frivolous and ordered the parents to prove why they should not be required to pay attorneys' fees and double costs to the school district and school officials as damages (*Shinn v. College Station I.S.D.*, 1996).

One may wonder how schools can be affected by the Fourteenth Amendment, phrased as it is in terms of states. As we already have noted, local school districts legally are viewed as political subdivisions of the state. Therefore, the Fourteenth Amendment applies to public school districts and personnel, but not to private schools, since they are not state-related. Neither the Bill of Rights, the Fourteenth Amendment, nor most provisions of the Texas Education Code apply to private schools. This is an important point, for many educators assume they are entitled to the same rights in the private-school setting as in the public. In reality, the "rights" that a person has in private schools depend to a large extent on the wishes of the private school. For the private school, contract law is of great importance, since it defines not only the teacher-institution relationship but also the relationship of the student to the school. Thus, it is important that contractual provisions be carefully developed and reviewed.

Over the years the U.S. Supreme Court has held that almost all provisions of the Bill of Rights are binding on the states through the Fourteenth Amendment. In other words, the Supreme Court gradually has incorporated these rights into the Fourteenth Amendment, specifically through the "liberty" provision of the due process clause, thereby ensuring that neither the federal government nor the states can abridge them. Courts have differed, however, on the extent to which teachers and, particularly, students in the public schools enjoy the same protections as do other persons.

Neither liberty rights nor property rights are without limits. They can be regulated, even denied, provided that the state or school follows due process: "nor shall any State deprive any person of life, liberty, or property without due process of law," meaning that, if due process *is* followed, the curtailment of rights *can* occur. Due process rights for employees will be discussed in some detail in Chapter 4 and those for students in Chapter 8.

Behavior that is not constitutionally protected as a liberty or property right can be regulated relatively easily. Smoking and the possession and/or use of hallucinogenic drugs or alcohol fall into this category. The legislature has banned smoking by all persons at school-related or school-sanctioned activities on or off campus (TEC §38.006) and has made student possession or use of hallucinogenic drugs an expellable offense (TEC §37.007). Moreover, the use of alcohol is banned at all school-related or school-sanctioned events on or off school property (TEC §38.007).

In sum, the Fourteenth Amendment protects persons from state government repression of basic civil liberties guarantees, such as those in the Bill of Rights of the U.S. Constitution. Since public schools are part of state government, the Fourteenth Amendment applies to them and to their employees, but not to private schools. Exactly what constitutional rights students and teachers have in the public-school setting will be discussed in subsequent chapters.

A second major source of constitutional litigation in the public-school setting relates to the Fourteenth Amendment equal protection clause: "nor [shall any state] deny to any person within its jurisdiction the equal protection of the laws." This clause, coupled with civil rights laws designed to enforce it, has furnished the grounds for antidiscrimination suits against schools.

Important Federal Statutes

There are a number of federal statutes that directly affect the day-to-day operation of Texas public schools. Several also apply to private schools. The most important are briefly set forth here and will be referred to periodically in later chapters.

42 U.S.C. §1981 accords all persons the right to make and enforce contracts free of racial discrimination in both the public and private sectors. This law applies to discrimination occurring during the contract term as well. Thus, a minority child subject to discrimination after being admitted to a private school would have a cause of action. Penalties include both injunctive relief and compensatory damages.

42 U.S.C. §1983 allows suits for injunctive relief and compensatory damages against public school districts that through policy or practice deprive persons of U.S. constitutional and federal statutory rights. Public employees also are subject to suit under this statute.

This law is very important in the enforcement of federal rights under the Fourteenth Amendment and will be discussed in some depth in Chapter 10.

Title VI of the 1964 Civil Rights Act prohibits intentional discrimination with respect to race, color, or national origin in federally assisted programs. Injunctive relief and monetary damages are available. This law was instrumental in the desegregation of schools during the 1960s and '70s. The law provides exemptions for small businesses and religious entities.

Title VII of the 1964 Civil Rights Act prohibits discrimination on the basis of race, color, religion, sex, or national origin in all aspects of public and private employment. In addition to equitable relief such as back pay and reinstatement, this law allows money damages for intentional discrimination.

Age Discrimination in Employment Act of 1967 (ADEA) prohibits discrimination against individuals age forty or over unless age is a bona fide qualification reasonably necessary to carry out job responsibilities. While an employer always has the right to terminate an employee who is not performing satisfactorily, with few exceptions, there no longer is a permissible mandatory retirement age. The law applies to both public and private employers. Penalties for violating the Act are similar to those for Title VII.

Americans with Disabilities Act of 1990 (ADA) accords persons with disabilities meaningful access to the programs and facilities of public and private schools as well as most businesses in the country. The statute also prohibits discrimination against persons with disabilities in public and private employment and requires employers to make reasonable accommodation to enable them to perform the job. Money damages are available for intentional discrimination. The ADA Amendments Act of 2008 expands coverage by broadening the interpretation of "disability."

Individuals with Disabilities Education Act (IDEA) requires public schools to identify children with disabilities and provide them a free, appropriate public education in the least restrictive environment. Together with §504 of the 1973 Rehabilitation Act, IDEA provides a comprehensive legal framework for serving children with disabilities. Both statutes will be discussed in detail in Chapter 3.

Title IX of the 1972 Education Amendments prohibits discrimination against persons on the basis of sex in any federally assisted education program. Penalties against school districts under this statute can encompass compensatory damages, as well as termination of federal funding. Title IX has gained major significance in the context of student and employee sexual harassment. For example, the school district can be liable when an administrator sexually harasses a teacher or when a principal fails to act when a student complains about unwelcome sexual advances from a teacher or another student. Liability under this statute is discussed in Chapter 10.

No Child Left Behind Act (NCLB), an amendment to the Elementary and Secondary Education Act of 1965, attempts to raise student achievement levels by holding states and school districts to strict accountability standards. Sanctions are imposed for low-performing Title I schools, and all schools are subject to a "safe schools" option. Read more about NCLB in Chapters 2, 3, and 4.

In addition to these, there are other important federal laws that will be discussed in subsequent chapters. Among them are the Equal Access Act and the Family Educational Rights and Privacy Act (Buckley Amendment).

SCHOOL FINANCE

School finance is a complex subject, generally beyond the scope of this book. However, it is important to have an overview of the subject since it is central to the operation of the school system and remains contentious. In recent years the issue of equalization in school finance has been the focus of a dramatic struggle between the Texas judicial and legislative branches of government.

As previously noted, the 1876 Texas Constitution left to the legislature the duty to establish an efficient system of public education. That same year the Texas Legislature established the Available School Fund, which consisted of revenue from an endowment and from designated state taxes. Funding was meager, and most of the funding for public education originated at the local level.

With the growth of population centers, the imbalance between urban and rural districts created by reliance on local property taxation became increasingly apparent. But it wasn't until the enactment of the Gilmer-Aikin Bill in 1949 that substantial reform occurred. The Gilmer-Aikin Bill later became the focus of the *San Antonio I.S.D. v. Rodriguez* equalization lawsuit filed in federal court in the late 1960s. The bill established a Minimum Foundation Program (MFP), through which state funds for personnel and operations were distributed via a complicated economic index that established a basic minimum below which no district could go. The MFP involved both local and state contributions to a special fund. Each local district had to levy a property tax to support its contribution. But inequities continued because local districts remained free to enrich contributions to their schools beyond the MFP local fund assignment.

In *San Antonio I.S.D. v. Rodriguez*, the U.S. Supreme Court ruled that the plan had a rational purpose, did not deprive anyone of a fundamental constitutional right, and did not discriminate against any particular group in violation of the Fourteenth Amendment equal protection clause. The high court noted that, while not perfect, the Texas MFP program did alleviate some of the vast differences in school finance among districts. However, the Court urged the Texas Legislature to end the glaring discrepancies between rich and poor districts. Inequities persisted despite the passage in 1984 of House Bill 72, which established a basic allotment for each student in the state and introduced other mechanisms intended to foster equalization.

After *Rodriguez*, the next episode in the Texas equalization fight was *Edgewood I.S.D. v. Kirby*, filed in state district court in Travis County. The property-poor districts, having failed to find an enforceable right under the U.S. Constitution in *Rodriguez*, sought to find such a right under the Texas Constitution in *Edgewood*. In 1987 Judge Harley Clark declared the existing system of school finance in Texas unconstitutional. Judge Clark ruled that, because education is a fundamental right and because wealth is a suspect classification under provisions of the Texas Constitution, disparities between property-rich and property-poor districts violate the equal rights provision of the Texas Constitution, Article I, §3.

The Third Court of Appeals reversed the decision; however, the plaintiffs prevailed at the Texas Supreme Court (*Edgewood I.S.D. v. Kirby (Edgewood I)*, 1989). The court noted that "if the system is not 'efficient' or not 'suitable,' the legislature has not discharged its constitutional duty" and directed the state legislature to remedy the inefficiencies in the Texas school financing system. The court noted that "districts must have substantially equal access to similar revenues per pupil at similar levels of tax effort. . . ."

While the Texas Legislature enacted yet another finance plan during the summer of 1990, in January of 1991 the Texas Supreme Court once again unanimously declared the plan unconstitutional because it did not correct the deficiencies noted in *Edgewood I*. The court suggested in *Edgewood II* that the legislature could effect systemic change by consolidating school districts, thus removing duplicative administrative costs, and by consolidating tax bases.

Shortly thereafter, the property-poor districts asked the Texas Supreme Court to overrule its 1931 *Love v. City of Dallas* decision holding that local property taxes could not be used to educate students outside the district. In an order of February 25, 1991 (known as *Edgewood II½* and appended to the court's published *Edgewood I.S.D. II* decision), the court refused to overrule *Love,* noting that tax base consolidation could be achieved through the creation of new districts with the authority to generate local property tax revenue for all of the other districts within their boundaries. But the court also stated that unequalized local enrichment was still possible under the state constitution.

The Texas Legislature once again, in 1991, tried to reform the system by enacting Senate Bill 351, which sought to consolidate school district tax bases by creating 188 county education districts (CEDs) to levy, collect, and disburse property taxes in a way to minimize interdistrict disparities. But in January of 1992 the Texas Supreme Court declared Senate Bill 351 unconstitutional in *Carrollton–Farmers Branch I.S.D. v. Edgewood I.S.D. (Edgewood III).* The central problem was that the county education districts violated constitutional provisions requiring local voter approval of local property taxes and prohibiting a state property tax. Now expressing considerable frustration and uncertainty, the Texas Legislature opted to let the voters have a chance to pass a constitutional amendment upholding the CED plan, which effectively would moot the Supreme Court decision. The voters rejected that measure in the spring of 1993.

The legislature then passed Senate Bill 7, which required school districts above a certain wealth level (now known as "Chapter 41 districts") to engage in tax base reduction by transferring wealth to poorer school districts through various means. This is what has become known as the "Robin Hood" approach. No sooner was the ink dry than lawsuits were filed by both property-poor and property-wealthy school districts. In 1995, the Texas Supreme Court upheld Senate Bill 7 as constitutional "in all respects" (*Edgewood I.S.D. v. Meno (Edgewood IV)*). The court found that the plan provided an efficient system of education. However, the court cautioned that "Our judgment in this case should not be interpreted as a signal that the school finance crisis in Texas has ended."

Litigation continued, and in 2005 the Texas Supreme Court concluded that the state's cap on local property tax rates had become a prohibited statewide property tax because many districts had to tax at the maximum rate in order to provide a constitutionally adequate education (*Neeley v. West Orange–Cove C.I.S.D.,* 2005).

At the third called special session in 2006 the legislature changed the laws governing school finance in response to the Texas Supreme Court's ruling. The five-part package lowered property taxes for school operations in an effort to provide districts meaningful discretion in setting tax rates and tied funding levels to school district tax effort.

Subsequent legislative sessions have brought more changes to school finance. The 2009 legislature reduced recapture and increased equity among school districts using a formula-driven system tying fund-

ing to statewide increases in property value. The 2011 legislature revised the formula, tying funding increases to appropriations. However,
the 2011 legislature significantly reduced educational funding by about
$5.5 billion while imposing more rigorous academic standards. At this
point, more school finance litigation ensued, involving two-thirds of
the school districts in the state, including both rich and poor. In 2013,
a state trial court once again ruled the school finance system unconstitutional due to insufficient funding to provide a "general diffusion of
knowledge" and unequal distribution of wealth (*Texas Taxpayer and
Student Fairness Coalition v. Williams*). The court also declared that
the system created an unconstitutional property tax by forcing many
districts to tax at the highest rate just to meet minimum standards.
Although the school districts prevailed, as of the time of this writing,
the case has been returned to the trial court to consider the effects of
changes made during the 2013 legislative session. In 2013 the state re-
stored over $3.5 billion in education funding, helping to offset the deep
cuts imposed in 2011. The legislature also reduced the amount of required state testing and created more flexibility in public school graduation requirements. The ongoing saga continues. See Table 3 for a brief
history of the school finance controversy in Texas.

PARENT RIGHTS

In 1923 the U.S. Supreme Court observed that parents have a constitutionally protected right to control their children's upbringing (*Meyer
v. Nebraska*). However, its extent in the education context is limited.
While constitutional law generally does not support parent rights in
public schooling, Texas statutory law provides significant support for
parents. Indeed, the first objective of the public education system, as
specified in the state education code, is that "Parents will be full partners with educators in the education of their children" (TEC §4.001).
In recent years, the legislature has sought to expand the role of parents.
We begin this section by examining in what way Texas law enfranchises
parents with rights in public schools. We then discuss the right of parents to choose private schools or to educate their children at home.

Rights within Public Schools

In the recodification of Texas school law in 1995, the legislature added
Chapter 26, entitled "Parental Rights and Responsibilities," to the
Texas Education Code. The first section of that chapter, §26.001, recognizes parents as partners in the educational process and encourages
their participation in "creating and implementing educational programs
for their children." To that end, the statute requires boards of trustees

Table 3. School Finance at a Glance

1876	Texas Legislature established the Available School Fund, with funding provided on a per capita basis.
1949	Gilmer-Aikin Bill established Minimum Foundation Program involving local and state contributions, but districts could contribute extra local money.
1973	*San Antonio I.S.D. v. Rodriguez*—U.S. Supreme Court ruled Texas MFP program constitutional, but Court urged Texas Legislature to develop more equitable system.
1984	House Bill 72 established basic allotment for each student.
1989	*Edgewood I.S.D. v. Kirby (Edgewood I)*—Texas Supreme Court found school finance system unconstitutional ("[D]istricts must have substantially equal access to similar revenues per pupil at similar levels of tax effort").
1990	Texas Legislature developed new school finance system.
1991	*Edgewood II*—Texas Supreme Court again declared school finance plan unconstitutional; suggested consolidation of school districts and tax bases.
1991	*Edgewood II$\frac{1}{2}$*—Texas Supreme Court refused to overrule 1931 decision prohibiting use of local property taxes outside the district; again suggested tax base consolidation.
1991	Texas Legislature created 188 county education districts to levy, collect, and disburse property taxes equitably.
1992	*Carrollton–Farmers Branch I.S.D. v. Edgewood I.S.D. (Edgewood III)*— Texas Supreme Court declared CED plan unconstitutional; constitution requires voter approval of local property taxes and prohibits state property tax.
1993	Voters rejected CED and other school finance plans.
1993	Texas Legislature passed Senate Bill 7, which required property-wealthy school districts to reduce their tax base by transferring wealth to property-poor school districts ("Robin Hood").
1995	*Edgewood I.S.D. v. Meno (Edgewood IV)*—Texas Supreme Court declared Robin Hood plan constitutional, while indicating that school finance crisis was not over.
2001	Property-wealthy school districts challenged constitutionality of Robin Hood plan.
2003	*West Orange–Cove C.I.S.D. v. Alanis*—Plaintiffs stated valid claim; case returned to trial court.
2004	Special session of Texas Legislature called to develop new school finance system; session ended without plan.
2005	*Neeley v. West Orange–Cove C.I.S.D.*—Finance plan unconstitutional; local property tax cap had become prohibited statewide property tax.
2006	Third special session—Texas Legislature passed House Bill 1, which lowered property taxes in effort to give districts meaningful discretion in setting tax rates; increased state funding through other means.
2007	*Neeley v. West Orange–Cove C.I.S.D.*—$4.2 million in legal fees awarded to plaintiffs who successfully challenged school finance system.

2009	Texas Legislature passed House Bill 3646, which reduced recapture and increased equity, using formula-driven system tied to property values.
2011	Texas Legislature revised formula, tying funding increases to appropriations; significantly reduced educational funding while imposing more rigorous academic standards.
2013	Texas Legislature partially restored educational funding; reduced required testing; and eased graduation requirements.
2013	*Texas Taxpayer and Student Fairness Coalition v. Williams*—State trial court declared school finance system unconstitutional; case returned to trial court to consider effects of 2013 legislative session.

to support the establishment of at least one parent-teacher organization in each school of the district and to establish a parent complaint procedure. Further, parents are entitled to be represented by an attorney when they present a grievance to the school board on behalf of their children (*James N. v. Sinton I.S.D.*, 1999). The term "parent" means anyone standing in a parental relationship to a child. Excluded are individuals whose parental rights have been terminated or who do not have access to or possession of a child under court order.

While TEC §25.031 gives school officials the authority to assign students to particular schools and classrooms within a district, parents have a right to petition the board to have their child placed at a different school or to contest the assignment to a given school under TEC §25.033. Section 26.003 of the Code also gives parents the right to ask the school principal to have the child reassigned from a particular class or teacher within a school if the change would not affect the assignment of another student. Parents have a right to request, with the expectation that the request will not be unreasonably denied, the addition of an academic class to the curriculum if it would be economical to do so, the right to request placement of their child in a class above the child's grade level, and the right to have their child graduate early if all course requirements have been completed. If the child graduates early, the child has a right to participate in graduation ceremonies. The board's decision in these matters is final and nonappealable. This curtails the ability of parents to enforce the statutory provisions against a recalcitrant school board unless they can convince the commissioner or a judge that the board has acted illegally—for example, by engaging in illegal discrimination. In this sense nothing is ever truly "final and nonappealable."

Children attending low-performing schools are eligible to attend another school in the district that is not low-performing or to receive a public education grant ("PEG") to attend a school in another district (TEC §§29.201–29.202). Under the public education grant program, a low-performing school is defined as one having 50 percent or more of the students performing less than satisfactorily on state assessment tests for any two of the preceding three years or one that failed to meet any performance standard adopted by the commissioner under §39.054 in any of the three preceding years. The PEG program is funded through the traditional Foundation School Program. A PEG student is counted in the average daily attendance (ADA) of the receiving district rather than the home district. The financial aspects of the program are detailed in TEC §29.203.

Districts have the right not to accept students from other districts under the PEG program, but they may not refuse to accept them for reasons of race, ethnicity, academic achievement, athletic abilities, language proficiency, sex, or socioeconomic status. This essentially leaves lack of available space as the basis for refusal. Where a school district uniformly rejects all applicants due to expanding enrollment and limited facilities, the district does not discriminate when it denies a transfer to a PEG student (*Michael H. v. Eagle Mountain I.S.D.*, 1996). If a district does accept PEG transfers and there are more applicants than places, the law provides that the district must select by lottery, giving preference, first, to choosing students from the same family or household and then to at-risk students. The residential district is required to provide transportation to the school the child would have attended. The parent is responsible for transportation beyond that point.

Texas law reinforces federal law in giving parents access to all written records concerning their child, including attendance records, test scores, disciplinary records, psychological records, and teacher and counselor evaluations (TEC §26.004). Under federal law, the parent rights in this context transfer to the student when the student turns eighteen or is attending a postsecondary institution, though parents do not lose their right of access if they claim their child as a dependent. The federal Family Educational Rights and Privacy Act (FERPA) is discussed in Chapter 9. In addition, parents have a right to see state assessment instruments administered to their children, with the exception of questions that are being field-tested and that are not used to compute a student's score.

Parents also have a right to review all classroom teaching materials and tests previously administered to their child. School districts are required to make these materials readily available to parents and may charge a reasonable copying fee. TEC §26.007 reinforces the right of parents to attend school board meetings.

With the exception of child abuse reporting (discussed in Chapters 2 and 10), parents have a right to all information concerning the activities of their child at school. School employees who encourage or coerce a child to withhold information from the child's parents are subject to contract termination or suspension without pay. TEC §26.009 requires school employees to obtain written parental consent before conducting a psychological examination, test, or treatment unless such tests are related to child abuse reporting requirements or required by law for children with disabilities. In addition, the district must obtain written parental consent before referring a student to an outside counselor, must tell the parent about any relationship between the district and the counselor, and must provide the parent information about other sources of treatment in the area. Referral also requires approval of appropriate school personnel in order to prevent collusion between districts and outside counselors (TEC §38.010). Written consent is required under TEC §26.009 before making a videotape of a child or recording the child's voice unless for safety purposes in common areas of the school or on school buses, for cocurricular or extracurricular activities, for classroom instruction, or for media coverage. Videotape and audiotape recordings that contain personally identifiable information about students constitute protected records under FERPA and cannot be revealed to third parties without parental consent (see Chapter 9). TEC §33.004 requires districts to retain signed consent forms in the student's permanent record.

Under TEC §26.010, a parent is entitled to a temporary exemption for his or her child from a class or activity that conflicts with the parent's religious or moral beliefs upon written request to the teacher. This provision may not be used to avoid a test, to prevent the child from taking a subject for the entire semester, or to exempt a child from satisfying grade-level or graduation requirements.

Choosing Private Schools

The right to control a child's upbringing identified by the U.S. Supreme Court in the 1923 *Meyer* decision does not restrict the state from requiring all children to attend school. However, the state cannot require all children to attend *public* school. Such a law, the high court noted in its unanimous 1925 *Pierce v. Society of Sisters* ruling, "unreasonably interferes with the liberty of parents and guardians to direct the upbringing and education of children under their control." For this reason, the Texas compulsory public school attendance law provides an exemption if the child "attends a private or parochial school that includes in its course a study of good citizenship" (TEC §25.086). This right extends to children of public school teachers and administrators, as well. In one Fifth Circuit case, a teacher was denied the position of assistant principal because she refused to remove her children from private school and enroll them in public school. The Fifth Circuit determined that the woman had a constitutional right to educate her children in the private school and that the district could not take adverse employment action against her for exercising that right unless it "materially and substantially" affected the district's interest. The woman's constitutional right to choose a private school for her children outweighed the district's interest in preserving public confidence (*Barrow v. Greenville I.S.D.*, 2003).

The parents' right to direct their child's upbringing, however, does not confer a constitutional right to control every aspect of their child's education. Parents who choose private schools for their children may be forced to give up certain rights available to children in public schools. For instance, in 2009 the Fifth Circuit upheld the University Inter-scholastic League's refusal to allow a private school to participate in UIL athletic competition. The private school was ineligible according to UIL rules, and the UIL's enforcement of its rules did not violate the parents' right to practice their faith or to enroll their child in a private, religious school (*Cornerstone Christian Schools v. University Inter-scholastic League*).

In the past several years, private schooling has received considerable attention from educational reformers who view the public school system as too resistant to change to be successfully improved. These commentators urge the adoption of some type of voucher system whereby public money, rather than being provided directly to public schools, goes to parents, who then choose a public or private school for their children. Not only would such a system stimulate healthy competition within the educational system, proponents assert, it also would give parents a greater stake in their children's education. Critics assert that a voucher system would destroy the common learning experience fostered by the public schools and would be both economically and racially discriminatory. They also point out that private schools likely would experience an increase in state regulation.

In a major decision, the U.S. Supreme Court ruled 5-4 in June 2002 that the publicly funded voucher program in Cleveland, Ohio, does not violate the establishment clause of the First Amendment. That program channeled money to families whose children attended the Cleveland city schools so they could attend out-of-district public schools or religious or nonreligious private schools. The fact that nearly all students chose to attend religious private schools did not trouble the majority. Participating parents had many options from which to choose, and program benefits were available without reference to religion (*Zelman v. Simmons-Harris*).

Voucher measures have been unsuccessful in recent Texas legislative sessions. Article I, Section 7 of the Texas Constitution precludes appropriations "for the benefit of any sect, or religious society, theological, or religious seminary," while Article VII, Section 5 prohibits use of the permanent and available school fund "for the support of any sectarian school." This matter is discussed in more detail in Chapter 7.

Educating Children at Home

The word *school* in the Texas compulsory education statute is not defined. This uncertainty led to the dispute surrounding what generally is called "home schooling." A state district judge ruled in 1987 that in Texas a home in which students are instructed qualifies as a private school, subject to certain conditions. Chief among them are that students actually are taught by parents or those standing in parental authority, that there is a specific curriculum consisting of books and other written materials, and that the curriculum is designed to meet the basic educational goals of reading, spelling, grammar, mathematics, and a study of good citizenship. The court further held that TEA lacked the authority to enforce a more restrictive interpretation of the compulsory education law previously adopted by the State Board of Education. The decision was affirmed by the Texas Supreme Court in 1994 (*Texas Education Agency v. Leeper*). The high court recognized that TEA has the authority to set guidelines for enforcement of the compulsory attendance law, including requesting achievement test results to determine if students are being taught "in a bona fide manner." To date, the State Board of Education has not promulgated rules relating to home schooling.

Since the case was brought as a class action lawsuit by several home-school families, the holding applies in all Texas public school districts. Attendance officers are prohibited from initiating charges against parents simply because they are instructing their children at home. The trial court did recognize, however, the legitimate need of attendance officers to make reasonable inquiry of parents to determine whether a child is in attendance in a home school that meets the requirements approved by the court. Thus, information can be requested about the students, the curriculum being offered, and student test scores, if they exist.

In 1992 the commissioner of education upheld a school district's refusal to enroll a home-schooled girl in a one-period choir class based on the district's need to maintain discipline and supervision, obtain state funding, and avoid violating UIL rules concerning choir competition (*Michelle S. v. Beeville I.S.D.*). The U.S. Court of Appeals for the Tenth Circuit ruled similarly in a high-profile case in 1998, rejecting parent arguments that such a policy denied their child equal protection of the laws and interfered with both religious and parental rights (*Swanson v. Guthrie I.S.D.*). However, school districts must permit students who are home-schooled to participate in the Preliminary Scholastic Aptitude Test (PSAT), the National Merit Scholarship Qualifying Test (NMSQT), and college advance placement (AP) tests offered by the district at the same cost that students in the district pay (TEC §29.916).

When home-schooled students seek to return to the public school, placement decisions are left to the school. There is no requirement that school districts recognize the previous grade-level placements of home-schooled children. In 1998, a federal district court rejected a complaint concerning Buffalo I.S.D.'s policy that required a transfer student to take a proficiency test for each course in order to receive credit. The student who filed the lawsuit had attended an unaccredited Christian school prior to transferring to the district, and the girl claimed that the policy violated her right to the free exercise of religion. The court found no evidence that the policy interfered with religious freedom. The policy applied to all students who transferred from unaccredited or home schools, not to just those transferring from religious schools (*Hubbard v. Buffalo I.S.D.*).

SUMMARY

In this chapter we have reviewed the several sources of education law and their relationship to the structure and operation of the Texas public school system. It is apparent that local school districts have considerable authority to operate schools. Included in this authority is the right to develop local policy manuals and handbooks. School employees are required to follow these rules and regulations as they go about their assignments. At the same time, both federal and state law impose restraints on school boards and personnel by requiring compliance with certain constitutional and statutory provisions.

Education reform has been a central concern of the Texas Legislature since the early 1980s. At first, the legislative focus was on establishing state-level mandates that all districts and personnel had to follow. More recently, the legislature has sought to return greater decision-making authority to local districts and educators. At the same time, the legislature has recognized the need for innovation in schooling. A system of charter schools was enacted in 1995 to give local communities, campuses, and entrepreneurs the opportunity to develop new educational approaches and thereby stimulate reform across the education landscape. While the U.S. Supreme Court has ruled that interdistrict disparities in per-pupil expenditures do not violate the federal constitution, the issue of school finance continues to generate litigation under the Texas Constitution.

Parent rights have increasingly come to the forefront of the policy-making agenda. The Texas Legislature has given parents more influence over the schooling of their children, including the right to request exemptions from programs and activities they find objectionable on religious or moral grounds. Further, parents with children in low-performing schools can take advantage of a public education scholarship to enroll their children in the schools of another district. Constitutional law gives private schools the right to exist and accords parents the right to choose them for their children, though the state has no obligation to finance the choice. Texas law affords parents the right to educate their children at home, imposing few regulations on either home or private schooling. In short, the trend in Texas is decentralization of the educational enterprise, together with parental empowerment.

Student Attendance and the Instructional Program

THE MISSION OF THE Texas public education system is "to ensure that all Texas children have access to a quality education that enables them to achieve their potential and fully participate now and in the future in the social, economic, and educational opportunities of our state and nation" (TEC §4.001). To that end, the Texas Legislature has specified ten objectives for public education: participation of parents as full partners in the educational enterprise, development of full student potential, reduction of the dropout rate to zero, a well-balanced curriculum, recruitment and retention of highly qualified personnel, exemplary student performance, a safe and disciplined learning environment, use of creative and innovative techniques to improve student learning, implementation of technology, and preparation of students to become productive citizens. This is an ambitious agenda, and the legislature has enacted a host of measures to address it.

In this chapter, we discuss the law governing student attendance and the instructional program. Included will be a discussion of topics that are closely related to enrollment and instruction, such as a safe school environment, technology and the Internet, library censorship, the federal copyright law, and extracurricular activities. The chapter then will address how the school program must accommodate the needs of special groups of students.

ATTENDANCE

With limited exceptions, schools may not begin instruction before the fourth Monday of August (TEC §25.0811). Class size may not exceed twenty-two children for grades K–4, unless the district has received a waiver from the commissioner of education and provided written notice to the parent of each student affected (TEC §25.113). Children who are at least five years old and under twenty-six on September 1 of the school year are eligible to attend school on a tuition-free basis (TEC §25.001), while children from ages six to seventeen generally are required to attend school (TEC §25.085) (see below). This section begins with a discussion of various forms of discrimination in attendance, then looks at the specific requirements of school attendance in Texas.

Impermissible Discrimination

In 1954 the U.S. Supreme Court began the effort to eliminate de jure racial segregation (segregation by law) in our society. The means to accomplish this was the last sentence in the first section of the Fourteenth Amendment: "nor [shall any state] deny to any person within its jurisdiction the equal protection of the laws." Beginning with the *Brown v. Board of Education of Topeka* ruling, the Court repeatedly struck down laws that treated people differently solely on the basis of their color or racial heritage. In 1964 Congress added its legislative backing by passing the monumental Civil Rights Act, which prohibits discrimination on the basis of race, color, or national origin in public education, in any federally assisted program or activity, in public and private employment, and in privately owned places of public accommodation (hotels, restaurants, and so on). In 1968 the Court upheld this law as constitutional. About this time, the Court began to require not only that de jure segregation be ended but also that adequate remedies be provided to the victims of prior purposeful segregation.

The remedial mandates of both the federal courts and Congress have been the focus of controversy for some time. Since desegregation alone would not place the victims of segregation where they would have been had there been no segregation in the first place, the Supreme Court, Congress, and federal enforcement agencies have required good-faith integration and affirmative action efforts. It is beyond the scope of this book to describe the history of school desegregation. However, Table 4 provides a kaleidoscopic view of important U.S. Supreme Court rulings in the years since 1954, some of which have provided the basis for lower federal court rulings on racial attendance patterns in Texas public schools.

Districts still involved in the original desegregation suits conduct their affairs in accordance with the court orders issued in their respective cases. Those under court orders must file with the responsible courts periodic status reports describing their progress toward desegregation. The ultimate goal of this process is to be declared "unitary," a status denoting the eradication of all aspects of a segregated, dual school system.

In 1991 the U.S. Supreme Court handed down a decision in the most important school desegregation case since the mid-1970s. By a 5-4 vote, the Court concluded in a cautiously worded opinion that once all the vestiges of de jure segregation have been eliminated, federal court supervision may end, even if one-race schools reemerge (*Board of Education of Oklahoma City v. Dowell*). Justice Thurgood Marshall, who as an attorney in private practice was the architect of the original *Brown v. Board of Education* litigation, vigorously dissented. The 5-4 split among the Justices was an indication of disagreement on the Court over the

Table 4. Major School Desegregation Decisions, 1954–2007

Supreme Court Cases	Decision	Significance
Brown v. Board of Education of Topeka, 1954	Public education facilities that are racially segregated are inherently discriminatory even if equal.	Overruled the "separate but equal" doctrine of *Plessy v. Ferguson*, 1896, and began the movement to end de jure segregation in the public sector.
Griffin v. Prince Edward County, 1964	Ordered public schools that had been closed to avoid desegregation to be reopened.	Beginning of increased Supreme Court involvement in implementing its *Brown* mandate.
Green v. County School Board, 1968	Outlawed freedom of choice plans that do not result in integrated schools.	Demands more than a color-blind approach in areas of previous de jure segregation in the interest of establishing unitary school systems in which discrimination is eliminated "root and branch."
Swann v. Charlotte-Mecklenburg Board of Education, 1971	Approved a variety of court-ordered remedies, including cross-town busing, to achieve school integration.	High tide of Supreme Court support for remedies designed to achieve integration in formerly de jure segregated school systems.
Keyes v. School District No. 1, 1973	Burden of proof placed on school officials to show that intentional discrimination in one section of a school district has not been repeated elsewhere in the district.	First northern desegregation case; majority now speaks in terms of "segregative intent."
Milliken v. Bradley, 1974	Five-to-four decision limiting remedies to the school district(s) where de jure segregation previously occurred.	Makes it clear that the federal courts will not use Fourteenth Amendment to eradicate de facto segregation in North and West; for remedial efforts to be required, there must be evidence of illegal segregative acts by school officials.
Runyon v. McCrary, 1976	Used 1866 civil rights laws to prohibit racial discrimination by most nonpublic schools.	Dampened efforts to start "white academies" but raised questions about bona fide exemptions and meaningful enforcement.
Pasadena City Board of Education v. Spangler, 1976	Struck down court directives to enforce periodic adjustments to original desegregation plan.	Demographic changes occurring after desegregation order is in place are beyond judicial remedial powers.

(continued)

Table 4. (*continued*)

Supreme Court Cases	Decision	Significance
Columbus Board of Education v. Penick, 1979 Dayton Board of Education v. Brinkman, 1979	Upheld systemwide desegregation orders for two northern school systems.	Appeared to be reaffirmation of Court's willingness to uphold extensive remedies for past segregative acts.
Crawford v. Board of Education, 1982	Upheld a California constitutional amendment forbidding state courts to order busing unless necessary to remedy a violation of the U.S. Constitution.	States are under no legal obligation to go beyond the equal protection clause to require busing as a remedy for de facto segregation. This California constitutional amendment caused state courts to lift a busing order in the Los Angeles school system, which had never been found to have engaged in intentional segregation.
Washington v. Seattle School District No. 1, 1982	Struck down a state law prohibiting local school boards from using busing to desegregate schools.	Majority found the law unduly restricted local schools trying to integrate by lodging decision power regarding busing at the state level.
Board of Education of Oklahoma City v. Dowell, 1991	Held that once all vestiges of de jure segregation have been eliminated, federal court supervision may end, even if one-race schools reemerge.	Described the process by which federal district courts must decide whether a district has become unitary.
Freeman v. Pitts, 1992	Held that federal courts can relinquish supervision of those areas of school operation that have become unitary.	Unitary status can be achieved incrementally.
Missouri v. Jenkins, 1995	Held federal judge exceeded his powers in ordering adoption of a magnet school plan to attract white students from the suburbs.	Curtails federal judicial power to foster integration, even if schools remain substantially one-race and student test scores remain low.
Parents Involved in Community Schools v. Seattle School Dist. No. 1, 2007	Held that use of race in student assignment to particular schools violates equal protection clause in absence of compelling governmental interest.	Where a district has been declared unitary or has not engaged in prior racial segregation, use of racial classifications will be more difficult to justify.

appropriate time to end judicial efforts to eradicate the effects of prior state-maintained segregation. The question the trial court should ask, wrote Chief Justice William Rehnquist for the majority, is "whether the board had complied in good faith with the desegregation decree since it was entered, and whether the vestiges of past discrimination had been eliminated to the extent practicable." In making this determination, the court must consider "every facet of school operations," ranging from student assignment to faculty hiring, facilities, and extracurricular activities. A year later, the high court unanimously ruled that a trial court can relinquish supervision over those areas where a school district has achieved unitary status yet still retain authority to oversee continued desegregation in other areas. In effect, unitary status can be achieved in incremental stages (*Freeman v. Pitts*, 1992).

In 1991 the Fifth Circuit ruled that once unitary status has been declared, plaintiffs bear the burden of proving in a new lawsuit that a school board's actions were based on intent to discriminate. This is very difficult to do. The case involved an Austin I.S.D. student assignment plan that increased the number of racially identifiable elementary schools from six to twenty. The appeals court determined that the school district had redrawn elementary school attendance zones in the interest of curtailing crosstown busing time and promoting neighborhood schools, not with intent to discriminate. The fact that the minority schools were in a state of disrepair was attributed to budgetary problems, not racial animus (*Price v. Austin I.S.D.*).

In recent years, school desegregation plans have been ended in many school districts across the country, including the statewide school desegregation order handed down by U.S. District Court Judge William Wayne Justice in 1971 in *United States v. Texas*. The order, known as Civil Order 5281, requires integrated bus routes; an end to discrimination in extracurricular activities and use of school facilities; nondiscrimination in personnel decision-making; a prohibition on student enrollment and assignment on the basis of race, color, or national origin; TEA approval of student transfers; nondiscrimination against students on the basis of their first language; and the establishment of a complaint procedure. The order requires compensatory education in racially and ethnically isolated schools and restricts interdistrict student transfers that impede desegregation.

Civil Order 5281 originally applied to all districts in the state except those under separate federal court order or declared unitary by other federal district courts. In 2010 the U.S. Court of Appeals for the Fifth Circuit ruled that Civil Order 5281 should be modified to exempt from TEA's monitoring requirements and from federal trial court continuing jurisdiction school districts that (1) have been declared unitary in federal cases, (2) currently are under federal court desegregation orders or are parties to pending federal desegregation litigation, or (3) were not a party to the original 1970 litigation (*United States v. Texas (LULAC VI)*). As a result, most Texas school districts were released from the modified order's requirements by a federal trial court order dated September 27, 2010. However, a complaining party still can file a lawsuit on the issue of a school district's current unitary status. Districts must continue to implement language programs for students with limited English proficiency, discussed later in this chapter.

Can a school district assign students based on race if the motive is to maintain racially integrated schools? In June of 2007, the U.S. Supreme Court ruled that the use of race as a factor in assigning students to particular public schools in an effort to maintain racially integrated schools is unconstitutional, unless it is used to remedy the effects of past intentional segregation. The case involved two different school districts. The Jefferson County schools previously were under a court order to eliminate the effects of prior segregation but had since achieved unitary status, and the Seattle school district had never engaged in past racial segregation. In a 5-4 decision, the Supreme Court ruled that both school districts had violated the equal protection clause of the U.S. Constitution by using race as a factor in student assignment. Under the "strict scrutiny" standard, the use of race must be "narrowly tailored" to serve a compelling governmental interest. The Court has recognized only two interests that qualify as compelling in this context: (1) remedying the effects of past intentional discrimination and (2) providing student body diversity in the context of higher education. Neither of those interests was present in this case, and neither district produced any other compelling reason for the use of racial classifications in student assignment (*Parents Involved in Community Schools v. Seattle School District No. 1*, 2007).

However, in providing the fifth vote to constitute the majority opinion in the *Parents Involved* decision, Justice Anthony Kennedy differed with the four other justices that race can never be considered in promoting an integrated learning environment. "To the extent the plurality opinion suggests that the Constitution mandates that states and local authorities must accept the status quo of racial isolation in schools," he wrote, "it is, in my view, profoundly mistaken" (p. 788). He pointed out that in his view, more general use of race would be permissible to assure equality of educational opportunity regardless of race. As examples of permissible strategies, he cited site selection for new schools; redrawing of attendance zones; allocating resources for special programs; targeted recruiting of students and faculty; and tracking enrollment, performance, and other statistics by race. Since the four dissenters would defer to school districts in how they use race to further integration, Justice Kennedy's opinion is of great importance. However, crafting such an integration plan is no easy task, particularly in districts that are largely one-race to begin with.

The U.S. Court of Appeals for the Fifth Circuit, which has jurisdiction over Texas, ruled similarly in *Lewis v. Ascension Parish School* (2011). In that case a Louisiana school district redrew its boundaries and formulated a new student assignment plan to address population changes and overcrowding. The district previously had been declared unitary in a long-standing desegregation case. A parent challenged the new plan as discriminatory because one high school allegedly ended up with a disproportionate share of minority and at-risk students. The evidence indicated that the district had considered racial demographics in rezoning the schools in an attempt to maintain racial balance and retain its unitary status. The Fifth Circuit returned the case to the trial court to determine whether the assignment plan had a racially discriminatory motive and disparate impact on minority students.

A significant development in school desegregation law occurred in the context of Texas higher education in 1996. The U.S. Court of Appeals for the Fifth Circuit ruled in *Hopwood v. State of Texas* that preference given blacks and Hispanics in the admissions process at the University of Texas School of Law violated the Fourteenth Amendment equal protection clause. The admissions process set aside 5 percent of the spaces in the entering class for blacks and 10 percent for Hispanics. To achieve these goals, lower admissions criteria and greater individual attention were necessary for blacks and Hispanics than for other students. Significantly, while the appeals court rejected the use of race or ethnicity as a criterion in admissions, it did recognize that other criteria that may correlate with race and ethnicity would be permissible as long as they are not used for discriminating on the basis of race. Thus, the law school could consider such factors as the applicant's residence, parents' education, and economic and social background.

Taking a cue from this observation, the Texas Legislature enacted a measure in 1997 entitling students in the top 10 percent of their high school graduating class to automatic admission to Texas public higher education institutions (TEC §51.803). Top 10 percent students must complete at least the "distinguished" level of achievement under the foundation high school program or its equivalent, if available; they must meet certain college readiness benchmarks on the American College Test (ACT) or Scholastic Aptitude Test (SAT); and they must comply with application deadlines and paperwork requirements (TEC §§51.803–.807). The 2009 legislature placed a 75 percent cap on the number of entering freshmen who could be admitted under the top 10 percent rule at the University of Texas at Austin, due to UT's increasing inability to admit quality students who are not in the top 10 percent of their high school class. The cap applies through the 2017–2018 school year, assuming UT's current admissions policy remains in effect.

Since the *Hopwood* decision, other university admissions policies have been scrutinized. The U.S. Supreme Court took up the issue of race as an admissions criterion in two 2003 cases involving the University of Michigan. The Court ruled that the "narrowly tailored" use of race in admissions decisions to further a "compelling interest" in achieving a diverse student body is permissible under the equal protection clause. The law school admissions policy was upheld because the university reviewed each applicant's file individually and considered various ways in addition to race that an applicant might contribute to a diverse educational environment, including intellectual achievement, employment experience, nonacademic performance, and personal background (Grutter v. Bollinger, 2003). However, the university's policy regarding undergraduate admissions to the College of Literature, Science, and Arts was struck down. Under that policy, each minority candidate automatically received a twenty-point bonus to his or her "selection index" score, thus virtually guaranteeing the admission of every applicant from a minority group. That policy violated the equal protection clause because it was not narrowly tailored to further the compelling governmental interest of achieving diversity (Gratz v. Bollinger, 2003).

A 2011 opinion of the U.S. Court of Appeals for the Fifth Circuit considered an appeal regarding UT's use of an admissions policy similar to that of the Michigan Law School, which was upheld by the Supreme Court, for selecting the remainder of students who were not admitted under the top 10 percent rule. After admission of the top 10 percent, the remaining applicants were admitted under the "AI/PAI Plan," a review process that gave individuals scores according to (1) an Academic Index, based on class rank, standardized tests, and curriculum, and (2) a Personal Achievement Index, based on leadership, extracurricular activities, honors, work experience, community service, and other circumstances, including race. A Texas resident whose scores fell close to the admissions mark would receive a second review. Two students sued the university after being denied admission and asked the court to require the university to reevaluate their applications without consideration of race. The Fifth Circuit held that UT's policy complied with the Supreme Court's mandates in that (1) the policy did not establish a quota or award a fixed number of points to minority students; (2) applicants of every race were permitted to submit supplemental information concerning their potential contributions to the university; and (3) the university had a compelling interest in increasing the enrollment of underrepresented minorities who would add unique perspectives and better prepare all students to function in a diverse workforce (Fisher v. The University of Texas, 2011).

The students appealed to the U.S. Supreme Court, which in 2013 reversed the decision and returned the case to the Fifth Circuit for reconsideration. The Supreme Court concluded that the Fifth Circuit had applied the legal standard incorrectly by according too much deference to UT's good faith belief in its use of racial classifications. Instead, to establish that its admissions policy was narrowly tailored to meet the compelling interest of achieving diversity, UT had to establish that its use of race as a factor was "necessary" to achieve that goal and that no race-neutral alternatives would produce the same benefits. The litigation thus continues.

Moving on to other forms of discrimination, Section 504 of Title V of the Rehabilitation Act of 1973 prohibits discrimination against individuals with disabilities in federally assisted public school programs. The Individuals with Disabilities Education Act (IDEA) requires any state receiving financial assistance under the act to assure a free, appropriate public education to children with disabilities within the state and to protect the rights of these children and their parents. Both statutes and the obligations they place on school districts to serve children with disabilities are discussed in Chapter 3.

Title IX of the 1972 Education Amendments prohibits intentional discrimination on the basis of sex in programs that receive federal assistance, while §106.001 of Title 5 of the Texas Civil Practices and Remedies Code prohibits discrimination by public officials and employees against persons on the basis of race, religion, color, sex, or national origin. In addition, Article I, §3a of the Texas Constitution, known as the Equal Rights Amendment, provides that "equality under the law shall not be denied or abridged because of sex, race, color, creed, or national origin." Title IX, together with these other laws, restricts discrimination on grounds of gender, marriage, or pregnancy in a number of areas, including school attendance and participation in programs and activities.

In the context of athletic activities, the federal regulations accompanying Title IX require equal opportunities for males and females but at the same time recognize that schools may have separate male and female teams where selection is based upon competitive skill or the activity involved is a contact sport. However, if a school offers a team for one sex but not for the other, the excluded sex may try out for the team unless a contact sport is involved. Contact sports are defined to include boxing, wrestling, rugby, ice hockey, football, basketball, or other sport involving bodily contact. Note that in Texas, UIL rules permit a female athlete to try out for the football team. A school district is not required to offer an equal number of sports for each sex, but it must consider the athletic interests and abilities of each sex in choosing sports.

The U.S. Supreme Court has upheld the right of victims under Title IX to sue for compensatory damages (*Franklin v. Gwinnett County Public Schools*, 1992). Prior to that the only remedy available was the termination of federal funding. The *Franklin* case involved a female student who alleged that she was harassed and pressured into sexual intercourse by one of her teachers. She sued the school district for damages because of its failure to take corrective action. The addition of damage remedies, coupled with increased sensitivity to employee-on-student and student-on-student sexual harassment, has made Title IX claims a major concern of school districts. In Chapter 10, we discuss the liability standards under this important law.

Residency, Guardianship, and the Right to Attend a District's Schools

The cases discussed so far address the right of children present in Texas to a free public education. The more troublesome question has been whether a student has a right to attend school in a particular district. Under TEC §25.001 students are entitled to attend the schools in a district on a tuition-free basis under any of the following scenarios.

- One: The student and either of the student's parents live in the district.
- Two: One of the student's parents who is a joint managing conservator or sole managing conservator (with custody) or possessory conservator (with visiting rights) lives in the district but the student does not.
- Three: The student and the student's guardian or other person having lawful control of the student under a court order live in the district.
- Four: The student is younger than eighteen, unmarried, and has established a residence in the district separate and apart from the student's parents, guardian, or other person having lawful control of the student, as long as the student's presence is not for the primary purpose of participating in extracurricular activities and the student has not committed certain types of misconduct.
- Five: The student is homeless and lives in the district, regardless of the residence of the student's parents, guardian, or person having lawful control of the student. As defined by federal law, homeless children are those who lack a fixed nighttime residence or live in a shelter.
- Six: The student is a foreign exchange student placed by a nationally recognized foreign exchange program with a host family in the district, unless the district has received a hardship waiver from the commissioner of education.
- Seven: The student lives at a residential facility located in the district.
- Eight: The student is at least eighteen and lives in the district.
- Nine: The student is eighteen and lives in the district or is younger than eighteen and has had his/her minority

status removed through marriage or because the student manages his/her own affairs.

- Ten: The student has been placed in foster care and lives in the district. The student may not be required to serve a period of residency before participating in any activity sponsored by the district. Further, a student placed in the conservatorship of the state outside the attendance zone of the school where the student was enrolled may continue attending that school until completing its highest level.
- Eleven: The student's grandparent is a resident and provides a "substantial" amount of after-school care, as determined by the board (TEC §25.0001(b)(9)).

A district may allow a person showing evidence of legal responsibility for a child (e.g., power of attorney) to substitute for one possessing legal guardianship or lawful control under an order of a court. TEC §25.001(c) gives districts the right to request evidence of the student's eligibility to attend school and requires districts to establish what constitutes the minimum level of proof of residency. A person who falsifies information on an enrollment form to admit an ineligible student is liable for the student's tuition (TEC §25.001(h)), as well as criminal penalties under Penal Code §37.10. School officials cannot require the person with whom the student lives to secure legal guardianship (*Byrd v. Livingston I.S.D.*, 1987). However, they can encourage persons with whom students are living to secure a power of attorney for use in emergencies.

A school district is not required to provide a free public education to a student after both the student and the family have moved to another district (*Daniels v. Morris*, 1984). The Education Code implies neither a right nor a duty on the part of the student to continue attending, tuition-free, the school in which he or she enrolled at the beginning of the school year. Likewise, a student is not entitled to continue attending school in a district tuition-free after it is discovered the family home lies outside the district's boundary lines (*Argyle I.S.D. v. Wolf*, 2007).

TEC §25.002 provides that the parent, other person having custody of the child, or the former school district must provide the enrolling district with the child's birth certificate or other document proving the child's identity, a copy of the child's records from the previous school, and an immunization record. The former school district has ten working days after receiving a request to provide school records or a copy of the birth certificate. A parent or person with lawful control of a child has thirty days to produce the required documentation (TEC §25.002(a-1)). According to the attorney general, the Texas Department of Health may prohibit a newly enrolled child from attending school during the thirty-day period if the child does not produce immunization records or proof that the child has begun the immunization process or is exempt (*Att'y. Gen. Op. GA-0178*, 2004). The district must post on its website a list of immunizations required and recommended for admission and provide a link to the health department website containing the exemption procedure. Upon enrollment, a school district also must inquire whether a child has a food allergy and must develop policies to address the care of students who are at risk for anaphylaxis (TEC §38.0151).

If the admissions-related information is not provided in a timely manner, the enrolling district is to notify law enforcement authorities and request a determination of whether the child has been reported as missing (TEC §25.002(c)). Failure of those enrolling the child to furnish the enrollment data at the request of the police is a Class B misdemeanor, which is punishable by a fine not to exceed $2,000 or a jail term not to exceed 180 days or both. School districts are required to inform those enrolling children that presenting a false record is an offense under Texas Penal Code §37.10 and may require the payment of tuition or costs under TEC §25.001(h). A student must be identified by the student's legal surname as it appears on the student's birth certificate, a court order changing the student's name, or other document proving the student's identity (TEC §25.0021). If the child is enrolled under a different name than the name on the submitted documents, the enrolling district is to notify the Missing Persons Clearinghouse, a section of the Texas Department of Public Safety. A district must accept for enrollment a foster child under the care of the Texas Department of Family and Protective Services, and the Department has thirty days to furnish the required documentation (TEC §25.002(g)).

TEC §25.07 requires TEA to assist in the transition of students in foster or other substitute care from one district to another by such means as helping to ensure (1) the transfer of records within fourteen days, (2) the award of credit for prior course work, (3) the exchange of information with the Department of Family and Protective Services, and (4) acceptance of special education referrals by the previous school district. In addition, the Interstate Compact on Educational Opportunity for Military Children, set forth in TEC Ch. 162, facilitates the transition of children of military families between public school districts, for instance, by requiring school districts to transfer records, honor prior course placement and program enrollment, and allow additional excused absences.

A student who is twenty-one or older and who returns to school after not attending for three years may not be placed in any class or activity with a student age eighteen or younger. The district must revoke the student's admission if the student engages in misconduct warranting assignment to an alternative education placement (TEC §§25.001, 42.003(a)).

The Compulsory School Attendance Law

While the free public school is open to students who are as much as twenty-six years of age, the compulsory school law requires that a person who is at least six years of age (or younger than six but previously enrolled in first grade) and who has not turned eighteen "shall attend school" (TEC §25.085(b)). A child who enrolls in prekindergarten or kindergarten also shall attend school (TEC §25.085(c)). By "attend school," the provision means that the student shall attend for each day of instruction. Currently, the school year consists of at least 180 days of instruction, and the school day shall be for at least seven hours, including intermissions and recesses, except for prekindergarten and kindergarten. TEC §25.084 allows schools to operate year-round on a single-track or multitrack schedule (staggered instructional blocks and vacation periods) for the same length of time.

A student who is at least seventeen years of age and has a high school equivalency certificate or high school diploma is exempted from the compulsory school law. TEC §25.086 includes a long list of others who are also exempt. Among them are students attending a private school (including home schooling) that "shall include in its course a study of good citizenship," students who are at least seventeen and taking instruction for the high school equivalency certificate, students who are at least sixteen and preparing for the equivalency certificate upon recommendation by the public agency responsible for the child under a ·court order, students who have been expelled in a district that does not participate in a mandatory juvenile justice alternative education program, and students temporarily absent for physical or mental reasons.

Kindergarten and Prekindergarten Programs

Districts must provide either half-day or full-day kindergarten classes to children who are at least five years of age at the beginning of the school year (TEC §§29.151–.152). Districts may offer half-day prekindergarten classes for younger children but must do so if there are fifteen or more children at least four years old who (1) are unable to speak and comprehend English, (2) are educationally disadvantaged, (3) are homeless, (4) have a parent or stepparent in active duty in the armed forces or killed while serving in active duty, or (5) are or have been in the conservatorship of the Department of Family and Protective Services (TEC §29.153(b)). The commissioner of education may grant a waiver to this requirement where facilities are lacking. Students who are at least three years old are eligible to attend the prekindergarten program if they meet any of the above conditions.

Notices of prekindergarten classes must be in English and Spanish (TEC §29.153(e)). A district need not provide transportation for prekindergarten, but if provided, it is part of the funded transportation program. If a school contracts with a private agency to provide prekindergarten, the agency must comply with state licensing standards (TEC §29.1532). The content of prekindergarten programs must be designed to develop skills necessary for success in the regular public school curriculum, including language, math, and social skills. A district may charge tuition for prekindergarten, as long as the tuition charge does not exceed the cost of providing the program. The tuition rate must be submitted to the commissioner of education for approval (TEC §29.1531). A district that offers prekindergarten must furnish demographic information about its students, including the number of students who are eligible for classes, in the district's Public Education Information Management System (PEIMS) report (TEC §29.1532). The goal behind these laws is to provide special help to students who need it as early as possible.

Absences

Under TEC §25.095 a school district or open-enrollment charter school must notify parents at the beginning of the school year that both the parent and the student are subject to prosecution if a student is absent from school on ten or more full or partial days within a six-month period in the same school year or on three or more days or parts of days within a four-week period. If a student is absent from school without excuse on three days or parts of days within a four-week period, the district must notify the student's parent that it is the parent's duty to require the student to attend school and that the parent is subject to prosecution for failing to do so. The notice also must request that a parent attend a conference to discuss the absences.

If the student age twelve through seventeen fails to attend school without excuse on ten or more full or partial days within a six-month period in the same school year, the district must file a complaint against the student, the parent, or both in an appropriate court or refer the student to a juvenile court for conduct indicating a need for supervision (TEC §25.0951(a)). The district has ten days from the date of the tenth absence to file a truancy complaint. If the student fails to attend school without excuse on three or more full or partial days within a four-week period, the district may file a complaint in an appropriate court or refer the student to a juvenile court (TEC §25.0951(b)). A court must dismiss a truancy complaint if it fails to (1) specify whether the student is eligible for special education, or (2) include a statement that the school applied truancy prevention measures, which failed to "meaningfully address" the student's attendance (TEC §25.0915(c)).

Failure to have the child attend school is a Class C misdemeanor and carries a maximum $500 fine. Each day the child remains out of school may be considered a separate offense. One-half of any fines collected are remanded to the school district, thus increasing the incentives for districts to pursue truant students. If the court probates the sentence, it may require the parent to render personal services to the school as a condition of probation. A court may order the parents of truant students to attend a class offered by the school district that provides instruction in effective parenting skills relating to school attendance. The truant student also may be charged with a Class C misdemeanor under Family Code §51.03(b)(2). Legislation from 2013 requires the development of a uniform truancy policy for school districts in certain larger counties.

Texas Education Code §25.087 allows temporary student absences from school for any reason acceptable to the teacher, principal, or superintendent. In addition, this section requires school districts to excuse a student for (1) observing religious holy days; (2) attending a medical appointment for the student or the student's child, if the student attends classes the same day either before or after the appointment (including receiving services for autism spectrum disorder); (3) attending a required court appearance; (4) participating in a court-ordered activity, for students in the conservatorship of the state; (5) appearing at a governmental office to complete U.S. citizenship paperwork; (6) taking part in a U.S. naturalization oath ceremony; (7) serving as an election clerk; (8) serving as an early voting clerk up to two days per year; and (9) visiting a parent, stepparent, or legal guardian up to five days either within sixty days before or thirty days after a four-month military deployment. In addition, a district may excuse a high school student for visiting a college or university up to two days each year during the student's junior and senior years or a sixth-through-twelfth-grade student for playing "Taps" at a military honors funeral for a deceased veteran. Students absent under TEC §25.087 are not to be penalized and are to be counted as present for purposes of calculating the average daily attendance. They also are to be allowed to make up missed work. If they do so satisfactorily, the days of absence are to be counted as days of compulsory attendance.

A school district may adopt a policy requiring a person at least eighteen years old but under age twenty-one who voluntarily enrolls in school to attend for the remainder of the school year (TEC §25.085(e)). If the student accrues more than five unexcused absences in a semester, the school may revoke the student's enrollment for the remainder of the year; however, the adult student cannot be criminally prosecuted for failure to attend school under the compulsory attendance laws (*Att'y. Gen. Op. GA-0946*, 2012).

A student in any grade level must attend a class for at least 90 percent of the days a class is offered in order to receive credit or a final grade for the class (TEC §25.092(a)). However, a student may be given credit or a final grade if the student has 75 percent attendance, as long as the course requirements are met pursuant to a plan approved by the principal (TEC §25.092(a-1)). A student under court jurisdiction may receive credit only with the consent of the presiding judge. Students who do not meet the attendance requirement may petition an attendance committee for class credit or a final grade based on extenuating circumstances. School boards must define "extenuating circumstances" and specify alternative ways for students to make up work or regain lost credit. If credit or a final grade is not given, a student may appeal the committee's decision to the school board and from there to a state trial court. School districts may seek permission from the commissioner to provide a flexible school day program for students in any grade who will be denied class credit for failure to meet the attendance requirement (TEC §29.0822). TEC §25.092 does not apply to a student who receives credit by examination pursuant to TEC §28.023, which is discussed later in this chapter.

MAINTAINING A SAFE SCHOOL ENVIRONMENT

Concern about school safety has become paramount among educators, parents, and the general public. Here we discuss provisions of the Texas Education Code that relate to keeping schools safe. Chapter 8 focuses on student discipline. Preventive measures such as metal detectors, restrictive dress codes, and student drug testing are covered in Chapter 9.

Students, like other citizens, are subject to the laws of the community, state, and nation. Under certain circumstances, they can be held accountable for their illegal acts on school premises in the criminal or juvenile justice systems whether or not they are subject to the authority of the school. The legislature in 2013 enacted new measures designed to reduce the number of youth referred to the criminal justice system. To be subject to the juvenile justice system, a student must meet the statutory definition of a child. The term "child" is defined in §51.02(2) of the Texas Family Code as a person who is (a) from ten to sixteen years of age, or (b) seventeen and has either been charged with or engaged in delinquent conduct or conduct indicating a need for supervision for acts committed before turning seventeen. Persons under the age of ten cannot be held legally responsible for their acts. But as noted below, parents may be held responsible for the actions of their children. Upon reaching age eighteen an individual is considered an adult and is within the jurisdiction of the criminal justice system. However, an individual may not be arrested for a Class C misdemeanor committed when the person was under age seventeen (TEC §37.085). Further, a child accused of a Class C misdemeanor may be referred to a first offender program prior to the filing of a criminal complaint or referral to juvenile court.

TEC §37.101 provides that the criminal laws of the state apply to areas under the jurisdiction of the school board. In addition, school boards have the authority to adopt their own safety rules, including rules governing the operation and parking of vehicles on school property (TEC §37.102). Except in the case of an emergency or official business, Transportation Code §545.4252 makes it an offense for motorists to use cell phones on school property or in a school zone, unless the vehicle is stopped or they are using a hands-free device. TEC §37.103 authorizes a school district to commission an officer to enforce rules, and §37.081 allows school districts to set up a school district police force.

Public school officials can request identification of any person on school property, can refuse to allow those with no legitimate business to enter onto school property, and may eject a person from the property if the person refuses to leave (TEC §37.105). A person who trespasses on school grounds commits a Class C misdemeanor (TEC §37.107). TEC §38.022 permits a school district to require visitors to campus to present a driver's license or other government ID. The district may store information concerning visitors in an electronic database. The district also may use the database maintained by the Department of Public Safety, or another database, to verify whether a visitor to campus is a registered sex offender. The board of trustees must adopt a policy concerning what action to take when a campus visitor is identified as a sex offender (TEC §38.022(d)).

The U.S. Court of Appeals for the Fifth Circuit upheld a district's policy requiring school visitors to provide personal identification upon arrival so the district can determine whether they are registered sex offenders. The district scans the visitor's driver's license and uses a private company to conduct a criminal background check. The court found no fundamental right to access secure areas of the school while students are present. Moreover, the district has a compelling interest in determining whether a visitor is a registered sex offender, and the policy is narrowly tailored to further that interest (*Meadows v. Braxdale*, 2010). A school district also can conduct criminal history background checks on parent volunteers (TEC §22.0835).

It is a Class B misdemeanor for a person alone or with others to engage intentionally in disruptive activity on the campus or property of any public or private school (TEC §37.123). "Disruptive activity" is defined to include such acts as obstructing entrances or hallways, preventing school administrators from conducting assemblies, and preventing persons from entering or leaving the campus. The person must have *intended* to engage in the prohibited conduct to be held liable (*Att'y. Gen. Op. JC-0504*, 2002). Where a parent entered a school building without a visitor's pass and disrupted her daughter's class, the school district was justified when its police officer warned the parent of the potential criminal liability for her actions and escorted her off campus. School districts have the authority to bar individuals, including parents, from school property to maintain order and prevent disruption to the educational environment. Parents do not have "unfettered access to school property" (*Mitchell v. Beaumont I.S.D.*, 2006).

It is a Class C misdemeanor to disrupt classes or other school activities within 500 feet of a public school or to disrupt the district's transportation of children to and from public school or a school-sponsored activity (TEC §§37.124, 37.126). Children under twelve may not be criminally charged for disruptive behavior, but they may be subject to discipline under the student code of conduct. The law requires districts to address behavior on school vehicles in the student code of conduct.

A public school campus has been added to the list of places where "disorderly conduct" is prohibited, which includes intentionally or knowingly using vulgar language, making offensive gestures, creating a noxious odor by chemical means, making unreasonable noise, fighting with or threatening others, displaying or discharging a firearm, exposing oneself, and looking into restroom or shower stalls for lewd purposes. The first five offenses do not apply to students younger than twelve if they occur during school hours (Penal Code §42.01).

A peace officer may not issue a citation to a child (age ten through sixteen) who commits a "school offense," defined as any Class C misdemeanor other than a traffic offense that is committed on school property (TEC §37.141). A school district that commissions peace officers may develop a system of graduated sanctions to be imposed before filing a complaint for disruption of classes or transportation or certain categories of disorderly conduct, which may include a warning letter, behavior contract, community service, referral to counseling, or other service. Schools that do not adopt such a system or commission peace officers may file a complaint against a child in criminal court, which must (1) be sworn to by a person having knowledge of the facts and (2) state whether the child is eligible for special education and whether the graduated sanctions were imposed.

School boards and open-enrollment charter schools may appoint a "school marshal" for every four hundred students in average daily attendance (ADA) pursuant to TEC §37.0811. A school district need not create a school law enforcement agency in order to appoint a school marshal since the marshal is not a peace officer. However, the marshal must be certified by the Texas Commission on Law Enforcement Officer Standards and Education (TCLEOSE). To receive certification, the marshal must (1) be an employee of a school district or open-enrollment charter school; (2) hold a concealed handgun license; (3) undergo eighty hours of training; and (4) pass a psychological fitness exam devised and administered by TCLEOSE. A marshal may possess and carry a handgun only at a specified school in accordance with regulations adopted by the school board and may act only as necessary to prevent or abate an offense that threatens serious bodily injury or death to students, faculty, or school visitors.

If the marshal's primary duty involves "regular, direct contact with students," the marshal may not carry the handgun but must keep it locked in a safe within immediate reach. The marshal is permitted to access the gun only in a situation that justifies the use of deadly force based on a reasonable belief that such force is necessary for the protection of himself or others against an individual's attempted use of deadly force or imminent commission of a Title V felony. The marshal's identity is confidential and not subject to disclosure under the Public Information Act, discussed in Chapter 9.

Aside from the laws concerning a school marshal, state law permits a person who obtains a license from the Department of Public Safety to carry a concealed handgun. However, there are several laws restricting the right to carry guns and other weapons onto school property. Section 46.03 of the Penal Code makes it a third-degree felony to intentionally, knowingly, or recklessly possess a firearm, illegal knife, club, or prohibited weapon on public or private school premises, on grounds or in buildings where school-sponsored activities are being conducted, and on school transportation vehicles, "unless pursuant to written regulations or written authorization of the institution." Section 46.035 of the Penal Code makes it an offense to intentionally, knowingly, or recklessly carry a concealed handgun on the premises of a school sporting or interscholastic event unless the license holder is a participant and the handgun is used in the event. The term "premises" means a building or portion of a building, not a nearby driveway, street, sidewalk or walkway, parking lot, or parking garage. Penal Code §46.035 also makes it a Class A misdemeanor for a license holder to intentionally, knowingly, or recklessly carry a handgun into a meeting of a governmental body, including a school board meeting, if the individual is given effective notice pursuant to Penal Code §30.06 that handguns are prohibited. Section 46.035 provides a defense to prosecution for certain federal and state judicial officers, district and county attorneys, and bailiffs escorting judicial officers. A Class A misdemeanor is punishable by a fine not to exceed $4,000 and a jail term not to exceed one year, or both. A person licensed to carry a concealed handgun may lawfully carry the weapon onto property owned or leased by a school district if not off-limits under §§46.03 and 46.035 (Penal Code §30.06(e)).

TEC §37.125 provides that a person commits a third-degree felony by intentionally exhibiting, using, or threatening to exhibit or use a firearm on any property owned by a public or private school, including parking lots and garages, or on a public or private school bus transporting children. Penal Code §46.11 provides for a weapon-free school zone and enhances penalties for violations committed within 300 feet of a school, school function, or University Interscholastic League (UIL) event.

The federal Gun-Free Schools Act of 1994 (20 U.S.C. §7151) requires a one-year expulsion for students who come to school with guns. However, the superintendent can modify the expulsion requirement in writing on a case-by-case basis, and districts may continue to serve an expelled student in an alternative education setting. The Act provides exceptions if the student lawfully possessed the gun (e.g., with a permit) and had it stored inside a locked vehicle, or if the student brought the gun to school for an activity authorized by the district. TEC §37.007(k) provides that a student may not be expelled for the use, exhibition, or possession of a firearm at an off-campus, approved target range facility or while participating in or preparing for a school-sponsored shooting sports competition or shooting sports activity sponsored by the Texas Parks and Wildlife Department or an organization working with the Department. However, the student may not bring a firearm on campus to participate in or prepare for one of these activities.

Section 28.04 of the Texas Penal Code makes it a Class C misdemeanor to recklessly damage or destroy property without the consent of the owner. It is a crime to deface property with paint, an indelible marker, or an etching or engraving device, and the penalties escalate from a Class B misdemeanor to a felony depending upon the extent of the damage (Penal Code §28.08). When a minor engages in conduct resulting in damage to district property or personal injury, the district may seek restitution from the minor in juvenile court or from his or her parents (Family Code §54.041). For a child from age ten through seventeen, the parent or other person responsible for the child is liable for property damage reasonably related to the failure to exercise the duty of a parent or caused by the willful and malicious conduct of the child (Family Code §41.001). The limit of liability is fixed at $25,000 per act plus court costs and reasonable attorneys' fees.

Causing the bodily fluids of a person or animal to come into contact with a public servant, including a teacher, with the intent to assault, harass, or alarm constitutes a criminal offense under Penal Code §22.11, if the action occurs while the public servant is on duty or is done in retaliation for the exercise of the person's official duties. The offender must submit to diagnostic testing for HIV/AIDS, hepatitis A and B, tuberculosis, and other reportable diseases and must make restitution to the victim for any testing or treatment necessary due to the offense (Code Crim. Pro. Arts. 21.31, 42.037(q)). A positive test result may necessitate additional testing.

School districts must ban all smoking, use, or possession of tobacco products at school-related or school-sanctioned events on or off school property (TEC §38.006). Similarly, school districts are required to prohibit use of alcohol at school-related or school-sanctioned activities on or off school property and must attempt to provide an alcohol-free environment for students coming and going from school (TEC §38.007). It is a Class C misdemeanor for a person to possess an intoxicating beverage at a public school or on the grounds of an athletic event (TEC §37.122). Each public school with a grade level of seven or higher is required to post an antisteroid-law notice in the gymnasium and other locations where physical education classes are conducted (TEC §38.008).

Further, each school district is required to develop a multihazard emergency operations plan and conduct a security audit of its facilities every three years. Results must be reported to the school board and the Texas School Safety Center (TEC §37.108(b)). In addition, each district must establish a school safety and security committee to participate in developing and implementing emergency plans and providing the necessary information to make the audits and reports (TEC §37.109). A school district may be awarded safety certification pursuant to TEC §37.1081. Thus, in addition to internal disciplinary measures described in the school's student code of conduct, there are numerous measures available to school administrators for maintaining a safe and orderly environment conducive to teaching and learning.

THE INSTRUCTIONAL PROGRAM

Since the early 1980s, the state has focused increasingly on improving student learning. As a result, a host of measures are in place to strengthen the curriculum, assess student achievement, and hold schools and districts accountable. The changes appear to have had a positive effect, as more students are passing statewide assessment tests. At the same time, Texas still struggles to reduce high dropout rates. In this section, we examine what the law requires in the context of the instructional program, as well as the mandates imposed by the NCLB. We also discuss book censorship, controlling computer and Internet use, and the federal copyright law.

The Required Curriculum

To assure consistency across the state in the instructional program, Texas requires a well-balanced curriculum in public school districts, including both a foundation curriculum and an enrichment curriculum (TEC §§28.001–.002). The foundation curriculum consists of English language arts, mathematics, science, and social studies. The enrichment curriculum adds other languages, health, physical education, fine arts, economics, career and technology education, technology applications, and Bible study. In association with educators, parents, and corporate representatives, the state board is to designate the essential knowledge and skills of the required curriculum and ensure that they be taught in the state's public schools as a condition of accreditation. These are known as the Texas Essential Knowledge and Skills (TEKS), which are located in Chapters 110–128 of volume 19 of the Texas Administrative Code, a collection of rules adopted by the State Board of Education (SBOE) and the commissioner. The SBOE also has been directed to incorporate college readiness standards into the TEKS of the foundation curriculum for grades nine through twelve (TEC §28.008).

The 2013 legislature eliminated the minimum, recommended, and advanced programs for graduation and replaced them with a foundation program of twenty-two credits, including four in English language arts; three in each of math, science, and social studies; two in foreign language; one in each of fine arts and physical education; and five electives (TEC §28.025). The SBOE was directed to develop standards for "endorsements" for students who exceed the required curriculum and complete additional credits in (1) science, technology, engineering, and math (STEM), (2) business and industry, (3) public services, (4) arts and humanities, or (5) multidisciplinary studies. Each school district must at least provide an endorsement in multidisciplinary studies but may provide more.

To graduate with a "distinguished level of achievement" (DLA) a student must complete the requirements of the foundation school program plus Algebra II and at least one endorsement. A school district must make an Algebra II course available to each high school student. As noted earlier, only students who achieve the distinguished level or equivalent course of study are eligible for automatic college admission under the top 10 percent rule. A student may earn a "performance acknowledgment" based on outstanding performance (1) in a dual credit course; (2) in bilingualism and biliteracy; (3) on a college advanced placement (AP) or international baccalaureate (IB) exam; or (4) on the PSAT, SAT, or ACT. All of these data must be reported to TEA disaggregated by race, ethnicity, socioeconomic status, gender, and special education.

Upon a student's entering ninth grade, a school counselor or administrator must meet with the student and parents to discuss graduation options and develop a personal graduation plan (PGP) (TEC §28.02121). The PGP must identify the student's chosen course of study and indicate which endorsement the student intends to earn. The plan must be designed to promote college and workforce readiness and career placement and advancement and must facilitate transition to postsecondary education. A student graduating with an endorsement earns four credits (one math, one science, and two electives) in addition to those earned in the foundation plan. A student may graduate without an endorsement only with written parental permission after being advised about the benefits of graduating with an endorsement. TEA must provide each school district with information in English and Spanish explaining the advantages of the DLA and endorsements, and the district must post the information on its website. In addition to meeting with incoming freshmen, districts must provide students counseling concerning post-secondary education each year of high school.

The SBOE must ensure that at least six advanced career and technology courses, including courses in personal financial literacy and statistics, are approved to satisfy a fourth credit in mathematics (TEC §28.00222). A school district may offer an apprenticeship or training program that would enable a student to obtain an industry-recognized credential or associate degree as part of its college credit program, whereby students can earn college credit while still in high school. A district also may apply to participate in a Texas Workforce Innovation Needs Program to enable a student to attain career and technical certification.

A state virtual school network offering online courses is available for any student who is younger than twenty-one on September 1st and has not graduated from high school or who is younger than twenty-six and has been admitted to a school district or charter school to complete graduation requirements. The network is administered by the commissioner in conjunction with an education service center pursuant to TEC §30A.

The Texas Legislature allows school districts to teach courses on sex education and to select the teaching materials. TEC §28.004 requires districts to establish a local health education advisory council with at least five members to assist in ensuring that local community values and health concerns are reflected in the district's human sexuality instruction. Before each school year, districts must notify parents in writing of their right to review the materials and remove their child from class without penalty.

TEC §29.085 authorizes public school districts to offer an integrated program of educational and support services for students who are pregnant or who are parents. A district also is required to implement in its health curriculum a parenting and paternity awareness program developed by the SBOE and the attorney general (TEC §28.002(p)). Districts may implement the program at the middle or junior high school level with parental consent for students under age fourteen (TEC §28.002(p)). The health curriculum also must address binge drinking and alcohol poisoning and must provide instruction in cardiopulmonary resuscitation (CPR).

All students in kindergarten through eighth grade must participate in thirty minutes of daily physical activity or longer blocks of weekly activity (TEC §28.002(l)). At least 50 percent of the class per week must be used for moderate to vigorous physical activity (TEC §28.002(d)(3)). A district annually must assess the physical fitness of students in grades three through twelve and provide the results to TEA and to parents (TEC §§38.101–.106).

Student Assessment

Districts must establish a policy that provides for parent-teacher conferences and requires notice to parents of their student's performance in each class or subject at least once every twelve weeks (TEC §28.022). Grade notices must be signed by the parent and returned to the school. Such notice is not required if the student is eighteen or older and living separate from the student's parents, is married, or has had the disabilities of minority removed by a court. If a student's performance is consistently unsatisfactory in a foundation curriculum subject, the district must provide written notice to the parent or legal guardian at least once every three weeks or during the fourth week of each nine-week grading period. TEC §32.258 requires the Texas Education Agency (TEA) to establish a website for maintaining student assessment data for access by students, parents, authorized school district employees, and college admissions offices. General assessment data must be made available to the public.

The statewide testing program has undergone considerable modification over the years. The legislature has directed the State Board to establish a statewide student knowledge- and skills-based assessment program, currently the State of Texas Assessments of Academic Readiness (STAAR) (TEC §39.022). The testing provisions require TEA to adopt or develop appropriate criterion-referenced tests, for administration at various grade levels from third through eighth, in reading, writing, mathematics, social studies, and science (TEC §39.023). "To the extent practicable" assessments should measure a student's performance as well as growth in achievement (TEC §39.023(a-1)). The Texas Legislature specifically rejected use of the national "common core" standards developed by the Common Core State Standards Initiative (CCSSI). Common core standards may not be adopted by the SBOE or used by schools to comply with TEKS requirements, and TEA may not develop testing instruments based on common core standards.

Yearly testing is not required under the state system; however, a student who fails a reading or math assessment will be required to retest the following year. To the extent the state requirements conflict with federal law requiring yearly testing, the commissioner must seek a waiver. The commissioner sought such a waiver in 2013, but it was denied. Unless required by federal law, a student is not required to take an assessment if the student is enrolled (1) in an above-grade-level course in the same subject, and the student will be tested in the more advanced course, or (2) in another course in the subject for which the student will receive high school credit and be administered an end of course (EOC) exam.

At the secondary level, districts must provide EOC exams designed to ensure a student's readiness for college. TEC §39.024 defines "college readiness" as the level of preparation a student needs in English language arts and math to succeed, without remediation, in a beginning-level course in those areas at a university or junior college. The commissioner determines the college readiness standards on the EOC exams in conjunction with the commissioner of higher education (TEC §39.0241(a-1)). A student must retake an EOC exam for failure to meet the minimum score (TEC §30.025(b)).

Pursuant to TEC §39.023(c), districts must provide EOC exams in the following five subject areas: Algebra I, English Language Arts (ELA) I, ELA II, biology, and U.S. history. The reading and writing portions of the English tests must be combined into a single assessment instrument to be administered in one day. EOCs may not be used to determine class rank, including entitlement to automatic college admission under the top 10 percent rule, and may not be used as the sole criterion in determining admission to state colleges and universities. Optional assessments for Algebra II and English III may be administered beginning in the 2015–2016 school year, but they may be used for diagnostic purposes only.

Each student who fails to perform successfully on a state assessment instrument in grades three through eight or on an EOC exam shall be provided, subject to adequate funding, accelerated instruction in the deficient subject area (TEC §§28.0211(a-1), 28.0217, 39.025(b-1)). The school district must provide accelerated instruction to any student who fails an EOC exam required for graduation prior to administration of the next test (TEC §29.081(b-1)). The instruction may be provided before or after normal school hours or outside the school year.

A fifth- or eighth-grade student who fails either the reading or math portion of the assessment must complete accelerated instruction in order to be promoted to the next grade level and must be given three attempts to pass the test. After the third attempt, the student may be promoted upon passing an approved alternate assessment (TEC §28.0211).

In addition to the accelerated instruction required at certain grade levels, a district shall offer an intensive program of instruction, pursuant to TEC §28.0213, to any student who fails a state assessment or who is not likely to graduate in four years. The district must provide a college preparatory course to a twelfth-grade student who has failed an EOC assessment or does not demonstrate readiness for entry-level college courses in math or English language arts. The student may use the score on the end-of-course assessment for that class toward meeting graduation requirements (TEC §§28.014, 39.025(b-2)). The commissioner also is directed to implement a method whereby a student may fulfill EOC test requirements for a subject through satisfactory performance on an AP test, IB test, SAT subject test, SAT, ACT, or other comparable test (TEC §39.025(a-1)).

A student may not be removed from class for remedial tutoring or test preparation if the student would miss more than 10 percent of the school day. Tests must be administered so as to minimize disruption to normal school operations. Schools may not administer more than two benchmark tests for each state assessment, unless so requested by the parent of a special needs child.

TEC §39.023(h) requires TEA to report test results to districts within twenty-one days. Results must be shared with the child's teacher in the subject tested. TEA also must report the amount of improvement needed to pass the test (TEC §39.304).

Certain children with disabilities or with limited English proficiency (LEP) may be permitted to take an alternate assessment. LEP students also may be granted a temporary exemption or permitted to take the exam in Spanish (TEC §§39.023(b), 39.027).

The commissioner must establish procedures to ensure the security of the assessment instruments. Criminal penalties may be imposed for intentional violations of test security (TEC §39.0303), and the superintendent must report violators to the State Board for Educator Certification (SBEC) if they are terminated because of the misconduct (TEC §21.006). TEC §39.023(e) requires the State Board of Education to release STAAR test question and answer keys when they are no longer in use.

A district must develop a personal graduation plan (PGP) for each middle school or junior high student who does not perform satisfactorily on the state assessment or is not likely to graduate on time. The plan must (1) identify educational goals; (2) include diagnostic information and evaluation strategies, such as monitoring and intervention; (3) include an intensive instruction program; (4) address parent participation and expectations; and (5) provide innovative methods to promote student advancement (TEC §28.0212). This PGP is to be distinguished from the plan required for all students entering ninth grade, noted earlier.

A student may receive a diploma when the student completes the required curriculum and achieves satisfactory performance on the required assessment instruments (TEC §§28.025, 39.025). Students with disabilities can receive a diploma when they meet these requirements or complete the components of their individualized education programs. School districts may award a "certificate of coursework completion" to students who complete the curriculum requirements but fail the state assessment requirement, and the district may permit these students to participate in graduation ceremonies (TEC §28.025(d)). The transcript must specify whether a student received a diploma or certificate of coursework completion.

In addition to the STAAR tests, districts must provide nationally norm-referenced college preparation assessments at various grade levels, as well as college entrance exams, at state expense (TEC §39.0261). Districts may use other criterion-referenced or norm-referenced tests at any grade level, pursuant to TEC §39.026. Further, districts shall administer reading assessments to kindergarten through second-grade students and to seventh-grade students who fail the reading portion of the sixth-grade STAAR test in order to assess reading comprehension and provide appropriate intervention. The commissioner is required to approve at least two multidimensional assessment tools to add to the options for kindergarten assessment (TEC §28.006).

A related area concerns teacher evaluation and accountability. The teacher evaluation system requires that one of the appraisal criteria must encompass the performance of the teacher's students (TEC §21.351). The appraisal of a school principal also must reflect how well students on the campus perform (TEC §21.354(e)). To what extent can an educator's success depend upon student performance? Suppose a teacher gives all the students in the class grades of 70 or above but only a small proportion are actually at or above grade level as demonstrated by test score results. Most commentators agree that a teacher probably can be held accountable, at least to some extent, for student test performance and that discrepancies between grading practices and student test performance can be negative factors in teacher evaluations. The best advice for teachers is to be honest in grading. The best advice for administrators is to have sufficient documentation linking teacher behavior to poor student performance prior to issuing a negative evaluation in this area. For a helpful manual that describes how to document effectively in the classroom and how to link teacher behavior to student behavior in growth and assessment plans, see F. R. Kemerer and J. A. Crain, *The Documentation Handbook*, Fifth Edition, published by the *Texas School Administrators' Legal Digest*.

School districts must adopt a policy prior to the beginning of each school year concerning the grading of class assignments and exams. The policy (1) must require the teacher to assign a grade that reflects the student's relative mastery, (2) may not require the teacher to assign a minimum grade without regard to quality of work, and (3) may allow a student the reasonable opportunity to make up or redo an assignment or exam for which the student received a failing grade (TEC §28.0216). A teacher cannot be required to change a student's grade on a course or exam, unless the board of trustees determines the grade is arbitrary, erroneous, or not consistent with the school district's grading policy (TEC §28.0214). Any such determination by the board is final and may not be appealed. However, a decision concerning extracurricular participation still may be appealed pursuant to TEC §33.081. See Chapter 6 for a discussion of teacher grading as related to the concept of academic freedom.

School District Accountability

TEC §39.053 directs the commissioner of education to establish a set of student achievement indicators that include such items as results on state-mandated assessment instruments, results of retesting on assessments required for graduation, success in meeting the college readiness standards, dropout rates, high school graduation rates, the percentage of students who earned the distinguished level of achievement or an endorsement, and the number of students who earned postsecondary credit. The indicators also may include the percentage of students who failed student assessments or did not meet college readiness standards but who met the standard for annual improvement as determined by TEA. The indicators must be reviewed biennially and must be based on data that are disaggregated by race, ethnicity, and socioeconomic status. TEC §11.253(c) requires that school principals consult annually with each campus-level committee in reviewing and revising the campus improvement plan relative to performance on the student achievement indicators.

Every year the commissioner must set a state standard for each indicator and project the standard for the next two years. The performance on the student achievement indicators is compared to the state standard and to the required improvement, i.e., the progress necessary to meet the state standard. The commissioner periodically must raise the standards with the goal that by the 2019–2020 school year student performance in Texas will rank in the top ten states nationally in terms of college readiness, with no significant achievement gaps by race, ethnicity, and socioeconomic status.

Besides being accountable for the student achievement indicators, districts are required to report on a variety of indicators listed in TEC §39.301(c), which include such items as the percentage of students who graduated under the foundation school program, including the percentage who earned the DLA or an endorsement; results from the SAT, ACT, and certain postsecondary degree and workforce training programs; the performance of retesters on required state assessment instruments; the percentage of students pursuing an endorsement at each campus, disaggregated by the type of endorsement; the percentage of students provided accelerated instruction, aggregated by grade level, or passing a retest after accelerated instruction; and the percentage of students promoted by grade placement committee and their test performance the following school year, among others. The performance of students receiving treatment in a residential facility in a district, whether or not pursuant to a juvenile court order, will not be considered by the district for accountability purposes (TEC §39.055).

In 2013 the state was transitioning to a new accountability system whereby the commissioner designates every district and campus as either "Met Standard" or "Improvement Required" based on performance in four Index Areas: (1) student achievement, (2) student progress, (3) the closing of academic performance gaps, and (4) postsecondary readiness. The commissioner also awards "distinction designations" to campuses in the following areas: (1) Top 25 Percent Student Progress, (2) Academic Achievement in Reading/English Language Arts, and (3) Academic Achievement in Mathematics.

Beginning in the 2016–2017 school year, TEA will rate districts with a letter from A through F based on the district's state rating with regard to academic and financial performance and a local self-rating system that accounts for community and student engagement (TEC §39.054(a)). Campuses will be rated exemplary, recognized, acceptable, and unacceptable.

Each year, TEA prepares a "campus report card" that compares the performance of the campus with previous campus and district performance, current district performance, and state standards based on current data disaggregated by student groups. The matters to be addressed include performance on the student achievement indicators and the first five reporting indicators listed in TEC §39.301(c), as well as student/teacher ratios and administrative and instructional costs per student (TEC §39.305(b)). These campus report cards are to be distributed annually to the parents and published on the district's website. A student's first report card each year must indicate whether the campus has been awarded a distinction designation or has been identified as needing improvement and must explain the significance of the label (TEC §39.361).

By the tenth day of instruction, a district must include on its website: (1) information from the most recent campus report card of each campus, (2) information from the district's most recent performance report, (3) the district's most recent accreditation status and performance rating, and (4) an explanation of each performance rating (TEC §39.362). In addition, school boards are required to publish an annual report describing the educational performance of the district and each of its campuses on student achievement and other measures, indicating the district's accreditation status and identifying each campus awarded a distinction designation or rated requiring improvement, and demonstrating the progress of each campus in meeting campus performance objectives (TEC §39.306). The campus annual report must include the number, rate, and type of violent or criminal incidents that occurred on the campus, as well as the violence intervention policies and procedures employed by the campus. The annual report also must include information on special education compliance. The annual reports are to be subject to public discussion at a hearing and thereafter widely disseminated.

School districts and individual schools also are held accountable to TEA through the accreditation process. Each year the commissioner shall designate a school district as accredited, accredited-warned, or accredited-probation after considering the district's performance on the student achievement indicators (TEC §39.053(c)) and the financial accountability rating system (TEC §39.082). The commissioner also may consider data from the Public Education Information Management System (PEIMS) and other required reports, high school graduation requirements, the effectiveness of the school district's special education and career and technology programs, and any other matter listed in TEC §7.056(e)(3)(C)–(I) related to school district programs. Districts falling in the lower two ratings categories must notify parents and property owners of the rating and its possible ramifications (TEC §39.052(e)).

Sanctions for low-performing districts can range from a public notice of deficiencies to closure and annexation by another district if the deficiencies last two years or more (TEC §39.102(a)). Sanctions designed to improve high school completion rates may be imposed if a district fails to satisfy any of the student achievement indicators based on dropout rates for two years or more (TEC §39.102(a)(11)). Sanctions for low-performing campuses can include establishment of a school-community partnership to render assistance or participation in a hearing before the commissioner to explain low performance (TEC §39.103). For a campus that fails to meet state performance standards, the commissioner must, for year one, assign a campus intervention team; for year two, order reconstitution of the campus; and, for year three, order repurposing, alternative management, or closure of the campus. The commissioner may waive closure for one year if certain conditions are met (TEC §39.107). A charter school may have its charter revoked or modified (TEC §39.104). If a campus receives an unacceptable performance rating for three consecutive years after having been reconstituted, parents may specify whether they want the campus to be repurposed, assigned alternative management, or closed. If presented with a written petition signed by at least one parent of a majority of the students at a campus, the commissioner must grant the parents' request; however, if the board requests a different option in writing, the commissioner may grant the board's requested relief (TEC §39.107(e-2), (e-3)).

The commissioner may order TEA to conduct (1) an on-site investigation of a school district to answer questions concerning any federally funded program, pursuant to TEC §39.056, or (2) a special accreditation investigation for one of several reasons outlined in TEC §39.057, many of which deal with assessment practices and unsatisfactory student performance. The results of these investigations may change the accreditation status of a school district or the accountability rating of a district or campus or may cause the withdrawal of a distinction designation. In addition, the commissioner may impose interventions designed to improve performance.

The Effect of the No Child Left Behind Act

The No Child Left Behind Act (NCLB) of 2001 was signed into law by President George W. Bush in January 2002 (20 U.S.C. §§6301 et seq.), amending the Elementary and Secondary Education Act (ESEA) of 1965 and greatly expanding the federal government's role in public education. The primary objective of the Act was to raise student achievement by holding states and school districts to high standards with strict accountability requirements. Each state was to have a timeline that ensured all students met or exceeded the state's "proficient level of academic achievement" not later than the 2013–2014 school year (34 C.F.R. §200.15). While the NCLB is in transition, the law currently requires that students make "adequate yearly progress," or AYP, demonstrated through the statewide assessment test.

Congress tied AYP to the state's receipt of Title I funds; thus the requirement currently applies to all public schools in the state. However, only schools that directly receive Title I funds are subject to the low-performance sanctions outlined below. All students, regardless of ability levels, are expected to meet the yearly progress requirements. To make AYP, a school not only must show that its student body as a whole met the standard, it also must show that each subgroup met the same standard (i.e., Anglo, African American, Hispanic, low-income, limited-English-proficient, and special education) (20 U.S.C. §6311(b)(2) (C)(v)). In other words, states must disaggregate the data to show AYP in each subgroup, as well as the group as a whole. NCLB requires a 95 percent test participation rate for each subgroup and the school as a whole. NCLB also requires that school districts employ "highly qualified" teachers for the core academic subjects.

If a school fails to make AYP for two consecutive years, then the school enters "school improvement." Sanctions range from offering public school choice to restructuring for continued failure to make AYP in subsequent years. Restructuring involves a "major reorganization of a school's governance" that makes fundamental reforms, which could include reopening the school as a public charter school, replacing staff, or turning the operation of the school over to the state educational agency (34 C.F.R. §200.43). Throughout the "school improvement" process, the state, local educational agency, or school must communicate with parents concerning the school's status and their options. The U.S. Department of Education has granted waivers from the Act's accountability measures to many states, including Texas.

Removal of Objectionable Library and Study Materials

Controversy over school censorship of library and study materials continues. Behind the controversy are two conflicting ideas about the purpose of schooling. Should schools inculcate community values as reflected in school board decisions, or should schools foster a marketplace of ideas? There is no consensus on the answer, and this is clear from a 1982 decision of the U.S. Supreme Court. In a murky 5-4 decision, the Court affirmed a lower court decision ordering a trial to determine why a school board removed controversial books from the junior and senior high school libraries (*Board of Education of Island Trees v. Pico*). The fact that five Justices ordered the case returned to the lower court supports the view that the First Amendment is involved at least to some extent when books are removed from public school libraries. Some of the books involved in the *Pico* case were *Slaughterhouse Five* by Kurt Vonnegut, Jr., *The Naked Ape* by Desmond Morris, *Down These Mean Streets* by Piri Thomas, *Soul on Ice* by Eldridge Cleaver, and *A Hero Ain't Nothin' but a Sandwich* by Alice Childress.

The majority, however, was not consistent in its reasoning, so no definite set of guidelines can be derived from the decision. Prior to trial, the school board voted to replace all the books, and, as a result, a trial was never held. Most school districts have developed a set of criteria for both book selection and book removal, as well as for describing the steps a person can follow when bringing a complaint. Some criteria are easy to defend as legitimate reasons for a book removal: obsolescence, mutilation, absence of shelving space, redundancy, lack of funds for repair or replacement of worn books. Others are harder to defend: bad taste, inappropriateness to grade level, threatening to the emotional or intellectual growth of students. In some districts, a school psychologist serves on a screening committee to lend credence to recommended removal decisions based on such criteria.

The U.S. Court of Appeals for the Fifth Circuit had an opportunity in 1995 to apply the *Pico* ruling to a Louisiana school district's removal of a controversial book on African tribal religion from the school library (*Campbell v. St. Tammany Parish School Board*). After the parent of a middle school student sought to remove *Voodoo & Hoodoo* by Jim Haskins, study committees were instituted at both the school and district levels to review the complaint. Both committees recommended that the book be retained but with restricted access. *Voodoo & Hoodoo* traces the evolution and practice of religious subcultures in African American communities in the United States and offers a prescription for over 220 spells to bring about certain events. Most of the parent's objections centered on the spell portion of the book. With the support of the Louisiana Christian Coalition, the parent continued her quest to have the book removed by appealing to the school board. In a 12-2 vote, the board voted to remove the book from all school libraries in the district.

Following this action, a lawsuit was filed by other parents who objected to the removal. The federal district court granted summary judgment for the parents, whereupon the school district appealed. Noting that the plurality of justices in the *Pico* ruling viewed the library as a marketplace of ideas not subject to school board plenary control, the Fifth Circuit sent the case back for a determination of what motivated the school board's action. The appeals court added, "we are moved to observe that, in light of the special role of the school library as a place where students may freely and voluntarily explore diverse topics, the School Board's noncurricular decision to remove a book well after it had been placed in the public school libraries evokes the question whether that action might not be an unconstitutional attempt to 'strangle the free mind at its source.' That possibility is reinforced by the summary judgment evidence indicating that many of the School Board members had not even read the book, or had read less than its entirety, before voting as they did" (p. 190). The court also was troubled that by not considering the recommendations of the two review committees, the board disregarded its own procedures for channeling and resolving complaints of this kind. School boards thus must adhere to their own well-developed criteria and procedures when considering book censorship.

Technology at School: Computers, the Internet, and Cell Phones

Increasingly, computers are becoming an integral part of the instructional program. Their use is not restricted just to school-purchased software but encompasses the Internet as well. Internet access is prevalent in the nation's classrooms, school libraries, and media centers. While access to what is considered the world's largest library has immense payoffs for the instructional program, it also carries legal risks. Unfettered access to the Internet enables users to tap into websites detrimental to the interests of the school, such as sites promoting pornography and violence. Yet overly restrictive controls may lead to charges of unconstitutional censorship. Letting students develop their own websites solicits student interest in technology but puts them at risk from unscrupulous viewers. While e-mail facilitates communication, it can lead to harassment and abuse. In this section, we consider how school districts are attempting to control the use of technology in the instructional program. Copyright issues are discussed in the next section, and how student and teacher free speech rights are implicated in regulating computer use is explored in Chapter 6. A teacher's privacy rights concerning materials stored in a school district computer are discussed in Chapter 9.

As computers have become a feature of American life, students have been among the fastest to master the technology, usually far outpacing their parents and teachers. Unlike the school library, where the school can control what information is stored on the shelves, the Internet enables users to touch the world at innumerable points—including some the school would just as soon avoid. The federal Children's Internet Protection Act (CIPA) requires both libraries and schools using federal

"E-rate" or Elementary and Secondary Education Act funds for Internet use or connections to have filtering devices in place. (The federal E-rate fund allows eligible schools and libraries to purchase networking equipment, telecommunication services, internal connections, and Internet access at substantial discounts.) Failure to implement filtering devices could result in loss of federal money. Filters screen out sites where certain words are used, e.g., "sex." CIPA also requires districts to monitor student use of the Internet and to develop an Internet safety policy that addresses such issues as access to inappropriate material, use of e-mail, "hacking," cyberbullying, interaction on social networking sites and in chat rooms, and disclosure of personal information about minors. Schools and libraries must certify that they have an Internet safety policy and technology protection measures in place in order to receive E-rate funding.

The American Library Association filed a lawsuit against CIPA in the spring of 2002, charging that it unconstitutionally censors academic material. The case made its way to the U.S. Supreme Court, which upheld the statute as constitutional (*United States v. American Library Association*, 2003). The governmental interest in protecting children from harmful materials was great, and the burden on adult library users to request that the filter be removed for their use was minimal. CIPA permits an authorized person to disable blocking or filtering devices for adult use, research, or other lawful purposes.

In addition to accessing information from the Internet, students and teachers also can post information on the Internet. The school has an interest in preventing the posting of messages on its website and on the websites that students construct at school that are abusive, obscene, pornographic, threatening, harassing, damaging to another's reputation, or illegal. Further, students easily could post information on the Internet that would place them in danger from child predators. Thus, some districts require students to use pseudonyms and to avoid posting photographs. Further, the posting of personally identifiable information about students on a school website could violate the terms of the Family Educational Rights and Privacy Act (FERPA). This federal law is discussed in detail in Chapter 9. Accordingly, schools need to monitor what is being posted on the Web at school but not violate student and teacher privacy rights in the process. TEA has been directed to compile a list of resources concerning Internet safety that are available to public schools (TEC §38.023).

Unrestricted use of e-mail by both students and teachers raises similar issues. To deal with these concerns, school districts use what are called "acceptable use policies" (AUPs). AUPs set forth the conditions for using the Internet and other technology at school. AUPs typically require the execution of waiver and consent forms, inform users that they are being monitored, provide for adequate supervision, limit computer access times and places, set clear guidelines for student and employee use, and teach safety in using the Internet. A school district may discipline students or employees for misconduct involving school computer equipment, as long as the consequences have been spelled out in the AUP or in the student code of conduct. An AUP should warn users that they have no privacy rights in information stored on school computers and that the computers are subject to search at any time. An AUP also should notify students and employees that violation of AUP guidelines will result in the revocation of computer privileges and may trigger other sanctions under board policies and regulations. The rationale behind AUPs is that the school has the authority to place restrictions on the use of its own technology and to impose sanctions on those who violate the conditions. The federal Electronic Communications Act (18 U.S.C. §§2510–2520) permits the interception of electronic communications where one of the parties has given prior consent.

With the prevalence of cell phones carried by students, school districts also should adopt policies concerning the possession and use of cell phones at school, outlining any time or place restrictions. The student code of conduct should specify disciplinary consequences for violation of the cell phone use policy. School districts also may prohibit possession of "paging devices" at school or school activities (TEC §37.082(a)). A school district may charge an administrative fee of no more than fifteen dollars for the return of a confiscated cell phone or paging device to a student and may dispose of the device after thirty days' notice to the cell phone company and the parent of the student (TEC §37.082(b)).

The Federal Copyright Law

The 1976 revised copyright law (17 U.S.C. §§101 et seq.) places restrictions on the duplication of copyrighted material for classroom use. Specifically, teachers may make a single copy for scholarly use for class preparation, or multiple copies for classroom use, of a chapter from a book, a newspaper or magazine article, a short story or poem, or a chart, graph, diagram, cartoon, picture, and the like if the following conditions are met:

1. The copying is at the instance and inspiration of the teacher.
2. There is not sufficient time prior to use to request permission from the publisher.
3. The copying is only for one course in the school.
4. Each copy includes a notice of copyright as it appears in the book or periodical.

The intent of the copyright law is to allow "fair use" but to avoid wholesale copying of complete works as a substitute for purchase. "Fair use" does not extend to copying of the same item by the same teacher from term to term. If a teacher wishes to use the item again, the best avenue is to write the publisher requesting permission to do so. Some publishers are very accommodating, asking only that the teacher indicate on the copied work that permission has been granted for duplication in the manner requested. Others will charge a fee for use of the work; in some cases, it may be cheaper to purchase the work. Another option is to have the library purchase several copies of the work and assign it as reserve reading.

While the law does not specify any number of words, lines, or illustrations that legally may be copied from printed materials, a committee of educators, authors, and publishers has agreed upon guidelines for copying by not-for-profit educational institutions. In a similar manner, guidelines for educational use of copyrighted music have been developed by music educators and publishers, and guidelines for off-air copying of television programs and copying of computer software have been developed by representatives of educational institutions, copyright proprietors, and creative guilds and unions. Table 5 uses these guidelines to show what and how much may be copied from a variety of sources. Extensive guidelines also exist concerning fair use in educational multimedia projects (see, e.g., http://copyright.lib.utexas.edu/ ccmcguid.html).

Microcomputer software copying is of particular concern; commentators and vendors alike warn that piracy of software is the biggest threat to its continued development. The 1976 Copyright Act specifies in §117 that computer programs are covered by the law. A computer program is defined as "a set of statements or instructions to be used directly or indirectly in a computer in order to bring about a certain result" (§101). Laws concerning copying of computer software protect both the disk and the manual accompanying it. The Digital Millennium Copyright Act (DMCA) of 1998 strengthened laws against software piracy, while providing protections for Internet service providers against copyright infringement under certain conditions.

To control downloading of information from the Internet, offline browsers allow districts to create their own "mini-Internet" that is limited to the files that are downloaded in creating it. Like any kind of downloading, that of content for offline browsing is subject to copyright challenges. Schools are best advised to contact the webmaster for each Internet site being downloaded for later offline use and get permission.

The Technology, Education, and Copyright Harmonization (TEACH) Act of 2002, an amendment to the federal copyright act, expanded the rights of educators in accredited nonprofit educational institutions that have copyright use policies in effect and provide copyright information to their employees and students. Under TEACH, an educator may show or perform certain works related to the curriculum "face-to face" in the classroom, regardless of the medium. However, there are some limitations concerning students participating in distance education. For example, the work may be digitized for use with distance learners but may not be shown in its entirety. The Act applies to "nondramatic" literary and musical works, reasonable and limited portions of any other work, and any work in an amount comparable to a typical classroom display. The Act does not apply to works produced for the digital distance education market, unlawfully made copies, or course materials typically purchased by individual students. Supplemental materials a teacher may assign for reading or viewing outside of class are subject to the fair use guidelines. Since lawsuits over duplication of copyrighted materials are becoming more common, it is important for school districts to develop guidelines for employees and students, and to monitor compliance.

EXTRACURRICULAR ACTIVITIES AND THE UIL

Here we look at the role of the State Board of Education, the commissioner of education, and the University Interscholastic League (UIL) in extracurricular activities. In Chapter 8 we discuss the restrictions that removal of students from classrooms by teachers and placement in an alternative education program impose on attending or participating in extracurricular activities.

TEC §33.081 leaves to the State Board of Education the establishment of rules limiting participation in extracurricular activities during the school day and school week, including practice times. TEC §33.081(g) provides that the decision of the Texas Commissioner of Education or the commissioner's designee in a dispute over student eligibility for extracurricular activities may not be appealed into state court except on the grounds of being arbitrary or capricious. Since the commissioner's jurisdiction is limited to decisions of local districts that violate the school laws of Texas or the terms of a written contract, allegations of unfairness or failure to follow local policy normally are not appealable to the commissioner. Thus absent allegations of illegal action, most disputes involving participation in extracurricular activities stop at the school board level.

The "no pass–no play" law specifies that a student who does not maintain a grade of 70 in all courses except certain honors or advanced classes must be suspended from extracurricular activities sponsored by the district or UIL for at least three school weeks or until the grade is raised to 70 or higher (TEC §33.081(c)). The law specifically excludes advanced placement (AP) and international baccalaureate (IB) courses

Table 5. Complying with Copyright Guidelines

Type of Copyrighted Material	School Personnel May	School Personnel May Not
Books, newspapers, magazines (specific items)	Make single copies for class preparation, or make multiple copies for classroom use of the following: • 250 words or less from poems • complete prose works if less than 2,500 words • excerpts from prose if not more than 1,000 words or 10% of entire work • one chart, graph, diagram, or illustration from a book or periodical • up to two pages or 10% of text from a work of fewer than 2,500 words	Copy consumables such as workbooks or standardized tests Copy items for use from term to term Copy more than one poem, article, or essay or two excerpts by the same author, nor more than three items from a collection (except current news) Make over nine copies for one class in one term (except current news)
Music	Make emergency copies to replace purchased ones Copy excerpts for academic preparation if less than a performable unit or 10% of entire work Make single copies for exercises or exams Make single copies of performable units if out of print or unavailable except in a larger work Copy student performances if for evaluation or rehearsals	Edit in a way that distorts the fundamental character of the work Add or alter lyrics Copy complete works Copy consumables
Television	Record local broadcast for instructional use within 10 days (some permit longer)	Use cable program without permission, but may retain program for years
Software	Make backup copies of purchased software	Make copies (other than backup) unless pursuant to lease or purchase

and honors and dual credit courses in English language arts, mathematics, science, social studies, economics, and foreign languages. TEA will review the list biennially. The student still can practice or rehearse with other students. Application of the "no pass–no play" rule against a student who has a disability that interferes with meeting regular academic requirements must be based on the student's failure to meet the terms of the individualized education program (IEP). The school board may develop a policy limiting the number of times beyond ten in a school year that a student can be absent from class for the purpose of participating in extracurricular activities sponsored by the district, UIL, or an organization approved by the board (TEC §38.0811). Further, no UIL competition is permitted on Monday through Thursday (or the last testing date) during the week of statewide assessment (TEC §33.0812).

State law prohibits a school district from holding an extracurricular activity, including practice time, in an athletic club that discriminates on the basis of race, color, religion, creed, national origin, or sex (TEC §33.082). Section 38.024 allows the board to purchase insurance for school athletes as a cost of operating the district's athletic program. Failure to obtain insurance is not to be construed as placing any legal liability on the district or its employees.

The Austin Court of Appeals in 2010 held that, as part of the University of Texas, the UIL is a governmental unit entitled to sovereign immunity, meaning it is immune from liability under state law unless imposed by statute (*University Interscholastic League v. Southwest Officials Association, Inc.*). The Texas Legislature requires that the UIL deposit its funds with the University of Texas at Austin, its parent organization, and file a fiscal report annually with the governor and the legislature. The UIL also must submit its rules and procedures to the commissioner of education for approval or modification (TEC §33.083). Finally, the legislature requires the UIL to establish an advisory council to review its rules and propose recommended changes to the governor, legislature, and State Board of Education (TEC §33.084). These actions tie the organization more closely to the state.

In *Niles v. University Interscholastic League* (1983) the U.S. Court of Appeals for the Fifth Circuit ruled that the UIL one-year-residency requirement for eligibility to participate in interscholastic events is rationally related to a legitimate state purpose and does not infringe on any constitutional rights. The court observed that there is no constitutional right to engage in an extracurricular activity. The Fifth Circuit also upheld the UIL's exclusion of a private school from participation in UIL competition. The UIL rule was rationally related to the state's interest in preventing unfair competition and did not violate the students' free exercise of religion or the right of the parents to enroll their children in a private, religious school (*Cornerstone Christian Schools v. University Interscholastic League*, 2009).

A federal court upheld the UIL's nineteen-year-old eligibility rule in *Blue v. University Interscholastic League,* 1980. The nineteen-year-old eligibility rule provides that any student who reaches his or her nineteenth birthday on or before the first day of September preceding a league contest is ineligible to participate. However, UIL rules add one extra year of UIL participation for students with disabilities who qualify for services under the Individuals with Disabilities Education Act (IDEA) or Section 504 of the Rehabilitation Act, if the student's education was delayed one or more years due to the disability. Students enrolled in courses for joint high school and college credit also maintain their eligibility to participate in UIL competition (TEC §33.087).

The Texas Supreme Court has advised courts to avoid interfering in the UIL's eligibility and forfeiture decisions involving high school athletics, emphasizing that student participation is considered a privilege and not a right and that judicial intervention often does more harm than good. In the spring of 2000 the UIL required the Robstown I.S.D. to forfeit all games the baseball team played with an ineligible player, causing the district to lose its place in the state tournament. A trial court ordered the UIL to permit Robstown to enter the playoffs and held the UIL in contempt for refusing. The Texas Supreme Court held that the trial court had abused its discretion and vacated the trial court's order (*In re University Interscholastic League,* 2000).

Coaches, trainers, sponsors, and marching band directors are required to complete an extracurricular activity safety training program developed by the commissioner that includes instruction in the recognition of catastrophic injuries, emergency action planning, and cardiopulmonary resuscitation (CPR), and they must obtain certification in the use of automated external defibrillators (AEDs) (TEC §§22.902, 33.202). Head coaches, directors, and sponsors must submit proof of current certification in first aid and CPR (TEC §33.086). Coaches also must take certain safety precautions, including ensuring students are hydrated, prohibiting students from returning to an activity after being unconscious, and preventing students from participating in unreasonably dangerous activities (TEC §33.204–.205)

Students who participate in extracurricular activities must receive training in recognizing serious injuries and the dangers of taking dietary supplements (TEC §33.202). Students and parents also must complete and sign UIL forms requiring the student to undergo a physical evaluation and provide a medical history and acknowledging the rules (TEC §33.203). Further, a student who participates in UIL athletic competitions must agree to submit to random testing for illegal steroids, and the parent must sign a statement acknowledging agreement (TEC §33.091). The UIL must provide an educational program for students, parents, and coaches regarding the health effects of steroid use.

ADDRESSING THE NEEDS OF SPECIAL GROUPS

At-Risk Children

Over the years, the legislature has tried various measures to reduce the dropout rate in Texas schools. The law leaves districts considerable discretion to deal with the problem, holding them responsible for the results through the accountability system.

The student achievement indicators adopted by the commissioner must include dropout rates and district completion rates for students in grades nine through twelve (TEC §39.053). Sanctions designed to improve high school completion rates may be imposed if a district fails to meet the standard for dropout rates for two or more years (TEC §39.102(a) (11)). In determining dropout and completion rates for accountability purposes, TEC §39.053(g-1) lists several exclusions. Districts do not include students who are expelled, students who have engaged in delinquent conduct or conduct indicating a need for supervision, students who have been convicted and sentenced for crimes, students who are being held in a county detention center, students who are incarcerated and certified to stand trial as adults, students who originally were enrolled in grades seven through twelve as unschooled refugees or asylees, students who are in the process of obtaining a court-ordered GED, students who do not count for ADA purposes, or students who previously were reported to the state as dropouts, including those who reenrolled then dropped out again.

TEC §29.081 requires each district to develop appropriate compensatory or accelerated programs for students who are not performing well. Accelerated instruction is required for students who are at risk of dropping out of school or have not performed satisfactorily on an end-of-course assessment. Districts are required to document the effectiveness of accelerated instruction in reducing the dropout rate and increasing student achievement. The statute applies to students under age twenty-six and specifies several factors for determining potential dropouts, including weak academic performance, limited English proficiency, child neglect or abuse, pregnancy, expulsion, criminal activity, and homelessness. Note that a prekindergarten or kindergarten student who did not advance to the next grade level at the parent's request is not considered at risk for dropping out of school (TEC §29.081(d-1)).

Districts may operate an extended-year program for students in kindergarten through grade eleven who are identified as unlikely to be promoted to the next grade or students in grade twelve who are not likely to graduate before the beginning of the next school year (TEC §29.082). Each class is limited to not more than sixteen students and must be taught by a specially trained teacher. If a student attends at least 90 percent of the classes and completes the requirements, the student must be promoted to the next grade unless the parent or guardian objects. Districts that have an extended-year program are required to phase out student retention. Further, a district may provide an optional flexible year program, pursuant to the requirements of TEC §29.0821, for students who did not or likely would not perform successfully on an assessment instrument or who would not be promoted to the next grade.

A district or charter school with a high dropout rate must submit a dropout prevention plan to the commissioner explaining how it will use its compensatory education allotment or high school allotment to implement dropout prevention strategies (TEC §29.918). The commissioner has developed an extensive dropout prevention strategy plan for this purpose, set forth in 19 TAC §89.1701. Further, the commissioner is required to develop a process for auditing school dropout records electronically (TEC §39.308). The system must be able to identify districts at high risk of having inaccurate dropout records, thus necessitating on-site monitoring of the records. Each district-level planning and decision-making committee and each campus-level committee for a junior high, middle school, or high school campus must analyze information about dropout prevention and use that information in developing campus or district improvement plans (TEC §11.255). Pursuant to TEC §29.908, the commissioner has established a program of early college high schools and middle colleges for students who are at risk of dropping out or who want to accelerate completion of high school. The program allows students to combine high school and college-level courses during the ninth through twelfth grades and receive a high school diploma and an associate degree or sixty hours toward a baccalaureate degree upon graduation. Students are given postsecondary educational and training opportunities, flexible class scheduling, and academic mentoring. Rules for implementing this program are found at 19 TAC §§4.154 et seq.

In certain larger counties, a school district with a dropout rate higher than 15 percent may partner with a public junior college to provide a dropout recovery program on the junior college campus, whereby students may complete their education and receive a high school diploma. The junior college may partner with a public technical institute to provide career and technology courses leading to certification as part of the curriculum. Such a program is open to students under age twenty-six who lack no more than three course credits to graduate or who failed the state assessments required for graduation (TEC §§29.401–.402). The SBOE also is directed to provide online administration of high school equivalency exams for persons eighteen years of age and older (TEC §7.111).

Education Code §§33.151–.159 outline the "Communities in Schools" program, a youth dropout prevention program. An elementary or secondary school receiving funds under TEC §33.156 is required to participate in a Communities in Schools program if the number of at-risk students enrolled in the school is equal to at least 10 percent of the average daily attendance (ADA) (TEC §33.157).

Bilingual Children

In 1974 the U.S. Supreme Court decided in *Lau v. Nichols* that federal guidelines enforcing Title VI of the 1964 Civil Rights Act require school districts to eliminate language deficiencies where school board policies discriminate against minorities, even in the absence of an intent to do so. The California case involved Chinese students who were not receiving any instruction in learning English, yet were enrolled in all-English classes. Section 601 of the Act at the time banned discrimination based on the grounds of race, color, or national origin in "any Federal program or activity receiving Federal financial assistance." The Court noted that California requires English to be the primary language of instruction (as does Texas) and that proficiency in English is a graduation requirement. Concluding that "those who do not understand English are certain to find their classroom experiences wholly incomprehensible and in no way meaningful," the Court also ruled that the school system had to comply with government regulations issued pursuant to the 1964 Civil Rights Act requiring affirmative steps to rectify language deficiencies. As do most districts, the California school district received substantial federal funds.

Lau had a spillover effect on school districts around the country. The chief problem with the ruling, however, was that the Court did not specify exactly what form bilingual programs are to have in order for school districts to comply with the 1964 act. In providing funds for meeting the needs of limited-English-proficient (LEP) students, the federal government has issued broad guidelines that have been interpreted in various ways by the states and the school districts. Two basic interpretations have resulted in reference to bilingual education programs: (1) providing students with instruction in their primary language and ensuring that English-language instruction be part of the students' daily curriculum until the students can understand enough English to function adequately in an all-English curriculum, and (2) immersing students completely in English-as-a-second-language (ESL) programs until the students can function adequately in an all-English curriculum. Variations that resulted from these two basic interpretations have only served to complicate the implementation of the instructional programs geared to meet the needs of the LEP student. Few exemplary programs that meet all the legal requirements exist.

Subchapter B of Chapter 29 of the Texas Education Code sets forth state law with respect to bilingual education. These provisions, originally adopted in 1973, were revised substantially during the 1981 legislative session, as a result of a federal court decision handed down by Federal Judge William Wayne Justice (*United States v. Texas (Bilingual)*). They remain little changed in the present Texas Education Code. As noted earlier, though most Texas school districts have been freed from TEA's monitoring requirements and from federal trial court continuing jurisdiction under Civil Order 5281, districts must continue to implement language programs for students with limited English proficiency (*United States v. Texas (LULAC VI)*, 2010). The U.S. Court of Appeals for the Fifth Circuit sent the case back to the federal trial court for a determination whether the state has provided equal educational opportunity to English language learners.

TEC §29.051 asserts that English is the primary language of Texas. The provisions require each school district with twenty or more students of limited English proficiency in the same grade to offer bilingual education in kindergarten through the elementary grades; bilingual education, instruction in English as a second language, or other transitional language instruction approved by TEA in postelementary grades through the eighth grade; and instruction in English as a second language in grades nine through twelve. Section 29.055 of the Texas Education Code requires dual-language instruction to be full-time, with basic skills instruction in the primary language of the students and with intensive instruction as well in English-language skills. The program also is to incorporate the cultural aspects of the students' backgrounds. Bilingual classes must be located in regular schools, not separate facilities.

A district that is required to offer bilingual or special language programs must offer a voluntary school program for children of limited English proficiency who will be eligible for kindergarten or first grade at the beginning of the following school year (TEC §29.060). Under §29.056, TEA is required to develop standardized criteria for identifying, assessing, and classifying bilingual students. Parents are to be kept fully informed and must approve the placement of their children in the program. Both school district and parents are provided with the right to appeal a placement decision. If a student makes a failing grade during the first two years after being transferred out of a bilingual or special language program, a language proficiency assessment committee (LPAC) must review the student's performance and evaluate whether the student should be readmitted to the program (TEC §29.0561).

Gifted Children

State law requires that school districts address the needs of gifted and talented students. A gifted and talented student is defined as one "who performs at or shows the potential for performing at a remarkably high level of accomplishment when compared to others of the same age, experience, or environment and who exhibits high performance capability in an intellectual, creative, or artistic field; possesses an unusual capacity for leadership; or excels in a specific academic field" (TEC §29.121). Using criteria developed by the State Board of Education as part of a state plan for serving these students, each district is required to adopt a process for identifying gifted and talented students and to establish a program for those students in each grade level. TEC §28.023 requires school districts to develop advanced placement tests for each primary grade level and secondary academic subject for advancing talented students from one grade to another under SBOE guidelines. The commissioner is required to adopt standards for evaluating gifted and talented programs to ensure they meet the requirements of the state plan set forth in TEC §29.123 (TEC §39.236).

Abused and Neglected Children

Provisions of the Family Code require that anyone having cause to believe that a child's physical or mental health or welfare has been or may be adversely affected by abuse or neglect shall immediately make a report to any local or state law enforcement agency, the Department of Family and Protective Services, or other appropriate agency (Family Code §§261.101, 261.103). A report of abuse occurring in a juvenile justice program should be made to the Texas Juvenile Probation Commission as well (Family Code §261.405).

A child is defined as a person under the age of eighteen. Definitions of "abuse" and "neglect" are contained in §261.001. Generally, abuse includes mental or emotional injury by any person that impairs the child's growth, development, or psychological functioning; physical injury or threat of physical injury by any person against a child; failure to prevent another person from physically injuring a child; inappropriate sexual conduct; obscene or pornographic photographing of a child; and injury to a child caused by a person's use of a controlled substance. Neglect encompasses failure by the person responsible for the child (including a teacher) to protect a child from a situation that could endanger the child; failure to obtain medical attention for a child; failure to provide food, clothing, or shelter for a child; and failure by the person responsible for the child's care to provide care after the child returns home from an absence.

Section 261.101(b) provides that a professional who has cause to believe that a child has been or may be abused or neglected has forty-eight hours to make a report. This responsibility cannot be delegated to someone else. A professional is defined as a person who is licensed or certified by the state or an employee of a state-licensed facility who has direct contact with children. The term includes teachers, nurses, and day-care employees, among others. Anonymous reports are not encouraged but will be received and acted upon. The identity of the person

making the report is confidential and may be disclosed only under narrow circumstances specified by law (TEC §261.101).

Section 261.109 of the Family Code makes the failure to report suspected child abuse or neglect a Class A misdemeanor, except it is a
state jail felony if it involves a child with an intellectual disability in
a residential facility who suffers serious bodily injury as a result of the
abuse or neglect. Section 261.106 expressly shields from civil or criminal liability those who in good faith report suspected child abuse. Immunity extends as well when one participates in any judicial proceeding
resulting from the report (*Chaney v. Corona*, 2003). (See Chapter 10
for more on liability and immunity.) Section 261.108 provides for an
award of attorneys' fees and other expenses incurred by persons who
report suspected cases of child abuse and then have frivolous lawsuits
filed against them for doing so. An employer may not discriminate by
suspension, termination, or other negative action against an employee
who reports suspected child abuse or neglect in good faith. An employee
who is the victim of such action may recover damages, court costs, and
attorneys' fees and may be entitled to reinstatement. The statute sets
limits on the damage awards (Family Code §261.110).

Under Family Code 261.302(b), child abuse investigations can take
place while children are in school, but interviews should not be conducted in a classroom in view of other students and the faculty. The
Texas Public Information Act permits investigators to access student
records in connection with a child abuse case. TEC §38.004 requires
school districts and open-enrollment charter schools to adopt a policy
concerning cooperation with law enforcement during investigations
of child abuse and neglect and requiring each employee to report child
abuse and neglect in accordance with the Family Code. Districts also
must adopt a policy promoting teacher, student, and parent awareness
of sexual abuse and describing intervention and counseling options
(TEC §38.0041). Schools must post a sign in English and Spanish containing the toll-free number of the Department of Family and Protective
Services to receive reports of child abuse or neglect (TEC §38.0042).

In addition to observing the reporting requirement under the Family Code, a superintendent or director of a school district, regional education service center, or shared services arrangement is required to notify the State Board for Educator Certification (SBEC) upon reasonable
cause to believe that an educator: (1) employed or seeking employment
has a criminal record, (2) was terminated based on abuse of or other
unlawful act with a student or minor, or (3) resigned based on such misconduct and reasonable evidence supports a recommendation for termination based on abuse of or unlawful act with a student or minor (TEC
§21.006). The superintendent or director must file a written report with
SBEC no later than the seventh day after learning of the misconduct and
notify the board of trustees or other governing body that such a report

was filed. A superintendent or director who makes such a report in good faith and while acting in an official capacity is immune from civil or criminal liability, but sanctions may be imposed by SBEC for failing to make the report.

Our society continues to be troubled with the state-versus-family issue; this makes prompt reporting coupled with documented evidence particularly important. Only under these circumstances are state agencies likely to be successful in intervening before it is too late.

SUMMARY

Significant changes have taken place in recent years in Texas regarding student enrollment. Segregation by law has ended, and most Texas school districts have been released from supervision in the long-running statewide desegregation order, *United States v. Texas.*

Virtually all students, including those who are homeless or have established a residence in a district separate from their parents or guardians, are entitled to a tuition-free education. The emphasis is on student inclusion.

Despite efforts to return more authority to the local district and its employees, significant top-down requirements remain, as demonstrated by the discussion in this chapter regarding the state-mandated curriculum, student testing, and controls on extracurricular participation. At the same time, both federal and state laws have strengthened school district, campus, and administrator accountability measures. The toughened standards may result in major changes for low-performing schools in the future.

THREE

Special Education

NO AREA OF SCHOOL LAW has experienced such explosive growth over the past forty years as special education. Since the early 1970s, the rights of students with disabilities have been increasingly a subject of legislation and litigation. Our purpose in this chapter is to present the legal requirements for identifying and serving children with disabilities in Texas schools. Included will be a discussion of procedures to be followed in disciplining these students, the impact of the No Child Left Behind Act (NCLB), and the standards required by Section 504. But first, a refresher course on acronyms is in order.

THE JARGON OF SPECIAL EDUCATION

Special educators and their attorneys often seem to have beamed down from another planet where initials and acronyms take the place of words. In order to walk the special education walk you have to talk the special education talk. Here is a quick overview of common terms.

P.L. 94–142:	This is the landmark legislation passed by Congress in 1975 guaranteeing every child with a disability a free, appropriate public education. The law more properly was known as the Education for All Handicapped Children Act, and now is known as the Individuals with Disabilities Education Act.
IDEA:	The Individuals with Disabilities Education Act (IDEA).
IDEA 2004:	Late in 2004, Congress passed the Individuals with Disabilities Education Improvement Act, a series of amendments to the law.
504:	Section 504 of the 1973 Rehabilitation Act, a federal law that prohibits discrimination against persons with disabilities in programs that receive federal funds. Section 504's counterpart in the private sector is the Americans with Disabilities Act. Both laws were amended as of January 1, 2009.

FAPE: Free, appropriate public education. The law mandates that FAPE be available to every child, regardless of the nature or severity of the disability.

IEP: Individualized education program. This is the basic planning tool for the child's education. It is to be collaboratively developed by school officials and parents.

ARDC: Admission, review, and dismissal committee. This refers to a committee of school officials and parents who have the responsibility for developing the IEP and placing the child in an appropriate program. Most states refer to this group as the IEP team, but Texas calls it an ARDC.

Placement: This refers to the instructional arrangement in which the child is educated. It can be anything from the regular classroom setting to a special residential school.

LRE: Least restrictive environment. The placement of the child must be in the LRE that is appropriate for the child. That is, it must enable the child to interact with his or her nondisabled peers as much as is appropriate in light of the nature and severity of the disability.

Related Services: Noninstructional services that are necessary for the child to obtain benefit from the educational program. These include such things as transportation, occupational therapy (OT), physical therapy (PT), counseling, and school health services.

Eligibility: In order to receive federally funded special education services, the child must meet eligibility criteria for one of several conditions. These include learning disabled (LD), emotionally disturbed (ED), other health impaired (OHI), visually impaired (VI), auditorially impaired (AI), along with others.

FIE: Full individual evaluation. Eligibility and services should be based on an FIE. This term replaced "comprehensive individual assessment" (CIA).

IEE: Independent educational evaluation. If a parent disagrees with the evaluation done by the school, the parent is entitled to an IEE, meaning an evaluation done by a qualified evaluator who is not employed by the school district.

ESY: Extended school year services. This refers to services beyond the normal school year that are

determined to be necessary for the student to
receive FAPE.

OSEP: The Office of Special Education Programs. This
is the federal agency with responsibility for the
implementation of the IDEA.

RtI: Response to Intervention is a process now mandated by federal law to provide more effective services to students in general education programs
in order to ensure that a child is not labeled as
having a disability erroneously.

FEDERAL LEGISLATION

Special education is governed by federal law more than any other aspect of school law. The notion that education is a matter to be left to
the sound discretion of the states and local communities went out the
window in 1975 when P.L. 94-142 was passed. Congress responded to
several court cases that were brought in the late 1960s and early 1970s
asserting that children with disabilities were being denied an equal
opportunity to public education. Just as racial minorities, who, at the
time, were seeking equal opportunity in schooling, parents of students
with disabilities sought redress through the courts.

By 1975, Congress declared that our public schools were failing to
serve over eight million students with special needs. So Congress made
federal money available to states, provided that the states adopted certain policies and procedures. Here is where we first encountered many
of the terms that have since become so familiar. To qualify for federal
financial assistance, a state would have to ensure that each student with
a disability was provided a "free, appropriate public education." That
education would have to include "special education and related services." Each child would be entitled to an "IEP" and a placement with
nondisabled peers to the extent appropriate.

It is difficult to conceive of a piece of legislation with better intentions. All children would be served; their parents would be directly
involved; their unique needs would be assessed and provided for; they
would not be segregated or hidden from the mainstream; each one
would receive an education that was appropriate; and there would be
procedural and legal requirements in place to make sure that all these
things really happened.

But from the beginning, there were concerns about cost, paperwork
burdens, litigation, and raised expectations. President Gerald Ford expressed many of these concerns when he signed the bill into law. His
message read, in part, as follows:

Unfortunately, this bill promises more than the federal government can deliver, and its good intentions could be thwarted by the many unwise provisions it contains. Everyone can agree with the objective stated in the title of this bill—educating all handicapped children in our nation. The key question is whether the bill will really accomplish that objective.

Even the strongest supporters of this measure know as well as I that they are falsely raising the expectations of the groups affected by claiming authorization levels which are excessive and unrealistic.

Despite my strong support for full educational opportunities for our handicapped children, the funding levels in this bill will simply not be possible if federal expenditures are to be brought under control and a balanced budget achieved over the next few years.

There are other features in the bill which I believe to be objectionable and which should be changed. It contains a vast array of detailed, complex and costly administrative requirements which would unnecessarily assert federal control over traditional state and local government functions. It establishes complex requirements under which tax dollars would be used to support administrative paperwork, and not educational programs. Unfortunately, these requirements will remain in effect even though the Congress appropriates far less than the amounts contemplated in [the law].

Indeed, the federal government never has come through with the amount of money that was first contemplated. The law authorized Congress to appropriate "up to" 40 percent of the excess costs states encountered in serving students with disabilities. Congress has never appropriated even half of that 40 percent figure. Thus, much of the burden of implementing this complex law has fallen on state and local shoulders.

So let's take a look at what the law requires.

Child Find

If you drive certain highways in Texas these days, you may notice a large, colorful billboard advertising IDEA. These public displays symbolize the local school district's responsibility to find each child residing in the district who needs special education services. "Child find" is the label attached to the requirement that school districts take an active approach toward identifying and serving students in need.

Schools are not permitted to sit back and wait for parents to ask for services. The law does not require billboards, but it does require school districts to publicize the availability of special education services. Teachers should be trained to identify the typical signs of disability so that students in need can be referred for services. Public schools should reach out to private-school administrators and home schoolers, to make sure that everyone knows that special services are available for those who need them.

Much of the litigation brought against school districts under IDEA alleges the failure to fulfill the child find requirement. Basically, such suits allege that "you should have known my child needed services, and you should have referred the child to the special education program." Since the school legally is required to be proactive, schoolteachers at all levels must be trained to recognize the typical indicators that a student might be eligible for special education. If the district fails to refer a child to the special education program when it is clear that the child needs these services, the school might later be required to provide compensatory services to the child.

As school districts have ramped up their efforts to provide RtI (Response to Intervention) services, the requirement to find every child who needs special education services has come into sharper focus. There is a natural tension between the child find principle and the RtI process. Child find emphasizes referring and testing every child who may need special education services. RtI, on the other hand, encourages school districts to fully explore services that are available in general education before moving toward special education. Child find encourages educators to think about special education services; RtI encourages educators not to do so.

Due to this natural tension, there has been, and likely will continue to be, considerable litigation over referral, eligibility, and services. In some cases, parents allege that schools have dillydallied around with RtI while the child falls behind. However, if RtI is implemented properly this will not happen. RtI requires careful progress monitoring, with adjustments to the program to be made based on results. Therefore a student who fails to make progress in the RtI program should be moved to a more intense level of RtI services, or referred to special education. The tension that exists between child find and RtI is a natural result of the effort to use all of the school district's resources appropriately. That tension is properly handled via progress monitoring, data analysis, individualized decision-making, and communication with the parents.

The communication with the parents must comply with IDEA's procedural safeguards. The federal law requires that schools provide parents with a copy of the state's "procedural safeguards" document when the parent requests a referral for special education testing. In Texas, this document is called the Notice of Procedural Safeguards. When the school refuses to conduct an evaluation requested by the parent, the school must provide PWN (prior written notice) in accordance with the procedural safeguards document. A school might refuse—at least temporarily—to conduct an evaluation of a child because the educators believe that the RtI process is producing good results. In such a case, the school must provide parents with PWN spelling out its rationale and advising the parents of how they can challenge the school's decision. If the parent can later prove that (1) she requested testing, (2) the school did not do the testing, and (3) the school also did not provide PWN, then the parent has a viable case alleging a child find failure on the part of the school district.

However, that parent will also have to prove one more fact in order to prevail on the "child find" claim—that the student would have qualified for special education. This came up in *D.G. v. Flour Bluff I.S.D.* (2012). The lower court had found the district guilty of a "child find" violation. The Fifth Circuit reversed, noting that there was no evidence in the record to establish that the student would have qualified for special education services. Thus the notion of "child find" is tied to the standards for eligibility. To fulfill the child find responsibilities, educators need to have a clear understanding of what makes a student eligible for special education. As we shall discuss shortly, not every struggling student will satisfy the criteria.

Evaluation

Years ago a school superintendent discussed with the school district's attorney a situation involving a student who, according to the superintendent, was emotionally disturbed but had never been identified as such by the school. When the attorney asked how the superintendent could know that the student was emotionally disturbed without a proper, formal determination, the superintendent explained, "He's crazy. His whole family is crazy. The acorn does not fall far from the tree!"

It is to avoid such untutored labeling that the law requires the school district to obtain a full individual evaluation (FIE) of the student's condition before applying any sort of label and before placing the child in a special education program. Evaluation procedures must guarantee that children are tested in their native language, that measurement instruments are not racially or culturally biased, that tests are validated for the specific purpose for which they are used, that tests are administered by trained personnel in accordance with their instructions, and that no single criterion (e.g., an IQ score) is used to determine an appropriate program for a child.

An initial FIE is required prior to a child's placement in special education and a reevaluation must be done at least every three years thereafter. Prior to a reevaluation, the members of the ARDC must review the existing data and decide what additional testing should be done. The idea behind this provision was to eliminate unnecessary testing. For example, if a child is blind, it really is not necessary to conduct a formal vision test every three years. So the parties can decide what tests should be done. Parents who disagree with the school's evaluation of their child have the right to obtain an independent educational evaluation (IEE). The IEE must be considered by the school, along with the school's own evaluations, and the school may be required to pay for the IEE, unless the school can demonstrate that its evaluation was properly done.

However, a parent cannot require the school district to accept an independent evaluation in lieu of the district's own evaluation. A decision from the Fifth Circuit has made this crystal clear. When Wesley Andress was due for an evaluation to reconsider his eligibility for special education, his parents objected to the school's conducting the testing. They argued that Wesley would be psychologically harmed by the evaluation process and offered to provide the school district with evaluations they had obtained privately. The school district, however, insisted on its right to conduct its own evaluation of Wesley, using personnel chosen by the school district.

The Fifth Circuit vigorously upheld the school district in this case: "If a student's parents want him to receive special education under IDEA, they must allow the school itself to reevaluate the student and they cannot force the school to rely solely on an independent evaluation" (*Andress v. Cleveland I.S.D.*, 1995).

This case is particularly important because evaluation data play such a critical role in the entire process. Evaluation data truly are the rudder that steers the ship in special education matters. All decisions concerning the student—the nature of the IEP, the level of inclusion with nondisabled students, the form of discipline to be used, the provision of related services—should reflect the evaluation data pertaining to that student.

The Fifth Circuit issued another important decision in 2006 that again illustrates the authority that schools have to conduct evaluations, even over parental objection. Shelby had a rare medical condition, dysautonomia, which made her vulnerable to sudden episodes that could result in unconsciousness, cardiac arrest, or death. She was also extremely sensitive to room temperature. Shelby was cared for by a medical specialist, and the school wanted information and guidance from the physician as to how to handle Shelby at school.

Shelby's grandmother, who served as her guardian, would not provide consent for the school to contact the doctor directly, or to obtain a medical evaluation from the doctor. She did permit written communication to occur, but only after she approved the school's questions and edited the doctor's answers. Frustrated with this situation, the school district requested a due process hearing, seeking an order that would override the lack of consent and permit the district to obtain the medical evaluation it wanted.

The Fifth Circuit ruled in favor of the school district, noting that "where a school district articulates reasonable grounds for its necessity to conduct a medical reevaluation of a student, a lack of parental consent will not bar it from doing so." Thus even in the very sensitive area of medical evaluations, a school district is entitled to obtain an evaluation over parental objection when the evaluation is educationally necessary (*Shelby S. v. Conroe I.S.D.*, 2006).

When a school district conducts an evaluation, it should discuss the results of the evaluation promptly at an ARDC meeting. In *R.P. v. Alamo Heights I.S.D.* (2012), the Fifth Circuit slapped the district on the wrist for its failure to do so. The ARDC had called for an evaluation of the student's need for assistive technology. The evaluation was to be completed by October 2008. The record showed that the district did not discuss the evaluation, however, until May 2009. The court inferred that the October date was selected so that the evaluation results could be incorporated into the IEP for 2008–2009. The court found that the failure to do this was an error, but a harmless one, because the district provided evidence that the student had made progress in the areas affected by assistive technology.

Eligibility

Students are eligible for special education services if they meet two requirements: First, the student must have a disability that qualifies under the law; second, the student must, as a result of that disability, need special education services. The ARD committee determines a child's eligibility based on these two factors.

The disabilities that would qualify for special education include just about everything that might present itself in school. The most common disability identified by school districts is a learning disability (LD). Other disabilities that schools can recognize are intellectually disabled (this used to be designated as "mentally retarded [MR]"); deaf, speech, and language impaired; visually impaired; seriously emotionally disturbed (SED, or ED); orthopedically impaired; autistic; traumatic brain injured (TBI); and other health impaired (OHI). This final designation, OHI, has proliferated in recent years. It is meant to be an umbrella, encompassing any condition that results in limited health, alertness, or vitality. IDEA was amended in 1997 to include attention deficit disorder (ADD) and attention deficit hyperactivity disorder (ADHD) as examples of conditions that could fit underneath that umbrella, thus tremendously expanding the notion of OHI.

Besides the disability, the student must demonstrate a need for special education services. The disability must adversely affect the student's performance to the point that the student requires services beyond those offered through regular education and other special programs.

Some students have a great need for special services, but do not have a disability that qualifies under the law. Consider the hypothetical case of José, whose family has just moved to Texas from Guatemala. José is fifteen years old and appears to be bright and healthy. But he has never been enrolled in an educational program of any kind. His family is extremely poor. José does not read or write, and he has no math skills beyond simple counting. He has virtually no English language skills. Does José qualify for special education? No. Though he clearly will need a great deal of special attention and special services from the school district, none of his special needs can be attributed to a disability. Indeed, based on what we know so far about José, he does not appear to have a disability of any kind, as that term is defined in IDEA. While José, as presented here, is an extreme case, there are many closer calls, where students with limited English proficiency or educationally disadvantaged backgrounds are tossed into special education programs inappropriately. When such students are placed in special education inappropriately, we see an overidentification of racial and language minorities in special education programs.

On the other hand, there are students who may have a disability but do not need special education services. Not all disabilities are severe enough to require special treatment by educators. Some students have disabilities of a relatively mild nature that can be accommodated effectively through good teaching practices.

Response to Intervention (RtI)

IDEA 2004 introduced the concept of "Response to Intervention" (RtI) as a means of identifying students who may have a learning disability (LD). LD is the largest category of students in special education programs, and Congress has clearly concluded that many of the students identified as LD should not be.

As noted at the start of this chapter, the move to RtI is designed to shrink the special education population by providing more focused interventions to students who are struggling in regular education. RtI requires the use of research-proven methods in a systematic way, while information on student progress is constantly gathered and analyzed. Decisions about students are to be based on the data of progress—how the student is "responding" to "interventions." This represents a major shift away from the somewhat mechanical approach Texas has used in the past, which is known as the "discrepancy model." That model required a comparison of an IQ test and an achievement test. If there was a "significant discrepancy" in one or more areas, and that discrepancy could not be explained in any other way, the student was considered LD.

Under RtI, individual testing of students will still be required, but eligibility decisions will not be based solely on the comparison of two tests. Moreover, the theory is that many students who would have ended up in special education in the past will instead make suitable progress in regular education programs that are supplemented with targeted "interventions."

We should point out that even though we discuss RtI in the special education chapter of this book, RtI is the responsibility of the general education staff. The theory is that if students can be given the kind of focused and intense interventions that they need in the general education program, then they will make progress without the provision of special education services.

ARD Committee

All of the important decisions about special education are made on an individualized basis by the student's ARD committee. The term "ARD" never appears in federal law. Instead, it refers to an "IEP team," which must develop the IEP, place the student, make decisions about disciplinary matters, and decide on evaluation activities. Texas has chosen to place those responsibilities under the banner of the admission, review, and dismissal committee. Thus we have ARDCs.

The ARDC is composed of (1) the parent(s); (2) a regular education teacher, if the student "is or may be participating in the regular education environment"; (3) a special education teacher or service provider; (4) someone who can interpret the instructional implications of the assessment data; (5) a representative of the school district; (6) others who, in the judgment of the parent(s) or the school, have special knowledge or expertise; and (7) when appropriate, the student.

The primary functions of the ARDC are to develop the student's IEP and decide on his or her placement. Since the IEP must be reviewed at least annually, there must be at least one ARDC meeting for every special education student each year. Some students will have many more than that.

Members of the ARDC are expected to work collaboratively to develop a program. When they do so and are able to reach consensus, few legal issues arise. When they fail to reach consensus, the school district usually must give the parents the opportunity to recess the meeting and then reconvene it in ten days or less. The recess is not required, however, when the student has committed an offense that calls for placement in a disciplinary alternative education program (DAEP) or expulsion. If consensus ultimately cannot be reached between the school and the parents, the parties may go to mediation, or the parents or school may opt for a special education due process hearing.

Individualized Education Program

If there is any single principle that applies to special education law across the board, it is individualization. The strengths, weaknesses, and needs of each child are to be considered on an individual basis throughout the decision-making process. Thus the individualized education program (IEP) is crucial. The IEP is a written statement of services to be provided and goals to be achieved. More specifically, the law requires that the IEP must contain:

- A statement of the child's present levels of educational performance;
- A statement of measurable annual goals, including short-term objectives if the student is assessed below grade level;
- A statement of the special education, related services, supplementary aids and services, program modifications, and supports for school personnel that will be provided to, or on behalf of, the child;
- An explanation of any exclusion of the child from the regular classroom and extracurricular activities;
- A statement of any accommodations the child will need to take statewide or districtwide assessments, such as the STAAR. If the student is assessed in some other manner (such as through an alternative assessment), the IEP must specify why this decision was made and how the student's progress will be assessed.
- Dates for services to be provided, along with the frequency, duration, and location where services will be provided; and
- A statement of how the parents will be regularly informed of the child's progress toward achieving the annual goals.

In 2011, the legislature directed the commissioner to develop a model IEP form for school districts to consider. The model form was to include only those provisions required by federal and/or state law. The purpose seems to be to provide a simple, streamlined form for schools to consider. That form is now posted on the TEA website in English and Spanish. Even this streamlined version is thirteen pages long, and TEA is careful to make note that use of the form does not guarantee that the school has fulfilled its legal duties. The model form is just that—a model. It is optional. We shall see how much it is used.

General Curriculum

IDEA now places a great emphasis on the subject matter that students with disabilities are to learn. This was one of the most significant new features of the 1997 amendments authorized by Congress (IDEA 1997). The original law, P.L. 94-142, required *that* students with disabilities be educated, but it said nothing about *what* the students were to be taught. Twenty-two years after the passage of P.L. 94-142, Congress sent the message that the students should be taught, as much as possible, the same subject matter that the regular education students are taught.

Throughout the law, the phrase "general curriculum" is repeated. The IEP is to be built around the "general curriculum" as much as possible. Students who move to an alternative placement still must be able to "progress in the general curriculum." The term "general curriculum" is not specifically defined. But in a "discussion" of its final regulations, OSEP states that "in each State or school district there is a 'general curriculum' that is applicable to all children." It appears, then, that the "general curriculum" simply refers to the things the regular education students are expected to learn.

In Texas, this is not hard to figure out. Texas has adopted the Texas Essential Knowledge and Skills (TEKS), which defines what students are expected to learn in each year, in each class, kindergarten through twelfth grade. This is the "general curriculum" for Texas students. With its emphasis on the general curriculum, IDEA 1997 simply takes the notion of "least restrictive environment" to the next logical step. The concept of LRE tells us that students with disabilities should be segregated from their nondisabled peers only to the degree necessary to accommodate each student's disability. The notion of teaching the general curriculum applies this same standard to the content of what students are taught. Students with disabilities should be taught the same things the nondisabled students are taught, except as necessary to accommodate each student's disability.

NCLB and Statewide Assessments

Students with disabilities also are expected to achieve at the same level as their nondisabled peers to the extent possible. But to what extent is that possible? How many students with disabilities realistically can be expected to achieve at the same level as nondisabled students? This issue has become more prominent since the passage of the No Child Left Behind Act (NCLB).

As outlined in Chapter 2, the NCLB requires states to hold all students to the same academic standards, and to see that students demonstrate "adequate yearly progress" (AYP) through statewide tests in certain subjects. (However, it is important to note that as of this writing, Texas has applied for a waiver from some NCLB requirements. Indeed, the future of NCLB is uncertain, given that it is up for reauthorization by Congress.) In reporting progress, states and local school districts are required to "disaggregate the data," meaning that results must be reported not only for all students, but also for certain subgroups. These subgroups include major ethnic groups in the district, low-income students, limited-English-proficient students, and students with disabilities. NCLB holds educators accountable not just for the achievement of the student body as a whole, but also for each of the subgroups. Thus, if the student body as a whole meets the AYP target, but one or more of the subgroups (e.g., students with disabilities) does not, the school will not have made AYP.

As a general rule, a student is held accountable under NCLB for proficient achievement at the grade level in which the student is enrolled. The statewide assessment (STAAR in Texas) should be aligned with the curriculum for the grade level of the student. Federal regulations allow for only a small departure from that standard for students with disabilities. The regulations permit schools to count as "proficient" the scores of students who have been identified as having "the most significant cognitive disabilities" even though those students are assessed at a level below their grade level. However, neither the district nor the state as a whole can use this designation for more than 1 percent of the students assessed.

An example will help. Suppose the Adequate I.S.D. has one thousand students in grades three through eight, and grade ten, which are the grades assessed under NCLB. If there are one thousand such students, then the school can count as "proficient" only ten of these students (1 percent of a thousand) based on below-grade-level testing. If twenty-five students are tested below grade level, only ten of them can be counted as "proficient," and the other fifteen must be reported as nonproficient no matter how well they do on the test.

Least Restrictive Environment

Federal law expresses a strong preference for placing the child with disabilities in the setting in which that child would be served if there were no disability. This preference goes by various names: least restrictive environment (LRE), mainstreaming, inclusion. All these terms refer to much the same thing. In making placement decisions, the ARDC is to consider first the regular classroom. If that placement will not afford the student an appropriate education, then the committee should consider providing supplementary aids and services to enable the student to remain in the regular classroom. If that will not afford the child an appropriate education, then a move to a more restrictive environment is necessary.

The LRE preference in the law is strong but must be considered in light of the primary responsibility of the school district, which is to provide an education that is appropriate. The law mandates LRE, but it also mandates a full continuum of alternative placements, some of them highly restrictive. Obviously it was never the intention of Congress that each and every child be served in a regular classroom all day, every day.

The Supreme Court has not yet handled a case dealing with the LRE component of the law. We can look to the U.S. Court of Appeals for the Fifth Circuit for the leading case on the subject, *Daniel R.R. v. State Board of Education* (1989). Daniel was a six-year-old with Down syndrome in El Paso, Texas. Due to his cognitive and speech impairments, Daniel's developmental age was less than three years, and his communication skills were those of a child two years old. Daniel's parents asked the school district to place Daniel for a half-day in an early childhood program and a half-day in the prekindergarten class. The latter would enable Daniel to interact with his age-appropriate, nondisabled peers. The school agreed to give this a try.

By November, the school was ready to pronounce the experiment a failure. The teacher reported that Daniel required almost constant one-to-one attention, that he failed to master any of the skills she was teaching, and that modifying the Pre-K curriculum sufficiently to reach Daniel would have gone well beyond "modification"—it would have been an entirely different curriculum. The school district called for an ARDC meeting and proposed moving Daniel out of the prekindergarten program. The parents, however, were determined to keep Daniel in the Pre-K regular program.

The Fifth Circuit upheld the school district's proposed change in placement for Daniel. In doing so, the court determined that LRE cases would turn on two critical questions: Can education in the regular classroom, with the use of supplementary aids and services, be achieved satisfactorily? If not, has the school mainstreamed the child to the maximum extent appropriate?

In answering the first inquiry, the Fifth Circuit indicated courts should examine carefully the efforts made by the school district to enable the child to succeed in the regular classroom. Genuine, good-faith efforts are expected. Teachers must modify the curriculum and the methodology for a student with special needs.

The appeals court did not establish a clear litmus test for determining the extent to which efforts should be made to serve children with disabilities in the regular classroom. Rather, three broad generalizations were offered. First, the school does not have to provide "every conceivable supplementary aid or service"; second, "the Act does not require regular education instructors to devote all or most of their time to one handicapped child"; and third, schools are not expected to "modify the regular education program beyond recognition." Applying these standards to a given case is a matter for individualized ARDC decision-making.

This much is clear. Regular education teachers must be prepared, supported, and trained to handle children with disabilities in the regular classroom. The old attitude of "If he's going to be in my classroom, he's going to have to meet the same expectations, do the same work, comply with the same standards, and achieve the same results as everyone else" is legally obsolete. In the words of the Fifth Circuit:

> States must tolerate educational differences. . . . As a result, the Act
> accepts the notion that handicapped students will participate in
> regular education but that some of them will not benefit as much as

nonhandicapped students will. The Act requires states to tolerate a wide range of educational abilities in their schools and specifically, in regular education—the EHA's [now IDEA's] preferred educational environment.

The court's second inquiry arises in those cases where mainstreaming is not appropriate. Even if a child is properly placed in a separate special education program, the school district has the duty to provide as much mainstreaming opportunity as possible. The school should look for opportunities for mainstreaming in art, music, and physical education. The student should have the opportunity to ride the regular school bus, eat with the other students in the cafeteria, attend assemblies, and play on the playground with the other students.

A 1996 case involving the Regional Day School Program for the Deaf provides an important clarification as to "mainstreaming." The case concerned Katie, a bright third grader with a hearing impairment. Everyone agreed that Katie should be served in the regular classroom with a sign language interpreter. The argument was over where that regular classroom should be. Katie and her parents argued that the school district should provide a sign language interpreter in Katie's neighborhood school. The school proposed to place Katie in the Regional Day School Program, which was in a neighboring school district. Katie and her parents based their argument on the "mainstreaming" language in the *Daniel R.R.* case, but the Fifth Circuit ruled that this was erroneous:

> First, this case does not raise the question of whether or not Katie should be mainstreamed. The regional day school Katie attended was attached to Calk Elementary and provided for fully mainstreamed classes when appropriate. Therefore, Katie's reliance on *Daniel R.R. v. SBOE* [cite omitted] and other cases concerning mainstreaming [is] not controlling.

Thus the court ruled that schools are required to "mainstream," that is, serve students in an instructional arrangement with their nondisabled peers as much as possible. But this does not mean that the parent has a right to demand that the appropriate services be available at the neighborhood school. Katie was being mainstreamed as much as possible. But she was not being served in her neighborhood school. She had to travel some distance to receive the services she needed. The Fifth Circuit said that this is perfectly acceptable:

> State agencies are afforded much discretion in determining which school a student is to attend. Under the regulations governing the placement of a student in the "Least Restrictive Environment,"

a child should attend his or her neighborhood school *unless* the child's IEP requires arrangements that do not exist at that school.

The court then held that there is no requirement, or even a "presumption," that students with disabilities will be served in their neighborhood schools. Proximity to home is just one factor to be weighed in the equation (*Flour Bluff I.S.D. v. Katherine M.*, 1996).

A decision from 2003 goes one step further. In *White v. Ascension Parish School Board*, the Fifth Circuit drew a clear distinction between "placement" and "site selection." The court ruled that the term "placement" refers only to the instructional setting in which the student is taught. Thus "placement" options would involve the regular classroom, the resource room, a self-contained setting in which the student is with other disabled students all day, a home or hospital setting, or a residential setting. "Site selection," on the other hand, has to do with the particular building in which the student is served. The court ruled that the ARDC's role is to decide the "placement," whereas the school district could decide "site selection" without parental input. Thus we have learned that LRE has to do with an instructional arrangement rather than a particular building.

Procedural Safeguards

Much of the federal law is procedural. Congress did not presume to tell educators how to educate children with disabilities. Instead, it set up an elaborate procedural system, assuming that if schools complied with the procedures, the end result would be an appropriate education delivered in the least restrictive environment. FAPE in the LRE.

Four aspects of the procedural safeguards are particularly significant—notice, consent, the right to an IEE, and the right to a due process hearing. Schools are required to give notice to parents prior to ARDC meetings. The notice must inform the parents of what the meeting is about and who is expected to attend, and it must be provided at least five days before the meeting. If the parent does not receive notice, the meeting cannot take place unless the parent is willing to waive the notice requirement. Notice also is required when the school proposes to initiate or change the student's evaluation, identification (as a special education student), or placement, or the provision of FAPE. Schools must also give notice if they refuse a parental request with regard to these same matters. Keep in mind that "notice" means a full explanation of what is proposed, why it is proposed, what alternatives were considered and why they were rejected, the data that support the proposal, and other relevant factors; a reminder to the parents of their procedural safeguards; and a list of sources for parents to contact to help them understand their rights. The notice must be in the parents' native language, unless this is "clearly not feasible." This same litany applies when the school refuses a parental request. Special education is a paper-intensive business.

The Texas Education Agency has amended its Notice of Procedural Safeguards to conform with IDEA 2004 and its regulations, including the latest changes dealing with the parent right to revoke consent for services, which is discussed below. This very important document is to be given to the parents in four situations: (1) upon initial referral or parent request for evaluation, (2) upon receipt of the first "State complaint" or "due process complaint" in a school year, (3) when a decision has been made to change the student's placement for disciplinary reasons, and (4) upon request by a parent (34 C.F.R. §300.504).

The reference to a "State complaint" is worth commentary. IDEA has long required each state to have a "complaint" process in place. There has been a marked increase in the use of this process in lieu of due process hearings over the past several years. The complaint process is simpler and less legalistic than the due process mechanism. Parents, or interested advocate groups, can file a complaint with the Texas Education Agency, which will then follow up with a review and/or investigation. The Agency is authorized by the law to order relief if appropriate.

Consent is required prior to any evaluation of a student, whether it be the initial consideration of the child for special education or the three-year reevaluation. This requirement is intended to apply to any individualized testing of the student. When a test is given to all of the students in a school, grade, or class, consent is not required. Besides consent for testing, consent also is required for the initial placement of a student in special education.

IDEA 2004 clarified what is to happen when consent is not given. If a parent refuses to give consent for an initial evaluation, the school district may initiate a due process hearing to override the lack of consent. However, this cannot be done if the parent refuses to give consent for services. In that event, the school district will not be guilty of a denial of FAPE due to the failure to deliver the services it offered to provide. Likewise with a reevaluation, if a parent refuses to give consent, the district can seek to override the parent through the due process hearing system.

In 2008 the Department of Education issued new regulations that permit a parent to revoke consent for the provision of services at any time. This marks a significant change in practice. Prior to this, parents could refuse services at the outset, but once the child received special education services the parents could not unilaterally remove the child from the special education program. If the parent became unhappy with special education services, the parent would have to ask the ARDC to agree to the dismissal of the student. Sometimes the ARDC would do so, and sometimes not.

With the new regulations, however, parents now can take their children out of special education at any time for any reason. The school is obligated to honor a parent's request whether school officials agree or not. The school must, however, provide a written notice to the parent outlining the services that will no longer be provided and the other consequences of the decision. Many educators have expressed concerns over this change, in fear that it may result in a denial of services to some of the students most in need. In its comments regarding the final regulations the Department of Education noted such concerns, but dismissed them by emphasizing that the law assumes that parents will act in the best interest of their children. Most of the time that is certainly true, but educators worry about the exceptions. We shall see how this plays out.

As should be clear from previous discussion, the evaluation of a student with a disability is crucial. Thus the parental right to demand an IEE (independent educational evaluation) is a key procedural safeguard. If the parent disagrees with an evaluation conducted by the school district, the parent has the right to obtain an independent evaluation, meaning one conducted by a qualified person who is not employed by the school district. The school district is required to consider the results of any IEE, as long as the evaluator is qualified and the testing was done under the same conditions as would apply to the school's own assessment of the student. Moreover, the school must pay for the IEE unless it is willing to ask for a hearing at which it must prove that its own assessment of the student was properly done. Many times school districts agree to pay for an IEE even when school officials believe their own assessment to be perfectly acceptable, simply to avoid the cost of a hearing.

Which brings us to due process hearings, the procedural safeguard that undergirds all the rest. The parent of a special education student can ask for a due process hearing on virtually anything—the content of the IEP, the placement of the student, a proposed disciplinary action, the label attached to the child, the amount of related services, or a request for reimbursement for expenses incurred by the parent. Parents of regular education students who are dissatisfied with their child's education must go through internal appeals (principal, superintendent, school board) before going outside the school district. Not so with special education. The parent of the student with a disability can go directly from the ARDC meeting to a due process hearing conducted by an impartial hearing officer. To access this process, the parent simply needs to file a written request for due process hearing with the Texas Commissioner of Education.

IDEA 2004 imposed some new requirements designed to reduce litigation and its costs. When a request for due process hearing is made, the school district is required to convene a "preliminary meeting" in which members of the ARDC and the parents attempt to resolve their differences. The law gives the school thirty days from the date it received the complaint to resolve the problem. Only after those thirty days have run can the parent obtain a due process hearing. The commissioner then will appoint an "impartial hearing officer" to hear and decide the case. The hearing officer will contact the parents and the school and schedule a hearing. The hearing will be conducted in the school district, unless the parties agree to some other arrangement. In some cases, the parties have agreed to hold the hearing at the regional education service center, but in most cases the hearing is held within the local school district.

In Texas, the hearing officers are independent attorneys, contractually retained by the Texas Education Agency (TEA). The hearing officers have considerable power. Their decisions cannot be overturned by a school board, the state board, or the commissioner. The only route of appeal from the hearing officer is to court, which is an expensive process.

The hearing process in Texas is very formal, adversarial, and attorney-driven. The Rules of Evidence apply, as do the Rules of Civil Procedure. Court reporters transcribe every word. The hearing officer and court reporter are paid by TEA, but the school district must pay its own attorney, if the district chooses to use one. Given the nature of the process, attorneys are a virtual necessity in these proceedings.

Attorneys' Fees

Parents who "prevail" in a special education dispute with a school district are entitled to recover reasonable attorneys' fees. To encourage nonadversarial dispute resolution, Congress put some limits on the recovery of attorneys' fees in IDEA 1997. Specifically, the law now says that parents may not recover attorneys' fees in connection with attendance at IEP meetings (ARDCs) unless the meeting is "a result of an administrative proceeding or judicial action." Thus a parent who brings a lawyer to a routine ARDC meeting is not entitled to recover the cost of the lawyer, even if the lawyer assists the parent in major ways to obtain services not previously offered.

When parties do go to litigation, the school can limit or even eliminate any payment of attorneys' fees with a well-timed settlement offer. If the parents reject a reasonable settlement offer, they may lose their opportunity to recover fees. The law specifically says that the parents may not recover fees if the relief they ultimately obtain is no greater than what was offered by the school district in a timely and written offer.

IDEA 2004 contains even stronger provisions designed to reduce or eliminate frivolous claims and unethical practices. The law now says that the attorney who represented the parents can be required to pay the school district's attorneys' fees if the case was "frivolous, unreasonable, or without foundation," or if the attorney "continued to litigate after the litigation clearly became frivolous, unreasonable, or without foundation." The law also authorizes the school district to recover its attorneys' fees from the parents or the parents' attorney if the case was brought for an improper purpose. The terms used in the law are "to harass, to cause unnecessary delay, or to needlessly increase the cost of litigation."

It has long been established that the parents can "prevail" even when they have fallen short of a slam dunk victory. If they have attained relief beyond what the school district has offered, they may claim victory. However, due to a U.S. Supreme Court decision from 2001, the parents must actually prevail in a hearing or otherwise obtain a judicial decree in their favor. Simply negotiating a private settlement with the school district will not suffice even if the settlement entirely provides the relief requested. In the case *Buckhannon Board and Care Home, Inc. v. West Virginia Department of Health,* the Supreme Court flatly rejected what had come to be known as the "catalyst theory" of recovery of attorneys' fees. That theory permits a plaintiff to recover attorneys' fees if the suit was the motivating factor for a change in position by the defendant. In other words, if the school district changed its position as a result of a parental request for due process hearing, the parents could recover attorneys' fees even though the school acted voluntarily and without a judicial order. The hearing request was the "catalyst" for the school's change of heart, and thus, fees could be awarded. The *Buckhannon* case rejected the catalyst theory and imposed a more difficult test. The parent must win the hearing, or at least obtain through settlement an enforceable judicial order. The *Buckhannon* case did not involve IDEA but rather another federal statute containing virtually identical language about recovery of fees for "prevailing parties." Since then, several courts have ruled that the Supreme Court's ruling does apply to IDEA cases.

In 2006, the U.S. Supreme Court ruled that parents who "prevail" in litigation over IDEA are not entitled to recover fees they have expended on educational experts. Thus, recovery of "attorneys' fees" means what it says—it does not extend to nonattorney experts (*Arlington Central School District Board of Education v. Murphy,* 2006). The ruling in this case was narrow, but the implications are broad. Justice Samuel Alito wrote the majority opinion. He opens discussion of the case by observing that "Our resolution of the question presented in this case is guided by the fact that Congress enacted the IDEA pursuant to the Spending Clause." Congress has no direct constitutional authority to pass legislation dealing with public education. There was no formal public education system at the time the Constitution was adopted, and so it is not surprising that the term "education" does not come up anywhere in the original document. Nor has public education been the subject of any of the amendments to the Constitution.

While Congress has no direct authority with regard to public education, it can assert its authority via the Spending Clause, which gives Congress the power to "provide for the common Defence and general Welfare of the United States" (U.S. Constitution, Art. I, Section 8). IDEA is a classic example of a statute enacted pursuant to the Spending Clause. Congress uses its authority to make money available for the "general Welfare" and attaches conditions to the receipt of the money. States and local school districts that want to receive IDEA money must agree to abide by its terms.

But what if those terms are not exactly clear-cut? What do you do with ambiguities as to what the statute requires? The Supreme Court has looked at this issue before. In 1981 the Court issued a very important decision in the case of *Pennhurst State School and Hospital v. Haldeman.* The statute at issue in the *Pennhurst* case was similar to IDEA—a "Spending Clause" statute that attached conditions to the receipt of federal money. The Court's ruling put the burden on Congress to be clear about what it was requiring: when Congress attaches conditions to a state's acceptance of federal funds it must do so "unambiguously." Recipients of federal funds can only be held accountable when they have accepted those conditions "voluntarily and knowingly." A state cannot be held to conditions of which state officials were "unaware" or which they were "unable to ascertain."

Thus the question was: does IDEA "unambiguously" indicate that those who accept its money are potentially liable to pay for an expert witness or consultant hired by a parent? In answering the question, the dissenters in this case put great emphasis on congressional intent. They quoted from conference committee reports and other portions of legislative history indicating that Congress fully intended for parents to recover expenses like this.

The majority, however, did not think congressional intent was that important:

> In a Spending Clause case, the key is not what a majority of the Members of both Houses intend but what the States are clearly told regarding the conditions that go along with the acceptance of those funds.

Thus the majority framed the issue from a different perspective:

> We must view the IDEA from the perspective of a state official who is engaged in the process of deciding whether the State should accept IDEA funds and the obligations that go with those funds. We must ask whether such a state official would clearly understand

that one of the obligations of the Act is the obligation to compensate prevailing parents for expert fees. In other words, we must ask whether the IDEA furnishes clear notice regarding the liability at issue in this case.

Justice Alito and the majority did not consider this a close call. There is nothing in the law itself that "unambiguously" would put a state agency, such as TEA, on notice that by receiving IDEA funds it was taking on this potential liability. As to "attorneys' fees" the statute is unambiguous. As to "expert fees" the statute is not. Thus the majority concluded that "this provision does not even hint that acceptance of IDEA funds makes a State responsible for reimbursing prevailing parents for services rendered by experts."

This case deals with a fairly obscure issue, and one that does not affect the day-to-day operations of the public schools. In that respect, the case is of more interest to school district lawyers than school administrators and teachers. Nevertheless, the Court's majority opinion sends a strong message about how IDEA should be interpreted.

Moreover, this case may represent a turning point in IDEA litigation. This possibility becomes clear from the dissenting opinion written by Justice Stephen Breyer. He admitted that the statute did not "*clearly* tell the States that they must pay expert fees to prevailing parents" (emphasis in the original), and then added:

> But I do not agree that the majority has posed the right question. For one thing, we have repeatedly examined the nature and extent of the financial burdens that the IDEA imposes without reference to the Spending Clause or any "clear-statement" rule.

Indeed. And that's why this case may be more important than the narrow issue it specifically resolves. Justice Breyer is quite right. In previous cases, the Supreme Court never posed the question the way the Court does in this case. Perhaps the best example of this is *Cedar Rapids Community School District v. Garret F.* (1999). This is the case in which the Court held that full-time, one-to-one nursing services were available as a "related service" if needed by the student. There is nothing in IDEA which "unambiguously" makes that clear. But in 1999, the Supreme Court was not emphasizing the origins of IDEA, the Spending Clause, and the *Pennhurst* case. In 2006, a majority of the Court told us that this is how we should interpret IDEA.

Hearing officers and lower courts should keep this in mind as they deal with future cases. The main point of the *Arlington* case is that IDEA's obligations are not binding on schools unless they are expressed in the law with clarity. If Congress wants to make itself more clear, it can always do so by amending the statute.

FAPE

The U.S. Supreme Court heard its first case pertaining to IDEA (then known as EAHCA) in 1982. The *Board of Education v. Rowley* case is significant for two reasons. First, it established the principle that school districts are not required to maximize the potential of a child, but rather, to provide some educational benefit to the child. Since this federal standard is fairly low, advocates for students with disabilities frequently point to state law in an effort to establish some higher standard. To date, such efforts have not succeeded in Texas.

Second, the case told us how courts in the future would examine disputes under IDEA. The Supreme Court in *Rowley* instructed federal courts to ask two questions in such cases: (1) did the school district comply with the procedural mandates of the law; and (2) is the IEP reasonably calculated to confer educational benefit on the child? If both questions are answered affirmatively, then the school is providing the student FAPE, a "free, appropriate public education."

The case involved a deaf student, Amy Rowley, and the issue was whether she was entitled to a sign language interpreter to enable her to secure a free, appropriate public education under the terms of the law. The lower courts had ruled that while Amy was progressing from grade to grade and performing above average, she was not achieving up to her potential because of the absence of the interpreter and thus was not receiving a free, appropriate education as spelled out in the law. The Supreme Court, however, ruled that Amy was not entitled to the sign language interpreter. The goal of Congress in enacting the law, wrote Justice William H. Rehnquist for the majority, was not to maximize the potential of students with disabilities but rather "to identify and evaluate handicapped children and to provide them with access to a free public education." Since Amy Rowley was progressing from grade to grade and was receiving an adequate education under the program approved by the school administrators to meet her needs, no sign language interpreter was necessary.

While the Rowley case told us how much progress is enough for Amy Rowley and others like her, that same issue is still difficult to deal with in many other cases. Amy was being served in a regular classroom setting. She was able to master the essential elements of the curriculum just as her peers were. She passed from one grade to the next at the same time that they did. Thus it was easy for the Court to conclude that the school district was providing Amy with an education that afforded her some benefit.

The question is much tougher when dealing with students whose cognitive abilities are significantly lower than their peers'. For the severely impaired child, how much progress is enough? For the medically fragile child, how do you define "benefit" or "progress"? This is where the IEP plays a crucial role. If properly written, the IEP should contain measurable annual goals and short-term objectives. If the student has achieved those goals or at least made substantial progress toward achieving them, then a court or hearing officer is likely to determine that reasonable progress has been made. If the goals are so vague as to be unmeasurable, or if the student truly has made little or no progress, then the school has failed in its mission.

The Fifth Circuit has expanded on *Rowley* with its own four-part test to determine if an IEP offers FAPE. To pass muster, the IEP must (1) be individualized on the basis of the student's assessment and performance; (2) be administered in the least restrictive environment; (3) include services that are provided in a coordinated and collaborative manner by the key stakeholders; and (4) produce positive benefits, both academically and nonacademically (*Cypress-Fairbanks I.S.D. v. Michael F.*, 1997). Hearing officers in Texas are using these four factors to assess the quality of IEPs in due process hearings.

It is not easy for a parent to prove that the school has failed to meet this standard. In *Houston I.S.D. v. Bobby R.* (2000) the Fifth Circuit concluded that a school district's failure to implement all elements of the student's IEP is not necessarily a deprivation of FAPE. The court required that the parent must "show more than a *de minimis* failure to implement all elements of that IEP, and instead, must demonstrate that the school board or other authorities failed to implement substantial or significant provisions of the IEP."

In the same case the court ruled that students with disabilities should be compared only to themselves, not the rest of the class. The parent had presented evidence that the student's academic progress, as measured by percentile ranking, was in decline. But the court did not find that to be meaningful:

> [A] disabled child's development should be measured not by his relation to the rest of the class, but rather with respect to the individual student, as declining percentile scores do not necessarily represent a lack of educational benefit, but only a child's inability to maintain the same level of academic progress achieved by his non-disabled peers. As with the argument in *Rowley* that an IEP must maximize a child's potential, the argument that [the student] should not experience declining percentile scores may be an unrealistic goal, and it is a goal not mandated by the IDEA.

The most recent illustration of what FAPE means came in the case of a student with an IQ of 142, and SAT scores north of 600 in both reading and math. How did such a bright student end up in a special education program? He had a learning disability that severely affected his writing ability. The case drew considerable national attention because of the question it posed: Do we look at the student's progress solely in the area affected by the disability? Or do we take a more holistic approach? By a 2–1 margin, the Fifth Circuit held that the statutory goal is overall educational benefit, not just remediation of the disability. By that standard, the district provided FAPE in *Klein I.S.D. v. Hovem* (2012).

Finally, in *Adam J. v. Keller I.S.D.* (2003), the Fifth Circuit adopted a "no harm, no foul" approach with regard to procedural errors by school districts. Reversing an earlier case, the court held that an error in procedure would not be considered a denial of FAPE unless the error actually resulted in a loss of educational opportunity for the student. This "no harm, no foul" principle was made statutory by IDEA 2004. Thus parents who allege procedural errors will also have to show some actual harm to the student, or to the parent's ability to participate in the process.

Related Services

Besides receiving instructional services, students with disabilities also are entitled to an IEP that provides for related services that are necessary for the student to benefit from the instructional services. Many legal disputes concern disagreements over whether, and the extent to which, a student needs such services as occupational therapy (OT), physical therapy (PT), counseling, and special transportation arrangements. But the area that has received the most attention in the courts is that fine line between medical services and school health services.

Indeed, the second special education case to advance to the Supreme Court concerned this issue. And it happened right here in Texas. Amber Tatro's parents asked the Irving I.S.D. to provide their three-year-old child with a service known as "clean intermittent catheterization" (CIC). Amber had spina bifida, a condition that prevented her from voluntarily emptying her bladder. Without someone at the school to provide CIC, Amber would be confined to a homebound program. With CIC, Amber could attend school with her peers. The school district balked at the request, arguing that CIC was a medical service and thus beyond the legal responsibility of a public school district.

The Supreme Court disagreed, unanimously ruling in favor of Amber. If the services needed by the student were necessary for the student's attendance and could be provided by someone other than a physician or hospital, then the school was required to provide the service. This came to be known as the "bright line rule," since it drew a "bright line" between those services that could only be provided by a doctor and all other services (*Irving I.S.D. v. Tatro*, 1984).

But after the Tatro case was decided, some courts effectively said, "They couldn't have meant that." Instead of the "bright line rule," these courts created a multifactor test, taking into account the complexity of the requested service, its cost, whether it required constant or periodic care, and whether it required a medical professional as opposed to a trained layperson.

Then, in 1999, the issue came back before the Supreme Court in the case of *Cedar Rapids Community School District v. Garret F.* Garret was described by the Court as "a friendly, creative and intelligent young man." Indeed, he was. But he was also paralyzed from the neck down and required far more medical attention than the occasional CIC Amber Tatro needed. Garret was ventilator-dependent and on a tracheotomy tube. He needed a full-time nurse to tend to his needs alone, not just a trained aide two or three times a day. So the school district, citing the multifactor test approved by some courts, argued that it was not required to provide a full-time, one-to-one nurse as a "related service" for Garret.

Again, the school district lost. The Supreme Court, citing its earlier decision in the Irving I.S.D. case, reaffirmed its "bright line rule." If the student needs the service to attend school, and the service can be provided by someone other than an M.D., then the school district must provide or pay for the service.

Extended School Year Services

Special education's mandates have required educators to shift many a paradigm. For example, every state has a law mandating the number of days of instruction children are to receive. In general, those laws conform to the traditional schedule with school running from August to May, with a summer break. But what happens when a student's disability is so severe that the summer break will cause a loss of any progress that may have been achieved?

This has been the issue in several court cases. The most important for us is the Fifth Circuit decision *Alamo Heights I.S.D. v. State Board of Education* (1986). Like every other circuit court that has addressed this issue, the Fifth Circuit determined that for some children an "appropriate" education is one that goes beyond the normal school year. The court stated that "if a child will experience severe or substantial regression during the summer months in the absence of a summer program, the handicapped child may be entitled to year-round services." The court concluded, "The issue is whether the benefits accrued to the child during the regular school year will be significantly jeopardized if he is not provided an educational program during the summer months." The court held in this case that there was sufficient evidence of regression to justify requiring the district to provide summer services to the student.

Thus the paradigm of "Every child gets the same amount of services. That's fair" had to shift under the weight of the law. The new paradigm is "Every child gets an education that is appropriate. For some that requires more than nine months of services. That's fair."

Schools now routinely address ESY concerns for many children. Again, the key is individualized decision-making. A one-size-fits-all summer program does not comply with the legal mandate for individualized consideration. The program should be tailored to the child's needs rather than the other way around.

Unilateral Placements

In a 1985 case, the Supreme Court opened the door to unilateral parent-initiated placements in private-school settings. The scenario usually involves a disagreement between school and parent as to the appropriate placement. The school believes the child can be appropriately served by the local school district; the parent believes that only placement in a special, private school, or perhaps in a residential facility, will do the job. As a result of the Court's decision in *School Committee of Burlington v. Department of Education,* and subsequent legislation, it is now possible for parents to recover reimbursement for the costs of such a unilateral placement.

However, parents bear a heavy burden of proof in these cases. First, they must prove that the IEP and/or placement recommended by the school is inappropriate. Second, the parents must prove that the IEP and placement they have arranged for the child are appropriate. Three factors make this particularly difficult for the parents. First, there is a presumption in the law that the program recommended by the school is appropriate. Second, the law merely requires the school to propose a program that will confer reasonable benefit. Thus the existence of a superior school with a program and placement that will enable the child to reach new educational heights is irrelevant if the school can afford "reasonable benefit." Third, the school's proposed program almost always will be less restrictive than the private placement sought by the parents.

Even when the parent places the student in a facility that does not meet all of the requirements a public school would have to meet, the parents may be able to obtain reimbursement. This was the situation in *Florence County School District Four v. Carter* (1994). The school district argued that it should not be financially responsible for the private placement of the child, since the facility chosen by the parents did not use written IEPs and employed as teachers some staff who were not certified. The U.S. Supreme Court unanimously rejected the school's argument. Just because the school district could not have placed Shannon Carter in this particular school does not mean the parents cannot do so. Since the school's proposed program for Shannon was determined to be inappropriate, and the parents' chosen placement was conferring educational benefit, the public school was stuck with the tab.

After the *Burlington* and *Carter* decisions, schools had only one surefire defense to a claim for reimbursement of a unilateral placement. That defense was that the school district was then, and is now, ready, willing, and able to provide FAPE.

IDEA 1997 added one further procedural requirement for parents who seek reimbursement, and thus another line of defense for the school district. Parents now must give the school district notice of their intent to withdraw the student and seek reimbursement. The law provides some exceptions to this requirement, such as when compliance would cause serious physical or emotional harm to the student. But the general rule is that parents now must give notice so that the school has a chance to fix the problem. Absent notice, reimbursement is not available. The First Circuit relied on this provision to rule in favor of a school district on a reimbursement claim involving a private school that charged tuition at the rate of $16,000 per semester. The court noted that if parents want reimbursement for private schooling,

> they must at least give notice to the school that special education is at issue. This serves the important purpose of giving the school system an opportunity, before the child is removed, to assemble a team, evaluate the child, devise an appropriate plan and determine whether a free, appropriate public education can be provided in the public schools. (*Greenland School District v. Amy N.*, 2004)

Private-School Children

Public schools also have responsibilities toward private-school students with disabilities. The public school is required to locate and evaluate these children. The duty of "child find" applies to students who may be in need of special education services, regardless of what kind of school they attend. But beyond that, public schools are required only to spend "a proportionate share" of their federal special education funds on private-school children. Furthermore, the kids in private schools do not have an individual entitlement to FAPE, cannot insist on the same level of services provided to public-school kids, and cannot obtain a due process hearing. Public schools are required to consult with representatives of private schools, but the ultimate decision-making authority resides with the public school. The public school has the authority to determine what services will be provided, and also where they will be provided. In some instances, public-school educators may provide services at a private school, while in other cases the services may be available only at the public school. In short, under IDEA, parents who reject the public school in favor of a private school for a disabled child lose some of the rights they would have retained in the public school.

Texas has created an exception to this rule, but only with regard to students who are three or four years old. These very young children can still partake of "dual enrollment," whereby they may be simultaneously enrolled in a private school and a public school. These children will continue to receive an IEP and a greater degree of legal protection even though they are not enrolled in the public school full-time.

IDEA 2004 made a major change in the responsibilities of public school districts with regard to services available to children who are enrolled by their parents in private schools. Previously, the obligation to find and evaluate these children belonged to the school district *in which the parents resided*. IDEA 2004 changed that to the school district *in which the private school is located*. For example, consider a student who resides with her parents in the Round Rock I.S.D., but attends a private school within the geographical boundaries of the Austin I.S.D. Under prior law, Round Rock I.S.D. was responsible for finding and evaluating the student, and offering "proportionate share" services if the student were eligible. Under the newer version of the law, these responsibilities belong to Austin I.S.D. Keep in mind, though, that in this example Round Rock still has the "child find" duty because the child lives in the district. Thus this student should be "found" by two districts, but for different purposes. Round Rock has the duty to make FAPE available; Austin has the duty to consider proportionate share services. If the parents want FAPE, they would need to enroll the child in a public school in Round Rock. If they like the private school in Austin, they may be eligible for "proportionate share" services from Austin.

DISCIPLINE OF STUDENTS WITH DISABILITIES

When Congress discusses special education, discipline is always an emotional and contentious issue. This was the case both in 1997 and in 2004. The law is attempting to accomplish two purposes, which sometimes collide. The law is designed to guarantee an appropriate education to all students, even those whose behaviors are challenging. At the same time, the law hopes to encourage safe classrooms free of drugs, weapons, and disruptive activities. It is not easy to create a statutory framework that perfectly accomplishes both of those tasks.

Before we look specifically at IDEA and its impact on discipline, a brief history involving two key cases is in order. *S-1 v. Turlington*, a decision handed down by the U.S. Court of Appeals for the Fifth Circuit in 1981, arose when school officials in Florida, which then was included in the Fifth Circuit, expelled several students with disabilities for almost two years. This was the maximum penalty available under state law. The behavior of the students certainly was serious: masturbation, sexual acts against fellow students, willful defiance of authority, insubordination, vandalism, and profane language. The students each were classified as mentally retarded. None was classified as emotionally disturbed.

The parties to the suit agreed that it would be illegal for the school officials to expel a student for behavior that directly resulted from a student's disability. The school asserted that it had taken that factor into account with regard to the only student who had raised the issue—S-1. Both the school superintendent and the school board determined that S-1 was not emotionally disturbed, and, therefore, his inappropriate behavior could not have arisen from his disability.

The Fifth Circuit found fault with that analysis in three respects. First, the school officials should have made a determination as to whether or not there was a link between disability and behavior with regard to each of the students, not just the student whose advocate had raised the issue. Second, the court rejected the idea that the determination hinges on whether or not the student is emotionally disturbed. The school was required to make such a determination for a child with any disability. Third, the court found fault with the superintendent and board for making the determination. Rather, the determination should have been made by the knowledgeable group trained to make such decisions—in Texas that means the ARDC.

Perhaps the most confusing aspect of the *Turlington* case, however, was its treatment of the issue of whether or not expulsion can be imposed on a student with disabilities. The Fifth Circuit chided the trial court for dodging the issue, stating that "we cannot ignore the gray areas that may result if we do not decide this question." The court then proceeded to create a considerable gray area itself, by observing:

> We therefore find that expulsion is still a proper disciplinary tool under the EHA [now IDEA] and section 504 when proper procedures are utilized and under proper circumstances. We cannot, however, authorize the complete cessation of educational services during the expulsion period.

Most educators find this to be the functional equivalent of saying you can go swimming—just don't get wet.

In 1988, the Supreme Court spoke to the issue of special education and discipline in the case of *Honig v. Doe*. John Doe and Jack Smith were suspended from school for behavior that was believed to be dangerous. John had attempted to choke another student, leaving abrasions on the victim's neck. Jack had made lewd comments and on previous occasions had stolen, extorted money, and made sexual comments to female classmates. It was undisputed that these behaviors were related to the students' disabilities.

While it is unclear exactly how long Jack was suspended, John's suspension lasted five and one-half weeks (twenty-four school days). The suspensions probably would have lasted much longer had the lower court not issued an injunction forbidding the school from taking such disciplinary actions against Jack and John. Although the lower courts addressed several issues and made a number of findings, only one issue addressed by the Supreme Court is crucial to this discussion. This issue concerns the so-called "stay put" provision of IDEA, which states in relevant part: ". . . during the pendency of any proceedings conducted pursuant [to IDEA], unless the State or local educational agency and the parents otherwise agree, the child shall remain in the then-current educational placement of such child" (20 U.S.C. §1415(j)). The "then-current placement" of the student refers to the child's placement prior to the expulsion or other change of placement. The "stay put" provision is triggered by an appeal before a special education hearing officer under IDEA. Once the parents disagree and appeal the matter, the student must "stay put" in his or her current placement while the appeal is pending.

In the *Honig* case, San Francisco school officials argued that Jack and John were dangerous. Invocation of the "stay put" provision would put them right back in school, where they had endangered other students. The "stay put" provision, school officials asserted, was not applicable to situations where students presented a clear and present danger to others. However, the Supreme Court could find no support for that argument in the statute. There was no stated exception in the "stay put" provision for situations in which the student's behavior is determined to be dangerous to the student or to others. In addressing this issue the Supreme Court held in *Honig* that the "stay put" provision is unequivocal and is not subject to an exception for dangerous students. The Court concluded that when a suspension of a student with a disability for more than ten days is proposed and the student's parents do not agree to the suspension and appeal the matter pursuant to IDEA, thus triggering the "stay put" provision, the school district must seek the aid of a court if the school officials consider it necessary that a particularly dangerous student be enjoined from attending school. In such circumstances, the Supreme Court ruled, the school will have to overcome the presumption in favor of the student's current educational placement by showing a court "that maintaining the child in his or her current placement is substantially likely to result in injury either to himself or herself, or to others."

Expulsion

Against this backdrop, Congress revised special education discipline laws in IDEA 1997 and again in IDEA 2004. With regard to expulsion from school, Congress has not "leveled the playing field" as between disabled and nondisabled students. Instead, Congress requires that students must continue to receive FAPE after expulsion. This applies regardless of the linkage between behavior and disability. In other words, a student who commits an expellable offense that has nothing whatsoever to do with the student's disability is, under federal law, still entitled to receive a free, appropriate public education. Thus, under current law, two students can commit the same offense and receive very different consequences. The nondisabled student can be expelled, at least for a period of time, with no educational services provided. The student who has a disability that qualifies for special education services continues to receive an appropriate education. Keep in mind that in the larger Texas counties, schools are required to continue to serve all students through JJAEPs (Juvenile Justice Alternative Education Programs, discussed in more detail in Chapter 8). Thus in Harris County, Bexar County, and other large counties all "expelled" students continue to receive services. In smaller counties, the special education student is guaranteed a continued education, but her nondisabled counterpart is not.

Stay Put

With regard to "stay put," Congress has strengthened the hand of local school administrators since the *Honig v. Doe* decision. If a student possesses drugs or a weapon at school, or causes serious bodily injury to someone, the student can be assigned to an alternative setting for forty-five school days regardless of any other factor. The school must still conduct a manifestation determination to ascertain any linkage between the behavior and the disability. But the school can assign the student to an alternative program for forty-five school days regardless of any linkage. Furthermore, if there is a dispute with a parent over a disciplinary matter, the "stay put" placement will be an "interim alternative educational setting" rather than the student's original placement.

What about students who are dangerous, but do not use weapons or drugs, and do not inflict serious bodily injury? There is an exception to "stay put" in those cases also, but the school cannot implement it unilaterally. Instead, the school must seek relief from a hearing officer for a forty-five-day interim placement of a student while the hearing is pending. Schools must convince the hearing officer that maintaining the current placement of the child is substantially likely to result in injury to the child or others. Thus if the student inflicts "serious bodily injury," the student can be removed from a placement by order of the principal, but if there is only a substantial likelihood of injury, the hearing officer must approve.

Change of Placement

Many of the special procedures for students with disabilities come into play only when the school district seeks to "change the placement" of the student due to a disciplinary violation. Thus the definition of "change of placement" is important. Under the final regulations, a change of placement occurs if the student is removed for (1) over ten consecutive days, or (2) over ten cumulative days if the removals form a "pattern." A "pattern" exists if the child's behavior is "substantially similar" to the child's behavior in previous removals, and "because of such additional factors as the length of each removal, the total amount of time the child has been removed, and the proximity of the removals to one another" (34 C.F.R. 300.536(a)(2)). That is a very fuzzy definition that is sure to lead to confusion, arguments, and litigation.

Ten Days

School officials can impose short-term disciplinary consequences, such as suspensions and in-school suspensions, on students with disabilities for any violation of the code of conduct, so long as those consequences would also be applied to the nondisabled student and do not amount to a change of placement. For the first ten days of such removals in a school year, the school is not obligated to provide educational services. Some refer to these ten days as "the FAPE-Free Zone." After the student has been removed from the placement called for by the IEP due to disciplinary problems for ten days, any subsequent removal must be accompanied by services. Thus principals and assistant principals who impose short-term suspensions must always know how many days have been used up. If the student has already been removed for ten days, the next removal is "beyond the FAPE-Free Zone" and will require the provision of services. Moreover, it may amount to a cumulative change of placement, which will require an ARDC meeting and a manifestation determination.

MANIFESTATION DETERMINATIONS

The concept of a "manifestation determination" goes back to the *S-1 v. Turlington* case, but IDEA 1997 for the first time spelled out how to do it. IDEA 2004 simplified the process a bit. Under the current law the ARDC must review all relevant information and then answer two questions: (1) Was the conduct of the student caused by, or did it have a direct and substantial relationship to, the child's disability? (2) Was the conduct of the student a direct result of the school's failure to implement the IEP? If the ARDC decides that the student's conduct is a manifestation of the disability, then the student may not be expelled or placed in DAEP for a long term "unless the parent and the local educational agency agree to a change of placement as part of the modification of the behavioral intervention plan." Furthermore, the school must conduct an FBA (functional behavioral assessment) and implement a BIP (behavior intervention plan) for the student. On the other hand, if the behavior is not a manifestation, the school imposes the consequence it would normally impose, but must also continue to provide appropriate services.

The terms FBA and BIP are used in the federal law, but not defined. In educational practice, an FBA is generally meant to describe a focused effort to collect and analyze data pertaining to student behavior to identify the reason for the behavior. The theory is that educators will be effective in correcting the behavior only if the root cause is first identified. Based on the information thus gathered, the ARDC can then develop a BIP, which would include positive behavioral interventions, strategies, and supports for the student and teacher. The overall goal is to teach the student appropriate behaviors to substitute for inappropriate or disruptive behaviors.

While the law pertaining to the discipline of students with disabilities is largely federal, the Texas Legislature has enacted statutes addressing some of the more controversial techniques. TEC §37.0021 prohibits the placement of any student, with very limited exceptions, into "seclusion." That term is defined to mean confining the student in a locked space that is designed for seclusion and contains less than fifty square feet.

The statute also authorizes the commissioner of education to enact rules pertaining to the use of "restraint" and "time-out" with students with disabilities. "Restraint" is defined to mean "the use of physical force or a mechanical device to significantly restrict the free movement of all or a portion of a student's body." The rules adopted by the commissioner permit restraint to be used only in an emergency. The term "emergency" is defined to mean a threat of imminent, serious physical harm to the student or others, or imminent, serious property destruction. This would mean that physical restraint cannot be used on a student who is "merely" noncompliant, disruptive, and verbally abusive. It is reserved for cases of imminent threat to persons or property. Educators who use physical restraint must be properly trained, and each incident must be documented and reported to the parent.

"Time-out" is defined to mean a behavior management technique in which the student is separated from other students for a limited period of time. The separation must not be in a locked room or a room in which the exit is impeded by an inanimate object.

SECTION 504 OF THE REHABILITATION ACT OF 1973

Finally, let's take a look at "the other law"—Section 504 of the Rehabilitation Act of 1973. Careful readers will note that 504 pre-dates the law now known as IDEA by two years. The idea behind 504 was very simple—institutions that receive federal money should not be allowed to discriminate against persons with disabilities. Seventeen years later, Congress took that same concept of nondiscrimination and applied it to virtually all businesses and schools in the country with the passage of the Americans with Disabilities Act (ADA). In 2008, Congress significantly expanded the scope of both laws. In the discussion that follows, we will reference Section 504, but the definitions and standards under the ADA are the same.

Section 504 has a three-pronged definition of persons with disabilities. Persons are covered by 504 if:

1. They have a physical or mental impairment that substantially limits a major life activity;
2. They have a record of such an impairment; or
3. They are regarded as having such an impairment.

However, it is only the first group that is entitled to special treatment. Only the first group is entitled to an evaluation, an individualized program, decisions by committee, etc. The second and third groups are entitled only to be free from discrimination. In other words, a student who has a record of impairment, such as a record of treatment for drug abuse, should not be kept out of the band or the basketball team as a result of that record. But the school has no duty to refer, evaluate, individually accommodate, and place that student. So, too, with the student who is regarded by some as having a disability because of an unusual physical appearance. The school should assure that individual of nondiscrimination. But unless the student actually suffers from a physical or mental impairment, the school should not refer, test, individually accommodate, or place that student. In short, the second and third prongs of the 504 definition come up much more often in the employment context than they do in public school services.

Students are not eligible for special treatment under 504 unless they demonstrate two conditions: a physical or mental impairment and a substantial limitation of a major life activity. The student who is doing poorly in school is not covered by Section 504 unless the student's problems are attributable to a physical or mental impairment. Thus an LEP (limited-English-proficient) student who comes to the school from a dysfunctional family or a condition of extreme poverty may experience great difficulty in school. Unless the student has a physical or mental impairment, however, the student is not a candidate for 504 identification. Programs adopted pursuant to Section 504 and the district's "at-risk" program are not supposed to be equivalent.

Case law puts an emphasis on the requirement that people covered by 504 and the ADA must be *substantially limited* in a major life activity. Minor difficulties and weaknesses in certain areas are not considered sufficient. Moreover, persons seeking coverage under these nondiscrimination laws must demonstrate that they are unable to perform a major life activity that the "average person in the general population" can perform, or are at least significantly restricted as to how they can perform that major life activity in comparison with the "average person" (*Bercovitch v. Baldwin School, Inc.*, 1998).

Prior to 2008, the courts had held that this comparison to the "average person" was to be done after taking into account certain mitigating measures, which might include medication, eyeglasses, a hearing aid, or just plain hard work to compensate for a weakness (*Sutton v. United Air Lines, Inc.*, 1999). The Supreme Court emphasized in the *Sutton* case that the relevant inquiry is the present status of the person, not a potential or hypothetical situation.

In 2008, Congress expressly rejected the reasoning of the Supreme Court in the *Sutton* case and some others that had limited the scope of 504's coverage. By enacting the ADA Amendments Act of 2008 (ADAAA), which simultaneously amended Section 504, Congress expressed its desire for broader coverage. It is clear from the political and legislative history of the ADAAA that Congress was focusing on the effect of these laws on the American worker—not the student in school. Nevertheless, the amendments carry no exception or exclusion for public school districts. Thus the broader coverage will apply in the school setting.

One of the major changes is that mitigating measures must now be disregarded when determining identification. Keep in mind that Section 504 deals with "impairments" and "disabilities." The terms are not synonymous. An "impairment" is also a "disability" only if it substantially limits the individual in the performance of a major life activity. This raises the issue: do you make that determination before the hearing impaired person dons his hearing aids, or afterwards? In *Sutton*, the Supreme Court said that mitigating measures like hearing aids should be taken into account. Thus you measure the impact of the impairment *after* the hearing aids are in place. Congress expressly rejected that thinking with the ADAAA. Now, the mitigating measure of hearing aids is to be disregarded. How does he hear without the hearing aids?

The list of "mitigating measures" in the law begins with medication—a common factor in dealing with students. It goes on to include hearing aids, prosthetics, reasonable accommodations, auxiliary aids and services, and learned behavioral adaptations. It does not include ordinary eyeglasses or contact lenses. Thus under the new law, 504 committees in school districts must disregard the impact of these "mitigating measures" when determining whether or not the "impairment" substantially limits the student in a major life activity.

The dividing line between "504" kids and "IDEA" kids is not always easy to discern. When a student has an impairment that substantially limits one of the "major life activities" that are physically based, 504 coverage is fairly easy to determine. Consider, for example, a student who is orthopedically impaired but cognitively very capable. Such a student may meet the standards for 504 coverage, since she is substantially impaired in the major life activity of walking. However, unless the student needs specially designed instruction, the student may not be eligible under IDEA. Such a student is properly classified as "504 only." She is entitled to an appropriate education that may include "related aids and services" designed to meet her needs in the school.

On the other hand, a student whose disability affects the major life activity of learning, thinking, concentrating, or reading may have a difficult time meeting 504 standards without also meeting IDEA standards. Moreover, many students meet eligibility criteria under both statutes. Students who qualify for IDEA services must have a "disability" that requires "specially designed instruction." In most instances this will also satisfy 504's eligibility criteria—a "physical or mental impairment" that "substantially limits" the student in a "major life activity" such as learning. Schools are not required to duplicate paperwork and procedures for these students. Regulations adopted under 504 specifically say that compliance with IDEA satisfies 504 standards.

Once a student is identified as meeting the definition of a person with a disability under Section 504, a number of procedural requirements come into play. Procedures similar to those for students under IDEA are required, including evaluation, individual planning by a group of knowledgeable persons, placement in the LRE, and parental procedural safeguards. Discipline becomes more complicated as well. Long-term disciplinary action likely will amount to a "change of placement," which requires a meeting of the knowledgeable group (usually known as the student's 504 committee) and a manifestation determination. Moreover, parents and students covered by Section 504 have legal recourse that includes the recovery of damages if they can show intentional discrimination.

SUMMARY

Commentators on the American scene who decry the "litigation explosion" of the late twentieth century have a case in point regarding children with disabilities. There is no question that litigation has increased dramatically in special education, and it appears to be here for the long run. The litigation has had at least two effects. On the one hand it certainly has made the schooling process more adversarial and stressful for many. Decisions sometimes seem to turn on an attorney's advice as often as on what is best for the child. But on the other hand the litigation has moved a forgotten minority to the forefront of our consciousness. Americans can be proud of the fact that our schools have a "zero reject" philosophy. Services that had been denied to students with disabilities for decades now are routinely provided. This would not have happened in the absence of lawsuits challenging the way things used to be.

FOUR

The Employment Relationship

IN MOST COMMUNITIES in Texas, the public school district is the largest employer. It is not surprising that myriad legal disputes arise out of the employment of public school personnel. In this chapter we will focus on the laws that affect the employment relationship, particularly at the beginning and end of that relationship. We will review the constitutional concept of due process of law, the different employment arrangements that are available to public schools in Texas, the hiring and firing process, and the legal issues that arise in that context.

CONSTITUTIONAL ISSUES

The most fundamental factor that distinguishes public employment from employment in the private sector is the fact that the U.S. Constitution applies to the public employment relationship. In Chapters 6 and 7, we discuss how the constitutional guarantees of free speech, free assembly, and freedom of religion impact public employers. In this chapter, the emphasis will be on the constitutional requirements of due process.

Due Process of Law

A term that is overworked and often misapplied, "due process" is, nevertheless, a key concept in the arena of public employment. The Fourteenth Amendment provides that no state shall deprive a person of life, liberty, or property without due process of law. (The Fifth Amendment contains a similar limitation on actions by the federal government.) As noted in Chapter 1, we can restate this proposition to mean that rights can be regulated or even taken away altogether if due process of law is provided.

The concept of due process of law is a means of assuring that decisions made by government officials affecting people's essential rights are made fairly. Before any process is due, there must be (1) state action and (2) a deprivation of "life, liberty, or property." Since the U.S. Constitution only restricts governmental action, the due process clause is not invoked in the private sector. Moreover, the Constitution applies only when the government deprives an individual of "life, liberty, or property." We are not aware of any school district that has taken away an individual's life, so in practical terms, the focus is on a deprivation of "liberty" or "property." (Note: We are aware that many longtime educators experience a daily, incremental loss of life in the public schools, but the due process clause is only concerned with the more sudden and dramatic deprivations.) Unless there is a significant deprivation of liberty or property, the courts are loath to intervene in educational personnel disputes, even when the judge may disagree with the outcome. Indicative of this attitude is this quotation from Supreme Court Justice John Paul Stevens:

> The federal court is not the appropriate forum in which to review the multitude of personnel decisions that are made daily by public agencies. We must accept the harsh fact that numerous individual mistakes are inevitable in the day-to-day administration of our affairs. The United States Constitution cannot feasibly be construed to require federal judicial review for every such error. In the absence of any claim that the public employer was motivated by a desire to curtail or to penalize the exercise of an employee's constitutionally protected rights, we must presume that official action was regular and, if erroneous, can best be corrected in other ways. The Due Process Clause of the Fourteenth Amendment is not a guarantee against incorrect or ill-advised personnel decisions. (*Russell v. El Paso I.S.D.*, 1976, quoting from *Bishop v. Wood*, 1976)

Thus, an important initial inquiry in any proposed personnel decision is whether the employee is to be deprived of "property" or "liberty" within the meaning of the constitutional guarantee of due process of law.

In 1972 the U.S. Supreme Court ruled that teachers have a protectable Fourteenth Amendment property right in continued employment if state law gives them a "legitimate claim of entitlement" to it (*Board of Regents v. Roth*). Thus we look to state law to determine what "legitimate claim of entitlement" to continued employment a school employee may have.

The general rule in Texas is that an employee works "at-will" unless a contract of some sort says otherwise. We discuss this in more detail below. For constitutional purposes, once it is established that an employee is "at-will," there will be no constitutional right to due process. If there is no legitimate claim of entitlement to continued employment, there is no property right. If there is no property right, then termination of employment is not a deprivation of property. Thus, "process" is not "due."

The contractual employee clearly has a property right in the job during the term of the contract. Any effort of the school district to terminate the contract prior to its stated date of expiration is a deprivation of property. Thus, some amount of process is due.

In each of the following instances, the school district is seeking to terminate the contract prior to its normal expiration date and, therefore, must afford due process:

Case One: The employee has a contract for the 2014–2015 school year. In November 2014, the school district seeks to terminate the contract immediately, due to alleged theft of school property.

Case Two: The employee has a contract for the 2014–2015 and 2015–2016 school years. The school district seeks to terminate the contract in February 2015, due to alleged violation of school policies.

Case Three: The employee has a contract for the 2014–2015 and 2015–2016 school years. The school district seeks to "nonrenew" the contract after the 2014–2015 school year due to excessive absences. The school district considers this a "nonrenewal," since it is occurring as of the end of one school year and prior to the start of the next. In fact, however, it is a termination of a contract that has another full year to run. The employee has a property interest in the job for the entire length of the contract and, thus, is entitled to due process.

If the school seeks to terminate a contract prior to its normal expiration date, it is depriving the employee of property and must afford the employee due process. Note that the nature of the contract, in this context, does not matter. Whether the employee is a continuing contract teacher with twenty years on the job or a first-year probationary teacher, the *constitutional* analysis and the *constitutional* right to due process are the same.

What of the due process rights of teachers facing nonrenewal of a term contract? Suppose the district proposes to nonrenew a teacher's term contract, and the teacher requests a hearing. Make the further supposition that the district, required to give a hearing, fails to do so. Clearly the district has violated state law, and the employee can obtain any remedy available to the employee under state law. Below, we will discuss rights and remedies under state law for the improper nonrenewal of a term contract. But can the employee pursue a claim of violation of his or her federal constitutional rights to due process?

Federal and state courts originally came to different conclusions on this issue, but the Texas Legislature settled the matter by adopting TEC Section 21.204(e): "A teacher does not have a property interest in a contract beyond its term." Since the courts have always recognized that property interests are created, defined, and limited by state law, this clear-cut expression of state law resolves the issue: No property interest means that constitutional due process is not required in the case of a term contract nonrenewal. In fact, that is exactly how a Texas court of appeals ruled in *Stratton v. Austin I.S.D.* (1999). In that case, a nonrenewed teacher complained when the school board limited her hearing before it to a one-hour presentation. The teacher asserted that such a limitation violated her due process rights. The court easily disposed of this argument, noting that the language in the Education Code supersedes earlier court cases: "Stratton has no property interest under Texas law."

Thus it now is clear under Texas law that educators have a "property right" subject to protection under the due process clause when the school district seeks to terminate a contract prior to its stated ending date, but not when the school district chooses not to renew a contract that has run its course. This is one of the fundamental reasons why the "nonrenewal" of a contract is a much different process than the "termination" of a contract.

A 2010 decision from the Fifth Circuit illustrates the parameters of "due process" in the employment context. Dr. Gentilello was a tenured professor at the University of Texas Southwestern Medical Center, also serving as chair of certain divisions. He alleged that he was removed from the chair positions and demoted after he voiced concerns over what he considered substandard care at one of the Southwestern Medical Center's hospitals. The court dismissed the lawsuit, holding that the plaintiff had not identified any legal entitlement to remain as chair of certain divisions. As a tenured professor, Dr. Gentilello had a property interest in continued employment, but "the due process clause does not protect Gentilello's specific job duties or responsibilities absent a statute, rule or express agreement reflecting an understanding that he had a unique property interest in those duties or responsibilities" (*Gentilello v. Rege*, 2010).

Besides having a "property right" at stake, public employees sometimes have a "liberty" interest as well. The U.S. Supreme Court has recognized certain other rights to be implicit in the word "liberty" in the Fourteenth Amendment. Among them are the right of the parent to select a nonpublic school; the right to privacy, which will be discussed in Chapter 9; and the right to a good reputation. With regard to reputation, the Supreme Court recognized in a 1971 case that, "where a person's name, reputation, honor, or integrity is at stake because of what the government is doing to him, notice and an opportunity to be heard are essential" (*Wisconsin v. Constantineau*, p. 437). Thus there may be instances in which a government employee is "stigmatized" by disclosures made in the context of a termination of employment. In such a situation, the government, as employer, may be required to hold a "name clearing hearing."

However, such situations should be rare. In *Higgenbotham v. Connatser* (2011) the Fifth Circuit identified seven elements of a cause of action, all of which are necessary to make a case: (1) the employee was discharged; (2) stigmatizing charges were made about the employee in the process of the termination; (3) the charges were false; (4) the employee was not given notice, or an opportunity for a hearing prior to discharge; (5) the charges were made public; (6) the employee requested a hearing to clear his/her name; and (7) the employer refused to provide a hearing. Ms. Higgenbotham failed to allege facts that would satisfy all seven elements of the cause of action, and thus her suit against the superintendent and H.R. director of Clear Creek I.S.D. was dismissed.

How Much Process Is Due?

Understanding when process is due is only the beginning of a due process analysis. The next question is: How much process is due? Courts regularly intone that due process is not an absolute and that it varies according to the deprivation of property in question. In the case of dismissal of an educator with a property right, however, the concept of due process is reasonably well defined.

One principle applies regardless of the legal framework under which an educator's property right arises: Due process must precede the taking. The U.S. Supreme Court made this point abundantly clear in *Cleveland Board of Education v. Loudermill* (1985). Thus it no longer is permissible to fire an employee who has a property right and then "cure" any due process defect by providing notice of reasons and a hearing after the fact (*Wells v. Dallas I.S.D.*, 1983).

As for the level of formality of due process in a typical employee termination case, the essentials are timely notice of why dismissal is being sought, a fair hearing where the employee can present a defense and question the evidence against him or her, and sufficient evidence to establish good cause for dismissal. An early and important case is *Ferguson v. Thomas*, a 1970 Fifth Circuit Court of Appeals ruling. In *Ferguson*, the court stated that in a dismissal for cause action, a teacher must at a minimum:

1. Be advised of the cause or causes of the termination in sufficient detail to fairly enable him or her to show any error that may exist;
2. Be advised of the names and the nature of the testimony of witnesses against her or him;
3. At a reasonable time after such advice, be given a meaningful opportunity to be heard in his or her own defense; and

4. Be given an opportunity for a hearing before a tribunal that both possesses some academic expertise and has an apparent impartiality toward the charges.

As we shall discuss below, Texas has now adopted an independent hearing system for teacher terminations. The system incorporates the elements of due process the courts have required.

One issue that likely will continue to arise, however, involves the role of the school board. Can a school board, which makes final personnel decisions, be impartial? This question was raised in an important 1976 U.S. Supreme Court case. The case, *Hortonville Joint School District No. 1 v. Hortonville Educational Association*, involved striking teachers who were dismissed by the Hortonville, Wisconsin, school board when they refused to return to work. Instead, they continued their strike in direct violation of Wisconsin's no-strike law. The teachers were given a hearing before the board prior to their dismissals. They argued that the hearing they received was unfair because their employer, the board, was involved in the labor dispute and thus could not be impartial. Chief Justice Warren Burger for the majority ruled against the teachers, pointing out that the mere fact the board "was 'involved' in the events preceding this decision, in light of the important interest in leaving with the Board the power given by the state legislature, is not enough to overcome the presumption of honesty and integrity in policymakers with decision-making power" (p. 497). In short, for employees to succeed in charging members of the board with partiality, they must produce clear evidence that such is the case.

In *Washington v. Burley* (2013), a Texas federal district court allowed an employee to go forward with a due process claim based on allegations that a single board member was biased. The court noted that in a small governing board the bias of one member can taint the entire board. To show bias, the employee must prove one of three things: (1) that the decision-maker has a "direct personal, substantial, and pecuniary interest" in the outcome of the case; (2) that the board member has been "the target of personal abuse or criticism" from the party before him; or (3) that the board member has the dual role of investigating and deciding disputes and complaints.

This case points out the fine line local boards must walk in dealing with matters that may come before them in the future. Board members are not expected to be completely ignorant, but they must not be so involved in pretermination discussions that they lose their impartiality. Due to the independent hearing system now in place, school boards are less involved in teacher termination cases than they were in the past. Nevertheless, the decision to terminate a contract comes back to the board before it is final, and thus, issues concerning school board member neutrality likely will continue to arise.

To summarize, the U.S. Supreme Court has ruled that states and their political subdivisions can create property rights protected by the Fourteenth Amendment. Public employment may give rise to such a right; whether it does depends upon state law, local policies, and contractual provisions. Once a governmental entity has created a property right protected by the Fourteenth Amendment, it may not take that right away without providing the employee due process of law. Educators employed by contract have a property right that can be taken away only when due process of law is afforded.

This is a fundamental distinction between public and private employment and one of the factors that make it more difficult to fire a teacher than a privately employed worker. Donald Trump may be able to simply inform one of his minions that "you're fired." When dealing with a public employee protected by the U.S. Constitution, it is not so simple. How this plays out in practice will be discussed in detail below.

TYPES OF EMPLOYMENT ARRANGEMENTS

Employees of the public school system will fall into one of six categories, each of which has its own legal issues. First, there are "at-will employees." Second, those employed under a "non–Chapter 21 contract." Third are "probationary contract" employees. Fourth, "term contract" employees. The fifth category is for those under "continuing contracts." And finally, there are those with a "third-party independent contractor" status. The basic legal contours of each relationship will be explored below. Later in the chapter we will review the legal requirements for ending the relationship with each of the six categories of employees.

At-Will Employment

At-will employment simply means that either the employer or employee is free to end the relationship at any time and for almost any reason. In the private sector, at-will employment is the norm. Professional athletes and news anchors have contracts, but most of us do not. We may have worked for the Acme Widget Company for twenty-four years, but we can quit tomorrow. Or be fired tomorrow. Since at-will employment is the norm in the private sector, it is when dealing with at-will employees that public employment law most resembles employment law in the private sector.

School districts employ many people on an at-will basis. This, in fact, is the custom for clerical workers, bus drivers, custodians, grounds crew and maintenance, and food service workers. It is frequently said that at-will employees are those without a contract. But that is misleading. There can be a written contract that incorporates an "at-will" relationship. If the contract leaves each party free to end the employment relationship without notice, hearing, or good cause, then you essentially have an "at-will" relationship.

Employees who work without written contracts sometimes argue that they do, in fact, have a "contract," even though there is no specific document entitled "Employment Contract." The argument is that the statements in the employee handbook, or even the verbal assurances of the supervisor, create a "contract" that alters the at-will status. This argument is likely to fail in Texas courts after the Texas Supreme Court decision in *Montgomery County Hospital v. Brown* (1998). In that case, the Texas high court ruled that verbal assurances from an employer that the employee would not be terminated as long as her work was good did not create a "contract" and did not alter the at-will relationship between employer and employee. The court's decision represents a strong affirmation of the at-will doctrine in Texas. The court said:

> General statements like those made to Brown simply do not justify the conclusion that the speaker intends by them to make a binding contract of employment. For such a contract to exist, the employer must unequivocally indicate a definite intent to be bound not to terminate the employee except under clearly specified circumstances. General comments that an employee will not be discharged as long as his work is satisfactory do not in themselves manifest such an intent. Neither do statements that an employee will be discharged only for "good reason" or "good cause" when there is no agreement on what those terms encompass.

Texas courts have been strongly supportive of the at-will doctrine. In *City of Midland v. O'Bryant* (2000), the Texas Supreme Court was asked to impose on all employers a "duty of good faith and fair dealing." The court declined to do so, thus again affirming the validity of the at-will doctrine and the flexibility it provides to employers.

The Texas Supreme Court again affirmed the "at-will" doctrine for Texas employers in 2006. The case involved a ten-year employee of the Matagorda County Hospital whose employment was terminated. There was no written contract of employment, but the employee argued that the personnel manual created a contract. The manual stated that employees could be dismissed "for cause such as insubordination, serious misconduct, or for inability to perform the duties of their job satisfactorily." The court again stated that to alter the at-will relationship an employer must "unequivocally indicate a definite intent to be bound not to terminate the employee except under clearly specified circumstances." The personnel manual in this case did not satisfy that standard, and so the court concluded that the employee was "at-will" and could be let go for "good cause, bad cause or no cause at all" (*Matagorda County Hospital District v. Burwell,* 2006).

School administrators should take that final quote from the court with a grain of salt. As we shall discuss in more detail later in this chapter, it is simply not true.

Non–Chapter 21 Contracts

Only certain employees are entitled to a written contract under Chapter 21 of the Education Code. If the district chooses to employ other people by written contract, then the contract is, by definition, a "non–Chapter 21 contract." Therefore, we first must address the fundamental question: Which school employees are entitled to contracts under Chapter 21? The answer to that question turns on §21.002 of the TEC, which requires school districts to "employ each classroom teacher, principal, librarian, nurse, or school counselor" under a Chapter 21 contract, meaning a probationary, a term, or a continuing contract. That section goes on to say that a district is not required to employ a person, other than those listed, under a probationary, term, or continuing contract. Thus it would appear that *only* classroom teachers, principals, librarians, nurses, and school counselors are entitled to the rights and benefits of a Chapter 21 contract.

However, there are other sections of the Code that come into play. Section 21.201 sets out the definition of "teacher" for purposes of term contract law. It defines a "teacher" as "a superintendent, principal, supervisor, classroom teacher, school counselor, or other full-time professional employee who is required to hold a certificate issued under Subchapter B or a nurse. The term does not include a person who is not entitled to a probationary, continuing or term contract under Section 21.002, an existing contract, or district policy."

To further complicate matters, the term "classroom teacher" has its own definition. It is defined in the Education Code at §5.001(2) to mean "an educator who is employed by a school district and who, not less than four hours each day, teaches in an academic setting or a career and technology setting. The term does not include a teacher's aide or a full-time administrator." The term "academic setting" means that the Texas Essential Knowledge and Skills are being taught to students for course credit.

Based on these definitions, the Texas Commissioner of Education determined in one case that athletic trainers were not classroom teachers and, thus, were not entitled to a Chapter 21 contract (*Renteria v. El Paso I.S.D.*). In another case, the commissioner ruled that a woman who worked part-time in the library was not entitled to a Chapter 21 contract. The woman was neither a "classroom teacher" nor a "librarian." To be a "librarian" under Chapter 21, the person must be employed full-time and must hold a librarian's certificate. In *Robinson v. Memphis I.S.D.* (2003) the employee was neither, and thus the district was not required to offer her a Chapter 21 contract. The commissioner held that a "community liaison" was not an educator under Chapter 21 in *Gardner v. Wilmer-Hutchins I.S.D.* (2005).

In another case, the commissioner concluded that a "budget coordinator" was not entitled to a Chapter 21 contract and not entitled to the protections afforded under Chapter 21 (*Castillo v. Dallas I.S.D.*, 2003). It is, perhaps, significant in the *Castillo* case that the commissioner flatly stated, "Chapter 21 rights apply to teachers as defined in section 21.201 of the Texas Education Code." This refers to the broader definition, thus incorporating any full-time professional employee whose employment requires certification from the State Board for Educator Certification.

There are many school officials who occupy important positions that do not require certification. For example, there are the business manager, the director of maintenance, the director of transportation, and the director of construction and facilities.

The first thing to observe about non–Chapter 21 employees is that such employees are not entitled to a written contract. Nothing in state law requires that all employees have a written contract. Only those certified educators under Chapter 21 must be employed in that manner. While it is customary to employ certain noncertified administrators by written contract, the law does not require it.

Second, the commissioner has jurisdiction over disputes involving allegations that a written employment contract has been violated by the school board if the employee alleges monetary harm. Section 7.057 gives the commissioner jurisdiction to hear such cases, and it refers to any "written employment contract," not just those under Chapter 21. Thus, if the district employs non–Chapter 21 employees under a written contract, a dispute over the contract may be appealed to the commissioner.

Third, that right to appeal cannot be "contracted away." In *Nugent v. Dallas I.S.D.* (2003) the district employed a non–Chapter 21 employee with a written contract that specified that the decision of the school board regarding nonrenewal was "final and may not be appealed." Yes, it could, the commissioner ruled. While a non–Chapter 21 employee is not entitled to any specific "nonrenewal" appeal, he can appeal to TEA alleging that a written contract was broken, resulting in monetary harm to the employee. This right of appeal is statutory and may not be waived by contract, unless it is in the form of a settlement agreement.

Fourth, districts that issue Chapter 21 term contracts to employees may have to comply with Chapter 21, even if the employee's current assignment would not require a Chapter 21 contract. This was the situation in *Lynch v. North Forest I.S.D.* (2007), which involved a registrar. The commissioner relied on the fact that the contract was a Chapter

21 term contract, noting that "simply because Petitioner was not performing teaching duties does not exempt a district from ending a term contract in compliance with the statute." Similarly, in *Harris v. Royse City I.S.D.* (2009) the commissioner held that a district that gives a Chapter 21 contract to an employee when it is not legally obligated to do so must afford that employee Chapter 21 rights in connection with a proposed nonrenewal. In other words, the district must either renew the contract "in the same professional capacity" or go through Chapter 21 proceedings. However, the commissioner also held that "same professional capacity" does not require a continuation of Chapter 21 status. The upshot of that ruling is that a district that has employed someone under Chapter 21 when it did not have to do so can change its mind and offer the employee a non–Chapter 21 contract for the next year, as long as the person works in the same professional capacity.

Probationary Contracts

When an educator first goes to work for a school district under a Chapter 21 contract, the educator will usually serve a probationary period that is basically the same in all school districts throughout the state. TEC §21.202(b) authorizes schools to bypass the probationary period and offer a term contract to a new employee who comes to the district with experience as a classroom teacher or principal. But this is rare. The common practice is to hire the new employee on probation.

After the probationary period, educators will split into term contract employees and continuing contract employees. But while serving a probationary period, all employees are under the same system.

Probationary contracts are governed by §§21.101 et seq. of the Education Code. Probationary contracts go to teachers, principals, supervisors, school counselors, nurses, and all other full-time professional employees who are required to hold educator certification. However, a probationary contract is not to be given to a superintendent. In the discussion that follows, we will use the term "teacher" to cover the wide range of employees defined by the law.

The probationary period can be as long as three years, except for teachers coming to the district after having been employed in public education for five of the eight preceding years. For those experienced educators, the probationary period is just one year. During the probationary period, the teacher will be employed on a contract that cannot exceed one year in length. Thus, in the typical situation, the teacher will serve under three consecutive one-year probationary contracts.

There is nothing in the law that requires a probationary contract to be for a full school year. The district could contract with its probationary staff for shorter periods of time—for example, for a semester rather than a full year. This often happens when a new employee starts work in the district at midyear. However, such a situation frequently leads to a legal dispute.

Suppose, for example, that Ms. Young, an experienced teacher in District A, moves to a new job in District B, starting at midyear. You will recall that the probationary period for experienced teachers (those who have five years' teaching experience in the preceding eight years) is one year. Ms. Young completes that year, and is hired to come back for the next full year. By the time "nonrenewal season" rolls around in the spring, Ms. Young will have been with District B for more than a year. Is she still on probation? That was the issue in *Young v. Lipan I.S.D.*, a commissioner's decision from 1996. The commissioner ruled that Young was still probationary and thus could be nonrenewed without a formal hearing. The intent of the probationary period, according to the commissioner, was to give the school district a full year to evaluate a teacher new to the district. The term "year" must be interpreted, as it normally is in the school business, to mean a full scholastic year.

The school district can extend a probationary period for a fourth year if "the board of trustees determines that it is doubtful whether the teacher should be given a continuing contract or a term contract." So in some situations a teacher will be serving a probationary period that lasts four years.

The first year of a teacher's employment with a school district will be probationary, even if the district attempts to do something else. In *Smith v. Zapata I.S.D.* (1999) the district gave a brand-new employee a three-year term contract. After just one year, the district gave notice of its intent to terminate the contract. Even though the contract was labeled a "term contract" and ran for three years, the commissioner ruled that the employee was probationary. Since the district had given timely notice, the employment relationship effectively was terminated. The effect of this decision is to say that state law requires that the first year be probationary, and the district and employee cannot avoid that result by contract.

Probationary teachers can resign without penalty up to forty-five days before the first day of instruction. With school starting in late August in most districts these days, this means the teacher must resign or honor the contract by approximately mid-July. Teachers who wish to resign after the "no penalty" date must get the consent of the board or its designee. Teachers who leave without consent and thus fail to honor the contract are subject to sanctions imposed by the State Board for Educator Certification.

Teachers with either a term or continuing contract can be returned to probationary status under two circumstances. First, this can be done with the teacher's consent in the context of a possible nonrenewal. The district can seek the teacher's consent if the superintendent informs the teacher that she is prepared to recommend a nonrenewal of the teacher's contract. In effect, this provision in the law amounts to a one-year buy-out of a contract. By agreeing to a return to probation the teacher surely must realize that the district easily can terminate the teacher's employment with the district as of the end of the probationary contract. But the teacher might agree to this, in lieu of an earlier nonrenewal.

The second situation arises when a person under a probationary contract voluntarily accepts an assignment in a new professional capacity that requires a different class of certificate than the class of certificate required by the prior position. The most common illustration of this would be a classroom teacher who moves up to an administrative position. The exception to this rule is when the employee is going back to a professional capacity he or she previously held in the same district. Consider Teacher Jones who serves as a teacher in the district for three years, and then becomes an assistant principal. A few years later, Jones voluntarily accepts a reassignment back to teaching. Jones retains the term contract and cannot be put on probation.

Term Contracts

After a probationary period, the teacher must receive either a continuing or a term contract. It is up to the local school board to determine which type of contract to issue.

What distinguishes a term contract from a continuing contract is the length of the contract and the process for renewal, nonrenewal, or termination. Term contracts can be issued to "teachers" as that term is defined in §21.201. That section defines "teachers" to include "a superintendent, principal, supervisor, classroom teacher, school counselor, or other full-time professional employee who is required to hold a certificate issued under Subchapter B or a nurse" (TEC §21.201). Note that superintendents can be employed by a term contract, but schools are not permitted to offer a superintendent a probationary contract.

A term contract is any nonprobationary Chapter 21 contract for a fixed term. The length of the contract can be up to five school years. There is nothing in the law that prevents a school district from offering longer contracts to certain classes of employees as opposed to others. Typically, administrators have multiyear contracts, whereas teachers are employed year to year. The key factor is that the contract lays out a beginning date and an ending date. As the ending date of the contract approaches, some action must be taken.

The resignation date for term contract teachers is the same as it is for the probationary staff—forty-five days prior to the first day of instruction. Later in this chapter we will discuss the legal standards and requirements for the nonrenewal of the term contract.

Continuing Contracts

The key distinguishing feature of a continuing contract is that it automatically rolls over from one year to the next, without the necessity of board action. The law pertaining to continuing contracts is found in Texas Education Code §§21.151 et seq. Key features of continuing contracts are as follows.

State law authorizes issuance of a continuing contract to any person who is a "teacher" as that term is defined in §21.101. That section defines "teacher" as including principals, supervisors, school counselors, nurses, and other full-time professional employees, none of whom was eligible for continuing contract status in the past. However, §21.155 of the Code confuses the issue. It states that a district may grant an administrator a continuing contract as a teacher "at the completion" of the person's service as an administrator. This implies that continuing contracts cannot be granted to administrators, but may be issued to former administrators who move into teaching positions. No clear answer to this ambiguity exists at this time.

It is clear, however, that a "teacher" must be a teacher of children. In *Baggett v. El Paso I.S.D.* (2002) a classroom teacher accepted an assignment as a computer technology coordinator, which meant that she taught teachers how to use technology effectively. The commissioner determined that by accepting this position, Baggett lost her continuing contract status. She no longer was a "classroom teacher." Nor was she one of the "other full-time professional employees" entitled to a continuing contract, since she did not have regular contact with students, did not supervise them, and did not have control of the curriculum.

As noted, there is no specific length of time for a continuing contract. Once entered into, the contract remains in effect until the teacher resigns, retires, is terminated, or is returned to probationary status.

Decades ago there were significant differences between continuing contract employees and all others. Prior to the passage of the Term Contract Nonrenewal Act (TCNA) in 1981, all educators other than those on continuing contracts effectively were "probationary." While that term was not used, the legal relationship was the same as what now exists between a school district and a probationary teacher. There were cases in which teachers had worked for a school district for ten, fifteen, or twenty years, and then simply were nonrenewed without notice, hearing, or an explanation. Thus, the only educators who had legally protected contracts were the continuing contract teachers.

The adoption of the TCNA narrowed the distinctions between continuing contract teachers and all others. Once it became the law, all teachers, other than probationary teachers, were entitled to some sort of process before the relationship could be ended. The nature of that nonrenewal process is discussed in detail below. For now, suffice it to say that with the passage of the TCNA, the distinction in legal protection for the continuing contract teacher versus the term contract teacher is less pronounced. Regardless of the type of contract used by a school district, contracts with teachers must be in writing. In *Delgado v. Eagle Pass I.S.D.* (1989), a teacher had worked for a district from August to October, was paid for his work, and had accepted the position by relinquishing a job in another district. The school board had not given the teacher a written contract, however, and terminated the teacher in October. The commissioner of education held that the teacher had been an at-will employee, since only the school board is empowered with the authority to hire teachers and "no representative of a district has the power to create a binding teaching contract. No person may reasonably rely upon appearances to the contrary."

Furthermore, the general rule is that terms of the contract must be approved by the school board. In the 1987–1988 school year, the Katy I.S.D. employed its teachers with a contract stating that "the Board agrees to pay the employee an annual salary in accordance with the District's salary schedule as adopted by the Board." The Katy administration then issued "salary notification letters" to inform the teachers of the actual salary each would receive. The district began the school year paying each teacher pursuant to the salary notification letter. Midway through the year the district discovered that a number of the salary notification letters were erroneous. The district then reduced payments to those teachers who were receiving more than they were supposed to receive pursuant to the board-adopted salary schedule. The district did not take away any overpayment that had already been paid—it merely dropped the teachers down to the proper schedule for the remainder of the school year. The commissioner of education denied the appeal of the teachers: "The established rule is that salary statements unauthorized by a school district's board of trustees and unsigned by the parties do not form a part of the employment contract" (*Sones v. Katy I.S.D.*, 1992).

Indeed, teachers should be on notice that verbal commitments from school administrators may not be legally binding when it comes to employment contracts. In *Hudspeth v. Chapel Hill I.S.D. and the Texas Education Agency* (2007), a teacher alleged breach of contract when she was paid less than she believed she was promised by the principal. The court concluded that the school did not breach the teacher's contract. The contract itself did not specify the annual salary, and the verbal representations of the principal were not binding on the district. The principal was not authorized to act as the board's agent on the matter. Moreover, the principal had warned the teacher that the board would make the final decision about salary, and that it would be based on her creditable years of service. The teacher mistakenly believed she was entitled to more creditable years than the facts warranted.

The terms and conditions of a contract are always important. But it can safely be said that they are more important in a private-school setting than in the public-school setting. The relationship between employer and employee in the public schools is determined, in large part, by constitutional restrictions and statutory provisions in the Education Code and other legislation. Generally speaking, however, the constitutional restrictions do not apply to the private schools; and there are far fewer statutory provisions applicable to the private schools. Most of the Education Code, for example, applies only to public schools, not private schools. Thus the relationship between employer and employee in the private-school setting is almost entirely determined by the terms and conditions of the contract between the parties. With fewer legal restrictions, private schools retain more flexibility in their employment relationships, but need to be particularly careful as to what they say in those contracts.

Third-Party Independent Contract Educators and Retire/Rehire

A new phenomenon appeared in the early twenty-first century. Private companies offered to provide teachers for public school districts. The idea was that the teachers would not be employed by the public school at all. They would work for the private business and be assigned to the public school. In other words, the Acme Teacher Supply Company would contract with the local school district and then provide teachers who were employees of Acme. This model has been in place for a long time with regard to bus drivers and custodians—why not teachers?

Indeed, with the baby boom generation of teachers nearing retirement age, the arrangement looked very good to many. Educators who were "fully vested" in the Teacher Retirement System of Texas (TRS) could retire, begin drawing benefits, and then go to work for a third party that contracts with the school district. The "retired" teacher draws a salary equivalent to or better than what he had been making. School boards could hire experienced teachers and yet not be burdened with having to treat them as employees. What's not to like? Keep in mind that the general rule under the TRS is that an employee may not receive retirement benefits and work for a public school at the same time. The retired teacher can work for a private school, a private employer, or a public school outside of Texas, but cannot, as a general rule, return to work in a Texas public school. But we now have three exceptions to this general rule. The three exceptions are: (1) working as a substitute teacher; (2) working on a half-time basis; or (3) working in any position, including full-time, if the retiree has separated from employment from all Texas public educational institutions for twelve full, consecutive calendar months. Those who are employed by third parties that contract for services with the school district are considered to be employed by the school district unless they are not performing duties or providing services for the school district. In other words, if you are employed by the Acme Teacher Supply Company and are assigned as a full-time teacher in the Sunshine I.S.D., you are considered to be an employee of the school district. You cannot do this and also draw TRS benefits unless you have laid out for a year. Employees who retired prior to January 1, 2011, were "grandparented" under this statute, and thus allowed to draw TRS benefits and also work for a public school district in any capacity.

The attorney general has issued an opinion affirming that such arrangements are legally permissible and that retired educators may be employed in this manner without losing their benefits under TRS (*Att'y. Gen. Op. GA-0018*, 2003).

Many questions remain unanswered about these arrangements. It is not clear, for example, whether teachers employed by a third party enjoy the same constitutional and due process rights as do the teachers employed by the school directly. For this and other reasons, school districts that contract for staff with third parties should pay particular attention to the contract with the third-party employer to ensure the district will retain appropriate levels of control and protection from liability. The liability issues are discussed in Chapter 10.

SELECTION OF STAFF

Certification and the Role of SBEC

In 1995, the legislature created a new entity to govern teacher certification. The legislature directed the State Board for Educator Certification (SBEC, as it is commonly called) to "regulate and oversee all aspects of the certification, continuing education, and standards of conduct of public school educators" (TEC §21.031). In particular, SBEC was given the power to adopt rules to specify the various classes of educator certification, the period for which each certificate is valid, the requirements for issuance and renewal of certificates, the rules for out-of-state educators, and the disciplinary procedures by which a certificate may be suspended or revoked. Moreover, SBEC has the power to establish training requirements for obtaining a certificate and entering an internship or induction-year program, and to establish the minimum academic qualifications required for certification.

There are two restrictions on this broad grant of authority. First, SBEC must appoint an advisory committee with respect to each class of educator certificates. The advisory committee, composed of members of that class, will make recommendations for standards for the class. Second, rules adopted by SBEC must be submitted to the State Board of Education (SBOE) for review. However, it will take a two-thirds vote of the SBOE to reject any proposed rule. The power of the SBOE is further limited by a provision that specifies that the SBOE "may not modify a rule proposed by the State Board for Educator Certification." The SBOE must either accept or reject, and can only reject by a two-thirds vote. It is clear, then, that SBEC is the key entity in the certification business.

Not everyone who works for a public school district has to be certified. The law requires certification for teachers, teacher interns, teacher trainees, librarians, educational aides, administrators, diagnosticians, and school counselors. There are many other professional employees working for Texas public schools. What credentials must they possess? According to Texas Education Code §21.003, persons hired as audiologists, occupational therapists, physical therapists, physicians, nurses, school psychologists, associate school psychologists, marriage and family therapists, social workers, and speech language pathologists must be licensed by the state agency that licenses that profession.

SBEC has had a significant impact on teacher preparation programs in colleges and universities. The legislature has given SBEC the power to adopt rules to govern the approval and continuing accountability of all such programs. Among other things, the board is to "annually review the accreditation status of each educator preparation program" (TEC §21.045). Testing also plays a part in certification. SBEC now has the authority to propose rules prescribing comprehensive examinations for each class of certificate issued.

Finally, there are now three nontraditional routes to employment as a teacher in Texas public schools. The first such route is alternative certification (TEC §21.049). This process provides an avenue into the profession for those who have not gone through a formal teacher preparation program. The legislative scheme for alternative certification is pared down so as to leave all of the details to SBEC.

The second nontraditional route authorizes a school district to issue a "teaching permit" to a person who is not certified (TEC §21.055). Unless the individual is to be employed in career or technology education, he or she must possess a baccalaureate degree. Beyond that, there are no specific requirements for issuance of a permit. The district that employs a teacher by permit must inform the commissioner of the person's name and qualifications and the subject matter to be taught. The commissioner has thirty days to review the information submitted and may, if appropriate, determine that the individual is "not qualified to teach." The legislature has given the commissioner no guidance as to what makes a person "not qualified to teach." If the commissioner fails to act within thirty days, the permit is approved. Once that occurs, the permit remains valid unless revoked for cause by the district that issued it.

A teaching permit is not as flexible as a certificate obtained through alternative certification. The alternatively certified teacher can teach in any Texas public school district. The permitted teacher can only teach in the district that issued the permit. If the teacher wishes to move to another district, the new district would have to issue a permit and submit it to the commissioner, just as the original district did.

Moreover, the teacher operating under a district-issued permit has less legal protection than his counterpart with a certificate obtained through alternative means. A Texas court of appeals confirmed this in *Houston v. Nelson* (2004). The case involved a man hired as a music teacher with a teaching permit issued by the district. The court ruled that the man was not entitled to a term contract and thus not entitled to the procedures afforded teachers when term contracts are nonrenewed. Ironically, the man held a certificate to serve as a principal. But since he was hired as a music teacher by virtue of a district-issued permit, his principal's certificate was irrelevant to the legal analysis.

The authority of SBEC is illustrated by the fact that it enacted a third alternative route to the classroom, even though the legislature and the SBOE had rejected it (19 TAC §230.39). This route permits anyone with a bachelor's degree who passes a subject matter exam and a pedagogy exam to earn a two-year teaching certificate. This would only apply to teachers in grades eight through twelve. Proponents of this plan assert that it will enable school districts to employ people with extensive knowledge and experience in subjects taught in school. For example, a retired petrochemical engineer might be able to teach chemistry. A lawyer could teach civics or government. This proposal had run into strong opposition in the legislature and SBOE but has now been enacted by SBEC and currently is in effect.

One of SBEC's responsibilities involves adopting and enforcing an Educator's Code of Ethics. The Code creates twenty-two enforceable standards grouped into three general areas (19 TAC §247). First, "Professional Ethical Conduct, Practices and Performance" has to do with general honesty and includes enforceable standards related to falsifying records or job applications, compliance with laws, and misappropriation of funds. The second area, "Ethical Conduct toward Professional Colleagues," encompasses seven enforceable standards including such things as not retaliating against others, not discriminating in any unlawful way, and not revealing confidential information about colleagues. The third area is "Ethical Conduct toward Students." The educator is expected to respect confidentiality, avoid misrepresentation, refuse to discriminate, and eschew physical mistreatment of students. In addition, the Code requires the educator to neither solicit nor engage in sexual conduct or a romantic relationship with a student. Nor can the educator furnish alcohol or drugs to a student or knowingly allow such things to happen in the presence of an educator. This area also includes inappropriate communication with students or minors via electronic devices or social media sites.

Anyone is authorized to file a complaint with the Texas Education Agency alleging that an educator has violated the Code of Ethics. TEC Section 21.006 requires superintendents to report certain types of misconduct by certified employees to SBEC, including (1) that the employee has a criminal record; (2) that the employee violated testing security procedures; (3) that the employee was terminated due to certain types of misconduct; and (4) that the employee resigned in the face of "reasonable evidence" that supports a recommendation of termination due to such misconduct. The types of misconduct that are covered by this statute are (1) the abuse of or other unlawful conduct with a minor; (2) drug offenses; (3) misappropriation or theft of school funds; (4) attempted fraud or other improper means of altering a certificate or license to seek a promotion or additional compensation; and (5) commission of any part of a criminal offense on school property. The superintendent or director of a school district is required to complete an investigation of an educator that is based on reasonable cause to believe the educator may have "abused or otherwise committed an unlawful act with a student or minor." Thus, besides reporting this incident to SBEC, the superintendent must conduct and complete an internal investigation. Presumably the findings from that investigation will be used in any subsequent SBEC action.

The same section of the Education Code also addresses situations in which a district or open-enrollment charter school receives notice from SBEC that an educator's certificate has been revoked due to conviction of a Title V felony or any offense that requires the defendant to register as a sex offender, if the victim of the offense was under eighteen. In such a case, the district or open-enrollment charter school must remove the person immediately, and, if the person was under a probationary, term, or continuing contract, suspend the employee without pay, provide notice that the contract is void, and terminate the employment as soon as practicable.

This statute also authorizes districts and open-enrollment charter schools to suspend without pay, declare void the contract of, and terminate employment of any Chapter 21 contractual employee who is convicted of, or received deferred adjudication for, any other felony offense. Contractual employees whose contracts are voided pursuant to this section are not entitled to a Chapter 21 hearing or appeal.

Sexual interaction between a certified employee and a student may cause the employee to lose certification and also face criminal liability. The Penal Code Section 21.12 defines the criminal offense of "Improper Relationship Between Educator and Student" to cover certified or licensed employees who have "sexual contact" with (1) any student in the district, or (2) any student participant in an educational activity sponsored by a school district or public school if students are the primary participants in the activity and the educator provides educational services to the participants. It is an affirmative defense to prosecution that the actor was not more than three years older than the enrolled person, and, at the time of the offense, the actor and enrolled person were in a relationship that began before the actor's employment at a public school. A noncertified employee (custodian, secretary, grounds crew) commits an offense if he or she has sexual contact with a student at the school where he or she works—but not if the student attends school elsewhere. The certified employee, however, commits an offense by having sexual contact with any student in the district, but not a student in another district unless the student is present for extracurricular activities.

Nondiscrimination Laws

The laws that prohibit discrimination based on race, sex, religion, age, national origin, and disability apply to all major employers, including Texas public school districts. A detailed discussion of the specifics of these laws is beyond the scope of this book. However, educators should bear in mind a few key points that sometimes are overlooked.

First, the nondiscrimination laws apply to all employees, regardless of contractual status. Custodians, secretaries, and cafeteria workers usually do not have contracts, but they are protected from illegal forms of discrimination as much as the certified employees who have contracts with the school district. This is why the statement that at-will employees can be fired for "good reasons, bad reasons, or no reason at all" is inaccurate.

Second, the laws that prohibit discrimination have implications for the hiring process itself. Since the school district cannot make its decisions based on age, it should not be asking about age in the hiring process. However, questions about experience are appropriate. Since gender is irrelevant, the district must avoid asking questions in the hiring process along the lines of "Do you expect to get pregnant anytime soon?" Concerning disabilities, the district can ask, "Is there any reason you would not be able to fulfill the essential functions of the job?" but must avoid "Do you have a bad back?" Those who are directly involved in the process need specific training in this tricky area. Some questions that commonly spring to mind in the process of getting to know someone ("Are you married?") are not permitted.

Third, sexual harassment has received a great deal of attention over the past two decades, but many remain confused over why this particular form of harassment is singled out. A personnel administrator once asked why it was that harassment based on sex was considered illegal, whereas being an "equal opportunity jerk," the sort of boss who is obnoxious, rude, and harassing toward everyone, was not. The answer is that sexual harassment is considered a form of sex discrimination. By the same token, harassment based on race, religion, disability, or age also is illegal, but we hear much less about those issues than we do about sexual harassment. Your authors do not recommend the "equal opportunity jerk" approach to management, but we have to acknowledge that such a person might present fewer legal problems than the individual who harasses on the basis of gender, race, age, religion, or disability.

In the employment arena, discrimination based on sexual orientation is considered a form of sex discrimination. This was true even before the Supreme Court's landmark ruling striking down the Defense of Marriage Act (DOMA), *United States v. Windsor* (2013). Educators should be aware of the case of *Gill v. Devlin* (2012), in which a Texas federal court held that this principle of the law was "clearly established." As we will explain in Chapter 10, this means that individual administrators who discriminate on the basis of sexual orientation face potential personal liability.

The decision of the U.S. Supreme Court in the *Windsor* case dealt with same-sex marriage, but its broad language will have an impact on Texas education. In that case, the high court held that individuals whose same-sex marriage is legally recognized are entitled to all of the benefits of married people under federal law. The Court did not hold that every state must recognize same-sex marriage, but left that issue to another day. However, the Court's language was sweeping, broad, and unmistakable in intent: "[DOMA] tells those couples, and all the world, that their otherwise valid marriages are unworthy of federal recognition. This places same-sex couples in an unstable position of being in a second-tier marriage. The differentiation demeans the couple, whose moral and sexual choices the Constitution protects, and whose relationship the State has sought to dignify. And it humiliates tens of thousands of children now being raised by same-sex couples."

No doubt that language will be cited in future challenges to the Texas version of DOMA. The Texas Constitution states that marriage consists of "the union of one man and one woman." It further prohibits Texas or its political subdivisions from recognizing any "legal status identical or similar to marriage." In *GA-1003* (2013) Attorney General Abbott stated that certain programs designed to provide insurance benefits to domestic partners improperly created a "legal status identical or similar to marriage." However, the Opinion also noted the cases that were then pending before the Supreme Court and their possible impact on this issue. The U.S. Supreme Court did not strike down the Texas version of DOMA but it laid the groundwork for a later challenge. Stay tuned.

Protected Activity

Claims of illegal "retaliation" are closely related to claims of discrimination. This scenario is fairly common. The employee files a complaint of discrimination based on race, sex, age, disability, or religion. Several months later the employee alleges that the employer has retaliated against him for making the original complaint. Even when the "discrimination" claim lacks merit, the "retaliation" claim may be good.

The U.S. Supreme Court broadly expanded the scope of such claims in *Jackson v. Birmingham Board of Education* (2005). The case concerned a man who was a teacher/coach for the school district. He filed suit after being dismissed from his coaching duties. Mr. Jackson claimed that he was dismissed from coaching the girls' basketball team as a direct result of his complaints of unequal treatment for the girls' team. Thus he claimed he was the victim of sex discrimination. The Supreme Court ruled that this is a viable theory of legal liability. If Mr. Jackson can carry the burden of proof by showing a causal connection between his advocacy for the girls and his dismissal as coach, he will have proved a case of discriminatory retaliation, which violates Title IX. Thus a man can prove sex discrimination if he is punished for advocating for the girls. Even though the man's gender had nothing to do with the school board's decision, he has a viable claim of discrimination if he can show that the decision was improperly motivated.

By the same logic, a nondisabled person who advocated for people with disabilities may have a viable retaliation claim, and thus, a disability discrimination claim, if she can show the causal connection.

A decision from the Fifth Circuit illustrates the standards that apply to "retaliation" claims that come on the heels of "discrimination" claims. Sue Easterling, a high school teacher in Louisiana, alleged that she was discriminated against on the basis of sex when she was passed over for the job of girls' basketball coach. A man was hired instead. She later added a "retaliation" claim to the mix, arguing that the school had punished her for raising the original discrimination claim. This "punishment" did not take the form of termination or nonrenewal of contract, but rather a variety of actions ranging from assignment to an inferior office to exclusion from school-oriented social activities. The Fifth Circuit pointed out that such lower-grade actions could amount to "retaliation" even though the teacher was never fired. Thus the court kept the case alive so that Ms. Easterling would have the opportunity to prove her case. Her burden is to prove that these acts of retaliation really happened and were, in fact, done in retaliation for her claim of discrimination (*Easterling v. School Board of Concordia Parish*, 2006).

Educators should be aware that retaliation claims are on the rise. In fact, the Equal Employment Opportunity Commission (EEOC) has reported that "retaliation" cases are now the most common form of complaint filed with that agency, exceeding claims of discrimination based on race, sex, age, religion, and disability.

The Hiring Process

Most school districts post notices of vacancies, but the law only requires this for positions requiring a certificate or license, unless the position "affects the safety and security of students as determined by the board of trustees" (TEC §11.163(d)). There are also exceptions to this requirement for midyear vacancies in positions that require SBEC certification or that of school nurse. The posting is to be done on school bulletin boards or the district's website.

The actual selection of staff to fill a vacant position involves an interplay between the school board and the administration. The school board is to adopt policies regarding the employment and duties of personnel. But the law goes on to dictate two key provisions of that policy. The first deals with the relationship between the board and the superintendent. The policy must provide that the superintendent has the "sole authority" to make recommendations to the board regarding the selection of all personnel. The board can accept or reject any of the superintendent's recommendations, but it cannot simply choose someone who has not been recommended. If the board rejects the recommended person, the superintendent is to recommend someone else. Ultimately, then, the board cannot force the superintendent to hire a person the superintendent would not recommend.

Thus the superintendent must be "in the loop" in hiring people. But the school board, if it so desires, can take itself out of that loop. The law specifically allows the board to delegate final hiring authority to the superintendent. If the board does not do so, then all personnel will be recommended by the superintendent and approved by the board. Of course, a district could delegate final authority to the superintendent for certain categories of employees, such as nonprofessional personnel, while retaining the superintendent-board arrangement for others. This is the practice today in many districts.

The second provision that must be included in local policy addresses the relationship between the campus principal and the central office. It requires local policy to call for each principal to approve each teacher or staff appointment to the principal's campus, in accordance with §11.202 of the Education Code. That section reads, in part:

(b) Each principal shall:
 (1) except as provided by Subsection (d), approve all teacher and staff appointments for that principal's campus from a pool of applicants selected by the district or of applicants who meet the hiring requirements established by the district, based on criteria

developed by the principal after informal consultation with the faculty.

The Subsection (d) exception relates to necessary teacher transfers due to enrollment shifts or program changes. In those instances, the superintendent has "final placement authority for a teacher."

While principals do not actually hire staff, it should be clear that the principal plays a key role in the selection of staff for the campus. Challenges to hiring decisions in the future are likely to focus on the principal's role. If the principal asks an improper question (e.g., "How old did you say you are?"), the rejected applicant could seize on that as evidence of discrimination. Moreover, the principal's approval authority is not limited to the initial hiring decision. Reassignments from one campus to another also require approval of the principal (*Att'y. Gen. Op. DM-27*, 1991).

Criminal Records

In 2007, the legislature enacted sweeping new legislation designed to enhance student safety by requiring criminal background checks on virtually everyone in the school who will have direct contact with students. The law requires some form of criminal background check on certified employees, noncertified employees, substitute teachers, charter school educators, student teachers, employees of shared service arrangements, many school volunteers, and some employees of contractors who serve the school. For both certified and noncertified employees of a school district, the background check will involve fingerprinting—a requirement that some educators have found demeaning.

A special rule applies to contracted transportation services. When a school district contracts with another entity for transportation, it must obtain criminal history information regarding bus drivers. If the records check turns up information that the driver has been convicted of a felony or a misdemeanor involving moral turpitude, the individual may not, without the school's permission, drive a bus on which students are transported.

With regard to its own employees, schools are not required to fire or refuse to hire a person with a criminal history, unless the person has been convicted of a Title 5 felony (generally this refers to crimes of violence) or an offense whose victim was a minor or a student enrolled in public school, requiring registration as a sex offender.

What if an applicant lies on a job application about his or her criminal record? State law specifically authorizes termination of the contract of such a person if (1) the conviction is for a felony or for a misdemeanor involving moral turpitude and (2) the employee failed to disclose the conviction (TEC §22.085).

What if an employee has a clean criminal record when hired, but is convicted of an offense while working for the district? Section 21.006 of the Code requires superintendents and other chief executives to notify SBEC in writing when they have "reasonable cause to believe" that any certificate holder or applicant has a criminal record. TEC Section 22.087 goes even further than that by requiring superintendents and other chief executives to promptly notify SBEC if they know that a certificate holder "has a reported criminal history." According to the SBEC website, "criminal history" includes convictions, indictments, deferred adjudication, and even an arrest.

Administrative rules require that such reports must be made within seven calendar days after the employee's record has been discovered (19 TAC §249.14). While there is no requirement in state law compelling educators to report if they have been arrested or convicted of a crime, many school districts have adopted a local policy imposing such a requirement.

The Impact of NCLB

One of the primary goals of the 2001 federal No Child Left Behind Act (NCLB) has been to encourage the hiring of "highly qualified" teachers. This effort has brought federal law into the picture much more extensively than in the past. Education traditionally has been viewed as a function of state and local government. But federal money, which always comes with strings attached, has changed the landscape. This is still largely true, even though efforts are underway to dismantle NCLB. In fact, many states have been granted waivers from some of its provisions, and Texas has applied for a waiver.

As of the end of the 2005–2006 school year, all teachers of "core academic subjects" in any state that received NCLB funds must be highly qualified. Some local school districts considered turning down NCLB funding so as not to be burdened by NCLB requirements. The effort failed. As long as the state receives NCLB money, the vast majority of NCLB's requirements apply to all public schools in the state, unless the Department of Education grants a waiver.

A teacher must be "highly qualified" if he or she is teaching a "core academic subject." This term encompasses English, reading, language arts, math, science, foreign languages, civics, government, economics, arts, history, and geography. In short, just about everything is a "core academic subject" except physical education.

The "highly qualified" standard turns on education, certification, and demonstrated competence. The most basic requirement is that the teacher must hold a bachelor's degree and be "fully certified" under the standards of the state. In Texas, teachers who go through an approved alternative certification program are considered "fully certified." However, those who are issued a "teaching permit" from a local school district are not and, thus, cannot be considered "highly qualified." Teachers in charter schools are "fully certified" for NCLB purposes if they meet the certification standards applicable to charter school teachers in the state. In Texas, charter school teachers need not have educator certification unless they are working in a federally funded area, such as special education, where a higher standard applies.

Teachers who are "new to the profession," meaning that they were first hired as a teacher after the beginning of the 2002–2003 school year, will demonstrate their competence by testing or training. New elementary teachers must pass an approved test (the ExCET or TexES) to show competence. New teachers at the secondary level can pass a test, or have an academic major in the subject taught, or a graduate degree, or course work equivalent to a major.

Experienced teachers can demonstrate competence in any of these ways or by meeting the requirements of a "high, objective, uniform state standard of evaluation" (HOUSSE). Texas regulations use a "Rule of 24" to determine HOUSSE standards. Any combination of teaching experience in the subject (up to twelve years) plus college credit hours and approved professional development that adds up to twenty-four meets the HOUSSE standards. Detailed information about the standards is available at the Texas Education Agency website.

Special education presents a uniquely complex area. Suppose, for example, that a teacher works with high school students on all of the core academic subjects, but well below grade level. Must this teacher demonstrate competence at a high school level in all areas? Our most recent special education law, IDEA 2004, addressed this issue. It requires special education teachers to be highly qualified in all subjects taught, but provides some flexible means of demonstrating competence.

Restrictions on Employment

Three restrictions on employment in Texas public schools are worth our attention. First, public school employees under state law may not hold two legally incompatible offices—for example, being a teacher and also a trustee of the same school district. However, a teacher may serve without pay as a trustee in another school district or as a member of the governing board of a local government unit, such as a city or a town. Under a provision of the Texas Constitution, teachers have been ruled eligible to serve as justice of the peace, county commissioner, notary public, or postmaster and receive a salary (Texas Constitution, Art. XVI, §40, as interpreted in *Ruiz v. State,* 1976).

A second restriction is set forth in the Texas nepotism statutes, contained in Chapter 573 of the Government Code, which prevents school districts from employing persons related within the prohibited degree by blood or by marriage to a "public official." Who is covered by that term? Clearly, board members are, but what about the superintendent? Can the district hire the superintendent's husband? Can the principal hire his daughter?

TEC §11.1513 addresses the role of the superintendent. The statute states that if the board has given to the superintendent the final authority to hire certain personnel, then the superintendent is a "public official" with regard to those employees. This means that the nepotism laws apply to the superintendent insofar as those employees are concerned. It is common for school districts to give the superintendent the final say in hiring noncertified staff. But if that is the case, the superintendent will not be able to employ a close relative. The statute goes on to say that this rule does not apply in counties of less than 35,000 population. Thus in the smaller counties, there is no statutory rule making the superintendent a "public official," and so we revert to case law. The authoritative case is *Peña v. Rio Grande City C.I.S.D.* (1981), which held that the superintendent is not a public official for purposes of the nepotism laws. To summarize, the superintendent can recommend or hire his or her own relatives except for those positions for which the superintendent has final authority in counties of larger than 35,000 population.

If the superintendent has final hiring authority, does this mean that the board members are no longer restricted by the nepotism laws? In other words, if the superintendent has final authority regarding nonprofessional staff, can the superintendent hire a board member's daughter as his secretary? In *GA-0794*, the attorney general answered that question in the negative. There are exceptions in the smaller counties, but the general rule is that the superintendent cannot employ the board member's spouse, parent, or child even though the decision rests entirely with the superintendent. This interpretation by the attorney general should prevent board members from pressuring the superintendent into hiring a relative.

As far as principals and nepotism, the law has not changed since a 1992 attorney general's opinion. Although campus principals approve all appointments to their campuses, this does not amount to the power to actually hire the employee. Thus the nepotism laws do not restrict the hiring of relatives of the principal (*Att'y. Gen. Op. DM-132*, 1992).

The effect of the law is not changed by a public official's abstaining from voting on the employment of the relative. The statutes, however, permit the continued employment of an employee who, before his or her relative became a "public official," was continuously employed by the district for (1) at least thirty days, if his or her relative was appointed to the position; (2) at least six months, if his or her relative was elected at an election other than the general election for state and county officers; or (3) one year if the relative was elected at the general election.

A person who has served continuously for the required time prior to the relative's becoming a public official may be reappointed for subsequent school years and even promoted. In any such decision, however, the related public official must not participate in the deliberation or vote.

Employees who have not served continuously for the required period prior to the relative's becoming a public official may finish out their contracts but may not be rehired (Att'y. Gen. Op. M-862, 1971). The same rules apply when the employee's status changes by virtue of marrying a relative of a public official. If the employee had not been employed by the district for the required period of time prior to the date of the marriage, the contract may not be renewed. Nor does the fact that the employee is paid out of federal, not state, funds alter the thrust of the nepotism statute (Att'y. Gen. Op. LA-80, 1974).

Another nepotism issue concerns the application of this law to independent contractors. In 1992, the attorney general reversed an earlier opinion and decided that the nepotism restrictions apply to independent contractors as well as employees (Att'y. Gen. Op. DM-76, 1992). Thus the school must be careful in choosing outside consultants and contractors, as well as regular employees.

Finally, there are some general exceptions to the nepotism laws. They do not apply to the employment of a substitute teacher, nor to the employment of a bus driver if the district is located in a county with a population of less than 35,000.

The third restriction is a geographic one. Is it legal for a school district to require employees to live within the district? The answer is yes. Several circuit courts have upheld such restrictions with regard to school employees. The Fifth Circuit case in point deals with municipal employees, but the answer is the same. In *Wright v. City of Jackson* (1975), the Fifth Circuit upheld a municipal ordinance requiring city employees to have their principal place of residence within city limits. Given the mobility of Texans, few districts require all employees to live within the district. More often, this restriction is applied only to selected high-level administrators.

Such was the case in Dallas I.S.D., which terminated the employment of an administrator who failed to comply with district policy requiring certain high-level executive and administrative employees to reside in the district. The commissioner of education affirmed the man's termination, noting that it did not violate his constitutional right to travel (*Davis v. Dallas I.S.D.*, 1994).

ENDING THE RELATIONSHIP

The standards that apply to the ending of the employment relationship, and the process that is required, will vary depending on the employment relationship. Thus, we will review the basic types of employment arrangements in the context of the ending of the relationship.

At-Will Employees

An employee who serves at-will can be terminated at any time, and is not entitled to any pretermination form of due process. Moreover, the reason for termination does not need to amount to "good cause." However, school administrators should not develop a false sense of security in dealing with the at-will employee. An at-will employee enjoys every protection afforded by law to all other employees, except for those that directly arise from the contract or from teacher certification. Thus provisions in the Education Code that deal with contract renewal and nonrenewal do not apply to the at-will employee. However, all of the federal and state mandates prohibiting discrimination apply with equal force to the custodian and the superintendent. The constitutional requirement of due process does not apply to the at-will employee, since there is no property interest in his or her continued employment. But the constitutional rights of expression and association and the right to petition for redress of grievances apply. Therefore, the at-will employee may not be entitled to a pretermination due process hearing, but she can file a grievance charging that her termination was in retaliation for constitutionally protected conduct, or was otherwise illegal.

For example, in *Lake v. Dripping Springs I.S.D.* (2006), an at-will teacher's aide challenged her termination by filing a grievance, which was eventually heard by the commissioner of education. The aide claimed that she was terminated in response to her reasonable use of force to maintain order in the classroom. A Texas statute prohibits districts from firing teachers or aides for the reasonable use of force in the classroom. The district prevailed in this case, based on evidence that the aide acknowledged that she had "lost it and shoved a student." Thus the force was not "reasonable." Nevertheless, the case illustrates the fact that at-will employees have legal recourse also.

The terminated at-will employee also can file suit alleging that his discharge was in retaliation for his exercise of constitutional rights, that it was in response to her "blowing the whistle" on wrongdoing, or that it resulted from his refusal to carry out an illegal order (*Sabine Pilots Services, Inc. v. Hauck*, 1985).

A 2003 Fifth Circuit case provides an excellent example of the legal difficulty that can arise when an at-will employee is let go. A school secretary filed a charge of discrimination and sexual harassment against the principal she worked for in 1991. The Equal Employment Opportunity Commission (EEOC) investigated and concluded that the claims were unsubstantiated, uncorroborated, and directly contradicted by other witnesses. Six years later the woman still worked for the same

school district, albeit for a different principal. When that principal recommended termination of the woman's at-will employment status, the
district, pursuant to its policy, conducted a "review session." In that
review session, the assistant superintendent described the woman as
a "problem employee." In support of that description, the assistant
superintendent cited the unsubstantiated EEOC claim of 1991. The district then terminated the woman's employment. Based on the assistant
superintendent's comment, the Fifth Circuit refused to toss this case
out of court. The court noted that the secretary had proven two of the
three things she needed to prove to win her case: (1) she had engaged
in protected activity by filing an EEOC complaint in 1991, and (2) she
subsequently had been terminated. The secretary still had the burden
of proving causation: was she fired *because* of her EEOC complaint?
At this preliminary stage of the litigation, the court concluded that a
reasonable jury could draw that conclusion from the comment of the
assistant superintendent. On the other hand, the school district had produced ample evidence to show that the woman's poor job performance
was the reason for her termination. Thus the court remanded the case
for a full trial so that a jury could sort out the crucial causation issue
(*Fabela v. Socorro I.S.D.*).

So can at-will employees be terminated for "no reasons at all," as is
commonly said? The fact of the matter is that no employee is ever terminated for no reason. There is always a reason. Well, then, can they be
terminated for "bad reasons"? Not if those reasons are so bad that they
violate state or federal law. The reason may be "bad" in the sense that
it does not amount to "good cause." It may be "bad" in the sense that a
reviewing body (court or EEOC) may not agree with the wisdom of the
decision. But if the decision is so "bad" that it violates state or federal
law, then it is a wrongful discharge. So it is not accurate to say that at-
will employees can be terminated for "bad reasons."

The more appropriate statement is this: At-will employees can be
terminated for any legally permissible reason. They can be terminated
at any time, and there is no constitutional requirement of pretermination due process. The employee may, however, file a grievance or a lawsuit asserting that the termination was impermissibly motivated.

Non–Chapter 21 Contracts

School boards determine how and when non–Chapter 21 contracts are
to terminate, provided that the termination process complies with any
relevant constitutional requirements. By definition, such contracts are
not subject to the independent hearing system or to the statutory nonrenewal process for term contract teachers discussed below. Keep in
mind, however, that if a non–Chapter 21 contract contains a specific
term, and the district wishes to terminate the contract prior to the expi-

ration of that term, the employee will be entitled to constitutional due process. Recall our discussion earlier of the *Ferguson v. Thomas* case, which spells out the basics of constitutional due process. For example, if the district employs its director of transportation through a non–Chapter 21 contract that covers the 2014–2015 school year, but the district seeks to terminate the contract prior to its expiration date, the director would be entitled to some sort of notice and some sort of hearing. The director, in this example, would have a property interest in the contract that could be taken away only after due process was provided.

On the other hand, if the district wishes to nonrenew the contract as of its expiration date, no property interest is at stake. If the district chooses to create some process for a nonrenewal it may do so, but it has no such legal obligation.

Finally, we do know that if there is a written employment contract, and if the employee alleges that the district has violated the contract and thereby caused the employee monetary harm, the non–Chapter 21 employee can appeal the decision to the commissioner pursuant to TEC §7.057.

Probationary Contracts

The intent of the legislature was to make it easy to terminate the relationship between the probationary teacher and the school district if the termination is to take effect as of the end of the teacher's contract. The board simply gives notice to the teacher of its decision to terminate the teacher's employment. Notice must be given by the tenth calendar day before the last day of instruction required under the contract. If the district fails to give this notice in a timely fashion, the contract automatically is renewed. No specific reason for termination is required. The board can make this decision "if in the board's judgment the best interests of the district will be served by terminating the employment." The law does not require the district to afford the teacher a hearing, although the district could choose to do so. Whatever decision the board makes is "final and may not be appealed" (TEC §21.103). Keep in mind, though, that this statement of finality does not prevent the terminated teacher from filing suit alleging a wrongful discharge.

Such was the case in *Ramirez v. Red Oak I.S.D.* (2001), where the probationary teacher complained that the school board specifically and officially had failed to recite that termination of the teacher's employment was "in the best interests of the district." Ruling for the school district, the court made the commonsense observation that every decision of the school board is implicitly in the best interests of the school district, at least as far as the board is concerned. Thus, the law did not require the board to spell it out. In another affirmation of school board authority in this area, the commissioner has ruled that a probationary contract can be nonrenewed by the board despite the fact that the superintendent recommended that it be renewed (*Berry v. Kemp I.S.D.*, 2001).

Suppose a district is so dissatisfied with a probationary teacher's performance that the district wants to terminate the relationship immediately, rather than waiting for the contract to run out. In that case, the legal analysis is significantly different and the burden on the district significantly higher. In such a case, the district must provide the teacher with formal due process and must demonstrate a good reason for ending the employment relationship earlier than expected. State law permits early termination of a probationary contract, or suspension without pay for the rest of the school year, "for good cause as determined by the board of trustees, good cause being the failure to meet the accepted standards of conduct for the profession as generally recognized and applied in similarly situated school districts in this state."

The process to be followed would be the independent hearing system, described below. For present purposes, suffice it to say that the teacher is entitled to a full-blown due process hearing, including the right to present evidence, to cross-examine witnesses, to be represented by counsel, and so on.

Term Contracts

Schools can take one of three actions regarding a teacher's term contract. The school can (1) renew the contract, (2) nonrenew the contract, or (3) terminate the contract. The expression "termination" refers *only* to the action of the district to end the contract prior to its normal expiration date. This deprives the teacher of a property interest and thus requires good cause and procedural due process.

School law makes quite a distinction between "termination" and "nonrenewal" of a term contract. To the employee, it makes little difference—he or she is unemployed. But the legal analysis changes significantly depending on whether the school's action is a termination or nonrenewal. A nonrenewal of contract refers to the decision of the school district to let the term contract expire. When an employee is nonrenewed she is permitted to fulfill the terms of her existing contract. But the district offers no new contract to continue the employment relationship.

The situation is slightly more complex if the employee has a multi-year term contract. In those cases, the common practice is for the school district to *extend* the contract each year. Assume, for example, that Mr. Hudson has a two-year contract, covering the 2014–2015 and 2015–2016 school years. In most school districts, the custom would be to consider the extension of the contract in the spring of 2015. At that time the board would consider extending Mr. Hudson's contract through the 2016–2017 school year. However, if the board chooses not to extend the contract, Mr. Hudson still has a valid contract for the 2015–2016 school year. The board has not "nonrenewed" Mr. Hudson, it has merely "nonextended" him. Mr. Hudson could file a grievance over this nonextension but otherwise has no legal recourse. The decision to nonrenew the multiyear contract can be made only in the final year of the contract.

To understand the current state of the law with regard to term contracts, a little history is helpful. The Term Contract Nonrenewal Act (TCNA) was adopted by the legislature in 1981. Prior to 1981, a school district lawfully could inform a term contract employee at the end of the contract of the fact of nonrenewal with no further ado. A teacher's procedural rights at the end of the twentieth one-year term contract were no greater than his or her rights at the end of the first one-year term contract.

Contract Nonrenewal. There no longer is a specific set of statutes referred to as the "Term Contract Nonrenewal Act." However, many of the requirements of the TCNA are still in place. For example, the board must give notice of proposed nonrenewal by the tenth day before the last day of instruction in the school year. If the board fails to give the notice in timely fashion, the district, as a matter of law, has elected to "employ the teacher in the same professional capacity for the following school year." As noted above, if the contract is a multiyear contract, this notice requirement applies only during the last year of the contract.

School board policy must contain a statement of all of the reasons why a teacher's contract might be nonrenewed, and the notice of proposed nonrenewal that is sent to a particular teacher should contain a list of the reasons for the nonrenewal of that teacher.

The board must consider the most recent evaluations before making a decision not to renew a teacher's contract "if the evaluations are relevant to the reason for the board's action."

A term contract teacher is entitled to a hearing prior to nonrenewal. When the teacher receives notice of the proposed nonrenewal, the teacher has fifteen days in which to request a hearing. The board may either conduct the hearing itself, under rules adopted by the board, or choose to use the independent hearing system described below. In districts with over five thousand students, the board may choose to have an attorney conduct the hearing.

If the teacher's contract is nonrenewed, the teacher may appeal to the commissioner of education. The commissioner's review will be a "substantial evidence" review. This means that the commissioner may not substitute his judgment for that of the board of trustees unless the board's decision was arbitrary, capricious, unlawful, or not supported by substantial evidence. In conducting the review, the commissioner will simply review the transcript of the hearing before the local board, rather than rehear the evidence at the Texas Education Agency.

Although the appeal of a nonrenewal to the commissioner is governed by the "substantial evidence" rule, the initial nonrenewal hearing is not. Such is the lesson of *Whitaker v. Moses* (2001). In that case, the district provided a hearing and voted to nonrenew the employee's contract. In doing so, the board indicated that it was applying the "substantial evidence" standard, meaning that it could vote to nonrenew the contract as long as there was "substantial evidence" in the record to support that decision. The commissioner ruled that the district erred by using the *appellate* standard at the *initial hearing* stage. The district should have applied the "preponderance of the evidence" standard, thus putting the burden of proof on the administration to prove that the nonrenewal was justified. The case then went into the court system and ultimately was decided by the court of appeals. The court agreed with the commissioner about the burden of proof—it should have been based on a "preponderance." What saved the district, however, was the fact that the teacher did not object to the "substantial evidence" standard when the case was heard by the school board. Thus, he waived any complaint he may have had. The court noted that the employee clearly knew how to make such an objection since he had made forty such objections during the hearing. Apparently, he should have made forty-one.

Procedural compliance with certain nonrenewal requirements is absolutely essential. Nonrenewal decisions can be reversed due to a procedural error alone. For example, if the district gives "notice of nonrenewal" instead of "notice of proposed nonrenewal," the district has committed a fatal error. In the case of *Castaneda v. Lasara I.S.D.* (2002), the board voted to "approve non-renewal" before notice of proposed nonrenewal was given to the teacher. The commissioner concluded that the board's action violated the law and ordered the district to reinstate the teacher with back pay.

Timeliness of the notice of proposed nonrenewal is equally crucial. If the district fails to give notice at the proper time (at least ten calendar days before the last day of instruction), the employee automatically is renewed. In *Howard v. Walnut Bend I.S.D.* (2008) the school board renewed teacher contracts in March 2008, but failed to take action on Ms. Howard's contract. The following month the teacher filed a grievance, seeking a contract for the following school year. The board heard the grievance, and voted not to renew the contract. However, this came after the deadline (which, at that time, was forty-five days) and with no notice of the "proposed nonrenewal" to the teacher. The commissioner reversed the board's decision due to its failure to comply with the procedures of the law.

It is also important to conduct the nonrenewal hearing in a timely fashion. For example, in one case the district held the nonrenewal hearing for a school counselor after the fifteen-day deadline. This can only be done by mutual agreement. The district originally set the hearing for April 12, 2005. The counselor requested a postponement and stated when he was available beyond the fifteen-day limit. The district agreed to the postponement and set the hearing for April 28, which was one of the days when the man said he was available. Thus there was a mutual agreement to hold the hearing on April 28, but fate intervened. The district did not get the agenda posted seventy-two hours in advance of the April 28 hearing date. When the district realized this, it canceled the April 28 hearing and set it for April 29, but this was not mutually agreed to, and the counselor's attorney was not available. The board met on April 29 and decided to reschedule the hearing for May 3 or 5, depending on which worked better for the counselor. The counselor did not show up at his nonrenewal hearing, which occurred on May 5. The board voted to nonrenew the contract.

It may sound like the board was trying to be reasonable and fair, but the commissioner held that the board's actions did not comport with the law. The hearing was held outside the fifteen-day window, and there was no mutual agreement to hold it on the day it was held. The teacher's contract was renewed (*Barrientes v. Beeville I.S.D.*, 2005).

Other procedural glitches may not be as costly. In fact, TEC Section 21.303(c) specifies that the commissioner may not reverse the board's decision based on a procedural irregularity or error unless the commissioner determines that the irregularity or error "was likely to have led to an erroneous decision." For a case example of this "no harm, no foul" approach consider *Lewis v. Austin I.S.D.* (2003). The nonrenewed principal in the case asserted that the district had made numerous procedural errors, some of them in the appraisal process two years earlier. The court was unimpressed with that argument: "Complaints of procedural irregularities in the appraisal process may not be resurrected at the time of the contract nonrenewal process." Furthermore, the principal had not shown how the alleged errors were relevant to the nonrenewal decision.

In *Jeffery v. Fort Bend I.S.D.* (2008), the commissioner upheld the nonrenewal of a contract despite the fact that the teacher was never identified as a "teacher in need of assistance" or placed on an intervention plan. Furthermore, the decision notes that teachers do not have a "right" to have a chance to remediate their problems. The commissioner noted that evidence of remediation is much less likely to be required in a nonrenewal case than in a termination case.

If the school district dots its i's, crosses its t's, and acts in a timely manner, the substantive standard it must reach is not difficult. However, the school must produce some evidence of some sort of problem with the teacher's performance. For example, two teachers in a small district near Fort Worth were nonrenewed after they were charged with sexual harassment of a student, even though the district did not even attempt to prove that the charges were true. District policy provided that a teacher could be nonrenewed due to "any activity, school connected or otherwise, that because of the publicity given it, or knowledge of it among students, faculty, and community, impairs or diminishes the employee's effectiveness in the District." The allegations of sexual harassment, made by a former male student accusing two female teachers, were widely publicized and known throughout the community. Witnesses testified that the effectiveness of the teachers had been diminished by these allegations, true or not. The commissioner sided with the school district, holding that the district's policy was valid and the nonrenewal was proper: "One need not prove that a teacher has engaged in an inappropriate activity in order to nonrenew a teacher's contract." However, the court of appeals saw it differently. While the court found the school's policy to be valid, it focused its attention on the word "activity." The court held that the district had failed to show that the teachers had engaged in any "activity" meriting nonrenewal. While the evidence showed that the community was upset with the teachers, it did not show that the teachers had engaged in any "activity" that produced the criticism (*Peaster I.S.D. v. Glodfelty*, 2001).

When there is evidence of some sort of wrongdoing, a teacher may be nonrenewed even though the evidence is less than overwhelming. In *Freeland v. Pasadena I.S.D.* (2002) the teacher was charged with inappropriate physical contact with a student. The case was not clear-cut. Criminal charges were brought against the man, but the court acquitted him. Moreover, at the nonrenewal hearing, some students testified that the man's accuser had made up the allegations in an effort to get him fired. Thus there were direct conflicts in the testimony, putting the school board in the difficult position of determining whom to believe. In this case they believed the accuser and voted to nonrenew the man's contract. The commissioner upheld that decision. The commissioner noted that in cases of conflicting testimony the board must determine what evidence is more credible. There was evidence in the record to support the board's decision. Finally, the fact that the man escaped criminal conviction was not relevant. The criminal courts apply different standards and different burdens of proof. Thus the criminal acquittal did not prevent the school district from pursuing the nonrenewal.

Contract Termination. Districts still retain the power to terminate a term contract teacher prior to the end of the contract, but only for "good cause" or due to a financial exigency that requires a reduction in personnel. Boards of trustees will have the opportunity to define the term "good cause," there being no definition of that term in the relevant section of state law. Later in this chapter, we will provide some examples of what constitutes "good cause." Whatever the reason for a termination, since it involves a deprivation of a property interest, the teacher is entitled to a full due process hearing. State law now mandates that such a hearing be conducted pursuant to the state's independent hearing process, described below.

As is the case with nonrenewal, a procedural irregularity or error is not sufficient to overturn a board's decision unless the commissioner concludes that the error affected the outcome. Failure to comply with the Texas Open Meetings Act might be viewed as such an error. In *Spaniel v. Fort Worth I.S.D.* (2010) the commissioner noted that the district had presented good cause to justify the termination of a principal's contract. The termination was based on a well-publicized incident in which the principal had left her children unattended in a hotel room while she went to a nightclub. She allegedly got into a scrap with a bouncer, refused to cooperate with police, and was charged with resisting arrest and lying to the police. The independent hearing officer, the school board, and the commissioner all agreed that this amounted to "good cause" to terminate the principal's employment. But the agenda for the board meeting was too vague. The commissioner held that there was a great deal of public interest in this matter due to the fact that it involved a principal and an incident that was big news with Fort Worth media outlets. The agenda stated that the board would discuss "Recommendation for Proposed Terminations of Instructional Employees (2)." The commissioner held that this was too vague to satisfy the Texas Open Meetings Act. Consequently, the board's vote to propose the principal's termination was void, and the district was ordered to reemploy the principal.

Professional Capacity. If a school district fails to follow proper nonrenewal procedures, then it has, by law, renewed the teacher "in the same professional capacity." The key to determining an employee's "professional capacity" is the contract. In *Ramos v. El Paso I.S.D.* (2002), a high school principal was reassigned to serve as an elementary principal with no cut in pay. The commissioner concluded that the man still served in the same professional capacity and thus was not entitled to a nonrenewal hearing.

Educators would be wise to examine their contracts carefully. Mr. Skinner was employed as a teacher/coach for the 2001–2002 school year, but when he asked to be relieved of coaching duties due to physical ailments, the district agreed. Then for the 2002–2003 school year, the district offered him another teacher/coach contract. The man signed it. When he then refused to perform coaching duties, the district proposed to terminate his contract. The commissioner ultimately upheld Skinner's termination. Even though the district had agreed to relieve him of coaching duties for one year, the parties had entered into a new agreement for the next school year. The agreement called for the man to serve as both teacher and coach, and he could not refuse to perform either as teacher or as coach (*Skinner v. San Felipe Del Rio C.I.S.D.*, 2003). We will explore the parameters of "same professional capacity" in more detail in the next chapter when we discuss reassignments.

Dual-Assignment Contracts. The *Skinner* case provides a good segue into the entire topic of dual-assignment contracts, the most common of which is "teacher/coach." If the district wants to nonrenew the coaching duties, but renew the person as a teacher, must it comply with the statutory nonrenewal scheme? Again, the key appears to be the language of the individual's contract. As far back as 1985, the Texas Commissioner of Education observed that a school district can hire a person to serve as teacher and coach in one of two ways—either with a single, unified "teacher/coach" contract or with two contracts, one for teaching and the other for coaching. Under the two-contract arrangement, it might be possible to nonrenew the coaching contract without adhering to statutory nonrenewal provisions, while retaining the person as a teacher. Under the unified contract, however, nonrenewal of either portion of the contract means that the employee is not coming back "in the same professional capacity," and thus nonrenewal procedures are necessary. Moreover, under the unified contract, nonperformance of any of the duties could lead to nonrenewal of the entire employment relationship, provided the district complies with the statutory scheme for nonrenewal (*Hester v. Canadian I.S.D.*, 1985).

These principles were applied in *Carroll v. Wichita Falls I.S.D.* (2000), in which the commissioner concluded that the man had two separate contracts and, thus, could be terminated as a coach without a nonrenewal hearing. On the other hand, in *Dibble v. Keller I.S.D.* (2000), the decision went the other way. This was particularly interesting because there were two separate pieces of paper, one of them a "teaching contract" and one of them a "supplemental contract" for coaching duties. The commissioner, however, looked at the language of the supplemental contract and concluded that there was, in fact, a unified contract in place here, even though there were two separate pieces of paper, not stapled together. The key was that the "supplemental contract" specified that (1) the man could not quit coaching without also quitting his teaching job, and (2) he could be terminated from both positions for poor performance in either. Those are the very hallmarks of a unified contract, and thus the commissioner ruled that the two separate documents formed but one, unified contract.

To summarize, if a district uses a unified "teacher/coach" contract, it may nonrenew the employee in both capacities, or nonrenew the coaching portion only, provided it complies with the law concerning such nonrenewals. If, on the other hand, a district hires a person as a "teacher," with a separate, supplemental contract as a coach, it may terminate or nonrenew the coaching contract without meeting those requirements. However, termination or nonrenewal of the supplemental coaching contract would have no bearing on the employee's rights under the teaching contract.

So let's get to the nub of the matter: Can a coach be nonrenewed because of a lousy win-loss record? This happens in college ranks all the time, sometimes when the coach's record is quite good, but short of very high expectations. The case of R. C. Slocum at Texas A&M comes to mind. In high school ranks, however, the only case on record involved an assistant coach. The commissioner concluded that a win-loss record was insufficient evidence under the substantial evidence standard for nonrenewal under the TCNA. The commissioner noted that while a win-loss record is relevant to assessment of a coach's performance, "when considered in a vacuum, a poor record does not constitute even a scintilla of evidence that bad coaching was responsible for that record. Too many other factors influence a won-loss [sic] record over which the coach has no control." Here, the coach's contract was nonrenewed for "significant lack of student progress." His team failed to make the play-offs, a goal set by the school district. However, there was considerable evidence that the students had progressed during the evaluation period. The commissioner added that, even if it were appropriate to consider a win-loss record in a vacuum for assessing a head coach's performance, such a standard cannot apply to assistant coaches: "This philosophy— i.e., 'We win as a team and lose as a team'— . . . cannot stand as a reason for nonrenewing an assistant coach who is doing his job competently and in accordance with district policy. Nonrenewal must be based on personal accountability" (*Hester v. Canadian I.S.D.*, 1985).

Remedies. Suppose a school district wrongfully nonrenews a contract. What remedy is the employee entitled to? A very interesting section of the Texas Education Code may come into play here. Section 21.304 of the Code says that the commissioner may reverse the decision of the school board to nonrenew or terminate a teacher. In that event, the commissioner is authorized to reinstate the teacher and to issue an order for back pay and employment benefits from the time of discharge to reinstatement. However, the law goes on to give school districts an avenue to avoid reinstatement: "Instead of reinstating a teacher under Subsection (e), the school district may pay the teacher one year's salary to which the teacher would have been entitled from the date on which the teacher would have been reinstated." The argument likely will be made that these provisions preclude any further remedy, such as for breach-of-contract damages. But future litigation will decide the outcome of that argument.

Reduction in Force (RIF). One of the reasons for nonrenewal merits special comment. Reduction in force (RIF) clearly is a valid reason for the nonrenewal of a term contract. In decisions dating back to the 1980s, the commissioner has held that a district must give the employee an opportunity to apply for any position that is available at the time of his or her nonrenewal hearing and for which the employee is qualified.

For example, consider *Parr v. Waco I.S.D.* (1991). In that case the commissioner overturned the nonrenewal of an administrator based on reduction in force. At the time of the nonrenewal, the position of vocational coordinator was open. The administrator was certified for the position but was not considered by the selection committee to be qualified. However, no evidence was produced establishing qualifications for the position or the reasons why the selection committee judged the administrator unqualified. The commissioner observed that "once an open position is established and Petitioner has shown that she is certified and at least minimally qualified for the position, Respondent has the burden to prove that Petitioner was not qualified for the open position." Had the qualifications and standards of the position been introduced into evidence at the local hearing and had the rationale of the committee been established, "the outcome would have been different." The employee was entitled to reinstatement in the same professional capacity for the ensuing school year.

In the latest twist on this issue, however, the commissioner ruled that vacant positions are not to be simply handed to the employee. Rather, the employee can be required to actually apply for and interview for a vacant position. When Mr. Amerson failed to do so, his nonrenewal due to RIF was upheld by the commissioner (*Amerson v. Houston I.S.D.*, 2003). One thing that has remained constant in RIF cases is that the school board must follow its own policy. In *Bosworth v. East Central I.S.D.* (2003) the commissioner overturned a RIF nonrenewal after concluding that the board had deviated from its written policy. The policy called for the board to identify certain employment areas in which employees would be RIFfed. Then the superintendent would apply four criteria, starting with certification, to the contractual employees in that area. In this case, the commissioner concluded that the superintendent had deviated from that policy. Instead of applying the criteria to the employees in the specified employment area, the superintendent developed his own criteria for the elimination of entire programs. Thus, due to a failure to comply with board policy, the nonrenewal was reversed.

The 2011 legislature made drastic cuts in school funding, and also adopted some new standards for RIFs in the context of "financial exigency." The legislature required the commissioner to adopt minimum standards for "financial exigency," which the commissioner has now done. A district cannot declare a "financial exigency" unless it satisfies the standards in the rules.

However, a RIF does not have to be driven by a declaration of financial exigency. It can also arise from a board decision to make a "program change." Districts are likely to find the "program change" route more flexible. In *Butler v. Buna I.S.D.* (2011) the district sought to nonrenew a P.E. teacher's contract due to a program change. The commissioner affirmed the nonrenewal, and in the process, recognized that local boards have considerable discretion in this area. The teacher complained that there was no need for a program change. But the commissioner held that the board was not limited to making "necessary" program changes. Further, "the Commissioner does not get to determine whether a program change is necessary or unnecessary." Under the district's local policy DFF (promulgated by TASB), a reduction in force could take place when the board determined that a financial exigency or program change required the discharge of one or more employees. Under local policy DFBB, a program change was a preestablished reason for nonrenewal. Making a program change that is not "necessary" would not violate that preestablished policy reason for nonrenewal. If the board determines a program change is to be made, teachers' contracts may be nonrenewed in accordance with board policy. "Whether or not the program change was necessary or unnecessary, wise or unwise, does not affect the validity of a nonrenewal due to a program change."

In seeking to terminate the employment relationship, can the school district present evidence of events that occurred in prior years, or is the district limited to the latest contract year? TEC Section 21.352(e) requires schools to "use a teacher's consecutive appraisals from more than one year, if available, in making the district's employment decisions and developing career recommendations for the teacher." Thus it would appear that the district must consider the teacher's prior years' performance in most cases. This legislative enactment, effective with the 2013–2014 school year, may change the commissioner's view on the matter. Consider, for example, *Goodfriend v. Houston I.S.D.* (2003). Although the case involved a continuing contract teacher, its holding has implications for term contract nonrenewals. Thus we bring it up at this point in the discussion. The commissioner concluded that "the general rule that a district cannot take action against a teacher's contract for actions taken in a prior school year is not an absolute bar. It is a doctrine based on the principle of 'waiver.'" Thus, the commissioner reasoned, the school district has more explaining to do when it relies on prior year events when nonrenewing a term contract. Most term contracts run for one year only and thus are subject to annual renewal. The fact that the school district renewed the contract after learning of the problematic behaviors indicates that the matters may have been waived. Such an argument, however, is not so strong when dealing with continuing contracts, where there is no affirmative action by the school to renew the contract. In the *Goodfriend* case the teacher was on a continuing contract. The commissioner concluded that no waiver occurred, and so the district could rely on evidence of "repeated failure to comply with directives" and "repeated and continuing neglect of duties" even though some of the evidence went back to earlier years. The key here is notice to the teacher and fair play. The renewal of a contract does not automatically waive the concerns the district has expressed to the teacher, particularly if the documentation presented to the teacher makes it clear that improvement is needed.

Finally, we should make note of the timeline that applies when the superintendent's contract is up for nonrenewal. The superintendent is entitled to "reasonable notice of the reason for the proposed nonrenewal, not later than the 30th day before the last day of the contract term."

Perhaps the most important distinction regarding superintendents, though, concerns the cost to the district in buying out the superintendent's contract. Superintendents typically have multiyear contracts. School board members who are unhappy with the superintendent face a dilemma: Either produce sufficient evidence to justify firing the superintendent (thus likely embroiling the district in costly litigation); wait for the contract to run out (which still requires legal proceedings to nonrenew the contract); or negotiate a buyout. Superintendent buyouts have become commonplace.

However, the cost of a buyout is substantially increased due to a provision added to the Texas Education Code in 1995 designed to discourage buyouts. Section 11.201 requires that any buyout of a superintendent's contract be reported to the Texas Education Agency. If the payment to the superintendent exceeds one year of his or her salary, TEA must deduct the excess amount from the district's funding for the next school year. For example, if the superintendent's salary is $100,000, and the board makes a severance payment of $125,000, it will actually cost the school district $150,000. This is because TEA will deduct the excess amount ($125,000 - $100,000 = $25,000) from the district's subsidy in the next school year.

Continuing Contracts

In the continuing contract system, there is no such thing as a "nonrenewal." Since the contract does not require renewal, but rather, automatically continues from one year to the next, it would not make sense for the school district to "nonrenew" the contract. This means that districts need not give notice of proposed termination as of a specific date, as they must do with term and probationary contracts. Recall that both term and probationary contracts automatically renew if the district fails to give notice of possible nonrenewal by the tenth day before the last day of instruction. No such notice requirement exists with continuing contracts.

Continuing contract teachers may be terminated at any time "for good cause as determined by the board of trustees, good cause being the failure to meet the accepted standards of conduct for the profession as generally recognized and applied in similarly situated school districts in this state" (TEC §21.156).

Regardless of the reason for termination of the continuing contract, the procedure to be followed for such a termination must be in accordance with the independent hearing system described below. In lieu of discharge, schools can suspend a continuing contract teacher without pay for a period of time not to exceed the current school year. However, such action must be done through notice to the teacher, who then is entitled to an independent hearing, just as if the school were proposing termination. Keep in mind that the continuing contract teacher can be returned to probationary status, as outlined above, provided that the teacher consents to the move.

The Independent Hearing System

Teachers and other certified personnel are entitled to a hearing concerning a termination of contract or a suspension without pay. Note that the type of contract does not matter—probationary, continuing, or term. A teacher is entitled to a hearing concerning any termination of contract.

The commissioner is required to certify hearing examiners according to criteria developed by the State Board of Education, in consultation with the State Office of Administrative Hearings. State law requires only that the hearing examiners be licensed to practice law in Texas and not serve as agents or representatives of a school district, a teacher in a dispute with a school district, or an organization of school employees, administrators, or school boards. Furthermore, a hearing officer may not be associated with a law firm that serves as representative or agent of any of these entities. Thus the lawyers and law firms that have represented schools and school employees, as well as the lawyers at the Texas Association of School Boards, are disqualified. However, the law does not prevent the appointment of a lawyer who formerly represented schools or school employees.

A teacher must make a written request for a hearing to the commissioner, with a copy to the local district. The request must be made within fifteen days after receipt of written notice of the proposed action. The commissioner then has ten days to appoint one of the certified hearing examiners to the case.

Either party can reject the assigned examiner for cause. The rejection must be in writing and must be filed with the commissioner within three days after notification of the assignment. The commissioner must then decide if good cause for rejection exists. If so, the commissioner is to appoint the next person on the list.

Rather than taking potluck with the next person on the list, the parties are authorized to agree on a noncertified hearing examiner, provided that the individual chosen is licensed to practice law in Texas. It does not appear that the parties can agree to use an examiner who is certified. Certified hearing examiners are to wait their turn. The parties also are authorized to agree that the decision of the hearing examiner will be final and nonappealable on all or some of the issues.

The teacher has the right to be represented at the hearing, to hear the evidence on which the charges are based, to present evidence, and to cross-examine adverse witnesses. Rules of Civil Evidence apply, and a court reporter must be employed to record the hearing. In general, the hearing is to be conducted just as a nonjury trial, with the school district bearing the burden of proof.

The hearing examiner has extensive powers to control the process. The examiner can issue subpoenas, rule on motions and admissibility of evidence, and maintain decorum at the hearing. In this connection, it should be noted that the hearing will be private unless the teacher requests that it be open. Even then the hearing examiner can close the hearing to maintain decorum. Finally, the hearing examiner has the power to protect the privacy of a witness who is a child by closing the hearing to receive the child's testimony or issuing other orders consistent with practices in criminal cases in which children are the victims.

The hearing examiner and the court reporter are to be paid by the school district. The commissioner is to establish hourly rates for hearing examiners, along with a per-case maximum compensation.

The hearing examiner must issue a written recommendation no later than forty-five days after the date when the commissioner received the request for a hearing. This puts the hearing on a fast track, but again, the parties can agree to waive this timeline. The recommendation must include findings of fact and conclusions of law. It may include a proposal for granting relief, including reinstatement, back pay, or employee benefits. The hearing examiner may not propose recovery of attorneys' fees or other costs as relief. Copies of the recommendation are to go to the parties, the president of the school board, and the commissioner.

The matter then goes to the board. At this meeting, the board must consider the recommendation and allow each party to present an oral argument. In effect, the board is acting as an appellate body. The board can limit the amount of time each side has, provided that each side has an equal amount of time.

The board can adopt, reject, or change the hearing examiner's conclusions of law or proposal for relief, provided that the board states in writing the reason and the legal basis for a change or rejection of the recommendation. With regard to the findings of fact, however, boards are even more restrained. They can reject or change a finding of fact "only after reviewing the record of the proceedings before the hearing examiner and only if the finding of fact is not supported by substantial evidence." Again, such a change must be accompanied by a written statement as to the reason and the legal basis for the change.

Boards probably will want some legal advice in handling these matters and are authorized to get advice "from an attorney who has not been involved in the proceedings." Thus the attorney who represented the district before the hearing examiner should not be the attorney advising the board as to what to do with the hearing examiner's recommendation. Finally, boards can delegate all of these responsibilities to a committee of the board, thus keeping some members of the board out of the process altogether.

Gonzales v. Brownsville I.S.D. (2009) made it clear that this opportunity to contest the hearing examiner's recommendation to the school board is no mere formality. In this case, the board proposed the termination of the superintendent's contract and the hearing examiner supported the board's proposal. When the matter came before the board for action, the superintendent's attorney made only a brief statement and did not raise any specific legal objections to the hearing examiner's recommendation. The board voted to terminate the contract and the superintendent appealed to the commissioner, who did not rule on the merits. Instead, he held that the superintendent had failed to exhaust his administrative remedies. The commissioner noted that educators must "reasonably place a board of trustees on notice of claimed legal errors so that the school board has an opportunity to correct those legal errors." Because that did not happen here, the commissioner dismissed the appeal for lack of jurisdiction.

A teacher can appeal the board's decision to the commissioner by filing a "petition for review" within twenty days. The commissioner then is required to review the record and the oral argument before the local board. In most instances the commissioner will base his decision on the record review without hearing any new evidence.

With regard to nonrenewals of term contracts, the commissioner may not substitute his judgment for that of the board of trustees unless the decision was arbitrary, capricious, unlawful, or not supported by substantial evidence. The same standard applies in termination cases, but only if the board accepted the hearing examiner's recommended findings of fact without modification. A board that changes the findings of fact can be reversed if the commissioner determines that its decision was arbitrary, capricious, or unlawful, or if "the hearing examiner's original findings of fact are not supported by substantial evidence" (TEC §21.303(b)(2)). This is a curious provision. Why should the validity of the decision turn on fact findings that were reversed by the local board? Some attorneys are arguing that this is a simple case of legislative error.

We shall have to wait and see how this curious provision is interpreted in actual cases.

The commissioner must issue a decision thirty days after the last day on which a response to the petition for review could have been filed. If the commissioner fails to act, the decision of the local board is affirmed.

If the commissioner reverses the board's decision, he must order the district to reinstate the teacher and to pay any back pay and employment benefits from the time of discharge or suspension. However, the district is not required to accept the teacher back. In lieu of reinstatement, the district can pay the teacher one year's salary. Thus the worst situation for the school district would involve back pay for seventy days (unless the parties agreed to waive timelines), plus one year's salary.

Either party can appeal the commissioner's decision to the district court in the county in which the district's administrative offices are located. This is a significant change from prior law, which required all appeals to go to Travis County. The parties still can take an appeal to Travis County, but only with agreement of all parties. School districts that are light years, geographically and politically, from Travis County are not likely to agree.

The appeal involves a "substantial evidence" review of the record, meaning that the court can reverse the decision only if it finds that the decision was not supported by substantial evidence, or that the commissioner's conclusions of law were erroneous. Just as with the commissioner, the court cannot reverse the decision on the basis of a procedural irregularity unless it finds that the error likely led to an erroneous decision by the commissioner.

There are two leading cases that define the powers and processes of the independent hearing system. In the first, the Texas Supreme Court ruled in favor of a teacher whose contract had been nonrenewed by the Montgomery I.S.D. The board opted to use the independent hearing system for the nonrenewal and then lived to regret it. The independent hearing examiner issued "findings of fact" to the effect that the teacher's performance was satisfactory or better. He recommended renewal of the contract. The school board, however, voted to nonrenew the contract, relying largely on new findings of fact that it made. The case wound its way through the commissioner's office, the trial court, and the court of appeals before ultimately being decided by the Texas Supreme Court. The court ruled that the actions of the board violated the Texas Education Code. When an independent hearing officer issues findings of fact, those findings must be supported as long as there is any reasonable basis in the record to support the findings. The board might disagree with the findings, but it is powerless to change them, or add to them, as long as there is some support in the record for the hearing examiner's view. By adding new fact findings, the court concluded, the board had, in effect, changed the hearing examiner's findings (*Montgomery I.S.D. v. Davis*, 2000).

The second key case deals with changes to the hearing examiner's conclusions of law. In its decision, the court of appeals emphasized that such changes can be made only in the manner spelled out in TEC §21.259. The change may be made by the board, which must "state in writing the legal basis" for the change. In the case before it, the only explanation of the changes came in a letter from the board president, rather than coming from the board as a whole. Moreover, the explanation was deficient. It simply stated that the hearing officer's conclusions were "not supported by substantial evidence." The court concluded that this was inadequate as an explanation (*Goodie v. Houston I.S.D.*, 2001).

The commissioner has taken the same approach as the court in the *Goodie* case with regard to changes to the conclusions of law. Any such changes must be adequately explained. "We think the hearing officer is wrong" will not suffice as an explanation. This is the lesson of *Roberts v. San Benito I.S.D.* (1996). The explanation, according to the commissioner, must be specific enough to enable the teacher to make an informed decision about an appeal of the board's decision. Here, the explanation for the changes was inadequate, the hearing officer's findings were supported by substantial evidence, and the teacher was ordered reinstated with back pay.

In Sonora I.S.D. the board junked the hearing officer's recommendation but did not explain why. Moreover, the district did not come up with its own findings of fact and conclusions of law, but instead, delegated this responsibility to its attorney. The commissioner rejected this approach and ordered the teacher reinstated. The board cannot delegate its duty to its attorney, must explain any changes in findings of fact, and must not change findings that are supported by substantial evidence (*McNaughten v. Sonora I.S.D.*, 1997).

Moreover, the explanation for any changes to the conclusions of law or the proposal for relief must be done in a timely fashion. The Dallas I.S.D. rejected a hearing examiner's recommendation to reinstate a probationary teacher the district sought to terminate. However, the written explanation for the change was not provided until two days after the teacher's deadline for appealing the decision to TEA. This was untimely, said the commissioner, and thus the teacher was ordered reinstated. School administrators should take note of the fact that this case is a classic illustration of the problems with the independent hearing examiner system and why school districts generally will want to avoid it. The hearing examiner concluded that the teacher had violated the district's corporal punishment policies and had "used bad judgment" in interactions with parents. Nevertheless, the hearing examiner proposed that the woman should be reinstated to her teaching position since she had never been given notice of her deficiencies, counseled, or given an opportunity to remediate. As we shall explain a little further along in this chapter, the commissioner has expressly rejected the notion that all employees are entitled to remediation. This hearing examiner apparently disagreed and thus proposed that the teacher be reinstated. It was not surprising that the school board changed that proposal and refused to reinstate the teacher. It must have been disconcerting to see the case reversed due to a procedural glitch, particularly since the district could have terminated the teacher's probationary contract as of the end of the contract year without a hearing at all, much less one before an independent hearing examiner with his own ideas of what constitutes good cause (*Cox v. Dallas I.S.D.*, 2003).

Taken together, these cases show how important the hearing examiner's decision is. It is almost impossible for a board to alter the hearing officer's view of the facts. A decision to terminate the teacher's contract must be supported by fact findings. So the bottom line is that if the hearing examiner does not find facts sufficient to justify termination, then termination is a legally risky move.

One of the most crucial issues in a termination case is whether or not there is "good cause" to terminate the contract. This is inherently a judgment call, and one might think that the elected school board would retain the power to make that call. But prior to 2011, the commissioner had emphatically ruled that "good cause" is a fact issue to be decided by the hearing officer. In *Floyd v. Houston I.S.D.* (2003) the commissioner said it plainly: "There is no reason to defer to a board's opinion as to the definition of 'good cause.' In a termination case, a board does not retain the authority to make the ultimate decision based on a claim that it is interpreting its own policies."

The legislature addressed this issue in its 2011 special session, making a subtle but important change in the independent hearing system. The new law states that the determination of whether or not the district has presented "good cause" to justify contract termination will henceforth be deemed a "conclusion of law" rather than a "finding of fact." This is welcome news to school boards that have been hamstrung by hearing examiner rulings that they disagree with. It is virtually impossible for the board to alter a "finding of fact." So as long as the ultimate issue—good cause—was deemed a "finding of fact," the hearing examiner's opinion on that issue carried more weight than the board's.

It is not easy for the board to change a "conclusion of law," but it can be done. Thus the legislative change to make "good cause" a legal issue, rather than a factual one, will restore the authority of the school board to determine what types of conduct are intolerable within the district.

Finally, there are a few cases that were decided on procedural grounds. A teacher asked for a hearing to contest his proposed termination, but only after waiting for almost two months. The commissioner ruled that the request for hearing was untimely. Under TEC §21.253, the request for hearing must be made within fifteen days after receipt of written notice of the proposed action (*Putnam v. Harlandale I.S.D.*, 1997). One case involves a fifteen-day suspension without pay, appealed by a teacher from an adverse board decision all the way to the court of appeals level. The district failed to file the entire record with the commissioner in a timely fashion. Based on this procedural error, the commissioner granted the teacher's appeal. The court of appeals agreed (*Moses v. Fort Worth I.S.D.*, 1998). Another timeline came into play in *Horton v. Dallas I.S.D.* (1997). The hearing officer recommended termination of the teacher's contract, but the district failed to set a hearing within twenty days of receiving the recommendation, as required by the law. Based on that missed timeline, the commissioner ordered the teacher reinstated.

It should be clear to Texas educators that the independent hearing officers are expected to be truly independent. If the school administration cannot persuade the hearing officer that the teacher should be terminated, it is highly unlikely that the teacher is going to be terminated. Moreover, the cases emphasize the importance of procedural compliance with the various timelines imposed by the law.

Some of the most interesting termination cases of the past few years invoke a statute that is designed to protect educators from adverse action when they find it necessary to use force against students in an emergency situation. The statute, TEC §22.0512, protects educators from termination, nonrenewal, or SBEC sanction based on "the employee's use of physical force against a student to the extent justified under Section 9.62, Penal Code." That section of the Penal Code authorizes nondeadly force by someone who is charged with the "care, supervision, or administration of the person for a special purpose." Force is permissible "when and to the degree the actor reasonably believes the force is necessary to further the special purpose or to maintain discipline in a group." Thus, if a teacher reasonably believes that nondeadly physical force is necessary in the classroom, the teacher may not be discharged for using force.

A Few Final Thoughts on "Good Cause"

What constitutes good cause for dismissal? No mechanical test can be applied. Basically, good cause means that convincing evidence has been presented to indicate that the school district is justified in breaking off its contractual commitment to the teacher. Under the independent hearing system one is tempted to simply say that "good cause" is whatever the independent hearing examiner thinks it is. Nevertheless, there are some general principles we can rely on.

Conduct that is potentially harmful to students can justify termination. Sexual misconduct with students, of course, justifies termination. An employee who assaults another person and engages in violent conduct at school may be justifiably terminated for such conduct. Insubordination or refusal to comply with directives or policy may justify dismissal during the term of a contract. An employee's misappropriation of public funds is a criminal violation that may justify termination. Racist comments in a fifth grade classroom amounted to good cause to terminate a teacher (*Williamson v. Dallas I.S.D.*, 1998).

Other cases remind us that "good cause" for termination may arise based on incidents that occur off campus. A teacher allegedly had held his wife hostage with a hunting rifle one evening. The wife eventually escaped, and the teacher surrendered to police, but the incident caused a commotion in the school's community. The district terminated the teacher's employment due to his loss of effectiveness as a teacher. The commissioner affirmed the decision (*Humphrey v. Westwood I.S.D.*, 1996). Similar results occurred in *Moten v. Dallas I.S.D.* (1999), in which a teacher was given deferred adjudication and probation for an aggravated assault on his wife, and in *Massey v. Paris I.S.D.* (1999), in which a teacher had several DWI convictions.

Mid-contract terminations are not to be undertaken lightly. Most school lawyers routinely have advised that it is usually necessary to give the employee an opportunity for "remediation" prior to termination. This is still good advice if the problems are correctable and relatively minor. But in recent decisions, the commissioner has repeatedly made it clear that remediation is not always necessary.

Constructive Discharge

A significant footnote to the discussion of termination of employment involves the concept of "constructive" discharge. This is the situation in which an employee resigns and then claims that the resignation was not voluntary. The employee contends, instead, that the actions of the employer forced him or her into an involuntary resignation. The focus of a constructive discharge case is twofold. First, were the employee's working conditions "intolerable," and, second, was there "illegal conduct" on the part of the employer (*Young v. Southwestern Savings and Loan Assn.*, 1975)? A constructive discharge results when job conditions are so difficult or so unpleasant that a reasonable person in the employee's place would have felt compelled to resign (*Junior v. Texaco, Inc.*, 1982). If a case of constructive discharge can be proven, the employer is liable for the illegal conduct leading to the discharge, just as he or she would be in the case of formal discharge (*Kline v. North Texas State University*, 1986).

Those who allege constructive discharge face a demanding burden of proof, as illustrated by some recent decisions from the Fifth Circuit.

Robert Woods claimed that he was constructively discharged when the principal informed him that she intended to recommend that his two-year contract not be extended after the first year. Mr. Woods resigned, claiming that his work environment was intolerable. The Fifth Circuit did not agree. The court noted several factors that are important in constructive discharge cases: (1) demotion; (2) salary reduction; (3) reduction in job responsibilities; (4) reassignment to menial work; (5) reassignment to work under a younger supervisor; (6) badgering, harassment, or humiliation by the employer that is calculated to force a resignation; and (7) an offer of early retirement or continued employment on unfavorable terms. Mr. Woods cited none of these factors, and thus he fell short of proving constructive discharge. The principal did admit that on one occasion she wrote a note to the teacher that referenced "termination," but the court brushed this off, noting that a veteran educator like Mr. Woods should know that a principal could not unilaterally terminate his contract, and that he had other options (*Woods v. Sheldon I.S.D.*, 2007). The same court rejected another claim of constructive discharge in *Easterling v. School Board of Concordia Parish* (2006). Citing the same seven factors, the court held that Ms. Easterling's allegations fell short.

Complaints that the boss has second-guessed the teacher's judgment or held her responsible for things outside of her control will not be enough to prove constructive discharge. According to the Fifth Circuit, such claims are merely "ordinary work-related disagreements" that do not amount to constructive discharge. Thus the claim of Norma Cavazos, a high school principal who was reassigned to another school, was rejected (*Cavazos v. Edgewood I.S.D.*, 2006). Guadalupe Perez was reassigned from middle school principal to Pregnancy Education Program Coordinator in Laredo I.S.D. She resigned. The district accepted the resignation. Ms. Perez then charged the district with a "constructive discharge." The commissioner rejected that argument, and noted the heavy burden of proof employees face when making such a claim. The fact that the plaintiff was embarrassed and humiliated, received less pay, was demoted, or moved to a different professional capacity does not necessarily mean that there was a constructive discharge. An employee has a valid claim for constructive discharge only if his or her working conditions are "unendurable" (*Perez v. Laredo I.S.D.*, 2011).

SUMMARY

In this chapter we have concentrated on how the employment relationship begins and ends. We also have highlighted those aspects of public employment that make it distinct from employment in the private sector. Educators must be aware of the various types of employment arrangements available in Texas public schools and the legal ramifications of each. Regardless of the employment arrangement, certain constitutional principles will apply to the employment relationship in the public sector.

No area of school law generates more legal disputes than personnel. This is not surprising, since school districts employ so many people and have to comply with so many federal and state mandates. If it has done nothing else, this chapter should have made clear that personnel administration is no simple task. With the push toward site-based decision-making, it is all the more important that knowledge of the basics of the law move from the central office to each campus. The human resources director for the district needs to be an expert on the matters discussed in this chapter. But the principal needs to have a good grasp of the subject as well.

Personnel Issues

IN CHAPTER 4, we reviewed the legal issues surrounding the beginning and the ending of the employment relationship. In this chapter, we
discuss personnel issues that can arise during the employment relationship. These include disputes over reassignments, compensation, evaluation of performance, various types of employee leave, the right of public
employees to file grievances, and the role of employee organizations.

REASSIGNMENT

The Constitutional Issues

Most Texas teacher and administrator contracts contain a clause to the
effect that the employee may be assigned and reassigned at the discretion of the superintendent. In spite of such contractual language, reassignments frequently lead to litigation. The leading case on the constitutional aspects of a reassignment is *Jett v. Dallas I.S.D.* (1986). The
case arose when the athletic director and head coach at South Oak Cliff
High School in Dallas was reassigned to another school as a teacher
with no coaching duties. There was no reduction in salary or supplemental pay. Jett came out even financially, but he complained that he
was unfairly deprived of a "property right" in the position of athletic
director and head coach.

Jett served under a typical "teacher contract," which indicated that
he was employed "subject to assignment." The reassignment was done
without any formal notice or hearing—in short, without due process.
Recall from our discussion of due process in Chapter 4 that process is due
only when the state deprives a person of property or liberty. No doubt
Jett had a property interest at stake, as evidenced by his contract—but
to what extent? Did he have a property interest in being head coach and
athletic director? Or did he merely have a property right in the financial
aspects of the contract? The Fifth Circuit ruled that Jett's property right
included only the economic benefits of the contract. Since he received
all of those economic benefits, even after the reassignment, he was not
deprived of any property right. Therefore, he was not entitled to notice
and a hearing or any of the other aspects of due process.

However, a reassignment that is wrongly motivated still can lead to constitutional challenges. In *Anderson v. Pasadena I.S.D.* (1999), an area superintendent was reassigned to a position that he described as "dead end." According to the area superintendent, his reassignment was done in retaliation for his speaking out as a citizen on matters of public concern, specifically, an upcoming bond election. Though his pay was not cut, he was allowed to proceed with the suit. The Fifth Circuit ruled that if, in fact, retaliatory action was taken in response to the man's exercise of constitutional rights, he could seek relief in court, even in the absence of a monetary injury.

Same Professional Capacity

The superintendent's authority to assign and reassign certified staff is limited by the concept of "same professional capacity." Recall from our discussion of the nonrenewal of term contracts in Chapter 4 that an educator's probationary or term contract will be renewed in the "same professional capacity" unless the school district follows the procedures for nonrenewal of contract. In effect, this limits the superintendent's authority to reassignments that fall within the same professional capacity.

Fortunately for superintendents, "same professional capacity" covers a lot of ground. Laura Perales was employed under a contract that described her as an "administrator." In the middle of her third year serving under such a contract, the superintendent reassigned her from director of the Even Start Program to middle school assistant principal. The salary stayed the same for the rest of that school year. But the district informed Ms. Perales that her salary for the next year would drop by more than $7,500.

Ms. Perales appealed her grievance over this to the commissioner, and lost on all counts. According to the commissioner, this reassignment kept Ms. Perales in the "same professional capacity" and thus the district was not required to go through nonrenewal procedures. The commissioner reasoned that "administrator" was a broad enough term to encompass both director of Even Start and middle school assistant principal. Comparing the skills and responsibilities of the two positions, as well as their respective positions on the organizational chart, the commissioner concluded that they were sufficiently similar to fall within the same professional capacity (*Perales v. Robstown I.S.D.*, 2006). We will discuss the compensation issue later in this chapter.

When Margaret Lehr was reassigned by Ector County I.S.D. from executive director of special education to assistant principal at an elementary school, she tendered her resignation, which the district accepted. She then filed a grievance, complaining of her "demotion." The commissioner ruled that the case was moot due to the resignation. Moreover, since the reassignment was at the same rate of pay, there was no allegation of a violation of contract that caused monetary harm. On top of that, however, the commissioner made some interesting comments about "professional capacity." The commissioner observed that these two positions were within the same professional capacity, meaning that the reassignment would not trigger Chapter 21 nonrenewal procedures. Further, "the Texas Education Code does not prohibit a school district from demoting a teacher." And even though there was no salary reduction in this case, the commissioner noted that there could have been: "If the Legislature had intended that no reduction in salary could occur when a teacher's contract is renewed, it would have said so" (*Lehr v. Ector County I.S.D.*, 2011).

Lancaster I.S.D. reassigned Connie Fowler from high school librarian to elementary librarian, still maintaining her 207-day contract. This was neither a demotion nor a change in professional capacity that would trigger nonrenewal procedures, according to the commissioner in *Fowler v. Lancaster I.S.D.* (2010). The fact that Ms. Fowler's replacement at the high school was given a 226-day contract did not change the analysis.

As these cases illustrate, the key to determining an employee's "professional capacity" is the contract. "Administrator" is a broad term, but "professional employee" is even broader. In fact, the commissioner views it as too broad. Austin I.S.D. employed Robert Wheeler as a "professional employee." He was assigned to work as an assistant principal until the summer of 2007, when he was informed that he would be a classroom teacher the next year at a lower salary. The commissioner reversed the district's decision, noting that "assistant principal" and "classroom teacher" were not within the same professional capacity, even when the contract used the term "professional employee" (*Wheeler v. Austin I.S.D.*, 2011).

Compensation Issues

What if the employee's pay is cut? Can the superintendent order a reassignment that reduces the employee's compensation? Certainly this could not be done in mid–school year during the term of an employee's contract. Nor can it be done in the middle of a multiyear contract that establishes salary for each year. Cutting pay in the middle of a contract for which salary has been set is a deprivation of property and a breach of contract that would require due process. But in many instances an educator's contract does not spell out compensation in dollars and cents. Many contracts call for the educator to be paid according to a salary schedule that is not yet set. Consider the case of *Barnes v. Tyler I.S.D.* (2007). Mr. Barnes served as assistant superintendent for administrative services during the 2002–2003 school year at a salary of $83,360. On April 21, 2003, Mr. Barnes signed his contract for the next school year, agreeing to compensation at "an annual salary according to the compensation plan adopted by the Board." One month later, Mr. Barnes was reassigned as director of transportation at a salary $4,000 less than he had been receiving. The commissioner ruled for the school district on Mr. Barnes's grievance, noting that he could have resigned without penalty. The commissioner noted that the authority of the school board to set salaries is "significant but not unlimited." The board cannot reduce an employee's compensation from what it was the previous year after the "penalty-free resignation date."

The "penalty-free resignation date" is set out at TEC §21.105 (probationary teachers), §21.160 (continuing contract teachers), and §21.210 (term contract teachers). These statutes give contractual educators the opportunity to resign, with no penalty, as long as they give written notice of resignation to the school by the forty-fifth day before the first day of instruction the following school year.

In the *Robstown* case discussed above, the employee's compensation was reduced. Ms. Perales had her salary reduced by $7,500 from one year to the next, and yet the commissioner ruled that this was legal. Again, this is because of the "penalty-free resignation date." This statute may have been intended to benefit teachers, but it also has the effect of enormously increasing the authority of the superintendent to cut an educator's salary. The commissioner reasoned that employees who are not willing to work at a reduced salary can quit.

If a district intends to reduce a professional employee's compensation prior to the penalty-free resignation date, it has to give that employee clear notice. In *Brajenovich v. Alief I.S.D.* (2009), the commissioner had the opportunity to rule on what kind of communication must be provided to the employee. The notice to the educator, according to the commissioner, must be "formal" and "specific." Communication is "formal" if it is in writing, or at a meeting called for the specific purpose of advising educators of cuts in pay. It is "specific" if (1) the teacher actually knows the amount by which his salary will be reduced, or (2) a reasonable teacher would have known the amount the salary would be reduced. In this case, the man was reassigned from natatorium manager to teacher/coach. This was done during the school year, with no cut in pay. But he was informed that if he was brought back for the next year, it would be at a teacher/coach salary. The commissioner held that this notice was both formal and specific, and the reduction in pay of over $7,000 was upheld.

Thus educators should be acutely aware of the "penalty-free resignation date," which will vary from one district to the next, and from one year to the next depending on when school starts. By statute, the date is calculated to be not later than the forty-fifth day before the first day of instruction of the following school year. This usually falls within the first half of July in most districts in Texas.

Duties and Schedule

Sometimes a reassignment does not affect the employee's title, position, or compensation, but only the duties to be done on a daily basis. The typical teacher contract specifies that the teacher can be assigned and reassigned to such duties as the supervisor deems appropriate. Nevertheless, challenges can be made. For example, teachers at Garza Elementary School in Brownsville I.S.D. were required to report to work thirty minutes early one week out of every six, due to security concerns. Some of the teachers balked and filed a grievance that was appealed to the commissioner. The commissioner denied the grievance, noting that the contract called for the teachers to serve "according to the hours and dates set by the District as they exist or may hereafter be amended" (*Association of Brownsville Educators/TSTA v. Brownsville I.S.D.*, 2007).

North East I.S.D. v. Kelley (2010) probably holds the record for "Longest-Lasting Litigation Over a Single Day of Work." That single day of work was graduation day in 2001. Mr. Kelley was required to work that day, and he claimed that this was one day too many. The contract was for ten months "according to the hours and dates set by the district as they exist or may hereafter be amended." The work schedule adopted by the district called for 187 days of work. When Kelley was ordered to work at graduation—day 188—he filed a grievance. The case bounced around between the TEA and state courts in Travis and Bexar Counties until 2010, when the Austin Court of Appeals ruled in favor of Mr. Kelley. The court held that the contract was clear, and it called for 187 days of work. The district breached the contract by requiring Mr. Kelley to work another day. The class that graduated on the day in question would be celebrating its ten-year reunion just a few months after this decision came down. We hope those graduates invited Mr. Kelley as a guest.

The Commissioner's Jurisdiction

Complaints concerning an illegal reassignment likely will not receive a hearing at the Texas Education Agency, unless the employee has suffered financially. The commissioner's jurisdiction is limited to cases involving parties aggrieved by "the school laws of this state" or a "provision of a written employment contract between the school district and a school district employee if a violation causes or would cause monetary harm to the employee" (TEC §7.057(a)(2)). In *Smith v. Nelson* (2001) the court held that the commissioner did not have jurisdiction to hear the appeal of a man who was reassigned from head coach/athletic director to P.E. teacher. There was a written contract involved, but the man's salary remained the same after the reassignment. He tried the creative argument that his loss of status would make it harder for him to find good coaching jobs in the future. Not good enough, said the court. Allegations of speculative future losses are not enough to give the commissioner jurisdiction over such a case.

Reassignment of the Superintendent

The whole question of reassignment calls to mind the famous case of *Briggs v. Crystal City I.S.D.* (1972), in which the school board reassigned the superintendent to a teaching position. Briggs sued and won when a Texas court of appeals held that a superintendent occupies a unique position and that any reassignment would be a material change in the contract. In other words, a superintendent is one of a kind.

COMPENSATION DISPUTES

Educators are accustomed to thinking of their salaries in various increments. For example, there is a state pay scale that all districts must meet for its classroom teachers, full-time librarians, school counselors, and nurses. On top of the state minimum, many districts pay a "local supplement." When educators read in the newspaper that the legislature has raised their rate of pay, they sometimes are disappointed to see no real difference in the bottom line. That is because the legislature only raises the amount of the minimum that must be paid. The local school board then may cut the local supplement, leaving the teacher no better off. This is what happened in Weslaco I.S.D. in 1995. The state raised the minimums, but the local district lowered its local supplement. In terms of net dollars, teachers received at least the same amount as they had in the previous year. But they got less than they were expecting, and the changes occurred *after* the date when the teachers could resign without penalty. Nevertheless, the court of appeals ruled in favor of the school district, reasoning that as long as total compensation was not reduced, the local supplement could be (*Weslaco Federation of Teachers v. Texas Education Agency,* 2000). A similar result occurred in *Griffin v. Van I.S.D.* (1998) when the school lowered the band director's stipend but not his overall compensation. Again, the commissioner ruled that the district could do this, even after the penalty-free resignation date had passed.

If the board fails to set the salaries by the penalty-free date it will not be able to reduce any educator's pay, but it may still leave educators frustrated and angry. That's what happened in Arlington I.S.D. when the school board changed the salary schedule after the penalty-free resignation date in the summer of 2002. This locked in teacher compensation for 2002–2003 to at least the same as what it was in 2001–2002. The board did a bit better than that—it gave the teachers a 1 percent raise. However, the United Educators Association was not happy. UEA pointed out that if the old salary schedule had been retained, teachers would have enjoyed more than a 1 percent raise. Thus the argument was that the board had reduced salaries from what they would have been under the previous salary schedule. But the commissioner found that to be inconsequential. Actual compensation for each teacher was more than it had been the previous year. Thus the district was in compliance (*United Educators Association v. Arlington I.S.D.*, 2004).

Occasionally, a district erroneously makes an overpayment to a teacher. Can the district get the money back? A Texas court of appeals ruled against the district when it tried to recoup sick leave overpayments made the *previous* year by impounding funds due teachers on their *current* contracts (*Benton v. Wilmer-Hutchins I.S.D.*, 1983). The court held that the dispute over the previous year's overpayments was unrelated to and could not generate deductions from teacher paychecks. The current salaries were amounts lawfully due, reasoned the court, and were not subject to the proposed unilateral deduction by the district.

Canutillo I.S.D. was wise to include in its teacher contracts a provision allowing the district to withhold the final paycheck if the employee lost or damaged school equipment. The commissioner denied a teacher's grievance over the $1,699 that was withheld in two equal installments from her last two paychecks. The teacher failed to return or account for a laptop computer the district had provided her, and the commissioner noted that payroll deductions can be made with consent. Here, the contract language amounted to consent. Furthermore, although there is a statute that protects teachers from liability for equipment provided to students (TEC §31.104), it does not apply to equipment provided to teachers (*Flores v. Canutillo I.S.D.*, 2010).

TEACHER APPRAISAL

Prior to passage of the Term Contract Nonrenewal Act (TCNA) in 1981 there was no state law requiring any kind of teacher evaluation in Texas. Some districts devised their own systems, others did not. The TCNA required that those teachers serving under a term contract be evaluated in writing at least once a year. All other decisions about evaluation, including what instrument to use, were left to the local district.

In 1984, the legislature created the Texas Teacher Appraisal System (TTAS), the first effort to adopt a uniform system of teacher evaluation throughout Texas. This system, which included the very controversial career ladder, was ultimately junked in the early 1990s.

The current system is the PDAS (Professional Development and Appraisal System). Each district must either use this system to evaluate its teachers or develop its own. If the district chooses to use a locally devised system, it must develop the system through district and campus-level site-based decision-making committees. Any locally devised system must reflect the teachers' implementation of discipline management procedures and the performance of students. A locally devised system must be approved by the board, but the board's hands are restricted on this matter. In order to ensure that the site-based decision-making committees are real players in this system, the law requires that the local board accept or reject the plan in toto. The board cannot modify the plan.

The PDAS is based on observable, job-related behaviors. It involves a single appraisal by a single appraiser, assessing performance in eight "Domains." The teacher can demand a second appraisal by a different appraiser. The teacher is also specifically permitted to file a written rebuttal to the appraisal. If the teacher does so, the rebuttal must be kept in the personnel file along with the appraisal. As to whether or not a teacher is given advance notice of the date and time of the appraisal, this is a local matter. The law says that the teacher "may" be given such advance notice. The process must guarantee a diagnostic and prescriptive conference between the appraiser and the teacher. A teacher who also directs extracurricular activities is to be appraised only on the basis of classroom performance—not on performance in connection with extracurricular activities.

The eight "Domains" in the PDAS are (1) active, successful student participation in the learning process; (2) learner-centered instruction; (3) evaluation of and feedback on student progress; (4) management of student discipline, instructional strategies, time, and materials; (5) professional communication; (6) professional development; (7) compliance with policies, operating procedures, and requirements; and (8) improvement of academic performance of all students on the campus, based on indicators in the Academic Excellence Indicator System. In each Domain every teacher is rated (1) exceeds expectations; (2) proficient; (3) below expectations; or (4) unsatisfactory.

Although there are eight Domains on the PDAS, a single failure by the teacher may impact several. In Clyde I.S.D. a teacher admitted that for two months she had not been teaching phonics as required by the district. Based on this information, the principal rated the teacher "below expectations" in four Domains. In her appeal to TEA, the teacher argued that since the law requires each Domain to be rated "independently," it was improper for the principal to rely on a single factor to reduce her rating in four Domains. The commissioner did not agree with this line of reasoning (*Miller v. Clyde I.S.D.*, 2003).

Rules adopted pursuant to the PDAS require that a teacher be identified as "a teacher in need of assistance" if the teacher is evaluated as unsatisfactory in one or more Domains, or if the teacher is below expectations in two or more Domains. If the teacher is so designated, the supervisor and teacher must develop an intervention plan. However, the teacher can be nonrenewed without all this taking place. In *Kinnaird v. Morgan I.S.D.* (1999) the commissioner approved the nonrenewal of a teacher despite the fact that he was not first given an intervention plan.

The PDAS puts an emphasis on timely documentation by administrators. The theory is that incidents that may affect a teacher's rating should be verified, documented, and shared with the teacher promptly. In *Koehler v. LaGrange I.S.D.* (2002) the commissioner invalidated the teacher's entire appraisal due to the fact that the supervisor had failed to document and share with the teacher two incidents that had adversely affected the appraisal. Rules require such incidents to be documented and shared with the teacher within ten working days of the appraiser's knowledge of the incident. Despite the invalidity of the appraisal, the commissioner found no fault with the growth plan imposed for the teacher.

Indeed, even when incidents are not timely documented and shared, they can be relied upon for purposes other than the PDAS appraisal. This is what happened in *Taylor v. Wichita Falls I.S.D.* (2002). In that case the school district agreed with the teacher that certain incidents had not been promptly documented and shared with the teacher, and therefore, could not be used in connection with the PDAS appraisal. However, the teacher filed a grievance requesting that the information not be used by the school in any way. The commissioner ruled that the school was not obligated to go that far. In fact, in *Anderson v. Tyler I.S.D.* (2008), the commissioner upheld the nonrenewal of a teacher despite the fact that evidence at the nonrenewal hearing was not incorporated into the teacher's summative annual appraisal. The commissioner pointed out that a violation of the PDAS does not always mean that a nonrenewal was improper.

PDAS appraisal is an annual affair, unless the district decides to appraise some teachers less frequently and the teacher agrees. If a teacher's most recent appraisal reflects a rating of at least "proficient" with no areas of deficiency, the teacher can be appraised less than once a year, provided that it is done at least every five years. The district must have a written agreement with any such teacher.

Schools now are specifically authorized to send copies of a teacher's evaluation (along with any rebuttals) to a district to which the teacher has applied for employment if the new district requests such information. Time will tell if this becomes a common practice or not. To the general public, however, teacher evaluations are not accessible. Section 21.355 of the TEC states that "A document evaluating the performance of a teacher or administrator is confidential." This provision applies to charter school employees as well. Moreover, the confidentiality of a teacher evaluation goes beyond the general public. The attorney general issued an opinion in 2003 stating that the SBEC (State Board for Educator Certification), the governmental entity with authority over teacher certification, has no right of access to teacher evaluations (*Att'y. Gen. Op. GA-0055*, 2003).

The confidentiality of evaluations extends to documents other than the formal evaluation. This issue was decided in *Abbott v. North East I.S.D.* (2006). The attorney general had ordered the district to release, in response to a request under the Texas Public Information Act, a memo from the principal to a teacher. But the court of appeals reversed that ruling, noting that the memo reflected the principal's judgment regarding the teacher's performance. The memo ordered corrective action. Accordingly, it was a "document evaluating the performance of a teacher or administrator" and thus was confidential under the TPIA.

PDAS does not cover all professional employees. Librarians, for example, are not covered. The Texas Administrative Code specifies that the PDAS is for classroom teachers. In *Fenter v. Quinlan I.S.D.* (2002) the commissioner concluded that a librarian is not a classroom teacher and is not entitled to the PDAS process. Thus, if the district chooses to evaluate librarians in some other manner, it may do so.

Since the PDAS is for classroom teachers, there must be some other mechanism in place for administrators. For those administrators whose employment requires educator certification, state law requires a process quite similar to that used for classroom teachers. The local district is to use either its own locally developed system or the commissioner's recommended system. In either case, the district is authorized to include staff input as an evaluation tool, as long as it is not done anonymously. The law specifically prohibits the use of school funds to pay any administrator who has not been appraised within the preceding fifteen months.

For both principals and superintendents, the evaluation must include an assessment of student performance. If the school uses the commissioner-recommended process, principals and superintendents are not held accountable for student academic performance in their first year on the job, or for dropout and attendance data for two years—these are included as "report only."

In 2008 the commissioner decided a case in which a principal claimed that her appraisal failed to meet state standards. The commissioner agreed, noting that the district did not evaluate the principal in the Student Performance Domain as required. Thus the principal's annual evaluation was invalid. However, this did not provide much relief to the principal, who had been given an intervention plan and reassigned to assistant principal. The commissioner held that the intervention plan was valid, despite the invalid appraisal. The principal also complained of the use of "focus groups" by the district in the evaluation process. However, the commissioner pointed out that the regulations specifically permit the district to rely on "staff input" as long as it is not done anonymously. In this case, it was not. The staff meetings may have been private, but they were not anonymous (*Hall v. North East I.S.D.*, 2008).

School districts also employ administrators whose job does not require educator certification. How and when such administrators are evaluated are matters of local control. In *Tinnemeyer v. Pasadena I.S.D.* (2001) an associate superintendent of facilities and construction complained that the district had not conducted an annual appraisal of him. But the commissioner ruled that the district was not required to do so, since the man's employment did not require educator certification.

EMPLOYMENT BENEFITS

Planning and Preparation Period

Exactly what benefits an employee is entitled to depends to a great extent on the actual wording of the employment contract and the policies of the school district. State law does, however, set forth some demarcations on benefits with which school districts must comply. For example, each classroom teacher is to have at least 450 minutes within each two-week period for instructional preparation, parent-teacher conferences, evaluating students' work, and planning. Each planning and preparation period must be at least 45 minutes long and must be scheduled during the school day. During the planning and preparation period, the teacher may not be required to participate in any other activity (TEC §21.404). Thus the commissioner has ruled that a district may not require a teacher to attend an in-service meeting during the 45-minute period (*Strater v. Houston I.S.D.*, 1986). Nor can teachers be required to meet with the principal during planning time (*Gonzales v. San Antonio I.S.D.*, 2007).

The planning and preparation period must occur "within the instructional day." Teachers challenged Canutillo I.S.D. when the district scheduled the planning period from 3:00 to 3:45—right after the students were released. The commissioner ruled in favor of the teachers, noting that "instructional day" means "the time when students are receiving instruction at the school where the teachers are located" (*Canutillo Educators Association v. Canutillo I.S.D.*, 2010).

Duty-Free Lunch

Classroom teachers and full-time librarians also are entitled to at least a 30-minute lunch period free from all duties and responsibilities connected with the instruction or supervision of students, unless the district is faced with such dire situations as personnel shortage, extreme economic conditions, or unavoidable or unforeseen circumstances. In any event a teacher may not be required to supervise students during the duty-free lunch more than one time per week (TEC §21.405).

Personal Leave

Every school district employee is entitled to five days of personal leave per year. There is no limit on the accumulation of personal leave, and it moves with the employee from one district to another. Over a long career, therefore, employees who are able to accumulate these personal leave days will have a great job benefit. The school board is authorized to develop policies governing the use of personal leave, but there are some restrictions on that policy. Specifically, the policy cannot restrict the reasons for which personal leave can be taken. An individual can use personal leave for any reason. Nor can a school district dictate to the employee the order in which personal leave and any other type of leave offered by the district is taken (TEC §22.003(a)). In other words, employees who are eligible for both personal leave, which is paid, and unpaid leave will be able to take the paid leave first.

Although school districts cannot restrict the purposes for which employees take personal leave, it can impose other restrictions. If the employee wants to use personal leave to attend a mud wrestling convention, that's his choice. However, school policy can restrict the timing and limit the use of leave in other ways. The Castleberry I.S.D. adopted a policy containing three restrictions that were challenged. Employees were (1) not permitted to take more than two days of leave consecutively, (2) not permitted to take personal leave if another employee in the same category was already on such leave, and (3) not permitted to take personal leave on the day before a holiday. The court of appeals approved the district's policy. The policy did not restrict the purposes for which leave could be taken, it just limited the timing (*Amaral-Whittenberg v. Alanis*, 2003).

School districts can reward employees for not taking personal leave. Brady I.S.D. did this via a policy that provided a $1,000 stipend to any teacher who met certain conditions. One of the conditions was that the teacher could not use more than five days of personal or sick leave in a school year. A teacher who missed eight days of work did not qualify for the stipend and filed a grievance, complaining that the district's policy improperly punished teachers for taking personal leave. The commissioner disagreed. The policy did not restrict the purposes for which personal leave could be taken, and it did not punish anyone—it offered a reward instead (*Ceynowa v. Brady I.S.D.*, 2000).

Of course, a district can adopt a local sick leave plan or local personal leave plan to supplement what the state provides. Absent some abuse of discretion, a school district's interpretation of its local leave policies will be affirmed if challenged. For example, the mother of a quadriplegic son sought to use seven days of sick leave to assist him in enrolling in college and to locate an attendant to provide for his personal needs. The school district advised the mother that sick leave could not be used for this purpose. The principal advised her that two days of hardship leave could be used instead, with her salary docked for additional days. The mother subsequently filed a grievance asking that all seven days of her absence be taken from accumulated sick leave. The Texas Commissioner of Education noted that both state law and local policy limited sick leave to illness and to family emergencies. Neither applied in this case. "The district reasonably interpreted the provisions of its own sick leave policy as it related to the Petitioner's circumstances and such interpretation complies with state law and agency regulation" (*Waligura v. El Campo I.S.D.*, 1991).

Health Insurance

TEC §22.004 requires each school district to offer its employees health insurance. The insurance can be provided by a risk pool involving one or more districts, by an insurance company, or by a health maintenance organization (HMO). The insurance plan must be comparable to the insurance program the state offers its employees. Costs may be shared by employees and the district. Before a district contracts with an insurer or HMO, the latter must provide an audited financial statement showing its financial condition. Alternatively, a school district can opt to participate in the state health insurance program, subject to certain conditions. School districts must certify annually to the executive director of the Employees Retirement System that the district's coverage meets the requirements of the statute.

Districts with twenty or more employees also are subject to the provisions of a federal statute known by the cheerful acronym COBRA (Consolidated Omnibus Budget Reconciliation Act of 1985), which requires some continuation of coverage after certain events.

Health insurance for school employees is a major cost of doing business. Therefore it is not surprising that the board of trustees retains the power to change health plans in the best interests of the school district, even if it might impact employees adversely. In Ector County I.S.D. a teachers' organization challenged the board's decision to change the health coverage in the middle of the school year. As a result of the change, teachers had to pick up a greater amount of the cost. The teachers argued that their contracts incorporated the health plan coverage and, thus, could not be changed in midyear. The commissioner disagreed, citing TEC §22.005(c), which authorizes the board to "amend or cancel" the district's health care plan at any time (*Ector County TSTA/NEA v. Ector County I.S.D.*, 2000).

Assault Leave

The legislature has provided additional protection for school employees who are physically assaulted during the performance of their duties. Such employees are entitled to take "the number of days of leave necessary to recuperate from all physical injuries sustained as a result of the assault." This paid leave can continue, if necessary, up to two full years. Leave taken as a result of an assault may not be deducted from accrued sick leave. In other words, this is paid leave on top of other sick leave available to the employee. Furthermore, the employee is to be placed on assault leave status immediately upon request. Upon investigation of the claim, the district may change the assault leave status and charge the leave, first against accumulated personal leave, and then, if necessary, against the employee's pay (TEC §22.003(b)). To make sure that employees are aware of this job benefit, schools are required to include information about assault leave in any informational handbook the school provides to employees, as well as on any form used to request leave.

To be eligible for assault leave, the employee must be physically assaulted by a person who could be prosecuted for having committed an assault, or who "could not be prosecuted for assault only because the person's age or mental capacity makes the person a nonresponsible person" under the Penal Code (TEC §22.003(c)). In other words, an employee will be entitled to assault leave even if the perpetrator is too young or too cognitively impaired to warrant prosecution.

Whether or not to grant assault leave depends on the facts of each situation as determined by local school authorities. Assault leave is available after an assault—not an accident. But the line between the two is not always clear. In one case, a student was attempting to prevent a teacher from calling his parents. The student ripped the phone cord out of the wall. This caused a bookcase to tip over. The teacher tried to stop the bookcase from falling, and injured her hand in the process. Assault or accident? The commissioner concluded that the facts were such that a fact finder could decide the case either way, and either decision would be supported by "substantial evidence." In fact, the local school board had decided to deny leave to the teacher, and the commissioner affirmed (*Long-Walker v. Fort Bend I.S.D.*, 2006).

Ms. Charles-Washington was knocked down by a student who was rushing to get to class when the tardy bell rang. The student immediately apologized and stated that this was an accident. Nevertheless, the commissioner concluded that it was an assault. An assault can be done "intentionally, knowingly, or recklessly." Here, the student's actions were deemed "reckless." The commissioner laid down a rule—an intent to commit an assault is presumed to have occurred if the teacher is injured through an act of violence. That presumption can be overcome, but the school district must present evidence to do so. Here, there was an act of violence that resulted in injury, and thus, a presumption of an assault. The school failed to overcome that presumption, and the assault leave was granted (*Charles-Washington v. Fort Bend I.S.D.*, 2006).

Mansfield I.S.D. did overcome the presumption in the case of *Brown v. Mansfield I.S.D.* (2006). This was another murky fact situation involving the restraint of a student who fell, which caused the teacher to fall as well. Evidence before the board was conflicting, but the commissioner found sufficient evidence in the record to sustain the board's conclusion that the student merely tripped accidentally.

In *Cavazos v. Raymondville I.S.D.* (2009) the commissioner denied a request for assault leave in a case where a teacher claimed post-traumatic stress disorder after a student displayed a knife at school. The student never physically assaulted the teacher. The commissioner noted that the statute allows leave only for physical injuries, not psychological problems. The statute defines "assault" in a way that can include a threat of imminent bodily injury, but if it is only a threat, there will not be a physical injury.

The statute of limitations for filing a civil suit over an assault is two years, but that does not mean that an educator can wait that long to seek assault leave. Brenda Poole learned this the hard way in *Poole v. Karnack I.S.D.* (2011). The court noted that the statute authorizing assault leave does not include a deadline, and that in such cases courts generally apply the "reasonable time" standard. Here, the court did not define "reasonable time" other than to say that it is less than two years.

Teacher Retirement

School districts are not required to participate in the federal Social Security system for the majority of their employees, and most do not. However, Government Code §822.001 requires every employee of Texas public school districts who meets the membership criteria to belong to the Teacher Retirement System of Texas. In addition, school districts may establish their own supplementary annuity programs. School districts also may provide various insurance programs for their employees paid for out of local funds.

The 2011 legislature adopted measures that will affect teacher retirement. One such provision establishes a uniform school year of September 1 through August 31 for purposes of Teacher Retirement System of Texas (TRS) benefits. Thus, even if an employee starts a contract year in July or August, the TRS year will not begin until September 1.

Another provision changes the way certain members of the Teacher Retirement System of Texas may purchase additional service credit for time spent on active duty with the armed forces, for service in public schools outside of Texas, or for service that was previously unreported to TRS.

A third provision changes the rules with regard to the hiring of retirees. Under this provision, those who retire after January 1, 2011, may return to work for a Texas public school and still receive benefits if (1) they are hired as a substitute; (2) they serve in another capacity within the school system for no more than half-time; or (3) they serve as much as full-time if they have been separated from service with all Texas educational institutions for at least twelve full months after retirement. Those who retired prior to January 1, 2011, may return to work for a Texas public school in any position, full- or part-time. However, if the retirement date was after September 1, 2005, the employing district may be required to pay a surcharge.

Temporary Disability Leave

Section 21.409 of the Texas Education Code provides that each full-time educator employed by a school district is entitled to a leave of absence for temporary disability without fear of termination. Pregnancy is specifically listed as a temporary disability. Requests must be made to the superintendent and must include a physician's statement confirming the inability to work and indicating the date the employee wishes to begin the leave and the probable date of return. Insofar as pregnancy is concerned, teachers are allowed to take a leave of absence only for the period a physician certifies they are unable to work. This precludes taking a leave of absence under §21.409 for infant-nurturing purposes. Such a leave may be available, however, under the federal Family and Medical Leave Act.

Temporary disability leave is unpaid. The primary purpose of the leave is to assure the employee that he or she will have a job upon returning to good health. The employee is required to notify the superintendent at least thirty days prior to the expected date of return and include a physician's statement indicating the employee's physical fitness for resumption of regular duties. Section 21.409(e) provides that an employee who returns to work "is entitled to an assignment at the school where the employee formerly taught, subject to the availability of an appropriate teaching position. In any event, the educator must be placed on active duty not later than the beginning of the next term."

In 1992 the attorney general was asked about the effect of site-based decision-making on this guarantee. As already noted, TEC §11.202 gives campus principals the power to approve all appointments to the campus, except in cases involving program changes or enrollment shifts. In those instances, it is the superintendent who has the final word. But what happens if a teacher is due back from disability leave and there are no openings on the campus where the teacher taught? What happens if there is an opening, but the principal does not want to take the employee back? The attorney general concluded that the teacher returning from disability leave must be placed on his or her former campus unless another principal voluntarily accepts the employee. The returning employee is to go to the former campus if a position is available there. However, if no such position is available, the school cannot force some other principal to accept the employee. As of the beginning of the next school year, however, the school district has the duty to make sure a position is available. Again, if no other principal will take the employee, the principal of the campus where the teacher formerly taught must do so (*Att'y. Gen. Op. DM-177*, 1992). Thus when push comes to shove, the principal may be required to create an opening and take the employee back.

Section 21.409(f) leaves the length of leaves of absence up to the superintendent but provides that the school board may establish a maximum length for a leave of absence for temporary disability of not less than 180 calendar days.

The statute says that "the contract or employment of the educator may not be terminated by the school district while the educator is on a leave of absence for temporary disability" (TEC §21.409(a)). However, the contract termination process can take place during the temporary disability. This is what happened in *Nelson v. Weatherwax* (2001). The teacher asked for temporary disability leave on the same day that the school district gave her notice of intent to terminate the contract. The leave was granted, but the district also went forward with the termination proceedings. The termination hearing was conducted while the teacher was on leave. The board decided to terminate the teacher's employment, but the effective date of the termination was the date when the disability leave ended. The court of appeals concluded that this process did not violate the Education Code.

Educators customarily go on temporary disability when they ask to do so. However, sometimes an educator can be placed on leave involuntarily. The school board has the right under §21.409(c) to establish a policy providing for placing an educator on involuntary leave of absence "for temporary disability if, in the board's judgment and in consultation with a physician who has performed a thorough medical examination of the educator, the educator's condition interferes with the performance of regular duties." The policy must allow the employee the right to present testimony and/or other information to the board relevant to such a determination. As far back as 1983, the Texas Commissioner of Education concluded that such a "medical examination" might include a psychological review. The case of *Moore v. Dallas I.S.D.* involved a teacher who was placed on involuntary leave of absence without pay until she submitted a psychological evaluation pronouncing her fit to teach. The commissioner concluded that school districts inherently possess the power to require teachers to submit to a psychological examination. It is important to note that this inherent power can be applied only to educators in accordance with the statutes and local policies governing temporary disability leave.

Family and Medical Leave Act

Under the Family and Medical Leave Act (FMLA), eligible employees are entitled to up to twelve weeks of unpaid leave per year (1) to care for newborn, adopted, or foster children; (2) to care for a spouse, child, or parent with a serious health condition; (3) or when a serious health condition prevents the employee from performing the essential functions of the job. To be "eligible" an employee must have been with the district for at least twelve months and must have worked at least 1,250 hours. Since this is unpaid leave, its primary purpose is to assure the employee of a job upon his or her return. The district will be obligated to restore the returning employee to his or her former position or an equivalent position with equivalent pay, benefits, and terms and conditions of employment. Family and medical leave runs concurrently with other leave available to the employee. In other words, if the employee already has twelve weeks of sick leave accumulated, the employee is entitled under this law only to those twelve weeks, and not twelve paid weeks (sick leave) followed by twelve unpaid weeks (family and medical leave).

The FMLA is a statute of general application, and thus noneducational employees may be familiar with it. However, there are some special rules under FMLA that only apply to employees of local educational agencies. These address the taking of intermittent leave, leave on a reduced schedule, or leave taken near the end of an academic term by "instructional employees," a term that encompasses teachers, coaches, driving instructors, and assistants in special education programs. The special rules are set out at 29 C.F.R. §§825.600 et seq.

In *Matamoros v. Ysleta I.S.D.* (2012) a federal district court held that the district violated the FMLA when it refused to reinstate an employee after taking FMLA leave. The district argued that it was in the process of terminating the man's employment due to numerous performance deficiencies when he took leave. The court concluded that the employer's intent was not relevant—it was required to put the man back to work. The court seemed reluctant to come to this conclusion, noting that it defied numerous court rulings as well as "concerns for economic inefficiency, and even, perhaps, common sense itself." Despite all, the court felt obligated to follow Fifth Circuit precedent on this issue, citing the case of *Nero v. Industrial Molding Corporation* (1999). In the *Nero* case the employer vigorously argued that it had decided to fire the employee before he took leave, but the jury did not believe that. In that context, the court held that the employer was required to put the man back to work. If the jury had agreed with the employer, the case would likely have come out the other way.

USERRA

The Uniformed Services Employment and Reemployment Rights Act (USERRA) is designed to provide job protection for people who serve in military reserve units or the National Guard. The USERRA not only provides that no adverse action can be taken against the employee due to military service, it also contains an innovative provision designed to reinstate the person where he or she would have been had there been no call to active duty. The first reported case under this law involving a Texas school district is *Carpenter v. Tyler I.S.D.* (2006). Mr. Carpenter was a teacher who missed work from time to time when he was called up from the Air Force Reserves into active duty. The district did not offer the teacher a contract for the next year, and he sued, claiming a violation of USERRA. Among its many detailed requirements, USERRA prohibits discriminatory action against an employee as a direct result of military service. Based on the jury's verdict, the court ultimately held that the district had discriminated against Mr. Carpenter. The court did not order reinstatement, noting that the relationship between the parties was not good. Nor did the court order back pay, observing that Mr. Carpenter had not diligently sought other employment. But the court did order the district to pay Mr. Carpenter $48,000 in "front pay" to compensate him for the discriminatory actions.

State law also protects the military. Under Texas Government Code §431.005, employees who are members of the state militia or the U.S. reserve forces must be granted up to fifteen days per year of leave without loss of salary for participation in authorized duty. Teachers on military leave cannot be required to pay the cost of a substitute (*Att'y. Gen. Op. MW-240*, 1980). Section 431.001 of the Labor Code provides protections for members of state military forces who work in the public sector similar to the protections of USERRA.

Miscellaneous Leave Policies

School districts may offer local leave programs for a variety of purposes—for example, local sick leave, death leave, professional leave, and maternity/paternity leave. The policies governing local leave programs are developed by local school districts. The only restriction is that local leave must not be used to benefit a private organization or individuals contrary to a provision of the Texas Constitution. The Texas Attorney General has opined that this means a teacher may not be given paid leave to attend a meeting of a teacher's professional organization (such as TSTA, ATPE, or TCTA) if the primary purpose of the meeting is to pursue the business of the organization (*Att'y. Gen. Op. MW-89*, 1979).

Districts may offer a "developmental leave" as authorized by TEC §21.452. This is available to certified teachers who have served at least five consecutive years in the district for study, research, travel, or other suitable purpose. Such leave is limited to one school year at one-half salary or one-half school year at full salary. While on developmental leave, the teacher is entitled to the same employee benefits available to other employees of the district. Note that developmental leaves are discretionary with school districts; districts may, but do not have to, offer this benefit.

WAGE AND HOUR REQUIREMENTS

In 1985 the U.S. Supreme Court ruled that the minimum-wage and maximum-hour provisions of the Fair Labor Standards Act (FLSA) apply to local government functions. The Court overruled a 1976 decision to the contrary, thus restoring the application of FLSA to certain employees in local governmental entities, including public schools (*Garcia v. San Antonio Metropolitan Transit Authority*).

The FLSA provisions do not apply to everyone. Workers are divided into two general categories—"exempt" and "non-exempt." The term "non-exempt" means, specifically, not exempt from the FLSA rules and regulations. Thus, a "non-exempt" employee will be entitled to overtime pay, or "comp time," if she works more than forty hours in a week. Those who are "exempt," however, are not covered by FLSA and thus not entitled to extra benefits for work in excess of the forty-hour week.

Exempt employees fall into three broad categories: Executive, Administrative, and Professional. Moreover, teachers and school administrators who serve as principals and assistant principals and in other positions related to instruction are specifically exempt from FLSA coverage. The nonexempt employees generally will include secretaries, maintenance workers, bus drivers, custodians, and teacher aides.

The most interesting illustration of the FLSA in the school context arose when cafeteria workers in Greenwood I.S.D. were required to serve meals after hours for the monthly school board meetings. The school district did not pay the workers for this, contending that the workers had volunteered to provide this service. When the workers became vocal in their complaints, they were terminated, thus leading to allegations of violations of the Whistleblower Act, discussed in Chapter 6. The court determined that the workers were not volunteers and should have been compensated. The point, for purposes of our discussion of the FLSA, is that school districts should assume that school employees serving a school function are doing so as employees and should be compensated (*Knowlton v. Greenwood I.S.D.*, 1992).

Under the FLSA, the employer has the duty to provide good documentation to establish that employees have not worked overtime without proper compensation. Thus many districts have adopted "punch the clock" methods or other systems to show that workers are not required to work overtime without compensation.

Much of the litigation over FLSA has involved athletic trainers, such as in *Villegas v. El Paso I.S.D.* (2006). The federal court held that the athletic trainers were "learned professionals" in the jargon of the FLSA, and thus exempt from the requirements of the law. The court cited the earlier Fifth Circuit case of *Owsley v. San Antonio I.S.D.* (1999). The trainers argued that *Owsley* was old and irrelevant since it preceded the most recent Department of Labor regulations. The court did not agree, noting that those regulations themselves include athletic trainers as "learned professionals."

Professional employees have not been successful in efforts to be compensated at their regular rate for services beyond the normal school day. As professionals, they are exempt from FLSA regulations. Other legal theories have not availed. For example, a teacher in Lampasas filed a grievance seeking additional pay and reimbursement for child care costs when she was required to be a ticket taker at a night football game. She was unsuccessful at both the district and commissioner levels. The commissioner noted that the teacher had agreed in her contract to perform "such additional duties as may be assigned." The 8 A.M. to 3:45 P.M. attendance requirement specified in local policy simply established minimum working hours and did not preclude additional assignments (*Watson v. Lampasas I.S.D.*, 1989).

WORKERS' COMPENSATION AND UNEMPLOYMENT COMPENSATION

Two subjects of increasing financial significance to public education in Texas are workers' compensation and unemployment compensation. Although a detailed discussion of these matters is beyond the scope of this book, no discussion of employment issues would be complete without some attention to both.

In the case of workers' compensation, state law provides that a school district shall extend such benefits to its employees by one of the following options: becoming a self-insurer, providing insurance under workers' compensation insurance contracts or policies, or entering into interlocal agreements with other political subdivisions providing for self-insurance. In practice, almost all Texas school districts have chosen to meet their obligations through the option involving entering into interlocal agreements with each other.

One very important provision in the workers' compensation statute prohibits an employer from retaliating against an employee because the employee has filed a workers' compensation claim. In 1995, the Texas Supreme Court held that cities (and therefore, presumably, school districts) could be held liable for such retaliation despite the immunity generally enjoyed by governmental entities. But that changed with the decision of the Texas Supreme Court in *Travis Central Appraisal District v. Norman* (2011). The court noted its previous decision on this issue (*City of La Porte v. Barfield*) but pointed out that subsequent legislation had changed the analysis. The court concluded that the legislature did not clearly and unambiguously waive the immunity that local governments generally enjoy. Thus Ms. Norman's lawsuit, alleging that she was fired for filing a workers' compensation claim, was dismissed.

Districts frequently are perplexed about whether they must hold positions open for employees who are on sick leave and drawing workers' compensation, or create new positions for employees who want to return to work but cannot perform their normal duties. There is no legal obligation to hold positions open indefinitely or to create limited-duty jobs for employees who cannot return to their former jobs. However, the situation is sometimes influenced by the requirements of the Americans with Disabilities Act. Under the ADA, districts will have to "reasonably accommodate" injured workers whose injuries cause them to be classified as having a disability. Thus districts should consider such situations on an individual basis. In one case, a court of appeals ruled in favor of a school district that terminated the employment of a police officer based on the district's absence control policy. The man had used up all available leave and was still unable to return to work (*Larsen v. Santa Fe I.S.D.*, 2009).

Unemployment compensation is the state's effort to help people over the rough spots and is intended to provide compensation for a specified number of weeks to people who are unemployed through no fault of their own. As in the case of workers' compensation, most Texas school districts meet their obligations by entering a joint group account with other political subdivisions.

There are two situations in which an employee should not receive unemployment compensation benefits: if the employee is dismissed for misconduct or if the employee voluntarily quits. These matters are presided over by the Texas Employment Commission.

GRIEVANCES AND THE ROLE OF EMPLOYEE ORGANIZATIONS

One thing is for certain about all that we have said so far: Educators sometimes will have a disagreement with their employing school district about how these personnel issues should be applied in a given situation. Thus we turn to the dispute resolution mechanism of employee grievances.

Employee Grievances: A Little History

Any discussion of grievances must begin with Article I, §27 of the Texas Constitution, which in one form or another has been part of the Texas Constitution since 1845. It provides that "the citizens shall have the right, in a peaceable manner, to . . . apply to those invested with the powers of government for redress of grievances . . . by petition, address, or remonstrance."

There also are statutory provisions that guarantee the right of public employees to pursue grievances. TEC §11.171 requires that school district grievance policies must permit an employee to bypass his or her immediate supervisor with the grievance in certain circumstances. If the grievance alleges "the supervisor's violation of the law in the workplace or the supervisor's unlawful harassment of the employee," there must be a means of bypassing the customary chain of command. In other words, a teacher who alleges that her principal has unlawfully harassed her will be able to file the grievance with someone other than the principal. Grievance policies have traditionally included a "bypass" provision for sexual harassment complaints. This statute broadens that concept to other forms of harassment and/or violations of law. The same section of the TEC also now requires that the school permit the grieving party to tape-record any meeting at which the grievance is being discussed or investigated.

The basic right of public employees to file grievances can be found at Government Code §617.005, which acknowledges "the right of public employees to present grievances concerning their wages, hours of employment or conditions of work either individually or through a representative that does not claim the right to strike."

That language has been a part of the Texas legal landscape for a long time, but its meaning changed significantly in the 1980s when the scope of what is "grievable" expanded tremendously. Most school districts have had some form of grievance process for decades. But for many years the process was virtually unusable. A bold teacher would occasionally inquire about filing a grievance over a reassignment, or language in the teacher's contract, or perhaps teaching load, only to be informed that "that's not grievable." What was "grievable" appeared to many to be a moving target, diminishing in size. It was understood that teachers could grieve over "wages, hours, and conditions of work," but those terms were narrowly construed. Many "conditions of work" were considered management prerogatives or features of the board's exclusive authority, and thus not proper subjects for a grievance.

All that changed with an attorney general's opinion and a series of decisions from the commissioner. In 1984, Attorney General Jim Mattox opined that the term "conditions of work" could not be construed to "restrict, limit, narrow, or exclude" any aspect of the employment relationship from the grievance process. Mattox concluded his opinion (*Att'y. Gen. Op. JM-177*):

> [T]he term "conditions of work" should be construed broadly to include any area of wages, hours, or conditions of employment, and any other matter which is appropriate for communications from employees to employer concerning an aspect of their relationship.

The Texas Commissioner of Education followed up on this with a series of decisions confirming the broad sweep of "conditions of work." The most contested issue concerned teacher evaluations. Since the process of evaluating a teacher's performance inherently involves judgment, discretion, and subjectivity, school administrators argued that a teacher should not be able to grieve over an unfavorable evaluation. The commissioner concluded otherwise.

In *Etzel v. Galveston I.S.D.*, the commissioner held that the content of an evaluation was grievable as a "condition of work." In *Etzel*, a teacher grieved a procedural violation of the appraisal processes as well as the rating received. The commissioner concluded that the complaint concerning the evaluation *procedure* should have been allowed to be presented to the board under the district's policy. He also concluded that the complaint regarding the evaluation *content* could appropriately "be concluded" at the level of the district superintendent. The commissioner noted that a board, not trained to evaluate teachers, was not qualified to substitute its judgment for that of a trained evaluator on a professional matter of judgment on appraisal scores *unless* there was some evidence of a procedural defect that resulted in an incorrect rating. The commissioner then hedged on those statements about concluding grievances at the level of the superintendent, however, by observing that an opportunity to address concerns to the board (presumably including those about the content of an evaluation) in an open forum would satisfy the requirements of both Article I, §27 of the Texas Constitution, which allows persons to present complaints to governmental entities, and Texas statutory law.

Falvey v. Alief I.S.D. also dealt with grievances over the content of evaluations. A teacher demanded a hearing before the board to grieve her evaluation formally, but the board refused. The district had an open-forum policy at its board meetings, but the teacher did not request to be heard through that channel. Following the same reasoning as in *Etzel*, the commissioner concluded that the teacher was entitled to present her grievance by meeting informally with her evaluator and, ultimately, her superintendent. According to the commissioner, both are in a "position of authority" to address grievances over the content of evaluations under state law. The commissioner concluded by again noting that in most circumstances a board of trustees is not an appropriate entity to consider grievances concerning content of evaluations. However, he noted that a district's allotment of a forum wherein employees have the opportunity to present grievances to the board satisfies the statutory requirements of Texas law and the constitutional requirements of Article I, §27.

But what happens if the board insists on hearing and *granting* the grievance? Can a board, neither trained nor certified in the appraisal process, reverse the substantive decision of the appraiser? That interesting situation came before the commissioner in 1991. A teacher filed a grievance with the board of trustees over the contents of her appraisal. The assistant principal who conducted the appraisal denied credit to the teacher on two of the seventy-two indicators on the TTAS, the appraisal system in place at the time. The school board granted the grievance, thus awarding the teacher credit for the two indicators. Then it was the assistant principal's turn to grieve. Noting that she was certified and trained to conduct TTAS appraisals, whereas the members of the school board were not, the assistant principal asked the board to reverse itself and deny credit for the two indicators. Not surprisingly, the board refused to do so. So the assistant principal appealed to the Texas Commissioner of Education. Following his previous admonitions to school board members not to substitute their judgment for that of trained evaluators, the commissioner granted the assistant principal's grievance (*Navarro v. Ysleta I.S.D.*). This appeared to send a loud and clear message to school boards—don't change appraisal ratings for a teacher.

However, that was not the end of the story. The teacher took the case to Travis County District Court, where the judge took a slightly different approach. The judge ruled that the school board does have the authority to review the educational judgment of an appraiser and may award credit if the appraiser's judgment "was clearly erroneous or an abuse of discretion." Moreover, the judge ruled that the commissioner also had the authority to overrule the appraiser. "The Commissioner," according to the court's ruling, "must make an independent decision as to whether the appraiser's educational judgment was clearly erroneous or an abuse of discretion" (*Heredia v. Central Education Agency*, 1992).

This case then went back to the Texas Education Agency for a second time, where the commissioner again ruled in favor of the assistant principal. Applying the district court's criteria, the commissioner ruled that the decision of the assistant principal was neither clearly erroneous nor an abuse of discretion. The commissioner observed that "the abuse of discretion standard is not met simply because a disagreement exists as to who is correct" (*Navarro v. Ysleta I.S.D.*, 1994).

Thus the door opened wide. Now it is clear that employees have the right to grieve virtually anything. Grievances routinely are filed over assignments and reassignments, appointments to extra duty, salary and extra pay, and the wording of reprimands or other written communications. If an employee is terminated and has no other means of complaining of the decision, a grievance can be filed. Thus an at-will employee can grieve the termination. A probationary teacher whose contract is nonrenewed cannot invoke the independent hearing process but can file a grievance instead.

Hearing Employee Grievances

While the "grievable" door swung wide open in the 1980s, we also learned just what it means to present a grievance and what the employer must do to "hear" the grievance. In a nutshell, the case law has made it clear that a grievance significantly differs from a situation in which a due process hearing is necessary. For many years, the common operative term has been "stop, look, and listen." The early cases indicated that (1) not all grievances had to be heard formally by the school board; and (2) the school board could discharge its duty to "stop, look, and listen" through the "open forum" portion of a school board meeting. However, recent decisions, statutes, and rules from the commissioner have required school districts to go beyond "stop, look, and listen."

The term "stop, look, and listen" first appeared in print in *Professional Association of College Educators v. El Paso Community College District* (hereafter referred to as *"PACE"*). In *PACE*, the appeals court held that Article I, §27 of the Texas Constitution does not require school boards to negotiate or even respond to grievances and complaints filed by those being governed, "but surely they must stop, look, and listen." The constitution simply requires school boards to "consider" the grievances addressed to them by citizens, including the district's employees.

According to *PACE*, whether a board appropriately considers a grievance (or remonstrance) under the "stop, look, and listen" standard will be determined as follows. A board that, when presented with a remonstrance, immediately files it in a waste basket can hardly be said to have "considered" it. A board that delays action upon a remonstrance in order to study and deliberate on the issues presented quite clearly will have "considered" a remonstrance, particularly if it modifies or changes its decision upon the issue confronting it. In between these extremes, the board may "consider" the remonstrance by reading it, perhaps on occasion having discussions, and then proceeding to act contrary to the contentions raised in the remonstrance.

The "stop, look, and listen" standard is still cited by educators, and is an interesting piece of history, but it no longer accurately depicts how grievances must be handled. Two things have happened to change the landscape. First, the Texas Legislature enacted TEC §11.1513(i), which provides that each school district must have an employment policy that gives each school district employee the right to present grievances "to the district board of trustees." Thus a grievance policy that prevents the employee from appealing the superintendent's decision to the school board would not comply with that statute.

Second, the commissioner adopted rules pertaining to the local record a school district must develop in connection with any case that might be appealed to the commissioner. In combination these two developments mean that the local board must be prepared to do more than "stop, look, and listen" and the local administration must keep a detailed record of what has transpired.

The duty to create a record of the proceedings before the local board first came up in *Taylor v. Marshall I.S.D.* (1997). Taylor filed a grievance requesting the district to grant assault leave. The board denied the grievance, and Taylor took an appeal to the commissioner. The commissioner observed that TEC §7.057 requires him to decide these appeals "based on a review of the record developed at the district level under a substantial evidence standard of review." Marshall I.S.D. had presented no record. The commissioner ruled that it was the school district's responsibility to create a record so that he would have something to "review." The term "record" is defined in TEC §7.057 to include, "at a minimum, an audible electronic or written transcript of all oral testimony or argument." Since no such record was submitted, the commissioner ruled that he could not find "substantial evidence" to support the school board's decision. The case was reversed, thus granting Taylor assault leave.

Numerous cases since then have said the same thing. In *Green v. Port Arthur I.S.D.* (1998) the commissioner expanded on the statutory definition of "record" by adding that it also should include "all correspondence between the district and the grievant concerning the grievance, and all documents or exhibits presented by the grievant or the administration to the board."

This requirement that the district create a record does not mean that a grievance process must be as formal as a due process hearing. The commissioner went to some pains to explain this in *Sierra v. Lake Worth I.S.D.* (1998), in which he said:

> a grievance is not required to be a very formal process. There is no requirement that the rules of evidence apply. . . . The record to be reviewed is whatever was presented to the board of trustees. Statements need not be made under oath. Hearsay exceptions need not be proved up. . . . Board members need not limit their consideration to evidence that meets the standards of the Texas Rules of Civil Evidence.

The burden is on the school district to create a record of the grievance proceedings. Failure to do so can mean that the commissioner will grant the grievance. For example, in one case a teacher filed a grievance over her appraisal. The grievance went through levels one and two, but was never heard at level three by the school board. Counsel for the district wrote the teacher a letter informing her that the board would not hear the grievance. The teacher then took the case to the commissioner, who granted the appeal without looking into the merits of it. The commissioner noted that when a school board is presented with a proper grievance, the board must hear the matter. Here, the grievance was properly presented to the board, but never heard by the board. The commissioner concluded that the board had effectively denied the grievance, but had no evidence to support its "decision" (*De la Rosa v. South San Antonio I.S.D.*, 2006).

The requirement to develop a record is now spelled out at 19 TAC §157.1073(d). The record must include a tape recording or transcript of the hearing (if a recording, it must be complete, clear, and audible, and must identify each speaker); all evidence admitted; all offers of proof; all written pleadings, motions, and intermediate rulings; a description of all matters officially noticed; if applicable, the decision of the hearing examiner; a tape recording or transcript of the oral argument before the board; and the decision of the board. The very vocabulary of this rule is completely inconsistent with a simple "stop, look, and listen" process. Terms such as "evidence admitted" and "offers of proof" are associated with the Rules of Federal Civil Procedure governing litigation in court, not simple grievances. But this is how the law of grievances in Texas has evolved.

If the employee appeals a denial of her grievance, she will have to show that she presented the issue to the board. Failure to do so may mean that the appeal is dismissed for "failure to exhaust administrative remedies." Such a case went all the way to the Texas Supreme Court in *Wilmer-Hutchins I.S.D. v. Sullivan* (2001). The case involved an allegation that the district had retaliated against the woman for filing a workers' compensation claim. However, the employee had never presented her grievance to the local school board. She went directly to the courthouse. The Texas Supreme Court noted that a person must "exhaust administrative remedies" before filing suit. The first step in doing so would have been to present the grievance to the school board. Since that was not done, the suit was dismissed.

Moreover, the employee will want to make sure that any local record of the grievance reflects every issue raised. In a case from Laredo, an employee attempted to raise issues before the commissioner that were not presented to the local school board. The commissioner refused to hear those issues (*Rodriguez v. Laredo I.S.D.*, 2000).

If a grievance is to be placed on the agenda for board action, there are sure to be questions as to whether it will be heard in open session or behind closed doors. Of course, the Texas Open Meetings Act requires that the final action of the board on any matter be done in open session. But what about the presentation of the case and the board's deliberations? Open or closed? Who decides?

The Texas Open Meetings Act (Government Code §551.082) allows the school board to meet in closed session in a case "in which a complaint or charge is brought against an employee of the school district by another employee and the complaint or charge directly results in a need for a hearing." However, a closed door session is not permitted "if an open hearing is requested in writing . . . by the employee against whom the complaint or charge is brought."

When a grievance is presented, it may be done on an individual basis or on behalf of a group, according to the court of appeals decision in *Lubbock Professional Firefighters v. City of Lubbock* (1987). Like many school districts, the City of Lubbock prohibited its employees from filing "group grievances." The city's practice was held to violate state law. The court held the employees have the right either to present their grievances individually or to combine them for a group presentation. These are not "class action" grievances, however, since the court held that the grievance must name the individual employees bringing any group grievance. Although the case deals with firefighters rather than teachers, it is applicable to all political subdivisions, including school districts.

There are circumstances in which a professional organization can file a grievance in its own name, on behalf of its members, without naming each member. In both *Weslaco Federation of Teachers v. Weslaco I.S.D.* and *Association of Brownsville Educators v. Brownsville I.S.D.*, the commissioner spelled out three factors that are relevant. If (1) the association's members could have raised the claims themselves; (2) the interests at issue were of interest to the association, as well as the individual members; and (3) the claims were not such that individual members were required to participate, then the association could proceed in its own name with the grievance.

The Port Arthur Teachers' Association was unsuccessful in its effort to make a claim on behalf of itself and certain unnamed members of the organization. The Association alleged that the district had retaliated against its members—some named and some unnamed—for participating in the Association and otherwise engaging in political activity. The commissioner tossed out the grievance of the Association and the unnamed members due to a "lack of standing." The commissioner observed that cases like this depend on the individual facts presented, and thus each party must present facts that particularly showed individual retaliation. Neither the Association as an entity, nor parties unnamed, could satisfy that standard.

However, five named teachers also joined the effort, asserting that they had each been reassigned to a middle school improperly, in retaliation for their political and Association activity. While the named teachers had standing to pursue the matter, they lost on the merits. The commissioner concluded that the reassignments were all based on permissible reasons as indicated in the local record. In particular, the district was seeking to strengthen one of its middle schools, which had a high number of uncertified staff members. The district's case was bolstered by the fact that four other teachers who were not members of the Association were also reassigned to the same school at the same time (*Port Arthur Teachers' Association v. Port Arthur I.S.D.*, 2007).

A grievance can be denied on the basis of its being filed untimely. Most policies require grievances to be filed within fifteen days of the date when the employee knew, or should have known, of the action giving rise to the complaint. In *Ysleta Teachers Association v. Ysleta I.S.D.* (2009) the commissioner affirmed the dismissal of a grievance based on untimeliness. The teachers argued that the district had waived the timeline by hearing the merits of the complaint. But the commissioner held that filing on time is an element of the exhaustion of administrative remedies. Exhausting administrative remedies is a jurisdictional requirement. Citing case law, the commissioner held that jurisdiction cannot be granted by waiver. The district's policy did not permit the use of a "continuing violation" standard, and the policy did not violate the Texas Constitution and its Open Courts provision. As the commissioner noted, Texas courts have consistently upheld short timelines for grievances in the school setting.

The case of *Walker v. McKinney I.S.D.* (2003) presents a common wrinkle in the "should have known" analysis. The grievance involved allegations that the district had placed the employee on the wrong pay scale. The "event" that produced the grievance—the wrongful pay scale—occurred long before the grievance was filed. However, the woman argued that she consistently had been misled by administrators and did not realize her pay was wrong until much later. The commissioner ruled that the grievance was untimely. The timeline for filing a grievance runs from the date the employee knows, or should know, of the event complained of, not the date when the employee realizes the legal consequences of the event.

While the employee must file the grievance quickly, the administration cannot "run out the clock" by refusing to meet with the employee. Fort Bend I.S.D. had a policy that required employees to initiate the grievance process by meeting with the immediate supervisor within ten days of the event being grieved. In this case, the court of appeals concluded from the record that the employee had made numerous attempts to meet with her principal concerning her grievance. The court ruled that the principal's failure to meet with her effectively thwarted the employee's grievance. Under these circumstances, the district could not deny the grievance as being untimely (*Fort Bend I.S.D. v. Rivera*, 2002).

If a school district chooses to deny the grievance on the basis of its being untimely, it should make it clear that the decision is based on timeliness, rather than the merits. Employees have sometimes argued that the board waived the timeliness argument by considering and/or actually ruling on the merits of the grievance. For example, in *Hernandez v. Meno* (1992), a Texas court of appeals ruled that the local school district waived the argument that the employee's complaint was untimely by granting the employee a full hearing on the substance of the complaint. However, this "waiver" argument lost much of its power when the Texas Supreme Court considered the issue in 2005. The court held that waiver can be established only by conduct that is "unequivocally inconsistent with claiming a known right. Hearing the merits of a party's complaint while reserving a ruling on its timeliness is not unequivocally inconsistent with later denying the complaint on the latter ground" (*Van I.S.D. v. McCarty*, 2005). The *Ysleta* case, mentioned above, makes this point in even stronger language by making the timely filing of the grievance a jurisdictional matter.

If the district wants to dismiss a grievance because it is untimely, it must give the employee the opportunity to grieve that decision. The district cannot simply rule that the grievance is untimely and be done with it. It must make the ruling in the context of the grievance process. Such was the ruling of the commissioner in *Halpin v. Mansfield I.S.D.* (1998). This means, in effect, that the district must raise the issue of timeliness, and give the grievant an opportunity to address that issue, as well as the opportunity to appeal the ruling through all levels of the grievance process.

Harsh words sometimes are spoken at a grievance hearing, as was apparent in *Hernandez v. Hayes*, a 1996 Texas court of appeals decision. In that case, a school administrator sued both the teachers and their association over things said at the grievance hearing. The administrator claimed defamation and negligent infliction of emotional distress, but the court of appeals tossed the suit out. The court determined that a school district's grievance process is a "quasi-judicial" process. Witnesses who speak at such a proceeding are entitled to absolute immunity from civil liability.

Sometimes a citizen or employee will make critical remarks about a district employee during the "open forum" of a school board meeting. Most school districts have adopted policies that address this situation, often granting the board president the authority to redirect the complaining party to the district's grievance process as a more appropriate means of voicing complaints. The policies promulgated by TASB that address this problem survived a legal challenge before the Fifth Circuit in *Fairchild v. Liberty I.S.D.* (2010). The Fifth Circuit held that the board, in accordance with its policies, properly prevented Ms. Fairchild from criticizing a current school employee during the public comment section of a board meeting. The court recognized that the district had a legitimate interest in maintaining student and employee privacy. The case does not hold that school boards can shut down all criticism that might occur in the public comment section of the board meeting. Indeed, in this case the board heard critical remarks during its meeting. However, the case holds that the board can bar the public airing of individual complaints against a specific employee that would be better suited to the district's grievance process.

Employees who file grievances have the right to be represented by "a representative that does not claim the right to strike." This right of representation applies at all stages of the process, including the initial level. This issue was addressed in the *Lubbock Firefighters* case, discussed above. As in many school district grievance policies, the Lubbock policy provided an informal first level for employee grievances from which employee representatives were excluded. The court struck down this practice, holding that the employee has the right to legal representation at any level, including the informal stage of a grievance.

Keep in mind that this right to representation applies when the employee is filing a grievance, a process initiated by the employee. If the employee's supervisor initiates a meeting to discuss concerns, the employee does not have the right to bring a lawyer or professional representative. This issue was decided by the Texas Supreme Court in *City of Round Rock v. Rodriguez* (2013).

A teacher claimed a right to legal representation at a parent-teacher conference in a 1991 case. The school counselor set up the conference after the parent requested the meeting. When the conversation focused on the student's relationship with the teacher, the teacher walked out. Concerned about possible disciplinary action, the teacher maintained she was entitled to legal representation. The principal later placed a letter of reprimand in the teacher's file. The teacher complained of the reprimand and carried the matter to the Texas Education Agency. The Texas Commissioner of Education denied the teacher's grievance. Parent-teacher conferences in the district were found to be informal, noninvestigatory proceedings used as administrative tools. No disciplinary action stemmed from participating in them. Thus, the teacher had no need for representation. The commissioner noted that the conference involved confidential information about the student. Having a third-party representative present would undermine the confidentiality. The commissioner noted that "a teacher has no right to representation outside a formal grievance proceeding" (*Thrower v. Arlington I.S.D.*).

Though the *Arlington* case may seem to imply that teachers are entitled to representation in conferences that could lead to disciplinary action, the *Round Rock* decision from the Texas Supreme Court clearly rejects that implication. It appears, then, that an employee is entitled to representation when the employee initiates the conference to complain of wages, hours, or conditions of work. When the employer initiates the conference to discuss concerns or complaints, the employee cannot insist upon representation.

The best source for educators in understanding how the grievance process works is the policy of the local school district. Almost all schools in Texas subscribe to the policy service provided by the Texas Association of School Boards. That policy service includes a comprehensive grievance policy for employees at Policy DGBA. Most school district policies can be found online at the district's website, so access to the latest on grievances is as close as your laptop.

The Role of Employee Organizations

The expansion of the grievance process has raised the profile of employee organizations, but there is no doubt that those organizations (associations or unions) in Texas remain far less powerful than their counterparts in other parts of the country. The fundamental reason for this is the absence of collective bargaining in Texas. Let us begin with a brief description of collective bargaining as it exists on the national scene and then proceed to a discussion of Texas.

Collective Bargaining on the National Scene. Collective bargaining is a familiar feature of American labor relations. It has been allowed in the private sector since 1935, when Congress passed the National Labor Relations Act (NLRA), sometimes called the Wagner Act. Its passage followed years of labor strife in major industries.

However, the NLRA does not apply to public employment. The law pertaining to labor-management relations in the public sector is governed by state law. Thus the power of employee organizations and unions depends on the political muscle of those organizations in each state. It should not come as a surprise, therefore, to find that public employment unions have more power in states with a long history of strong labor unions in the private sector. Thus, the teacher unions in Michigan, Illinois, and New York are more powerful than their Texas counterparts.

For example, the Longview Classroom Teachers Association challenged the decision of the Longview I.S.D. school board when it reduced the number of "local leave" days from five to two. This happened after the penalty-free resignation date, and the teachers argued that it amounted to a breach of contract and violation of law. They took their case to the commissioner and lost (*Longview Classroom Teachers Association v. Longview I.S.D.*, 2012). If the same scenario had played out in a state with collective bargaining, the CBA (Collective Bargaining Agreement) would have addressed this issue and would have, no doubt, restricted the unilateral authority of the school board. But not in Texas.

While the NLRA does not apply to public sector employees, most of the states in the country have adopted some type of collective bargaining law for public employees. To varying degrees, the states have incorporated into their laws the NLRA's concept of full bargaining rights. Basically, full bargaining rights encompass:

1. The right to organize collectively or to refrain from doing so.
2. The right to be represented by a single bargaining agent.
3. The right to democratic internal union organization (one person has one vote; usually, only union members are allowed to vote).
4. The right to bilateral negotiations over conditions of employment.
5. The right to a binding contract between the employer and the union (individual employee rights are surrendered to the bargaining agent).
6. The right to strike or to negotiate binding arbitration of both grievance and contract term disputes.

Few states have come close to granting employees all of these statutory rights, believing that there exists a very real difference between the private industrial sector and government service. Thus, for example, most states that allow collective bargaining do not allow public employees to strike. The role of public employee unions remains a subject of political controversy and tension, as illustrated by recent developments in Wisconsin over this issue.

The Law in Texas. Three specific features in Texas law are particularly important for this discussion. First, Texas has a "right-to-work" law with regard to public employment. Section 617.004 of the Government Code flatly spells it out: "An individual may not be denied public employment because of the individual's membership or nonmembership in a labor organization." Thus an employee organization cannot insist that all employees in the school must belong to the organization.

Second, Texas specifically bans collective bargaining in the public sector (Government Code §617.002).

Third, Texas prohibits strikes or organized work stoppages by public employees and allows public employees to present their grievances only through organizations that do not claim the right to strike (Government Code §§617.003 and 617.005).

While Texas law outlaws collective negotiation, it does not prohibit unions from existing, nor public employees from joining them. In fact, Texas law repeats itself in an effort to make sure that employees are not forced into membership in any particular group. As already mentioned, §617.004 of the Government Code proclaims that an individual may not be denied employment because of the individual's membership or non-membership in a labor organization. On top of that, two sections in the Education Code (§§21.407 and 21.408, discussed in more detail below) reaffirm that membership in an employee organization is an individual decision that must be respected.

To facilitate membership in professional organizations, the legislature has added §22.001 to the Texas Education Code, requiring school districts to deduct from an employee's salary an amount equivalent to membership fees or dues in a professional association if the employee so requests. The district may charge an administrative fee for doing so.

Prior to 1995, the Education Code included a provision that authorized "consultation" between school boards and professional organizations regarding "matters of educational policy and conditions of employment." Consultation is not to be confused with collective bargaining, for the two are significantly different. Nevertheless, consultation was seen by some as a first step toward collective bargaining. As a result of that perception, the 1995 legislature scrapped consultation altogether. Texas no longer has a statute authorizing official consultation between teacher organizations and school boards.

Does this preclude a school board from "consulting" with various professional organizations? No. School boards are free to consult with whomever they choose in formulating school policy and budgetary decisions (see, e.g., TEC §11.251(g)). But boards that choose to engage in consultation should be careful not to do so in a way that effectively "coerces" teachers to join a particular organization. Such was the underlying concern behind the case of *San Antonio Federation of Teachers v. San Antonio I.S.D.* In that case the San Antonio Federation of Teachers challenged the school board's agreement with the San Antonio Teachers Council because the agreement recognized the Teachers Council as the sole agent for consultation. The Federation argued that this "exclusivity" provision was coercive, since the only way teachers could participate in consultation would be through the favored organization. The commissioner agreed. In a 1980 ruling the commissioner declared that such an exclusive agreement violated the provision in the Code that prohibits coercing teachers to join groups, clubs, committees, or organizations.

Just as school boards must be careful to avoid an appearance of favoritism toward a particular group, so must administrators. TEC §21.407 states that no school district, board, or administrator may directly or indirectly require or coerce any teacher to join any group, club, committee, organization, or association. TEC §21.408 affirmatively states that educators have the right to join or refuse to join any professional association or organization. School administrators are well advised to be circumspect about these provisions. Subtle endorsements by an administrator may be seen by some as "coercion." In *Att'y. Gen. Op. LO-95–047* (1995) the attorney general opined that "mere words of encouragement to join a particular teacher organization or association, when uttered by a high-level administrator in a particular context," could be construed to be coercive. Thus the beginning-of-the-year recruitment drives of the various organizations should be conducted exclusively by teachers.

An interesting illustration concerns an assistant principal in Ysleta I.S.D. The assistant principal stated at a faculty meeting that he was a member of the Association of Texas Professional Educators (ATPE) and would be available to talk with interested teachers about the organization. A faculty member objected to his statement, considering it a subtle form of coercion and thus a violation of the Code. Later, the school board approved a resolution stating that, since solicitation of membership by administrators can be construed as coercive, "administrators should not participate in the recruitment of members of professional organizations to which teaching personnel are eligible to belong." The resolution went on to specify that such presentations should be made by other teachers rather than administrators. Excluded from the board resolution were other organizations, such as PTA and booster clubs. ATPE appealed the resolution to the Texas Commissioner of Education, who ruled that the resolution was overly broad and, therefore, unenforceable. As the commissioner noted, the resolution as written prohibited administrators under *any* circumstances from recruiting members for professional organizations. The commissioner noted that a narrowly worded resolution would be valid "if specifically restricted to apply to administrators only at those times when the administrators are performing their duties of employment." The commissioner added that even in the absence of a policy "any administrator would be well advised to avoid soliciting membership in a professional organization at any time when a teacher might reasonably perceive that the administrator is acting in his or her capacity as a superior addressing his or her subordinate" (*Association of Texas Professional Educators v. Ysleta I.S.D.*, 1983).

SUMMARY

In this chapter we have reviewed the personnel issues that arise in the day-to-day interaction between school employees and their supervisors and employers. Much of the law in this area is set out in the Texas Education Code and subject to change with every legislative session. Some of what we have discussed, such as the FLSA and FMLA leave, is a reflection of federal law.

All of the issues discussed in this chapter provide fertile ground for the germination of employee grievances. The expansion of the notion of what is grievable, along with the clarification of the role of school administrators and boards in hearing such grievances, indeed has changed the labor-management landscape in Texas public schools and likely will continue to do so.

SIX

Expression and Associational Rights

IN A DEMOCRATIC SOCIETY, rights of expression are especially valued. Included in the term "rights of expression" are freedom of speech, freedom of the press, and freedom of assembly and association—in short, the key provisions of the First Amendment in the Bill of Rights of the U.S. Constitution. The First Amendment reads: "Congress shall make no law respecting an establishment of religion, or prohibiting the free exercise thereof; or abridging the freedom of speech, or of the press, or the right of the people peaceably to assemble, and to petition the Government for a redress of grievances." The religion components of the First Amendment will be discussed in Chapter 7. By virtue of the Fourteenth Amendment, the provisions of the First Amendment apply to public school districts.

The counterpart to the First Amendment in the Texas Constitution is Article I, §8, which states in part, "Every person shall be at liberty to speak, write or publish his opinions on any subject, being responsible for the abuse of that privilege; and no law shall ever be passed curtailing the liberty of speech or of the press." In a 1992 decision, the Texas Supreme Court noted that in some respects Article I, §8 affords greater protection to free speech than the First Amendment, adding that "it has been and remains the preference of this court to sanction a speaker after, rather than before, speech occurs" (*Davenport v. Garcia*). In 1995 the U.S. Court of Appeals for the Fifth Circuit noted that the drafters of the Texas Constitution rejected the language of the First Amendment, preferring instead broader support for free speech. Thus, a claim under Article I, §8 is not the equivalent of a claim under the First Amendment (*Carpenter v. Wichita Falls I.S.D.*). At the same time, it is important to note that the remedies available under the state provision are less extensive than those under the First Amendment. The Texas Supreme Court ruled in 1995 that, unlike federal law and the First Amendment, state law does not allow damages for a violation of free speech and assembly rights under Article I of the Texas Constitution. Remedies are limited to declaratory and injunctive relief and to such actions as reinstatement and back pay (*City of Beaumont v. Boullion*).

Expression issues often surface in disputes over employee contract nonrenewal or termination and student discipline. Employees and students often argue, sometimes with good reason, that the actions taken against them were in retaliation for the exercise of free speech. Exactly what rights of expression and association Texas public employees and students are entitled to is the focus of this chapter. We also will examine the extent to which parents and others may have expression rights on the school campus. Since private-school employees and students cannot assert a cause of action under either the federal or state constitutions in their schools (see Chapter 1 for a general discussion), the extent to which these rights are protected in that setting depends upon the policies of the school. Included in our discussion will be an examination of how teacher and student use of electronic communication devices on and off campus has posed challenges for school authorities and courts alike.

EDUCATOR RIGHTS OF EXPRESSION

Expression outside the School

Frequently, it is asserted that public-school teachers and administrators have the same civil rights outside school as do any other citizens. While this claim has some truth, it also is true that the educator's job may be in jeopardy if the exercise of a right undermines job effectiveness. A brief review of key U.S. Supreme Court decisions in this area will make this point clear.

The most important case insofar as educator rights of expression are concerned is *Pickering v. Board of Education* (1968). *Pickering* involved a teacher who was dismissed from his job for sending a letter critical of the school board to a local newspaper. Both the school board and the lower courts concluded that the letter, which contained some false statements, was detrimental to the interests of the school system and that the interests of the school should take precedence over the teacher's claim to freedom of expression. But the U.S. Supreme Court ruled unanimously that the school board was wrong in firing the teacher. Justice Thurgood Marshall, who wrote the opinion in *Pickering*, sought to balance the teacher's rights of expression on public issues outside school with the legitimate interests of the school board in assuring an efficient and orderly learning environment in school. Since the statements in the letter were not aimed at any person with whom the teacher would come in contact in carrying out his duties, and the falsehoods were not carelessly made nor did they impede school operations, the Supreme Court concluded that the teacher should not have been dismissed. In a later case, the U.S. Supreme Court extended the *Pickering* principle in a unanimous decision upholding a teacher's right to speak out at a school board meeting about employment matters (*City of Madison v. Wisconsin Employment Relations Commission*, 1976).

What is interesting about *Pickering* is that, while it does convey substantial support for teacher expression outside school, it also contains some caveats. The Court did not state that educators have an unrestricted, absolute right to freedom of expression outside school. In fact, Justice Marshall openly acknowledged that the government "has interests as an employer in regulating the speech of its employees that differ significantly from those it possesses in connection with regulation of the speech of the citizenry in general" (p. 568). If it can be shown that the statements are made recklessly or with knowledge of their falsity, that school functioning or the teacher's performance is impaired, or that the superior-subordinate relationship is undermined, then sanctions, including dismissal, might appropriately be brought against the employee.

Pickering is an important case, for it recognizes that educators—and, by implication, all public employees—do have a substantial right to freedom of expression as citizens in the community. It also is important because it conveys to administrators the burden of documentation they must shoulder to take adverse action against an employee who they believe has abused the right. For example, in *Alaniz v. San Isidro I.S.D.* (1984), the Fifth Circuit upheld a lower court ruling in favor of the school district's deputy tax assessor-collector, who was fired after an opposition political party won control of the board. Romula Alaniz had actively supported the policies and candidates of the incumbent party, headed by her brother-in-law. She maintained that she would not have been fired but for her First Amendment–protected political activities. The trial court awarded Alaniz $51,000 in back pay and $40,000 in compensatory damages for mental anguish and emotional distress and ordered her reinstated to her position.

In a 2013 unreported but instructive decision, the Fifth Circuit ruled that an assistant principal had established that her demotion back to her previous speech pathologist position was based in part on her support for a candidate for school superintendent. The candidate lost to the incumbent. Thereafter, the assistant principal's evaluations began to sour. The appeals court identified four factors that the employee must satisfy for *Pickering* to apply. The employee must establish, in order, that:

- The employee suffered an adverse employment action
- The speech related to a matter of public concern
- The speech did not cause disruption in the workplace
- The speech was a motivating factor in the adverse employment action

Once the employee has satisfied these four factors the burden shifts to the employer to prove by a preponderance of evidence that the same decision would have been made even in the absence of the protected speech. Here, the employee had satisfied the four factors, but it was not clear whether she would have been reassigned even if she had said nothing about the superintendency candidate. The Fifth Circuit sent the case back to the trial court (*Mooney v. Lafayette County School District*).

The extent of free speech rights under the *Pickering* ruling is more limited for public employees who occupy policy-making or confidential positions. This is clear from a 1992 ruling of the U.S. Court of Appeals for the Fifth Circuit involving the removal of the superintendent in the Salado I.S.D. The superintendent, Nolan Kinsey, had supported a losing slate of candidates in a school board election. While he had not openly campaigned or made financial contributions, he had voiced support for his choices in conversations with Salado citizens and expressed concerns about the opposition. When the opposition won and became a majority on the school board, the relationship between Kinsey and the board deteriorated. Eventually, he was removed from his position. Kinsey filed suit, claiming that his removal was in retaliation for his exercise of First Amendment rights in connection with the school board election. The litigation involved several trips to the courthouse, the last of which was in 1992 when the Fifth Circuit, sitting en banc—meaning all members assigned to the court participated—upheld his removal by a 13-2 vote (*Kinsey v. Salado I.S.D.*). The majority noted that the *Pickering* balancing test favored the public employer in this case, given the close working relationship between the superintendent and the school board. "[I]n light of his high-level policymaker and confidential position, Kinsey stepped over the line. . . . in so doing, he abandoned any shelter otherwise provided him by the First Amendment" (p. 996).

In 1977, the Supreme Court again addressed the issue of employee expression rights outside school. In *Mt. Healthy City School District Board of Education v. Doyle*, a marginally qualified teacher on a probationary contract made comments critical of the school's dress code for teachers over a local radio station. The teacher, Fred Doyle, was not given a continuing contract. He asserted that the primary reason was his radio presentation and argued that such expression is a constitutionally protected right. The Court agreed that it is but also was concerned that a marginal candidate not take unfair advantage of the *Pickering* decision by exercising protected expression rights just before an adverse employment decision is to be made. Thus, the Court ruled that the employee first has the burden of proving that the adverse employment decision was substantially based on the exercise of the right. Subsequent case law has established that the person bringing the suit must show at least some circumstantial evidence to prove illegitimate intent. Mere allegations will not suffice (*Thompkins v. Vickers*). This burden was not difficult for Fred Doyle in the *Mt. Healthy* case because the superintendent had sent him a memo in which he listed the radio talk show remarks as a factor in the nonrenewal decision. The lesson for administrators, of course, is not to rely on legally impermissible reasons in a negative employment decision.

If the employee is successful in sustaining his burden, the school district then must be given the opportunity to show that there are other valid reasons, unrelated to the exercise of the right, to support its decision. Where there is a history of inadequate employee performance, the exercise of expression rights is not likely to make any difference, assuming that the employee's evaluations document the deficiencies. The Supreme Court sent the *Mt. Healthy* case back to the trial court to make this determination, since Doyle had been involved in a number of employment-related incidents. The district court later upheld his termination, a decision affirmed by the Sixth Circuit in 1982.

The so-called *Mt. Healthy* test is often used in employment cases. For example, a white cafeteria worker protested her dismissal some years ago from a predominantly black public school in Mississippi, one of the states within the jurisdiction of the U.S. Court of Appeals for the Fifth Circuit. The worker alleged that the only reason she was released was because she had decided to send her son to a private school, which was largely segregated. As noted in Chapter 2, parents have a constitutional right to select a private school for their children. Since a constitutional right was involved, the burden of justification shifted to the school district to show that she was fired for reasons having nothing to do with the exercise of the right. The school was unable to shoulder this burden, and the court awarded the employee damages, including back pay, attorneys' fees, and reinstatement to her position (*Brantley v. Surles*, 1985).

The outcome was different in a 1989 decision involving the Longview I.S.D. Despite evidence that racial discrimination and retaliation for the exercise of First Amendment rights had played a substantial role in the nonrenewal of a black teacher's contract, administrators were successful in convincing William Wayne Justice, a controversial civil-rights-oriented Texas federal judge, that the nonrenewal was justified. The judge noted that the school district had carefully evaluated the teacher, even to the point of having scripted her classroom performance. The evaluations, he wrote, "form a compelling record of plaintiff's primary weaknesses." On the strength of the evidence, Justice concluded that the school district had established that even in the absence of racial bias and retaliation, it would have decided not to renew the teacher's contract (*Johnson v. Longview I.S.D.*). It helped that the district had replaced the teacher with another black teacher. The lesson for school administrators is clear: document *job-related deficiencies* carefully and thoroughly so that the *Mt. Healthy* test can be met.

One of the more interesting applications of the *Mt. Healthy* test involved a newspaper's claim of retaliation by a county board of supervisors for critical articles it published about the board. The newspaper argued that the county board became so upset over the articles that the board shifted most of its legal announcements to a competing paper. The newspaper maintained that the switch was in retaliation for its exercise of freedom of the press. The Fifth Circuit agreed and sent the case back to the trial court to determine if the county board could advance other reasons unrelated to the First Amendment to justify the switch. The appeals court added that in order to escape any legal liability the supervisors would have to show that "each and every one" of the legal notices had been placed in the competing paper for legitimate reasons (*North Mississippi Communications, Inc. v. Jones*). In 1996 the U.S. Supreme Court applied the same principle in two cases involving independent contractors. In one of the cases, the county board of commissioners terminated the contract of a trash hauler over the latter's criticism of the board for various matters relating to trash hauling. While the Justices ruled that the independent contractor's free speech rights were implicated, they noted that the board could prevail if it could show that its job-related concerns outweighed the free speech interests of the trash hauler (*Board of Commissioners of Wabaunsee County v. Umbehr*). The important lesson for Texas school boards from these rulings is not to retaliate against the media and independent contractors for critical comments they make about the school district.

School districts also are limited in their ability to file lawsuits against those who make critical comments about the district and its employees. This is the lesson from litigation involving an effort by the Port Arthur school district to sue a political relations firm for defamation. The firm had posted a story on its website about alleged misconduct at the high school prom. The school district argued that the owner of the firm didn't live in the district and thus lacked the right to comment on district matters. The Texas appeals court rejected the contention, noting that "This court agrees that prosecutions for libel on government have no place in the jurisprudence of the United States of America. If the government is permitted to use public resources to bring defamation claims against its critics, criticism of government will be silenced through, at the very least, fear of monetary loss" (p. 352). The Port Arthur district's argument, the judges observed, undermines the basic principle of free expression (*Port Arthur I.S.D. v. Klein & Associates Political Relations*, 2002). In 2011 the Texas Attorney General relied on this ruling to advise that a school district may not pay the expenses of an administrator who files a defamation claim on the district's behalf (*Att'y Gen. Op. GA-0878*).

In the employment context, reassignments ordinarily are within the discretion of school officials, and most contracts contain a statement that the employee may be reassigned. However, even a reassignment cannot be made in retaliation for an employee's exercise of expression rights. It makes no difference whether the employee has a contract of employment or is employed on an at-will basis. A case in point is a 1987 decision by the Fifth Circuit. The case involved Odessa Reeves, a school administrator of long standing. Reeves was reassigned from being a Chapter I coordinator to director of reading after she had testified on behalf of several teaching assistants who were suing the district over their employment terminations. She was moved from the central office to the kitchen of a home economics class in a junior high school. She supervised no employees in her new position and for some time did not have a job description. She was required to stay in her office until 5 P.M., while other administrators left at 4 P.M. Previous perquisites, such as reimbursement for attending conferences, were withdrawn. The appeals court agreed with the trial court that the reassignment was an unconstitutional retaliation for her previous trial testimony, a protected form of expression. "To allow a government employer to retaliate via demotion, transfer, or reassignment against an employee's unfavorable trial testimony would undermine the ability of the witness to speak truthfully without fear of reprisal" (p. 31). Since there were no other reasons to support the reassignment, the court, following *Mt. Healthy,* ordered Reeves reinstated to the Chapter I position. While she voluntarily had accepted the lower pay that went with the reassignment, she was entitled to the difference between her former and present pay rate (*Reeves v. Claiborne County Board of Education*).

Expression within the School

Expression within the school has three important dimensions. The first relates to expression outside the classroom but on the school grounds, the second concerns itself with classroom academic freedom, and the third relates to retaliation for speaking out about suspected wrongdoing under the Texas Whistleblower statute. The first is discussed in this section, and the next two in the following sections.

In 1979 the U.S. Supreme Court ruled that the First and Fourteenth Amendments to the U.S. Constitution can under certain circumstances protect private communication between a public-school teacher and a school principal (*Givhan v. Western Line Consolidated School District*). At the same time, the Court stated that, since subordinate-superior relations are particularly sensitive, the content of what is said, as well as the time, place, and manner in which it is said, can be taken into account in deciding what is and is not constitutionally protected. This employer-employee relationship factor, while briefly mentioned in *Pickering*, was not particularly stressed in that case.

Following the *Givhan* decision, the U.S. Supreme Court issued three important rulings pertaining to teacher expression within the workplace, the first involving mailboxes, the second involving teacher complaints over working conditions, and the third involving speech on public matters but made within one's scope of employment. All three indicate a trend toward giving public officials greater control over employee expression on the job.

The first is a 1983 ruling, *Perry Education Association v. Perry Local Educators' Association.* In *Perry,* the Court decided in a narrow 5-4 ruling that school mailboxes are not automatically "public forums" available to teachers, their associations, and others to disseminate information. A public forum is a place where persons and groups can come together for expressive purposes free from government control except in extreme situations, e.g., imminent threat of lawless action. Street corners and public parks are examples of public forums. At the opposite end of the spectrum from the public forum is the closed forum—government property that is traditionally not a place for public communication. A good example is a prison. The Supreme Court viewed the school mail system to be a closed forum under the school's control and reserved for its use so long as officials are not suppressing expression because they disagree with the message.

At the same time, the Court recognized that a school, as part of its control over the mail system, may decide to open up the mail system to certain types of communication but limit it regarding others—in effect, to create a "limited public forum" where certain categories of expression but not others are allowed. A limited public forum can be considered to be midway between a public forum and a closed forum. It is important to note that once a limited public forum is established for certain categories of speech, school officials cannot disallow certain types of speech *within* those categories. For example, if community groups are allowed to use the school mail system or website for announcements, it would be unconstitutional viewpoint censorship to deny access to Planned Parenthood for this purpose.

In the *Perry* case the school permitted its faculty collective bargaining agent to use the internal mail system pursuant to a contract provision but denied access to other employee organizations. "This type of selective access does not transform government property into a public forum," wrote Justice Byron White. Thus, the other employee organizations were not allowed to use the mailboxes.

It is doubtful whether Texas public school systems could grant exclusive use of the mail system to a single teacher organization, since Texas does not have a state law allowing schools to grant exclusive recognition rights to one organization, though employees have a right to join labor organizations (TEC §§21.407–21.408). This conclusion is supported by the Fifth Circuit in a 1985 decision involving Garland I.S.D. (*Texas State Teachers Association v. Garland I.S.D.*). The Fifth Circuit also ruled in the *Garland* case that, since the campus itself is not a public forum, the school district could deny all employee organizations access during school hours, yet allow other, unrelated groups, such as civic and charitable organizations, to meet with students and faculty during nonclass school hours. However, Garland could not prohibit its teachers from talking among themselves about TSTA or about labor relations matters on campus unless material and substantial interference with school activity could be shown, since such speech is protected expression. Nor could the district limit the mail system to official messages, yet at the same time allow teachers to communicate with each other through the system on any subject except for matters relating to employee organizations. The decision later was affirmed by the U.S. Supreme Court.

It is important to note that school district control over the mail system is not absolute. In *Ysleta Federation of Teachers v. Ysleta I.S.D.*, the Fifth Circuit applied the *Perry* ruling to a school policy limiting teacher organizations to a one-time-only use of the school mail system. The district had opened the mail system to all employee organizations and required prior administrative approval of the material to be circulated. Failure to secure approval would result in suspension of access to all means of in-school communication, including the mail system. The appeals court returned the case to the lower court to see if the Ysleta I.S.D. could justify its one-time-only rule as narrowly drawn and furthering a compelling state interest, a heavy burden of justification.

The Ysleta I.S.D. case also is instructive because it sheds light on the legality of a policy giving the superintendent complete discretion to review all material prior to its distribution by employees and their organizations. Since the superintendent could deny access not only to the mail system but also to school bulletin boards and similar communication vehicles if he or she determined the intended communication to be not in conformity with school board policy, the Fifth Circuit declared the regulation a clear violation of the First Amendment. The court noted that the *Perry* case involved only the mail system and that the Supreme Court explicitly denied school authorities the right to suppress expression through the mail system because they oppose the speaker's views. The Fifth Circuit agreed with the lower court that the prior-review policy was constitutionally unacceptable because it did not limit the discretion of the superintendent. The court referred to its 1982 ruling in *Hall v. Board of School Commissioners of Mobile County*, in which it required prior-review policies involving teacher expression to have sufficient guidance through clearly articulated prior-submission procedures and approval standards to prohibit "the unbridled discretion that is proscribed by the Constitution." The general format of these procedures and standards is discussed later in the chapter in connection with non-school-sponsored student publications.

Taken together, the *Perry* decision and the later Fifth Circuit rulings suggest that administrators must be sensitive to employee First

Amendment rights when making decisions about school mailboxes, websites, and similar types of communication systems, even when the decision is to make these school-sponsored channels of communication closed forums. This same sensitivity applies to the campus itself. While normally reserved for school business, the campus easily can become an open forum for parents and other members of the community by district policy and practice. For example, administrators in the Plano Independent School District organized a series of "math nights" some years ago to inform parents about its new math curriculum. Several parents were rebuffed when they tried to distribute material critical of the program at the evening meetings. They were told that they had to submit their materials for approval before the materials could be displayed or distributed. The parents filed a lawsuit against the district and the administrators. The Fifth Circuit ruled that the parents sought to speak on a matter of public concern—the district's math curriculum—and that the prior-review request was unconstitutional for the same reasons expressed in the *Ysleta* and *Hall* decisions: It subjected free speech to the will of school administrators. Furthermore, no evidence was presented that the flyers and petitions the parents planned to circulate at the meetings would prove disruptive. Because the administrators had violated the parents' First Amendment rights, the administrators were not entitled to immunity from possible liability (*Chiu v. Plano I.S.D.*, 2003).

The second important decision of the U.S. Supreme Court in the context of in-school employee speech is *Connick v. Myers*, handed down in April of 1983. That decision involved the issue of whether employee expression concerning on-the-job complaints is constitutionally protected and thus cannot be used in a negative employment decision. By another 5-4 vote, the Court ruled that such expression is *not* protected and thus *can* serve as grounds for dismissal. Referring repeatedly to the decision in *Pickering v. Board of Education*, the Court drew a distinction between expression involving the public interest and expression involving working conditions. Writing for the majority, Justice Byron White observed that "when close working relationships are essential to fulfilling public responsibilities, a wide degree of deference to the employer's judgment is appropriate. Furthermore, we do not see the necessity for an employer to allow events to unfold to the extent that the disruption of the office and the destruction of working relationships [are] manifest before taking action" (p. 1692). Justice White added, "We caution that a stronger showing may be necessary if the employee's speech more substantially involved matters of public concern."

The implications of the *Connick* decision for public school administrators are important. The administrator must determine if the expression is protected by the First Amendment before recommending a negative employment decision on the basis of that expression. According to a 1994 U.S. Supreme Court decision, this requires that the employer must "tread with a certain amount of care" by conducting a reasonable investigation to determine what the person said (*Waters v. Churchill*). Does the expression involve community interests? If the answer is no, it probably is not protected. For example, a teacher who refers to himself as a perfect "10" and to other personnel as "witches" or "bug-eyed troublemakers" is not engaging in protected expression, according to a decision of the Texas Commissioner of Education handed down the same year as the *Connick* ruling (*Bowen v. Channelview I.S.D.*).

On the other hand, a teacher who complains about the religious components of a school holiday observance program or about sexual harassment of female teachers may well be speaking out on matters of public interest. In *Wells v. Hico I.S.D.*, the Fifth Circuit in 1984 found sufficient evidence to support a jury verdict in favor of two teachers who complained about the school's handling of a federally funded reading program. The program had been the subject of debate in the community. Debate intensified when one of the teachers spoke out at a school board meeting about the program. The contracts of the two teachers subsequently were not renewed. They sued, arguing in part that their nonrenewals were in retaliation for their speaking out. The Fifth Circuit noted that after the school board meeting the two teachers received poor evaluations and that the evaluations included negative comments by the school principal regarding their appearance before the school board. The school was unsuccessful in arguing that the pair would have been nonrenewed even had the expression not occurred—an attempt to meet the conditions set forth in the *Mt. Healthy v. Doyle* ruling. It is important to note as well that Texas school employees have a right to present a complaint to the school board under Article I, §27 of the Texas Constitution, which allows citizens to "apply to those invested with the powers of government for redress of grievances or other purposes, by petition, address, or remonstrance."

The expression rights of administrators may not be coextensive with those of teachers. The same reasoning used in the *Kinsey* decision discussed earlier in this chapter regarding the school superintendent–board relationship may apply to some extent to lower-level administrators as well. Further, principals have the same burden as other employees in arguing that job actions taken against them were retaliatory because of the exercise of free speech. A principal in the Pittsburg I.S.D. who was notified of being reassigned the following year sent several memoranda to the school board, local newspaper, and the Texas Commissioner of Education requesting a buyout of her contract. She also complained in the memos that the board had mishandled allegations involving her management of the school activity fund and sought exoneration for her oversight of the fund. The board subsequently did offer her a buyout option, but she turned it down. Thereafter the board reassigned her to be the head of the district's alternative school. The principal resigned and filed suit, claiming the actions taken against her were in retaliation for speaking out in the memos. The Fifth Circuit agreed with the trial court that the woman had not proved her case. The memos dealt mostly with her job and reputation, not with any public dialogue over the student activity fund. Further, she sent the memos after her reassignment, thus indicating her speech was focused mostly on her own situation. "Post hoc metamorphoses," wrote the judges, "fall short of the constitutional threshold" (*Bradshaw v. Pittsburg I.S.D.*, 2000).

The third U.S. Supreme Court decision involved a deputy district attorney who claimed he suffered retaliation after he wrote an internal office memorandum to his supervisors noting serious deficiencies in a governmental affidavit used to obtain a search warrant. The deputy district attorney maintained that he was addressing serious governmental misconduct, a matter of public concern. The high court ruled that even if the memo involved a matter of public concern, it was not entitled to constitutional protection because it was written within the scope of his duties of employment as a prosecuting attorney (*Garcetti v. Ceballos*, 2006). At the same time, the Justices recognized that public employees who make such statements as citizens outside their official duties may be entitled to some degree of constitutional protection under the *Pickering* decision. The five Justices in the majority added two caveats to their ruling. First, they rejected the contention that employers can restrict employee expression rights by creating excessively broad job descriptions. Second, they observed that speech related to scholarship or teaching may be different. As noted below in the section on academic freedom, the Fifth Circuit issued a ruling in 1980 protecting the right of teachers to lead classroom discussion on controversial issues.

With regard to the Justices' concern about excessively broad job descriptions, a Texas federal judge addressed a matter related to it in an unreported but informative 2012 decision. The case involved a payroll clerk who had worked for the Cleveland I.S.D. for over twenty years. She engaged in small talk with a fellow employee during her lunch hour, at one point encouraging the fellow employee to participate in the upcoming school board election and vote for some particular candidates. The payroll clerk was later terminated from her position for violating a board policy restricting employees from engaging in activities that "result in any political or social pressure being placed on students, parents, or staff." The federal judge held that the clerk was speaking as a citizen and not an employee when she was chatting at lunch. The judge noted that rather than produce evidence that the payroll clerk's effectiveness had been undermined by the discussion, school officials sought to focus on the district's "incredibly broad ban on all political 'pressure.'" In so doing, the district violated the employee's free speech rights (*Ricci v. Cleveland I.S.D.*). The lesson here is that neither job descriptions nor board policies can be so restrictive that they prohibit school employees from engaging in any free speech at school protected by the *Pickering* ruling discussed earlier.

Shortly after the *Garcetti* decision was handed down, the Fifth Circuit applied the ruling to two Texas cases. In the first, a high school principal in Edgewood I.S.D. alleged that her midyear transfer to the directorship of an alternative high school enrolling a much small number of students constituted retaliation for her notifying her superiors and the police that a student had been in possession of marijuana on the campus. The student was the son of the vice president of the school board, and the principal maintained that she refused to grant him preferential treatment. The appellate court ruled that under *Garcetti* her speech clearly fell within her official duties and thus was not entitled to constitutional protection (*Cavazos v. Edgewood I.S.D.*, 2006).

The second case involved a Dallas I.S.D. high school athletic director who challenged his removal from the position as retaliation for exercising free speech. When Gregory Williams was unsuccessful in getting the office manager to clarify why the athletic account had a deficit, he sent a memo to the school principal detailing his concerns. Subsequently, the principal removed him from the athletic director position. Williams sued the district over his removal, alleging retaliation for speaking out on misuse of public funding much as Marvin Pickering had done in the *Pickering* case. Referencing *Garcetti*, the Fifth Circuit pointed out that the role of the speaker must be considered before considering the content of what is said. "Even if the speech is of great social importance," the court noted, "it is not protected by the First Amendment so long as it was made pursuant to the worker's official duties" (*Williams v. Dallas I.S.D.*, p. 692). While writing memos to the principal regarding athletic accounts was not specifically part of the athletic director's actual job description, the judges noted that Williams could not perform his job effectively without knowing about athletic accounts. Thus, his memo to the principal was made in the course of his employment and consequently was not entitled to constitutional protection. In a footnote, the judges pointed out that unlike Marvin Pickering, Williams did not write a letter to the local newspaper or school board expressing his athletic account concerns. The implication is that had he done so, the outcome may have been different.

Suppose in the *Williams* case the principal had asked the athletic director to send him an e-mail about his concerns over the athletic account. It may be that under the Texas Constitution, the principal would have opened the door to the director's expressing his concerns. As noted at the start of this chapter, the Texas Supreme Court has ruled that Article I, Section 8 of the Texas Constitution provides greater protection for free speech than the First Amendment (*Davenport v. Garcia*). Citing this decision, a state district court ruled in an appeal from a decision by the Texas Commissioner of Education that employee speech is protected under the Texas Constitution if it is invited, solicited, or encouraged by a governmental employer. The case involving the job termination of an at-will employee was sent back to the commissioner. Upon rehearing, the commissioner concluded that because the employee's speech was not solicited, the termination did not violate the Texas Constitution (*Rymkus v. Spring Branch I.S.D.*, 1996).

In sum, while a public employee cannot suffer a negative employment decision for exercising free speech rights, the latter are protected only under certain circumstances. We can draw several key lessons about public employee free speech from the U.S. Supreme Court's *Pickering, Connick, Mt. Healthy*, and *Garcetti* decisions. First, speech is constitutionally protected if it is made outside the scope of the job description, relates to matters of public concern rather than one's working conditions, and does not undermine the employee's effectiveness. Second, even if the speech is protected, the employer can still prevail if there is documented evidence of job-related deficiencies not related to the exercise of free speech. It is clear that simply speaking out on a matter of public concern will not automatically shield an employee from a negative employment decision. One caveat to our discussion is how Texas courts may construe the free speech clause in Article I, §8 of the state constitution in the future. In light of the complexity of the law in this area, it is wise to consult the school attorney when employee expression is the center of concern.

Electronic Communication

The newest form of communication is through electronic communication devices such as netbooks, iPhones, and Blackberrys that access social networking websites like MySpace, Facebook, Blogger, and Twitter. The extent to which one enjoys privacy in these forums depends in part on the privacy protection afforded by the website and in part on the creativity of hackers. While what a school employee says and does outside of school normally is the employee's own business, it becomes the school's business if the employee's ability to perform the job is significantly compromised. This could occur, for example, if postings on a networking website become accessible to the school community. Thus, it would be wise for school employees not to post particularly sensitive material on their websites.

Using social networking websites to interact with students can be particularly troublesome for teachers. There often is a tendency to engage in informal and abbreviated forms of communication that may not serve the teacher well if disclosed. A 2008 case involving a probationary high school teacher in Connecticut provides a good illustration. The teacher, Jeffrey Spanierman, opened a MySpace account after students asked him to view their MySpace pages. He called one of the profiles on his account "Mr. Spiderman" and used it to communicate with students because he thought he could relate to them better and could engage in discussions about nonschool matters. A teacher told a counselor at the school about the MySpace profile and about complaints from students relating to it. When they viewed the profile page, they found a picture of Spanierman when he was ten years younger, along with pictures of students at the school. They also said they saw pictures of naked men with inappropriate comments underneath them. The counselor said that blogs on the profile with students were very peerlike. Spanierman deactivated the Spiderman profile but then started another one that was similar and had the same people as friends. School officials later opted not to renew the teacher's contract.

Spanierman filed suit, arguing in part that the nonrenewal violated his rights of free speech and association. The federal judge first observed that Spanierman's statements on MySpace were made outside of school and not within the scope of his employment as a teacher, so *Garcetti* didn't apply. The judge noted that a poem the teacher had posted on the profile expressing opposition to the Iraq War was protected by the First Amendment because it dealt with a matter of public concern. However, the poem was not the basis for the contract nonrenewal. Rather, the concern of school officials was the communication with students, which they viewed as disruptive to school activities. The judge agreed, citing this exchange with a student who used the profile name "Repko":

Plaintiff: Repko and Ashley sittin in a tree. KISSING. 1st comes love then marriage. HA HA HA HA HA HA HA!!!!!!!!!!!!!!!!!!!!LOL [can mean "laughing out loud"]
   Repko: don't be jealous cause you cant get any lol:)
   Plaintiff: What makes you think I want any? I'm not jealous. I just like to have fun and goof on you guys. If you don't like it. Kiss my brass! LMAO [can mean "laughing my ass off"].

The judge pointed out that it was reasonable for the school to expect a teacher with supervisory authority over students to maintain a professional and respectful association with them. Here, the teacher was acting more like a peer than a teacher. The judge also rejected the teacher's assertion that his right of association was violated by the nonrenewal. The judge questioned whether the right of association applies to a medium like MySpace, which does not itself express views on matters of public concern, and, if so, whether such a right of association implicates a matter of public concern. The case was dismissed (*Spanierman v. Hughes*).

The decision raises several interesting points. First, the judge viewed Spanierman as a public employee linked to the school, not as a private citizen acting on his own time. Thus, the judge relied on cases like *Garcetti* and *Connick* in considering issues involving scope of employment and expression on matters of public concern. Second, the right of association was viewed in the context of social networking sites like MySpace as a medium that may or may not take positions on matters of public concern, and not as being with persons linked through the medium to the person doing the posting. Third, while the right of privacy never surfaced in the case, it is doubtful that anyone who posts on the Internet can expect much privacy, even though social networking sites like Facebook seek to provide some degree of privacy to users.

Some abuses resulting from electronic communication are addressed by Texas Penal Code Section 33.07. That section makes it a felony offense for a person to use the name or identity of another person to create a Web page or to post messages on a commercial social networking site without consent and with the intent to harm, defraud, intimidate, or threaten any person. A person commits a misdemeanor offense by sending an electronic mail, instant message, text message, or similar communication referencing another person's name, address, phone number, or other identifying information without consent and with the intent to make the recipient believe that the other person was the one who sent or authorized the communication. This law does not apply to employees of service providers and commercial social networking sites, among others.

It also is important to note that most school districts now have policies that govern employee use of electronic media. For school districts that have adopted the Texas Association of School Boards model policies, Policy DH (Local) includes such a section. Districts also routinely have teachers and administrators sign an acceptable use policy (AUP) that sets forth the conditions for use of school Internet access routes, e-mail directories, and electronic communication devices.

Academic Freedom

Expression in the classroom is one of the most sensitive areas of education law, for it involves four sometimes clashing interests: the interest of the state and the local school board in seeing that the curriculum reflects the collective will of the community, the interest of the student in having access to knowledge and ideas, the interest of the teacher as a professional in controlling class discussion and choosing instructional methodologies, and the interest of parents in controlling their children's education. Traditionally, legislatures and courts have accorded states and school boards broad authority to determine the curriculum and to control teacher classroom behavior in the kindergarten-through-twelfth-grade classroom.

While federal courts, including the Supreme Court, have supported the claim of public college and university professors in a number of cases to a constitutionally protected right of academic freedom in the classroom, academic freedom has never developed as a definitive legal right for public-school teachers, though it has surfaced from time to time in later Supreme Court rulings. For example, in *Epperson v. Arkansas*, a 1968 Supreme Court decision, Justice Abe Fortas, who wrote the majority opinion, observed that "our courts . . . have not failed to apply the First Amendment's mandate in our educational system where essential to safeguard the fundamental values of freedom of speech and inquiry and belief" (p. 104). He went on to comment that "it is much too late to argue that the State may impose upon the teachers in its schools any conditions it chooses" (p. 107). In his concurring opinion in that case, Justice Potter Stewart agreed that a state could decide that only one foreign language shall be taught in the public school system, but he doubted that a state could punish a teacher for asserting in the classroom that other languages exist.

While the dimensions of a teacher's academic freedom right remain unclear, the U.S. Court of Appeals for the Fifth Circuit has ruled that public-school teachers do have a First and Fourteenth Amendment liberty right to engage in classroom discussion (*Kingsville I.S.D. v. Cooper*, 1980). The case involved a teacher of American history in the Kingsville, Texas, school system. The teacher, Janet Cooper, had taught on one-year term contracts for several years, her contract being renewed annually. In the fall of 1971, Cooper employed a simulation exercise to introduce her students to the characteristics of rural life during the post–Civil War Reconstruction era. The role-playing triggered controversy in the classroom and in the community. In a subsequent consultation with her principal and the district personnel director, Cooper was admonished "not to discuss Blacks" in class and that "nothing controversial should be discussed in the classroom." However, she was not advised to discontinue the simulation exercise, and hence she completed the project with her class. In the spring Cooper was again recommended for reemployment by the principal and superintendent. But, contrary to their recommendation, the board of trustees declined to issue her a contract.

The appeals court upheld the lower court's finding that Cooper's constitutional rights had been violated, declaring that "we thus join the First and Sixth Circuits in holding that classroom discussion is protected activity" (p. 1113). The court went on to declare that the proper test to determine if a teacher has abused the right is "not whether substantial disruption occurs but whether such disruption overbalances the teacher's usefulness as an instructor." Here there was no evidence that Cooper's usefulness as a teacher had been impaired. Indeed, school administrators had recommended that her contract be renewed. The appeals court affirmed the trial court's order of reinstatement and asked the lower court to reevaluate the amount of back pay and attorneys' fees due her.

Nearly a decade later, the Fifth Circuit refused to extend academic freedom to encompass a teacher's selection of an unapproved supplemental reading list (*Kirkland v. Northside I.S.D.*, 1989). Noting that Timothy Kirkland had not availed himself of school guidelines for compiling history materials, the appeals court took particular offense at the teacher's testimony that he alone had the authority to control the content of his world history class, even to the point of using sexually explicit magazines in classroom discussion. The court likewise took offense at the comments of Kirkland's attorney, who stated that a teacher could limit discussion to subject matter consistent with his own political views. The appeals court summarized its position: "Our decision should not be misconstrued as suggesting that a teacher's creativity is incompatible with the First Amendment, nor is it intended to suggest that public school teachers foster free debate in their classrooms only at their own risk or that their classrooms must be 'cast with a pall of orthodoxy.' We hold only that public school teachers are not free, under the First Amendment, to arrogate control of curricula" (pp. 801–802). The court affirmed the nonrenewal of the teacher's contract.

The Texas Commissioner of Education also has viewed the authority of the school board over the curriculum broadly. Recall that §11.151(b) of the Texas Education Code states that the trustees "have the exclusive power and duty to govern and oversee the management of the public schools of the district." In a 1980 decision, the commissioner of education cited the predecessor to this provision in striking down a teacher challenge to school board authority to specify the materials and techniques for teaching sex education (*Vawter v. Bandera I.S.D.*). The teachers argued that the board resolution severely and unduly restricted their ability to teach sex education properly. In his ruling, the commissioner observed that "it is difficult to imagine an area over which the Respondent's Board of Trustees may more appropriately exercise its broad managerial powers than that of determining which teaching resources and techniques are to be approved for a given course of study. As the Respondent undoubtedly possesses the authority in its schools to cease the teaching in its schools of sex education altogether, how can it be argued that Respondent lacks authority to determine how and by what means and techniques the subject will be taught?"

In *Villa v. Marathon I.S.D.* (1984), the commissioner decided against a teacher who claimed his right to academic freedom was violated when he was ordered not to show a movie to his science class. Though there was no district policy governing use of movies, the commissioner noted that the movie, entitled *The Prejudice Film*, had been approved by the administration for showing to the teacher's health class but had been deemed inappropriate for his science class. Noting that "a school district must have the right to require its teachers to teach science during science class," the commissioner rejected the man's claim. He upheld the nonrenewal of the teacher's contract for failure to follow the film directive, as well as other directives relating to the teacher's performance as a coach.

While teacher discussion rights in the classroom—as contrasted with the right to control teaching methodology—are protected under the weight of judicial authority, they can be abused and lose their protection. A 1985 decision of the Texas Commissioner of Education makes this clear. The decision, *Whalen v. Rocksprings I.S.D.*, involved a seventh-grade science teacher who became involved in an extended question-and-answer session with her class that encompassed matters related to sex education. In the course of responding to questions about AIDS, contraceptives, and the development of sperm, the teacher engaged in what school officials considered unnecessarily graphic description harmful to the emotional well-being of students of that age and grade level in the largely rural community. For example, with regard to learning more about sperm, the teacher advised male students in her class to go home, lock the bathroom door, and masturbate. The teacher was dismissed in midyear following a due process hearing, a dismissal the commissioner of education upheld, though with some reservations. He noted that what might not be appropriate in a rural community very well could be acceptable in an urban setting. The commissioner stated that for a teacher to show that his or her comments were protected by academic freedom, the teacher has to show that the comments were reasonably relevant to the subject matter of the class, had a demonstrated educational purpose, and were not proscribed by a school regulation. The last condition is interesting in light of the *Kingsville* decision, where the Fifth Circuit found such a proscription unconstitutional. In any case, it is clear that at some point a teacher's classroom discussion will lose its protected status and could serve as grounds for contract nonrenewal or termination.

In 1995 the commissioner declared that "instructing students is part of the school's curriculum and therefore constitutes matters of private concern" (*Hammonds v. Mt. Pleasant I.S.D.*). The commissioner's statement seems at odds with the Fifth Circuit's *Kingsville I.S.D.* ruling that classroom discussion is protected expression, even in the face of a directive not to discuss controversial topics. The *Hammonds* decision involved the nonrenewal of a teacher who used sexually explicit plays in her drama class and had students read portions of books containing sexually explicit language, despite directives to the contrary from the principal. The commissioner noted that when classroom expression is related to the school curriculum, "a district may impose restrictions on the expression so long as they are 'reasonably related to legitimate pedagogical concerns.'" The two decisions might be reconciled in that the expression in *Kingsville* involved expression on social and political issues (race relations), while the expression in *Hammonds* involved sexually explicit language deemed inappropriate for high school students.

One type of expression in the classroom that clearly has no constitutional protection is profanity. The U.S. Court of Appeals for the Fifth Circuit concluded in *Martin v. Parrish* in 1986 that use of profanity in a college classroom to "motivate" students is not related to any matter of public concern and is not protected by the First Amendment. The instructor in the case had exhorted his class with words like *hell*, *damn*, and *bullshit*. He continued to do so after a warning and was terminated. The court found that since profanity was not germane to the subject matter of the course and had no educational function, it was not necessary to consider the instructor's claim of academic freedom.

In another decision, the Fifth Circuit ruled that academic freedom does not include the right to award a grade. The case involved a professor who contested the request by his department chairman that he award a "B" to a student in his class (*Hillis v. Stephen F. Austin State University*, 1982). The court noted that academic freedom is a murky concept whose "perimeters are ill-defined and the case law defining it inconsistent." The court did not choose to find a teacher's right to award a grade within it. In a 1987 decision, the Texas Commissioner of Education cited the *Hillis* ruling in a case involving a teacher who was told to regrade a paper based on a parent's complaint but delayed doing so. After repeated conferences, the teacher was told to assign the paper a specific grade. Continued delay resulted in termination of his contract. Holding that the teacher had no right to award a grade as a matter of academic freedom, the commissioner noted that the local school board guidelines on grading, which all schools now are required to have, did not support the teacher's contention that his grading system had to encompass matters of form—for example, neatness, legibility, accuracy. Thus, the teacher had failed to follow the directives of his superiors to award a specific grade based only on content (*Cooke v. Ector County I.S.D.*). In a 1992 decision, the commissioner rejected a teacher's assertion of a contractual right to award a grade. The commissioner added that when a school district grading policy lacks clarity, the principal has the authority to establish directives for its interpretation (*Fleming v. San Marcos I.S.D.*). In a 1994 decision, the commissioner extended the principal's authority to include directives for assignments as well as grading (*Rendon v. Edgewood I.S.D.*).

Given the tenuous nature of the teacher's claim to classroom academic freedom, the following guidelines should be observed:

1. Teachers should be careful not to use their freedom of expression rights within the school in such a way as seriously to erode their ability to work with school administrators and colleagues.

2. Before teachers make any determination for themselves about what they can or cannot do in the classroom, they should endeavor to ascertain what school policy is with respect to curriculum practices and the role of the teacher.
3. While teachers do have a constitutional right in Texas by virtue of the Fifth Circuit decision in *Kingsville* to engage in classroom discussion, the right has not been accorded much support by the Texas Commissioner of Education. Teachers should make sure that the discussion is germane to their subject-matter area, is balanced, and has not undermined their effectiveness.
4. Teachers should proceed with caution when it comes to selecting materials and teaching methodology, as well as awarding grades. It is always best to check with board policy and administrative directives before proceeding.

Texas Whistleblower Act

In 1983, the legislature passed a law known as the "Texas Whistleblower Act" prohibiting a governmental body from retaliating against an employee who reports a violation of law to an appropriate law enforcement authority if the report is made in good faith (Texas Government Code, Chapter 554). Governmental body as defined in the Act means a political subdivision of the state, including a county, municipality, public school district, or special-purpose district or authority. However, a Texas court of appeals has ruled that the Act does not apply to charter schools. Charter schools, the court noted, do not fall into any of these categories (*Ohnesorge v. Winfree Academy Charter School*, 2010). It is up to the legislature to change the law in order for it to apply to them. Each governmental body is required to post a sign in a prominent place informing employees of their rights under the act.

"Law" is defined to mean a state or federal statute, an ordinance of a local governmental body, or a rule adopted under a statute or ordinance. The Texas Commissioner of Education issued a decision in 1996 in which he observed that a violation of school policy is not within this definition (*Lane v. Galveston I.S.D.*). A Texas appellate court ruled in 2011 that a University Interscholastic League (UIL) rule requiring parental residency for a football player to participate on the team does not fall within the "law" category because no statute requires the UIL to adopt such a rule. The lawsuit filed by the athletic director challenging his reassignment to an athletic trainer position after he notified both the UIL and school officials about the noncompliance was dismissed (*Galveston I.S.D. v. Jaco*). Because exactly what constitutes a law violation under the Whistleblower Act is open for debate, it is always wise for school officials to consult the school attorney when a whistleblower action arises.

An appropriate law enforcement authority is defined as part of a state or local governmental entity or of the federal government that the employee "in good faith believes is authorized to: (1) regulate under or enforce the law alleged to be violated in the report; or (2) investigate or prosecute a violation of criminal law" (Texas Govt. Code §544.002). Texas courts have ruled in several cases that it is not enough that a governmental entity has general authority to regulate, enforce, investigate, or prosecute. The concern is whether the employee had a good faith belief that the governmental entity is authorized to regulate under or enforce the law alleged to be violated in the employee's whistleblower report.

The Texas Supreme Court added some clarification to whether an employee's supervisor can be an appropriate law enforcement authority in a 2013 decision involving a physician's challenge under the Whistleblower Act to his being removed from faculty chair positions after informing his supervisor of alleged violations of Medicare and Medicaid requirements. In dismissing the physician's lawsuit, the justices pointed out that the term "law enforcement authority" refers to those who actually promulgate regulations or enforce laws or to authorities that pursue criminal violations. "The specific powers listed in Section 554.002(b) [of the Texas Government Code] are outward-looking," wrote the justices. "They do not encompass internal supervisors charged with in-house compliance and who must refer suspected illegality to external entities" (*University of Texas Southwestern Medical Center at Dallas v. Gentilello*, p. 689).

A few months later, the high court cited *Gentilello* in ruling that a school district's director of facilities and transportation did not meet the good faith belief standard when he reported to the superintendent, internal auditor, and board of trustees that the district's disposal of grease trap waste violated El Paso city ordinances and the Public Service Board's regulations. The court noted that the director produced no evidence that any of these were authorized to enforce the city ordinances and regulations outside of the school district itself. Responsibility for internal compliance only is not sufficient to meet the good faith requirement (*Canutillo I.S.D. v. Fannan*, 2013).

While Texas school districts generally are immune from damage suits, the Whistleblower Act creates an exception. Thus, the district can bear a heavy burden of responsibility if it takes retaliatory action against an employee who reports in good faith an alleged violation of the law. The Texas Supreme Court has defined "good faith" to mean an honest belief that the conduct is a violation of the law, a belief that is reasonable in light of the employee's training and experience. The court noted that the act would protect a public employee from retaliation even if the report were erroneous and even if the employee had a malicious motive (*Wichita County, Texas v. Williams*, 1996).

An employee or appointed officer who is fired or otherwise penalized for reporting may sue for injunctive relief, money damages, court
costs, and attorneys' fees. The legislature in 1995 capped the amount
of damages available under the act. Compensatory damages that can be
awarded for such injury as future pecuniary loss, emotional pain, and
mental anguish now are capped at $50,000 for governmental organiza-
tions with fewer than 101 employees, $100,000 for organizations with
101 to 200 employees, $200,000 for organizations with 201 to 500 em-
ployees, and $250,000 for organizations with more than 500 employees.
Exemplary damages are no longer available. Supervisors can be liable for
taking adverse personnel actions against whistleblowers up to a maximum of $15,000. A civil penalty against a supervisor cannot be paid by
the employing governmental entity. The Texas Attorney General has
advised that a school district that prevails in a whistleblower lawsuit
is under no obligation to pay the nonprevailing employee's legal fees.
Indeed, were it to do so, the payment would be a gift of public funds
contrary to Article III, §52(a) of the Texas Constitution (*Att'y. Gen. Op.
GA-0062*, 2003).

The employee has the burden of proving that the adverse personnel
action against him or her was in retaliation for reporting a violation of
the law, though the law presumes this to be the case if the termination
occurs within ninety days of a report being made. In order to establish
a whistleblower claim, the complainant must cite some specific law
prohibiting the conduct objected to. Otherwise, as one Texas court of
appeals noted, every complaint, grievance, and misbehavior could be
actionable (*Llanes v. Corpus Christi I.S.D.*, 2001). The case before this
court involved a secretary who argued that the district's hiring process
was illegal after she was not selected for another position and later her
employment was terminated. But she did not specify what law had been
violated, referring only to a district policy titled "Employment Objectives: Equal Opportunity Employment." The appeals court concluded
that the complaints she was raising did not allege any type of discrimination against her and none could be construed as implicating board
policy.

The governmental entity is not liable if it can show that it would
have made the same negative employment decision in the absence of
the employee's reporting. Before filing a whistleblower lawsuit, the aggrieved employee must initiate action under the grievance or appeal
process within ninety days of the alleged violation or its discovery by
the employee. No particular words are required, nor is it necessary to
refer to rights under the Whistleblower Act (*Moore v. University of
Houston–Clear Lake*, 2005). The purpose is to give government employers a chance to remedy the problem short of expensive litigation.
But when the employer throws up roadblocks, the employee does not
have to exhaust internal processes before resorting to litigation. This

was the thrust of a 2002 Texas court of appeals decision involving a clerk in the Fort Bend I.S.D. who maintained that her school principal falsified enrollment documents so that the principal's niece and another child could attend the school. The clerk reported the infractions and then requested a transfer because she felt the principal was making her job uncomfortable by removing all student files from the clerk's office. The clerk further alleged that the principal would not respond to her efforts to file a level-one grievance and that the district's human resources office also was not accommodating. In rejecting the school district's efforts to dismiss the case because the woman had not exhausted the district's grievance process, the appellate judges noted that the statute requires the employee only to initiate the grievance process, not exhaust it. The court pointed out that it would frustrate the act to require an employee to exhaust the grievance process when the district refuses to meet with the employee (*Fort Bend I.S.D. v. Rivera*, 2002).

The ninety-day window for filing a grievance begins once the retaliatory action against the employee is taken, even though the employee might have suspected before this time that an adverse decision may occur (*Texas Southern University v. Carter*, 2002). Once the grievance is filed, the employer has sixty days in which to render a final decision. Can the employee file a lawsuit before the end of the sixty days while the grievance is pending, or does doing so automatically result in dismissal of the lawsuit? The Texas Supreme Court has ruled that if an employee does file suit prematurely, the jurisdiction of the court is abated until the end of the sixty-day period or until the grievance decision is rendered, whichever comes first (*University of Texas Medical Branch at Galveston v. Barrett*, 2005).

In a whistleblower case involving the Castleberry I.S.D., a probationary teacher who contended that her contract had been terminated because she reported a sexual assault on one of her students by another student filed a grievance within the ninety-day period. But it wasn't resolved within sixty days. So on the sixty-first day, she terminated the grievance and filed suit. The district contended that the court did not have jurisdiction over the matter because the lawsuit was filed ninety-six days after the contract termination had occurred, including the days the employee spent pursuing the grievance. The court rejected the assertion, noting that a fair reading of the act's provisions indicates that the ninety-day clock stops while the grievance is being processed. If it were otherwise, employees would be unfairly penalized for following the grievance process (*Castleberry I.S.D. v. Doe*, 2001).

What if an employee files a grievance but then does not participate in the grievance proceedings? Can the district get the whistleblower lawsuit dismissed? A Texas appellate court has ruled in the negative. The case involved a school administrator in the Fort Bend I.S.D. who filed a whistleblower lawsuit contesting her employment termination as retaliatory for reporting the school's failure to comply with certain requirements of the Even Start Family Literacy Grant. Before filing the lawsuit, the administrator submitted a detailed written grievance to the district but then did not participate in grievance proceedings. The court noted that all the Whistleblower Act requires is initiating a grievance. Here the administrator had done so in a detailed written statement. Rather than toss out the lawsuit because the employee did not participate in the grievance process, the court noted that the appropriate remedy would be abating the sixty-day requirement for reaching a final decision on the grievance to allow the district more time to conduct its own investigation and any hearing process (*Fort Bend I.S.D. v. Gayle,* 2012).

EDUCATOR FREEDOM OF ASSOCIATION

Closely related to the right of expression is the right to assemble and, by implication, to associate. The First Amendment as applied to the states through the Fourteenth Amendment has been construed to guarantee the public-school teacher the freedom to associate. A key ruling is *Shelton v. Tucker* (1960). There the Supreme Court struck down an Arkansas statute requiring teachers to file affidavits listing their membership in organizations for the previous five years. Justice Stewart wrote in his majority opinion that "the vigilant protection of constitutional freedoms is nowhere more vital than in the community of American schools" (p. 487). He concluded that "the statute's comprehensive interference with associational freedom goes far beyond what might be justified in the exercise of the State's legitimate inquiry into the fitness and competency of its teachers" (p. 490).

In *Burris v. Willis I.S.D.,* a 1983 decision, the U.S. Court of Appeals for the Fifth Circuit emphasized that a teacher's freedom of association "is closely akin to free speech" and that in a small community like Willis issues affecting local schools can become matters of great importance. Thus, the Fifth Circuit found sufficient evidence that a vocational director's association with former school board members in a dispute over teacher use of school vehicles went beyond mere friendship and may have triggered the nonrenewal of his contract by a realigned school board. The case was remanded to the trial court to see if the board could show that it was not retaliating against the employee when it nonrenewed his employment. In *Guerra v. Roma I.S.D.* (1977), a Texas federal district court found that the three-year contracts of four public-school teachers with long service in the district were nonrenewed primarily because of their support of and association with an unsuccessful candidate for the school board. While the board advanced reasons for its action, the court found them unconvincing in this pointed and colorful statement: "The court finds these reasons an incredible basis for unfavorable action upon the employment contracts of four demonstrably able and praise-worthy teachers whose records were without blemish and who enjoyed the full support of their principal and superintendent. There are too many fish in this milk for me to believe it has not been watered. I find the reasons given pretexts, and their insubstantiality adds weight to the allegations that these teachers suffered political retaliation" (p. 820). The court ordered that the teachers be offered reinstatement and be awarded monetary damages, as well as attorneys' fees.

Texas statutory law protects the right of association as well. While school districts are precluded by state law from recognizing teacher unions as bargaining agents and from engaging in collective negotiation, Chapter 617 of the Texas Government Code recognizes that "An individual may not be denied public employment because of the individual's membership or nonmembership in a labor organization." (An expanded discussion of the legal framework regarding teacher associations and collective bargaining activities will be found in Chapter 5.) Further, TEC §21.407 prohibits a school district from directly or indirectly requiring or coercing a teacher to join any group, club, committee, organization, or association or to refrain from participating in political affairs. TEC §21.408 provides that professional employees have a right to join or not join any professional association or organization. The commissioner cited both provisions in ruling in favor of a teacher in the Ysleta I.S.D. who was notified by a district administrator that, as president of the Ysleta Teachers Association, she was ineligible to run for the District Educational Improvement Council (*Valencia v. Ysleta I.S.D.*, 1999).

STUDENT RIGHTS OF EXPRESSION

Until the mid-1960s, students had few rights in the public school setting. Traditionally, young people were under the control of their parents at home and under the control of teachers and administrators at school. What rights they had within the school depended on the policies of the school district and the practices of its employees. The legal doctrine of *in loco parentis* described the relationship of school personnel to students. Meaning "in place of a parent," it cloaked school personnel with the authority of a parent in supervising students at school. State courts rarely (and federal courts almost never) intervened in the student-school relationship; it would take an extreme case of abuse of *in loco parentis* authority to involve them, much as is the case today with the parent-child relationship.

The 1960s saw dramatic expansion of student constitutional rights, especially in the context of expression and association. There are many reasons—the pressures of minorities for civil rights protection, the liberalism of the Warren Court, abuses of *in loco parentis* authority in the schools, and student radicalism triggered by the Vietnam War. These and other forces resulted in the U.S. Supreme Court's declaration in the momentous *Tinker v. Des Moines School District* decision in 1969 that "it can hardly be argued that either students or teachers shed their constitutional rights to freedom of speech or expression at the schoolhouse gate" (p. 506).

The student rights movement was short-lived. By the mid-1970s federal courts began to accord greater deference to school district decision-making. By the 1980s, the expansion of student rights ended; indeed, some retreat became evident. In the remainder of this chapter we will review some of the important developments pertaining to student constitutional rights of expression and association in the public school.

Communication among Students on Campus

The *Tinker* case involved several public school students who wore armbands in school signifying their opposition to the war in Vietnam. School officials had learned that something like this might happen and, as a result, had developed a rule that any student who wore an armband to school would be asked to remove it and, if compliance were not forthcoming, would be suspended until the armband was removed. Interestingly, the rule applied only to the secondary schools. Thus, when the elementary students wore their armbands to school despite the rule, they weren't suspended. Instead, the teachers used the opportunity to talk about dissent in a democratic society. The older students, who according to the evidence were sincere in their beliefs, were suspended when they defied the rule. Through their parents, they sued the school, claiming the regulation and its enforcement infringed their constitutional right of free speech. In essence, after losing at the lower court level, they asked the Supreme Court to grant freedom of expression rights to public school students.

The Supreme Court agreed with the students, noting that the public schools cannot be "enclaves of totalitarianism." "School officials do not possess absolute authority over their students," the majority noted. "Students in school as well as out of school are 'persons' under the Constitution. They are possessed of fundamental rights which the State must respect, just as they themselves must respect their obligations to the State. In our system, students may not be regarded as closed-circuit recipients of only that which the State chooses to communicate. They may not be confined to the expression of those sentiments that are officially approved" (p. 511). Supporters regard *Tinker* as the seminal case for opening the school to a variety of ideas. However, it is important to point out that the high court did not address the extent to which elementary students have expression rights in public schools. This area of the law remained unclear for Texas public schools until the U.S. Court of Appeals for the Fifth Circuit addressed it in its 2011 *Morgan v. Swanson* decision involving the Plano I.S.D. That decision is discussed in the section later in this chapter on student distribution of non-school-sponsored materials on campus. In it, the majority of judges ruled that elementary students also are entitled to free speech at school.

But the Supreme Court did not adopt an "anything goes" viewpoint in the *Tinker* ruling. At several points, the majority opinion emphasized that student expression in or out of class that "materially disrupts classwork or involves substantial disorder or invasion of the rights of others is, of course, not immunized by the constitutional guarantee of freedom of speech" (p. 513). Since the wearing of the armbands in the public schools of Des Moines had generated no significant disturbance within the school, the Court decided for the students.

What are material disruption and substantial invasion of the rights of others? A riotous situation that prevents students from getting to classes and prevents teachers from teaching certainly falls into this category. For example, in a 1966 case that the U.S. Supreme Court cited with approval in *Tinker*, the U.S. Court of Appeals for the Fifth Circuit upheld a school board regulation prohibiting students from wearing "freedom buttons" when students not wearing them were harassed and disturbances occurred in the halls (*Blackwell v. Issaquena County Board of Education*). Less clear are situations that *might* lead to disruption or invasion of the rights of others if allowed to continue. Consider, for example, the wearing of a *Tinker*-like armband that signifies a day of mourning for the slain leader of a neighborhood gang or that signifies minority student opposition to the school district's use of "Dixie" as its fight song. In these instances, if a suit is brought, the burden is upon school officials to make a convincing showing that their actions in prohibiting expression, or curtailing it once begun, were appropriate under the circumstances.

It is important to note that the *Tinker* case involved symbolic expression that was meaningful to the students and to other persons in the school and the community. By contrast, a male student who dons Mickey Mouse ears at his high school graduation ceremony, walks backwards through the school library, or wears earrings is not engaging in cognitive expression of the type protected in *Tinker*. To claim First Amendment protection, a student has to demonstrate that his conduct conveys a particularized message and to show a strong likelihood that the message is understood by those who view it.

The Fifth Circuit addressed a related matter in an unreported but informative 2010 decision. The case involved the removal of a female cheerleader from the cheerleading squad for refusing to cheer for a student at a basketball game. The cheerleader refused to do so because the male student had allegedly sexually assaulted her at a party. The grand jury had voted not to indict the male student. The cheerleader maintained that her removal violated her right not to cheer as a form of symbolic expression protected by the First Amendment. The Fifth Circuit affirmed the trial court's rejection of the claim, noting that cheerleading is a school-sponsored channel of communication and under the U.S. Supreme Court's *Hazelwood* decision discussed in the next section, the student served as the mouthpiece through which the district could disseminate support for its athletic teams. Even assuming that the cheerleader's refusal to cheer was a form of symbolic speech, her refusal constituted substantial interference with the mission of the cheerleading squad. Recall that under the *Tinker* ruling student expression loses its protection if it causes material disruption or substantial interference with school operation and the rights of others. The cheerleader appealed the decision to the U.S. Supreme Court, which refused to hear it (*Doe v. Silsbee I.S.D.*, 2011).

In 1986 the U.S. Supreme Court ruled that indecent expression is entitled to no constitutional protection. *Bethel School District No. 403 v. Fraser* involved a high school senior who used sexual innuendo in a nominating speech during a voluntary school assembly for electing student body officers. The short speech evoked a lively and noisy response from students, including sexually suggestive movements by a few. However, no riotous situation occurred, and the assembly continued on schedule. School officials suspended Matthew Fraser for three days and denied him permission to speak at the graduation ceremony, though he had been elected to do so by his peers. Fraser claimed he used sexual innuendo as a speech technique to gain audience attention. In addition to being an honor student, Fraser was a member of the debate team and the recipient of the top-speaker award in statewide debate championships for two consecutive years.

The Supreme Court upheld the sanctions against Fraser. Writing for the seven in the majority, Chief Justice Warren Burger noted that the school has an interest in having students express themselves in an acceptable manner. While *Tinker* protects political speech, there is no constitutional protection for lewd, sexually explicit speech in the educational setting, though such expression might be protected outside school. *Fraser* gives school officials the authority to restrict the wearing of T-shirts and other apparel emblazoned with slogans and diagrams deemed indecent or in bad taste. A Texas federal judge ruled in 2005 that a middle school student in the Needville I.S.D. enjoyed no constitutional protection when wearing a T-shirt with the message "Somebody Went to HOOVER DAM And All I Got Was This 'Dam' Shirt" (*Mercer v. Harr*).

Are students exercising free speech when they wear bracelets at school with provocative slogans some consider lewd or indecent? That matter came to the forefront in 2013 when the U.S. Court of Appeals for the Third Circuit was confronted with a challenge to disciplinary action taken against two middle school students in a Pennsylvania school district for wearing bracelets at school bearing the slogan "I [display of a heart] boobies! (KEEP A BREAST)" before and during a breast-cancer-awareness campaign. The case was heard en banc, meaning that all judges assigned to the circuit participated, and generated a lengthy opinion that is the first to analyze the application of *Fraser* in this context. The majority noted that the students wore the bracelets to commemorate friends and relatives who had suffered breast cancer and to promote awareness of the disease among their friends. There was no evidence of material disruption, so *Tinker* did not apply. While the boobies message on the bracelets may be ambiguously lewd, the judges pointed out that the message can be viewed as commenting on a social and political issue. Thus it did not fall within the context of *Fraser*. The judges added that if student speech is plainly lewd, it can be restricted under *Fraser* even though it could be interpreted as political or social commentary.

The school district argued that if the boobies message is permitted, then what about more provocative messages like "I [display of a heart] Balls" or "feelmyballs" to support testicular cancer awareness? The majority refused to address these matters, simply saying that they await future litigation. The judges added that they doubted many parents would approve having their children wear bracelets with such slogans. The five dissenting judges found the bracelets to fall within the lewdness context of *Fraser* and would defer to the decision of the middle school officials to ban them at school (*B.H. v. Easton Area School District*). Whether the Third Circuit decision will be followed by courts in Texas should the issue arise here remains to be seen. Right after this decision was handed down, a federal district court in Indiana reached the opposite conclusion (*J.A. v. Fort Wayne Community Schools*). Thus, school officials should consult with the school attorney if similar bracelet-wearing occurs at school.

In 2007 the U.S. Supreme Court rejected a high school student's claim that his holding up a large poster with the words "Bong Hits 4 Jesus" during released time to view an Olympic parade passing in front of the high school is protected by the First Amendment. Five Justices agreed with the school principal that the sign evidenced support for drug use and held that such speech is not constitutionally protected (*Morse v. Frederick*). But the decision was very narrow. Chief Justice John Roberts, who wrote for the majority on the First Amendment issue, refused to endorse the school's position that any student speech viewed as plainly offensive enjoys no constitutional protection. Justice Samuel Alito wrote a concurring opinion for himself and Justice Anthony Kennedy in which they agreed that the message on the poster was not protected but drew the line at extending the ruling to other forms of student expression.

However, the Fifth Circuit went a step further in 2007 in applying the *Morse* decision to a case involving a sophomore with the initials E.P. attending Montwood High School in the Socorro I.S.D. who had written a story in a notebook about a pseudo-Nazi group that takes over the high school during the author's senior year. A good student with no disciplinary record, E.P. had gotten the idea of writing the fictional diary in the first person from his mother, who was taking a creative writing course. The student showed his notebook to another student. That student contacted a teacher. Later, the assistant principal talked with the student about the story and then sent him back to class. But upon rereading the notebook, the assistant principal concluded that the writing posed a terrorist threat under the school's student code of conduct. He suspended the student from school for three days and recommended him for placement in the district's disciplinary alternative education program (DAEP). He also had E.P. arrested, but the county attorney's office declined to prosecute the case.

E.P.'s parents filed a lawsuit, seeking a court order to have their son reinstated in the high school; his records expunged of any mention of the incident; and school officials barred from reading, disseminating, or discussing the contents of his writing without the boy's consent. The trial court ruled in favor of the parents, concluding that the facts did not establish a terrorist threat. Thus the suspension and other actions constituted violations of the student's First Amendment rights. However, the Fifth Circuit reversed that decision. The appellate judges viewed the notebook story to be so threatening to the physical safety of other students, like the drug threat in *Morse*, that it was not entitled to any constitutional protection. "When a student threatens violence against a student body," the judges wrote, "his words are as much beyond the constitutional pale as yelling 'fire' in a crowded theater, and such specific threatening speech to a school or its population is unprotected by the First Amendment" (*Ponce v. Socorro I.S.D.*, p. 772). In reaching that conclusion, the judges interpreted Justice Alito's critically important concurring opinion in *Morse* as not confined just to student drug-related speech but to include any speech that school officials view as threatening the physical safety of other students. For those leery of stretching the *Morse* decision this far, the same result could be reached by utilizing the material disruption and substantial invasion of the rights of others rationale in *Tinker* for disallowing student speech.

To sum up, public school students have a constitutional right to express themselves on controversial topics on school grounds so long as they do so without causing material disruption or substantial invasion of the rights of others. Under *Tinker*, students' commentary can pertain to matters involving themselves, the school, or the community. However, the *Fraser* ruling denies constitutional protection for student expression that school officials deem to be lewd, profane, or indecent, and the *Morse* ruling denies protection for speech that can be viewed as promoting illegal drug use. Of course, school officials are relatively free to discipline students for engaging in conduct that enjoys no constitutional or statutory protection at all. Hair length, matters of dress, running in the halls, and many other kinds of student conduct fall into this category.

School-Sponsored Student Publications

In 1988 the U.S. Supreme Court ruled in *Hazelwood School District v. Kuhlmeier* that school administrators have broad censorship powers over student newspapers produced under the auspices of the school as long as their actions are based on "legitimate pedagogical concerns" and as long as the school has not by policy or practice converted the school-sponsored student newspaper into a public forum where controversial views can be freely expressed. Justice Byron White differentiated interstudent communication from communication by students through channels maintained by the school. The former is personal in character and protected by the Court's decision in *Tinker v. Des Moines School District*. The school has broad control over the latter, the five-person majority held, because it is part of the school curriculum. Channels of communication maintained by the school include not only school-sponsored publications, such as newspapers and yearbooks, but also theatrical productions and "other expressive activities that students, parents, and members of the public might reasonably perceive to bear the imprimatur of the school" (p. 569). For an activity to fall into the school-sponsored category, the Court noted, it must be supervised by a faculty member and be designed to impart particular knowledge or skills. Thus, a school literary magazine or school play produced under the supervision of a faculty member likely would be a school-sponsored channel of communication.

In the words of the Court, educators are entitled to exercise greater control over student expression through school-sponsored channels of communication "to assure that participants learn whatever lessons the activity is designed to teach, that readers or listeners are not exposed to material that may be inappropriate for their level of maturity, and that the views of the individual speaker are not erroneously attributed to the school" (p. 570). The Court thus recognized that, as publisher of a school newspaper or producer of a school play, a school may delete material that the school considers potentially disruptive, ungrammatical, poorly written, inadequately researched, biased or prejudiced, vulgar or profane, or unsuitable for immature audiences.

A Texas federal district court judge later applied the *Hazelwood* decision to a lawsuit brought by the author of an environmental textbook that was highly recommended by the commissioner of education but rejected by the State Board of Education (SBOE). The judge ruled that under Texas law selection of textbooks is a form of private speech exercised by government to instill its values in the instructional program and that under *Hazelwood* the decision not to accept a particular textbook serves a legitimate educational purpose. In affirming the judge's decision in 2005, the Fifth Circuit took a more expansive view of SBOE authority over the curriculum. Rather than rely on the *Hazelwood* rationale, the appellate judges simply concluded that TEC §7.102(c)(22) gives the SBOE responsibility through textbook selection to see that the state's own message is communicated through the curriculum. "The Board does not encourage a 'diversity of views' but instead 'enlists private entities to convey its own message,'" the judges observed (p. 615). Therefore, neither textbook authors nor students can claim violation of First Amendment rights when a particular textbook is not selected (*Chiras v. Miller*).

Non-School-Sponsored Student Publications and Materials

The leading Texas decision on non-school-sponsored publications dates back to 1972. *Shanley v. Northeast I.S.D.* involved a school effort to ban an underground newspaper produced by students from distribution near and on the school campus. *Shanley* is important for what it says about the limits of school authority. The case involved several seniors at MacArthur High School in the Northeast I.S.D. of San Antonio who were suspended for distributing a student-produced newspaper called the *Awakening* on a sidewalk across from the school one afternoon after school hours and one morning before school opened. The paper had been produced by the students outside school without using any school materials or facilities. The distribution of the paper created no disruption at the time it was handed out or during school hours. The court described the nonschool publication as "one of the most vanilla-flavored ever to reach a federal court" (p. 964).

The students were suspended pursuant to a board policy that "any attempt to avoid the school's established procedure for administrative approval of activities such as the production for distribution and/or distribution of petitions or printed documents of any kind, sort, or type without the specific approval of the principal shall be cause for suspension and, if in the judgment of the principal, there is justification, for referral to the office of the Superintendent with a recommendation for expulsion."

While the court did not say a school may never discipline students for off-campus behavior unrelated to a school activity, it did note that geographical location is an important determinant in deciding who has jurisdiction—school, parent, police. Thus, "the width of a street might very well determine the breadth of the school board's authority"

(p. 974). The court pointed out that students, like everyone else, are subject to disturbing the peace, inciting to riot, and littering laws. In this instance, the school board had clearly overstepped its authority, for the off-campus distribution of the student-produced newspaper had created no disruption or interference with the rights of others on campus. In short, the school board could justify neither the rule nor its enforcement.

A clash of interests occurred in the Plano I.S.D. some years ago when elementary school students were not allowed to discuss or distribute tickets to religious events or to distribute candy canes, brownies, and pencils with attached religious messages during winter break classroom parties and other school events. However, students were allowed to distribute nonreligious material. The parents obtained a court order halting enforcement of the policy.

Then in 2005 the Plano school board adopted a new policy. As applied to the elementary campuses, the new policy permitted students to distribute materials thirty minutes before and after school at any entrance or exit to the school and at any gathering places approved by the principal. Students were allowed to distribute materials during designated recess periods and could leave materials on a designated distribution table for pickup. Students were not allowed to distribute materials in classrooms during school hours except at three annual parties designated by the district. The policy gave the school principal authority to permit distribution in other areas subject to reasonable time, place, and manner rules. Time, place, and manner rules do not focus on the content of the message but rather on the mode of its delivery. For secondary students, the policy was more permissive, in effect permitting distribution of materials anywhere except in classrooms during school hours. For both elementary and secondary schools, no distinction was to be made between religious and nonreligious materials. Another policy adopted at the same time applied some of the provisions to parents and other third parties.

The new policy also permitted Plano school officials to exercise prior review of materials being distributed. Prior review is a procedure whereby school officials can review non-school-sponsored materials intended for distribution on campus during school hours and screen out those that are deemed inappropriate. Most Texas school districts have adopted a prior-review policy with these components:

1. Criteria that spell out what is forbidden, e.g., materials that constitute hate literature or are obscene, sexually inappropriate, libelous, or disruptive of school operations.
2. Procedures by which students submit proposed materials to be reviewed.
3. A brief period of time during which the principal or other school official must make a decision.

4. An appeal procedure.
5. A reasonable time during which the appeal is to be decided.

The parents in the Plano case continued their lawsuit, arguing that nothing prevented the district from reverting to its old policy and that the new policy was still too restrictive in light of *Tinker*. After considerable litigation, the matter reached the U.S. Court of Appeals for the Fifth Circuit. In 2009 the court upheld the new policy (*Morgan v. Swanson I*). Then two years later the Fifth Circuit addressed the matter of whether the two principals who had prevented the elementary students from distributing religious messages could be liable for money damages for violating student free speech rights. All the judges assigned to the Fifth Circuit examined this question in a very lengthy and divided opinion. A majority of judges ruled that the principals were entitled to qualified immunity because the extent to which elementary students had constitutional rights of free speech at school at the time the disputes occurred was unsettled (*Morgan v. Swanson II*). (For more information about potential liability of both school districts and personnel in the context of federal rights, see the last part of Chapter 10.)

But then a different majority of judges went on to construe the *Tinker v. Des Moines School District* student free speech decision to apply to elementary students. In the words of the majority, "We hold this right—to engage in private, non-disruptive, student speech—is protected from viewpoint discrimination under the First Amendment and that the right extends to elementary-school students" (p. 396). This is a significant development in the law of student expression. This means that elementary students have the same right to expression as secondary school students as long as the speech does not cause material disruption or substantial invasion of the rights of others; is not lewd, indecent, or profane; does not promote drug use; and is not subject to defensible time, place, and manner rules (e.g., no distribution of materials in classrooms during instructional time). With regard to religious expression at the heart of the Plano case, the majority ruled that elementary students have the same right to express religious viewpoints, in the same manner as secondary school students, as long as what they express does not fall within the exceptions above or the religious speech could be construed to be school-sponsored. The latter is significant, because as we will note in the next chapter, public schools must be neutral with regard to religion.

Electronic Communication

As we discussed in Chapter 2 regarding the Internet, when students use school computers and websites to send out their messages, the students must comply with conditions set forth in policies and guidelines. However, when students use their own electronic communication devices (ECDs) to communicate with others through non-school-controlled channels, the matter becomes more complex. The U.S. Supreme Court has not yet addressed the matter, and the Court's student expression decisions described earlier pre-date ECDs.

Clearly, the authority of school officials to control the use of student-owned ECDs at school is greater than controlling their use outside of school. For example, simple time, place, and manner rules can be used to restrict ECD use during class, in restrooms and locker rooms, and the like. When students use their ECDs to engage in expressive activity outside of school via instant messaging, blog postings, and other forms of electronic communication, the authority of the school is more circumscribed. How much authority school officials have to discipline students in this instance depends upon the circumstances surrounding the communication and how closely it affects the interests of the school. And here judges are not of one mind. Three 2011 decisions—two companion decisions from the U.S. Court of Appeals for the Third Circuit and one from the U.S. Court of Appeals for the Fourth Circuit—illustrate the point.

In the first, a student in Hermitage, Pennsylvania, created a MySpace parody in the school principal's name on a computer at his grandmother's house. The parody centered on the word "big" and included such comments as "big fag," "big hard-on," and "big steroid freak." The student, Justin Layshock, sent the profile to his MySpace friends, and word of the profile reached most students at school. Students were able to access the profile on school computers until it was eventually blocked. The school principal learned about the profile from his daughter. District officials did not argue on appeal that the parody created material and substantial disruption at school. Rather, they asserted that Layshock's entry onto the school district's website to copy the picture of the principal constituted a trespass violation. The fourteen appellate judges unanimously rejected the argument outright. Furthermore, "[i]t would be an unseemly and dangerous precedent," the judges wrote, "to allow the state, in the guise of school authorities, to reach into a child's home and control his/her actions there to the same extent that it can control that child when he/she participates in school sponsored activities" (p. 216). The judges also rejected the assertion that the U.S. Supreme Court's *Fraser* ruling allowed the school district to punish the student for offensive expression occurring outside of school, noting that in the absence of foreseeable and substantial disruption at school under the Supreme Court's *Tinker* decision, school administrators are without justification to discipline a student for off-campus speech. Here the *Tinker* test was not met (*Layshock v. Hermitage School District*).

In the companion case, another Pennsylvania student, J.S., and her friend used a home computer to create a parody MySpace profile of her school principal that insinuated the principal was a sex addict and pedo-phile. The page included a photo of the principal taken from the school website. Although the student allowed other students to access the pro-file, MySpace access was blocked on school computers, and no student viewed the profile while at school. After another student informed the principal and brought a printout of the page to school, the student and her friend were suspended for ten days. Eight of the fourteen judges who heard the case on appeal (called an en banc hearing) agreed that the suspension violated J.S.'s rights. They noted no substantial disruption at school had occurred. They also noted that J.S. had not intended for the speech to reach the school and had taken steps to limit access to the profile so that only her MySpace friends could view it. They declined to apply the *Fraser* lewdness exception to profane speech occurring outside the school and during nonschool hours.

The six dissenting judges asserted that while the speech did not cause material disruption, it had the potential to do so by undermining the principal's authority and by undermining classroom learning. J.S.'s limiting the profile to her Internet friends still meant that twenty-two students were involved in the matter. Thus, the suspension was war-ranted in their view (*J.S. v. Blue Mountain School District*).

The third decision follows the thrust of the dissenting judges in the *J.S.* decision. At issue in this case was West Virginia twelfth grader Kara Kowalski's creating a discussion group webpage on her home com-puter dealing with herpes and targeting a fellow student, Shay N. Some one hundred persons on Kowalski's MySpace friends list were invited to join the discussion. Photographs and messages were posted, most fo-cused on Shay N. Included were words like "slut" and "whore" and a photograph with a sign over the victim's pelvic area with the words "Warning: Enter at your own risk." The targeted student's father saw the website and called Kowalski, who was unable to delete it. After con-cluding that Kowalski had created a hate website in violation of school policy against bullying and harassment, school officials suspended her from school and from school social events. The policy applied to any school-related activity or during any school-sponsored event. A separate Student Code of Conduct stated that "a student will not bully/intimi-date or harass another student." Through her parents, Kowalski sought to have the suspension overturned and the school policy declared vague and overbroad.

The Fourth Circuit affirmed the district court's decision granting summary judgment for the school district (*Kowalski v. Berkeley County Schools*). The judges ruled that the student-created website created the kind of interference with school operation described in *Tinker* that is beyond First Amendment protection. The judges noted that Kowal-ski knew that her MySpace communication would become known at school, as happened. Indeed, the judges pointed out, the group's name was entitled "Students Against Sluts Herpes." Had the school not intervened, there was potential for more serious harassment against Shay N.

With regard to the challenge to the validity of the school rule, the appellate court concluded that while the prohibited conduct had to be related to the school, "this is not to say that volatile conduct was only punishable if it physically originated in a school building or during the school day. Rather, the prohibitions are designed to regulate student behavior that would *affect* the school's learning environment" (p. 575, emphasis in original). Here, that Internet-based bullying and harassment did disrupt the school learning environment by their effect on Shay N.

What is interesting about these cases is the difference among the judges on whether *Tinker* applies to off-campus student speech in the first place and, if so, in what way. This will be a matter that the U.S. Supreme Court eventually will have to address. The Court refused to do so in all three of these cases.

Two guidelines for school officials emerge from these and other recent cases involving student electronic communication off campus. The first is the *reasonably foreseeable* determination, meaning whether the student knew or should have known that the electronic communication would reach the school. This guideline places responsibility on the student who composes the message but minimizes this responsibility in situations where the student may have communicated with someone else and that person, seeking to humiliate or embarrass the student, forwards the message or image to the school. It should be noted in passing that the degree of privacy students can expect when posting on social networking websites in any case is probably quite limited.

The second guideline is the *material disruption/substantial invasion of the rights of others* determination from *Tinker*. Given that the communication occurs off campus, where First Amendment protection is strongest, taking the terms "material" and "substantial" literally would help assemble convincing evidence that the communication negatively affected the school environment. In situations involving student cyber-bullying and cyber–sexual harassment on or off campus via ECD use, it should not be difficult to establish substantial invasion of the rights of others.

Because this area of the law is developing rapidly, it is important for school personnel, students, and parents to keep current. It is also important to make sure that school policies and provisions of the student code of conduct are carefully developed so that expectations of acceptable behavior regarding ECD use are clearly set forth and the extent to which the school can hold students accountable is clearly delineated. This is particularly important for student social communication occurring off campus. While the Fourth Circuit didn't seem troubled by the lack of clarity in the school board policy and student rules as to whether or not they applied to student behavior off campus, a federal district court judge specifically addressed this matter in a case involving a Pennsylvania high school student who posted four messages to an Internet message board—three sent from his parents' home. The messages related to the school's volleyball team and an upcoming match against another school. Jack Flaherty's posts insulted the opposing team and its players, calling them "purple panzies," telling them to "eat my wad ho," and claiming that the mother (a teacher at Flaherty's school) of a player on the opposing team was a bad teacher. Flaherty was punished pursuant to provisions of the school's student handbook that directed students to "express ideas and opinions in a respectful manner so as not to offend or slander others," and to refrain from the "use of computers to receive, create or send abusive, obscene, or inappropriate material and/or messages."

The judge found the student handbook sections to be overbroad because they placed no geographical limitations on the authority to punish student speech—students could be disciplined for speech occurring outside of school premises and unrelated to any school activity. Thus, the judge concluded that the provisions were unconstitutionally overbroad. The judge also found that the handbook provisions were unconstitutionally vague because the terms "abuse, offend, harassment, and inappropriate" were not defined adequately to put students on notice of the sort of conduct that was prohibited (*Flaherty v. Keystone Oaks School District*).

The Flaherty decision illustrates the importance of carefully crafting policies and rules pertaining to ECD off-campus use so that they specifically describe when and under what circumstances disciplinary action may be taken so as not to violate student rights of expression.

STUDENT FREEDOM OF ASSOCIATION

High school students have a right to assemble peacefully for expressive purposes in the vicinity of the public school, and students at the collegiate level have a relatively unfettered right to assemble and to associate. The U.S. Supreme Court ruled as much in two 1972 cases (*Grayned v. Rockford* and *Healy v. James*).

The support given the right of association, coupled with the recognition of student free speech rights in the *Tinker v. Des Moines School District* and *Morgan v. Swanson II* decisions, indicates that students also have a right to come together for expressive purposes on the public school campus as long as no material disruption or invasion of the rights of others occurs. Because the public school is not a public forum, however, the right of association does not automatically extend to nonstudents. Provisions of the Texas Education Code make this clear. Thus,

TEC §37.105 allows the board of trustees or its representatives to refuse to allow persons having no legitimate business to enter school property. Undesirable persons may be ejected upon refusal to leave peaceably. TEC §37.107 makes trespass on school property a crime.

Does the right to associate restrict school officials in deciding which student groups may and which may not function as school-recognized organizations? The answer appears to depend upon the type of group and the legitimacy of the school's reasons in denying status as a campus organization to a student group. For example, a federal district court in Michigan ruled in the early 1970s that it "is patently unconstitutional" to deny recognition in the absence of disorder to student groups because they advocate controversial ideas or take one side of an issue (*Dixon v. Beresh*). As noted in Chapter 7, the federal Equal Access Act precludes discriminating on the basis of speech content against non-curriculum-related student groups that meet on school grounds during noninstructional time except in narrow circumstances.

State law makes it a crime for a student or nonstudent to be a member of, pledge membership in, or recruit others to join fraternities, sororities, secret societies, and gangs in public elementary and secondary schools (TEC §37.121). In addition to being charged with a Class C misdemeanor, a student who violates this provision may be placed in a disciplinary alternative education program (see Chapter 8). According to a subsection of the statute, a fraternity, sorority, secret society, or gang is defined as a group that "seeks to perpetuate itself by taking in additional members from the students enrolled in school on the basis of the decision of its membership rather than upon the free choice of a student in the school who is qualified by the rules of the school to fill the special aims of the organization." Specifically exempted are organizations for public welfare such as Boy Scouts, Hi-Y, Girl Reserves, DeMolay, Rainbow Girls, Pan-American Clubs, scholarship societies, and other similar educational organizations sponsored by state or national education authorities.

Can a school district refuse to recognize a controversial student organization such as a gay student rights club if the students obtain a faculty sponsor and meet other criteria for school recognition? In the spring of 2004, a federal district court dismissed a case filed by two students and their organization against the Lubbock I.S.D. and several school administrators for refusing to permit the organization known as Gay and Proud Youth Group (GAP Youth) to post notices at the high school about its off-campus meetings, to use the district's public address system, and to meet on campus. A faculty member wrote a letter supporting the group's desire to post notices at the high school. And in a letter to the school board, the students asserted that their goal was to provide guidance to youth about nonheterosexuals and to improve the relationship between heterosexuals and homosexuals. They also noted that GAP Youth would strive to educate willing youth about safe sex and enhance family relationships. District officials made their decision after reviewing the group's website, which contained hyperlinks to sexually explicit sites. The district had adopted an abstinence policy applying to all matters involving sexual activity.

The plaintiffs argued that the district's refusal to accommodate them violated their First Amendment rights and, as discussed in Chapter 7, their rights under the Equal Access Act. With regard to the First Amendment allegations, the trial judge noted that the district disallowed any discussion of sexual activity on campus, whether homosexual or heterosexual. Such action was in accord with the U.S. Supreme Court's *Hazelwood* decision giving school districts the authority to control their educational program. The inclusion of links to sexually explicit websites on the group's website bolstered the school district's desire to protect immature younger students from harm, a legitimate concern recognized in the *Tinker* and *Bethel* decisions. The group argued that the school accommodated other groups with an antihomosexual agenda, but the court found no evidence to support the assertion. Thus, the school district and its officials were not engaging in unconstitutional viewpoint discrimination in refusing to accommodate GAP Youth (*Caudillo v. Lubbock I.S.D.*). This decision has not been followed by courts in other jurisdictions.

The U.S. Supreme Court has not yet dealt directly with student organizations. However, in a 1989 decision, the Court ruled that the right of association protected by the First Amendment relates to expressive activities and not to those that are strictly social. The case involved a Dallas city ordinance that restricted admission to certain dance halls to persons between the ages of fourteen and eighteen. The Court rejected the assertion that the ordinance violated a right to associate for recreational purposes (*City of Dallas v. Stanglin*).

SUMMARY

While the U.S. Supreme Court and U.S. Court of Appeals for the Fifth Circuit have extended expression rights under the First and Fourteenth Amendments to the U.S. Constitution to teachers and students, in neither case are these rights absolute. Except when acting pursuant to their job descriptions, teachers and administrators have a right to expression on public issues and to association in the community and within the school as long as their effectiveness as employees is not jeopardized and as long as the educational environment is not disrupted. Teacher classroom academic freedom rights are much less extensive. In the Fifth Circuit, teachers have a right to engage in classroom discussion as long as any resulting disruption does not overbalance the teacher's usefulness as an instructor. Teachers in Texas generally do not have the right to select teaching materials and methodology unless given this right by school officials.

Students have considerable entitlement to freedom of speech, assembly, and association in the public school as long as there is no material disruption of classwork or of school activity and as long as there is no substantial interference with the rights of others. Speech that is lewd, profane, or indecent, or advocates illegal drug use, is not constitutionally protected. School officials retain considerable control over the contents of school-sponsored channels of communication, such as newspapers, yearbooks, literary magazines, and school plays. The extent of their authority to exercise similar control over the contents of non-school-sponsored materials that either students or teachers wish to distribute on campus appears more limited. Following an announced system of prior review will lessen the chances that authority will be exercised inappropriately. School authority over off-campus student speech, for example in the form of a website developed by the student, is more constrained. It will require school officials to show a clear linkage between the interests of the school and the off-campus speech. This could be done by clearly establishing that the student's off-campus speech endangers the safety of students and teachers on campus. School officials are empowered by state law to limit student association with fraternities, sororities, secret societies, and gangs while on campus.

Underlying the cases in the expression area for both teachers and students is the complex and controversial issue of the purpose of schools. Are schools to be places where community values are inculcated and respect for authority instilled? Or are they to be marketplaces of ideas where students shed the trappings of the past and seek their own identity? There appears to be no consensus on the answer among either educators or judges, and this fact largely accounts for the disputatious character of the law of speech, press, and association in the public school arena.

SEVEN

Religion in the Schools

FEELINGS ABOUT THE appropriate role that religion should play in public education run deep and often are conflicting. This is particularly apparent when shifting demographic patterns increase religious diversity in school communities. School officials often are caught in the middle and must navigate a narrow channel between what is legally permissible and what is not.

The first part of this chapter looks at the legal framework applying to the role of religion in public schools. The rest of the chapter is devoted to an in-depth examination of contemporary religious issues in Texas schools. Because charter schools are public schools, the law referenced in this chapter generally applies to them. As we noted in the first chapter, private schools are not subject to constitutional constraints and are free from most federal and state statutes. Yet, governmental assistance to sectarian private schools directly or indirectly through vouchers and tuition tax credits does raise constitutional concerns, and we address these in the final section of the chapter.

LEGAL FRAMEWORK

No Government Establishment of Religion

The First Amendment to the U.S. Constitution begins not with a statement about free speech or press rights but with a statement about religion: "Congress shall make no law respecting an establishment of religion, or prohibiting the free exercise thereof. . . ." This statement, which applies to state governments and public schools through the Fourteenth Amendment, has two distinct components: the *establishment clause* ("no law respecting an establishment of religion") and the *free exercise clause* ("or prohibiting the free exercise thereof"). In this first section we will discuss the establishment clause.

Note that the word *an* appears before the word *establishment*. The U.S. Supreme Court has construed this to mean that not only is government not to set up a state church, but it also is not to aid any particular religion. In short—the Jeffersonian principle of separation of church and state.

Beginning with *Everson v. Board of Education* (1947), the first major case involving the establishment clause and education, the U.S. Supreme Court struggled to find a consistent way to decide establishment clause cases. *Everson* involved a New Jersey plan to reimburse the transportation expenses of parents who sent their children to parochial and other private schools. The Court began by noting that "In the words of Jefferson, the clause against establishment of religion by law was intended to erect 'a wall of separation between Church and State'" (p. 512). Applying that principle here, the Court upheld the reimbursement plan because its purpose was to enable both public and private school students to get to school safely.

A year later in *McCollum v. Board of Education*, the Court ruled that a release-time program in which religious instruction was given to students on a voluntary basis in the public schools breached the wall of separation. But four years later in *Zorach v. Clauson*, the Court upheld a New York program that allowed students interested in religious instruction to leave school early so they could receive religious instruction at off-campus centers, a decision that still stands.

By what rationale were these decisions being made? It was difficult to tell, in part because the Justices did not agree and sometimes switched sides. Considerable criticism greeted the Supreme Court decisions, and much of it continues. Given the close traditional linkage among church, home, and school, the criticism is understandable. Indeed, the first federal act to aid education, the 1787 Northwest Ordinance, stated that "religion, morality, and knowledge being essential to good government and the happiness of mankind, schools and the means of education shall forever be encouraged."

By the early 1970s the Justices had developed a set of guidelines to use in resolving complex church-state issues. The guidelines were:

1. The purpose of a challenged law or practice must be secular (as opposed to sectarian, meaning religious).
2. The primary effect of the law or practice must be one that neither advances nor inhibits religion (and thus does not impair the practice of one's religious beliefs).
3. The law or practice must not involve excessive entanglement between state and church (this guideline is most often related to state efforts to aid religiously affiliated private schools).

For a law or practice to be constitutional, it had to pass all three of the so-called *Lemon* guidelines, named after the 1971 *Lemon v. Kurtzman* decision in which they were advanced. To withstand an establishment clause challenge, according to the Supreme Court, a law or practice must be neutral regarding religion—neither promoting nor retarding it. Such was not the case with the posting of the Ten Commandments in public schools, a case reaching the U.S. Supreme Court in 1980. The

Court struck down the classroom posting as lacking a secular purpose, since "the Ten Commandments is undeniably a sacred text in the Jewish and Christian faiths" (*Stone v. Graham*). The Court affirmed that decision in 2005 (*Van Orden v. Perry*).

While some members of the Court have urged that the *Lemon* guidelines should be modified or abolished altogether in favor of a more flexible approach to resolving establishment clause issues, the full Court has not done so. It is widely presumed that any modification would make it easier to include manifestations of religion in public schools. Additionally, the Court has used two other considerations: whether there is government endorsement of religion and whether there is a psychologically coercive effect on objectors (*Lee v. Weisman*, 1992). This often has led the U.S. Court of Appeals for the Fifth Circuit, which has jurisdiction for Texas, Louisiana, and Mississippi, and federal district courts in Texas to employ five guidelines in determining establishment clause issues involving public schools: the three from *Lemon*, plus the two from *Lee*.

Provisions of the Texas Constitution similarly reflect a desire to separate church and state. Prior to the revolution of 1836, Texans had been forced to observe the state religion of Mexico, Roman Catholicism. To preclude a similar situation from ever arising again, the authors of the 1845 state constitution included a compelled purpose provision in Article I, §6: "no man shall be compelled to attend, erect, or support any place of worship, or to maintain any ministry against his consent." Section 6 also states that "no preference shall ever be given by law to any religious society or mode of worship." Article I, §7 of the Texas Constitution is very specific in prohibiting the expenditure of public dollars for sectarian purposes. It reads: "No money shall be appropriated, or drawn from the Treasury for the benefit of any sect, or religious society, theological or religious seminary; nor shall property belonging to the State be appropriated for any such purposes."

Free Exercise of Religion

Constitutional Provisions. The second component of the First Amendment to the U.S. Constitution is the free exercise clause: "or prohibiting the free exercise thereof." This clause assures that people shall be free to exercise their religious beliefs without government restraint or persecution. Like the establishment clause, the free exercise clause applies to states and their political subdivisions, including public school districts and charter schools, under the Fourteenth Amendment. When coupled with the protection accorded speech, press, and assembly in the First Amendment, the free exercise clause provides extensive protection for religious expression and exercise.

Article I, §6 of the Texas Constitution expresses much the same concern about religious freedom: "All men have a natural and indefeasible right to worship Almighty God according to the dictates of their own consciences. . . . No human authority ought, in any case whatever, to control or interfere with the rights of conscience in matters of religion. . . . [I]t shall be the duty of the Legislature to pass such laws as may be necessary to protect equally every religious denomination in the peaceable enjoyment of its own mode of public worship."

Even though there is wide latitude accorded freedom of religion in the U.S. Constitution and in the Texas Constitution, the exercise of the right is not absolute. There are limits to what courts will allow under the free exercise clause. Thus, while the Supreme Court has never permitted the government to punish individuals for purely religious belief, religious belief when accompanied by action is another story. For example, the U.S. Supreme Court decided in *Reynolds v. United States* in 1878 that, while Mormons have a right to believe in polygamy, Congress has a right to prohibit its practice. In the course of his opinion, Chief Justice Morrison R. Waite made the interesting observation that "Congress was deprived of all legislative power over mere opinion, but was left free to reach actions which were in violation of social duties or subversive of good order" (p. 164). "Suppose one believed that human sacrifices were a necessary part of religious worship," he added. "Would it be seriously contended that the civil government under which he lived could not interfere to prevent a sacrifice?" (p. 166). Of course, by preventing the practice of polygamy, Congress did interfere with the Mormons' religious freedom.

Closely related to the belief-action issue is the definition to be accorded religion. Does "religion" refer to established denominational churches only, or does it extend to a strictly personal belief system? For First Amendment establishment clause purposes, courts generally define religion as deity-based and having general recognition as a bona fide religion. But for free exercise clause purposes, the definition is more relaxed and can extend to a belief system that is philosophically rather than theologically based. As the Supreme Court noted long ago, "Freedom of thought, which includes freedom of religious belief, is basic in a society of free men. It embraces the right to maintain theories of life and of death and of the hereafter which are rank heresy to followers of orthodox faiths. Heresy trials are foreign to our Constitution" (*United States v. Ballard*, 1944, p. 86). Thus, belief systems such as Wicca and probably even Satanism are entitled to constitutional protection under the free exercise clause, just as are more mainstream religions. However, while a person can believe in whatever the person wishes, the person cannot practice beliefs in such a way as to disrupt the learning environment or interfere with the rights of others. Rules of order apply to everyone.

There is inherent tension in both the federal and state constitutions between the principle of separation of church and state and the principle of religious freedom. Too much of one may interfere with the other. For example, public school officials are concerned that if they allow students and teachers to proselytize their religious views on campus, the school will be promoting religion and thus breaching the separation of church and state. Conversely, if school officials deny them the opportunity to do so, students and teachers will argue that their free exercise rights are being violated. Similarly, school officials who inquire into the credibility of a person's religion before they grant an exemption based on the free exercise clause or state law arguably violate the establishment clause because government is deciding which religions are worthy of belief. How courts have responded to these concerns will be discussed later in the chapter.

Federal and State Statutes. In addition to these constitutional provisions, there also are federal statutes that protect religious freedom. For example, Title VII of the 1964 Civil Rights Act outlaws discrimination on the basis of race, color, religion, sex, and national origin in public and private employment. The statute does allow religious preference in hiring by sectarian private schools. Chapter 21 of the Texas Labor Code has similar provisions. The state has a general antidiscrimination law, §106.001 of Title 5 of the Civil Practices and Remedies Code, which prohibits officers and employees of state and local government from discriminating in a variety of contexts on the basis of race, religion, color, sex, or national origin. When considered together with a unanimous 1993 U.S. Supreme Court ruling (*Lamb's Chapel v. Center Moriches Union Free School District*), this law prohibits school officials from denying religious groups the same access to school facilities afforded to other community organizations. The *Lamb's Chapel* case was decided on the grounds of free speech. Since the Long Island school district had created a "limited public forum" by allowing use of its facilities after hours for social, civic, and recreational purposes, it could not grant access to all but religious groups. The evangelical Christian church in the *Lamb's Chapel* ruling had asked permission to use a room at the school to show a six-part film series presenting a Christian perspective on family life and child rearing.

In 2001 the U.S. Supreme Court handed down an important ruling on access of religious and other groups to the public elementary school campus. The case involved the Milford Central School in Milford, New York, which had a community use policy allowing community groups access to school campuses for, among other things, "instruction in any branch of education, learning, or the arts" and for "social, civic, and recreational meetings and entertainment events and other uses pertaining to the welfare of the community." However, the policy excluded individuals and groups wanting access for religious purposes. Based on this provision, the district refused to allow the Good News Club, a private Christian organization for children ages six to twelve, to hold after-school meetings in the school cafeteria. At the same time, the school granted access to the Boy Scouts, Girl Scouts, and 4-H Club. Evidence established that the adult instructor of the Good News Club began each meeting by having a student read a Bible verse and receive a treat for doing so. After attendance was taken, the club sang songs, then engaged in games focused on Bible verses. The adult leader read a Bible story and explained its application to the students' lives. The meeting ended with a prayer and with the distribution of treats and Bible verses for memorization.

The Court ruled 6-3 against the school district. As in *Lamb's Chapel*, the school had created through its community use policy a limited open forum for educational and recreational purposes and could not discriminate on the basis of speech within that forum. That is, it must accommodate all groups that engage in either educational or recreational activities, including those that do so from a religious perspective. The Court rejected the school's argument that the club should be denied access because it might convey the message to impressionable children that the school endorses religion. The majority pointed out that the meetings were held after school, were not sponsored by the school, and were not limited just to club members. Further, parents gave permission for their children to participate in the meetings. Allowing the club to meet on school grounds, the majority maintained, "would ensure neutrality, not threaten it" (*Good News Club v. Milford Central School*).

Just prior to the *Good News Club* decision, the Fifth Circuit grappled with a Louisiana school district's refusal to allow the Louisiana Christian Coalition to use school facilities after-hours for a prayer meeting. The district permitted its facilities to be used after-hours but not for partisan political activity, for-profit fund-raising, and religious worship and instruction. The Fifth Circuit upheld the district, but that decision was vacated by the Supreme Court following its *Good News Club* decision. The matter ended up back at the federal district court, which ruled in an unpublished 2003 decision that the district had to permit the Louisiana Christian Coalition to use the facilities because the group was engaging in both religious worship and discussion of family and political issues (*Campbell v. St. Tammany Parish School Board*). Given these decisions, it would appear difficult for a school district with a community use policy to exclude religious groups from holding religious services on school grounds. However, they must be treated no differently from other community groups.

There are several provisions of the Texas Education Code that also protect religious freedom. Included among them is TEC §25.901, which tracks U.S. Supreme Court rulings in declaring that a public school student has an absolute right to pray or meditate voluntarily and individually in school so long as there is no disruption of instructional or other activities. The statute also provides that no person may require, encourage, or coerce a student to engage in or to refrain from prayer and meditation. TEC §22.901 prohibits asking about the religious affiliation of anyone applying for public school employment. The prohibition extends to persons or organizations used to obtain positions for public school employees. It tracks the prohibition against religious tests for public office contained in Article I, §4 of the Texas Constitution, except that the constitutional provision allows asking an applicant whether or not the applicant believes in the existence of a Supreme Being. That provision was struck down in an unreported decision of a U.S. district court in Houston in 1982 as a violation of the individual's religious freedom (*Roe v. Klein I.S.D.*). In 1961 the U.S. Supreme Court ruled that requiring public officers to declare a belief in God constitutes a religious test for public office that invades the individual's right to religious freedom (*Torcaso v. Watkins*). As we have noted, federal law takes precedence over state law, so the Texas constitutional provision is null and void.

Texas Education Code §§25.151–25.156 protect student religious expression in the state's public schools, based primarily on the free speech clause of the First Amendment. Known as the Religious Viewpoints Antidiscrimination Act (RVAA), the statute provides that when one or more students speak at a school event, a limited public forum has been created requiring that student religious expression be treated in the same manner as other forms of student expression. Neutral criteria must be used to select student speakers at school events and graduation ceremonies. Obscene, vulgar, offensively lewd, or indecent speech must be restricted, though phrases like "indecent speech" are sufficiently ambiguous to sometimes trigger litigation. The school is to have a disclaimer indicating that it does not endorse or sponsor what students say at these events.

School districts must have a policy that implements the RVAA based on a model policy set forth in the Act. The policy must stipulate that all school events at which a student is to speak publicly for a set amount of time are limited public forums. Specifically listed are football games, other athletic events, opening announcements for the school day, and other activities such as pep rallies and assemblies. Only students in the highest two grades of the school holding positions of honor, such as student council members, captains of football teams, and class officers, may speak at these events. The policy is to set forth how the speakers are selected and rotated in compliance with statutory provisions. Student expression of a religious viewpoint is to be treated in the same manner as any other viewpoint. The district may issue an oral or written disclaimer indicating that the student speaker was selected on neutral criteria and that the remarks are the student's private expression.

The policy also is to recognize that irrespective of grade level, students who have achieved recognition as student body officers, homecoming kings and queens, prom kings, captains of sports teams, and the like occasionally address school audiences. When they do so, a limited public forum has been created, and discrimination against religious viewpoints is prohibited. Other provisions of the statute and the model policy for dealing with religious papers and presentations, religious expression in class assignments, the organization of student prayer groups, and student religious speeches at graduation will be discussed later in the chapter.

This, then, is the general legal framework surrounding the role of religion in public education. It is important to note that two constitutions are involved: federal and state. These constitutional provisions, coupled with federal and state statutes, provide ample opportunity for litigation, as the rest of the chapter attests.

CONTEMPORARY ISSUES

Concerns about the role of religion in Texas public schools have surfaced over a variety of issues. Among them are:

- The pledge of allegiance
- School prayer
- The teaching of creation-science
- Promotion of secular humanism and pagan religion
- Religion in classrooms, choir programs, and holiday observances
- Clergy in the schools
- Distribution of religious literature in schools
- Wearing religious symbols
- Student religious groups
- Religious exemptions for parents and students
- State assistance to private religious schools

The remainder of the chapter explores these issues, in turn, from the perspective of both statutory and judicial law. Occasionally, where judicial law in Texas has yet to develop, references will be made to leading judicial decisions in other jurisdictions.

The Pledge of Allegiance

Beginning in 2016–2017, Texas Education Code §25.082 requires school districts and open-enrollment charter schools to have both the United States and Texas flags prominently displayed in each classroom. Students are to recite the pledge of allegiance to both the U.S. and Texas flags in all public schools each day. Subsection (c) provides that a student is excused from doing so upon written request from the parent or guardian. However, there is some question whether a parent can control the wishes of a student on the matter, given the free speech rights of students as discussed in the Chapter 6.

In 1954 Congress added "under God" following "one nation" in the U.S. pledge. The constitutionality of this addition came before the U.S. Supreme Court in 2004 after a California parent objected to the provision. The Court avoided ruling on this contentious issue by holding that the parent did not have the authority to make a decision for his daughter in this case. Under the divorce settlement with the child's mother, the latter had that right when the two parents disagreed, and she did not oppose the pledge (*Elk Grove Unified School District v. Newdow*, 2004).

TEC §1.004 permits public schools and institutions of higher education to post the national motto "In God We Trust" in each classroom, auditorium, and cafeteria. In 2007 the Texas Legislature modified the Texas pledge to read "I pledge allegiance to thee, Texas, one state under God, one and indivisible." Parents filed a lawsuit challenging this change. They first argued that the word "God" in the pledge shows preference for monotheistic belief over polytheistic belief. The Fifth Circuit rejected the argument, noting that the term "God" is sufficiently generic that it can apply to both. The judges also rejected the parents' assertions that the modified pledge does not meet the secular purpose and government neutrality tests set forth in the U.S. Supreme Court's *Lemon v. Kurtzman* decision. The judges noted that the words "under God" are secular in that they recognize the religious heritage of Texas and that the legislature was not advancing religion in making the change.

The parents also argued that having teachers lead students in reciting the pledge places psychological coercion on dissenting students contrary to the U.S. Supreme Court's *Lee v. Weisman* decision (to be discussed later in this chapter). The judges ruled that unlike clergy who lead invocations and benedictions, teachers are not religious figures and the pledge is a patriotic, not religious, exercise (*Croft v. Perry*, 2010).

School Prayer

Prayer at school has many dimensions. Among them are school-sponsored or employee-led prayer; silent meditation; invocation, benediction, and religious speeches at commencement; baccalaureate ceremonies; and student-initiated prayer at school and school events. Each will be discussed in turn in this section.

School-Sponsored or Employee-Led Prayer. More than fifty years ago, the U.S. Supreme Court handed down two major school prayer decisions. The first, *Engel v. Vitale* (1962), involved a denominationally neutral prayer composed by the New York State Board of Regents: "Almighty God, we acknowledge our dependence upon Thee, and we beg Thy blessings upon us, our parents, our teachers, and our Country." The second case, *School District of Abington v. Schempp* (1963), involved state laws requiring selection and reading of passages from the Bible and recitation of the Lord's Prayer.

The Court ruled against the state-endorsed prayers in both cases. Since the state had in effect made a law respecting an establishment of religion in these cases, the Court ruled that the Constitution was violated. Writing the majority opinion in the *Engel* case, Justice Hugo Black noted, "We think that the constitutional prohibition against laws respecting an establishment of religion must at least mean that in this country it is no part of the business of government to compose official prayers for any group of the American people to recite as a part of the religious program carried on by government" (p. 425). Certainly, the U.S. Supreme Court's school prayer decisions leave no doubt that officially prescribed school prayers with or without student exemptions are illegal in public schools.

Arguments have been advanced that prohibiting state-mandated prayer programs in public schools inhibits the religious freedom of those who wish to say such prayers. Two responses to this concern have been advanced. First, these rulings do not preclude individuals from praying on their own in school. Second, a state-mandated religious program likely would have a coercive effect on those whose religious beliefs are not in accord with the program. When school communities become diverse in family religious background, religious factions in the community often raise objections to various expressions of religion in schools. The question then becomes, "Whose religion should the school promote?" Favoring the religion of the majority imposes the very oppression on religious minorities and nonbelievers that the establishment clause was meant to prevent.

In 1995 the Fifth Circuit ruled in a long-running case involving the Duncanville I.S.D. that school districts and their employees may not lead, encourage, promote, or participate in prayers with or among students during curricular or extracurricular activities, including before, during, or after school-related sporting events (*Doe v. Duncanville I.S.D.*, known as *Duncanville II*). The appeals court rejected the contention that such a restriction denies school employees a constitutional right to join students in prayer activities. Participation by coaches and other school employees would "signal an unconstitutional endorsement of religion," the court noted, since they are representatives of the school. However, employees are not required to leave the room when students pray on their own, and they must not treat student religious beliefs with disrespect.

The model policy set forth in Texas's Religious Viewpoints Antidiscrimination Act (RVAA) specifies that the time for opening announcements and greetings for the school day is a limited public forum and no discrimination is permitted against religious viewpoints spoken by students. As noted earlier, only students in the highest two grade levels who hold positions of honor, such as being a member of the student council or class officer, may speak. The selection and rotation process is designed to keep the school a step away from religious speech. In effect, the statute uses the student as a "circuit breaker" between the school and religion. However, in light of previous judicial decisions dealing with prayer at the opening of school, there is some question whether courts will view the time period and the circuit breaker approach the same way as does the legislature. What is clear is that neither the public school nor its employees may sponsor prayer at school.

Silent Meditation. In 1985 the U.S. Supreme Court was confronted with an Alabama statute authorizing public schools to set aside time for silent meditation or prayer (*Wallace v. Jaffree*). The Court concluded that the legislative history behind the "or prayer" addition to an earlier statute authorizing meditation revealed an unconstitutional effort to restore prayer to public schools. However, in his opinion for the six-Justice majority in the *Jaffree* case, Justice John Paul Stevens wrote, "The legislative intent to return prayer to the public schools is, of course, quite different from merely protecting every student's right to engage in voluntary prayer during an appropriate moment of silence during the school day."

TEC §25.082(d) requires a minute of silent meditation following the pledge of allegiance at the beginning of each school day, during which time a student may reflect, pray, meditate, or engage in any other silent activity that is not likely to interfere with or distract another student. Upon review of its legislative history, the Fifth Circuit upheld this provision in 2009, noting that it was enacted for the secular purpose of providing time for thoughtful contemplation, it does not have the primary effect of advancing particular religious beliefs, and it does not create excessive entanglement between teachers and religion (*Croft v. Governor of the State of Texas*).

In 2013 the legislature enacted a measure requiring an anniversary-date minute of silence at the beginning of the first class period to commemorate the September 11, 2001, Twin Towers terrorist attacks in each year that date falls on a regular school day (TEC §25.0821). The period of observance may be held in conjunction with the minute of silent meditation following the pledge. Prior to the observance, the teacher is to make a statement of reference to the memory of individuals who died in the tragedy.

Invocations, Benedictions, and Religious Speeches at Graduation. In 1983 the Supreme Court upheld chaplain-led prayers before the convening of the Nebraska Legislature (*Marsh v. Chambers*). Given this ruling and indications of a shift among some of the Justices toward greater recognition of free exercise rights, many commentators expected that the Court might approve the inclusion of invocations and benedictions at school commencement ceremonies.

But in a 5-4 ruling in *Lee v. Weisman* in 1992, the Court declared that school-sponsored sectarian and nonsectarian invocations and benedictions at school graduation ceremonies, where the school selects the clergy and advises them what kind of prayers to give, violate the establishment clause. The majority based its decision on two points. First, the state in the person of the school principal is pervasively involved in directing the religious exercise to the point of "creating a state-sponsored and state-directed religious exercise in a public school." And second, the practice exerts undue psychological pressure on the objecting student to participate. The majority observed that graduation is a seminal event in the life of a student, and this being so, it could not be said that attendance truly was voluntary. Thus, the majority viewed commencement prayer differently from the legislative prayer it had upheld in *Marsh*.

When it decided the *Lee* case, the Supreme Court returned a somewhat similar case to the Fifth Circuit. In that case the Fifth Circuit had upheld the Clear Creek I.S.D. school board's resolution leaving the inclusion of invocation and benediction at graduation exercises to the discretion of the senior class. After reconsidering its ruling in light of *Lee*, the Fifth Circuit once again upheld the Clear Creek plan (*Jones v. Clear Creek I.S.D.*, known as *Jones II*). Under the resolution, if the senior class votes in the affirmative, then an invocation and benediction can be given by a student volunteer. The message must be nonsectarian and nonproselytizing. The Fifth Circuit pointed out that, unlike the disfavored *Lee* practice, the Clear Creek prayer program did not implicate school officials in prayer decision-making and did not have the same psychologically coercive effect on objecting students. That ruling was again appealed to the U.S. Supreme Court, which refused to hear it in June of 1993, thus leaving the Fifth Circuit decision standing. Many commentators, however, found it difficult to see much of a difference between the two manifestations of religion at graduation.

In 1999 the Fifth Circuit once again addressed student graduation prayer. *Doe v. Santa Fe I.S.D.* presented the appeals court with a school district policy that abandoned the nonsectarian and nonproselytizing condition of *Jones II* when students deliver invocations and benedictions. The school district argued that the condition was not central to the *Jones II* decision. The Fifth Circuit disagreed. Prayers departing from that condition, the two judges in the majority wrote, "would alter dramatically the tenor of the ceremony, shifting its focus—at least temporarily—away from the students and the secular purpose of the graduation ceremony to the religious content of the speaker's prayers."

Rather than solemnizing the event, "sectarian and proselytizing prayers would transform the character of the ceremony and conceivably even disrupt it." The dissenting judge noted that the U.S. Supreme Court itself had found no distinction between a sectarian and a nonsectarian invocation and benediction in the *Lee* decision—both are unconstitutional in the context of a public school graduation ceremony. But the majority disagreed, observing that the nonsectarian/nonproselytizing condition in *Jones II* when students deliver the invocation and benediction is central to the decision because it mitigates psychological coercion on objecting students.

The Santa Fe school district had a fallback position. It argued that it had created a limited public forum by eliminating the nonsectarian and nonproselytizing condition. In a limited open forum, government permits speech by certain categories of speakers, e.g., enrolled students, provided that there is no discrimination among them. If some students want to give a sectarian, proselytizing invocation and benediction, the school district argued, the First Amendment free speech clause gives them that right. For the school district to say they couldn't do so would amount to unconstitutional viewpoint censorship. The appeals court majority was not persuaded, noting that neither the graduation ceremony, nor the portion of it devoted to the invocation and benediction, is a traditional public forum. Rather than grant access to a broad range of speakers at graduation, the judges wrote,

> [the district] has simply concocted a thinly-veiled surrogate process by which a very limited number of speakers—one or two—will be chosen to deliver prayers denominated as invocations and benedictions. These speakers, moreover, will not be given free reign [*sic*] to address issues, or even a particular issue, of political or social significance. Rather, they will be chosen to deliver very circumscribed statements that under any definition are prayers. (p. 820)

To rule otherwise, the court noted, would undermine its *Jones II* decision that student-led prayers must be nonsectarian and nonproselytizing. As discussed later in the chapter regarding student-initiated prayer at school, extracurricular activities, and athletic events, the *Santa Fe* case was appealed to the U.S. Supreme Court. However, in accepting it, the Court refused to hear the portion involving student-initiated prayer at graduation, only addressing whether it is constitutional for a school district to let students decide whether to have a brief invocation or message before football games and, if so, select a student to deliver it. The Court ruled that it is not. Later, a federal district court confronted with a challenge to a student graduation prayer policy in the Round Rock I.S.D. observed that the high court likely would apply the same reasoning to strike down student-initiated-and-delivered prayer at graduation as well (*Does 1–7 v. Round Rock I.S.D.*, 2007). In the *Round Rock* case, the judge determined that the passage of the Religious Viewpoints Anti-discrimination Act (RVAA) mooted the Round Rock prayer policy and thus a court order against continuing it was not necessary. But the judge did not go further to address RVAA.

So how does RVAA affect student prayer at graduation in the form of an invocation, benediction, or graduation speech? The Act's model policy requires school districts to state that graduation ceremonies are limited public forums where graduating students who hold a position of honor (e.g., top graduating students, class officers) may speak. The district may not discriminate against a student who chooses to express a religious viewpoint. Pursuant to a random drawing, a student who does not have another speaking role at the ceremony can speak at its beginning and a second student at its ending for purposes of "marking the opening and closing of the event, honoring the occasion, and participants, and those in attendance, bringing the audience to order, and focusing the audience on the purpose of the event." Though the policy doesn't say so, these times are commonly known as the invocation and benediction. Other students who have attained positions of honor, such as the valedictorian, also can speak on matters traditionally addressed in these ceremonies (e.g., honoring participants, giving the student's perspective on purpose and achievement). Time limits are to be set on how long a student can speak. Once again, no discrimination is permitted against religious viewpoints. A written disclaimer must be included in the graduation program identifying student messages as private speech and not reflective of the school or its officers or employees. The disclaimer is to state that the district refrained from any interaction with student speakers regarding their viewpoints on permissible subjects, as set forth in the policy.

RVAA's model policy provisions relating to religious speech at graduation are based on a set of guidelines issued some years ago by the U.S. Department of Education. The guidelines provide that "Where students or other private graduation speakers are selected on the basis of genuinely neutral, evenhanded criteria and retain control over the content of their expression . . . that expression is not attributable to the school and therefore may not be restricted because of its religious (or anti-religious) content." The guidelines permit the district to use disclaimers to clarify that such speech reflects the view of the speakers, not the school.

Can any part of commencement be converted into a public forum for the exercise of free speech by graduating seniors as RVAA attempts to do? The Fifth Circuit's *Doe v. Santa Fe I.S.D.* decision focused on invocations and benedictions, not on graduation speeches. However, the majority decision seemed to imply that the entire graduation ceremony is inherently a closed forum: "Neither its character nor its history makes the subject graduation ceremony or the invocation and benediction portions in particular appropriate for such public discourse." The judges added, "For obvious reasons, graduation ceremonies—in particular, the invocation and benediction portions of graduation ceremonies—are not the place for exchanges of dueling presentations on topics of public concern." They concluded with this colorful remark: "The limited number of speakers, the monolithically non-controversial nature of graduation ceremonies, and the tightly restricted and highly controlled form of 'speech' involved, all militate against labeling such ceremonies as public fora of any type. Absent feathers, webbed feet, a bill, and a quack, this bird just ain't a duck!" (p. 822).

At this writing, there are no reported cases involving RVAA. However, in the *Round Rock I.S.D.* decision referred to above, the federal judge offered this whimsical comment in a footnote, "The Court doubts whether the new statute will do much to resolve the issue of prayers at graduations, but expects the new legislation will be quite effective at keeping attorneys in fees for the foreseeable future." The absence of a definitive ruling from the Fifth Circuit or from Texas state courts on the matter leaves school officials in a quandary. For this reason, the school attorney should advise the district on what policy to follow regarding graduation speakers.

Baccalaureate Ceremonies. Under the rationale of the Supreme Court's *Lee v. Weisman* decision, baccalaureate ceremonies that are pervasively religious, school-sponsored, and held on campus violate the establishment clause. To avoid constitutional problems, a religiously oriented baccalaureate service should be held off school grounds and without school sponsorship. Alternatively, the service could be held on campus if the school is not the sponsor and if the facility is rented to nonschool sponsors pursuant to a neutral school rental policy. Under the Supreme Court's ruling in *Lamb's Chapel v. Center Moriches Union Free School District,* if the school opens its facilities to private groups, then it must make them available on the same terms to both religious and nonreligious organizations. A Wyoming federal court ruled some years ago that accommodating baccalaureate services in this manner does not violate the establishment clause (*Shumway v. Albany County School District*).

Student-Initiated Prayer at School, Extracurricular Activities, and Athletic Events. After the Fifth Circuit upheld allowing students to decide the matter of invocation and benediction at commencement in the interest of solemnizing the event, there was speculation that the court would uphold the practice at other school activities. But the appeals court refused to do so. A case in point is *Doe v. Santa Fe I.S.D.* There the district extended the graduation public prayer policy to football games. The district had tried to modify the policy to make it less a matter of prayer and more a matter of free speech. Accordingly, the policy provided that it would be permissible for students to deliver a "brief invocation and/or message" during the pregame ceremonies of home varsity football games "to solemnize the event, to promote good sportsmanship and student safety, and to establish the appropriate environment for the competition." The policy provided that under the direction of the high school principal, the high school student council was to conduct an election each spring to determine whether to have an invocation or message and, if so, to select a student from a list of volunteers to deliver it. The invocation and/or message had to be consistent with the purpose of the policy and had to be nonsectarian and nonproselytizing. The district hoped that the election process would provide a "circuit breaker" between the district and prayer. The Fifth Circuit was not convinced. Nor was the U.S. Supreme Court, which affirmed the Fifth Circuit decision against the district in 2000.

The six-member majority pointed out that the district really had not created a limited open forum for the free exchange of ideas. Only one student had access to the forum for the entire season. Further, the Court was concerned that the majoritarian vote process in effect would silence the views of minority candidates. Moreover, the majority noted, the school district had not insulated itself from religion by the election process. The board had developed the policy, had evidenced support for religion through the words "invocation" and "solemnize," and was providing the setting. As a result, the pregame prayer was stamped with the school's seal of approval. The Court also was not convinced that the voluntary nature of football game attendance made any difference, noting that there are many students who have no choice but to attend. Among them are the players and cheerleaders. Thus, as with the student in the *Lee v. Weisman* graduation prayer case, the delivery of invocations at football games improperly coerces those present to participate in an act of religious worship (*Santa Fe I.S.D. v. Doe*).

Something similar arose recently in Kountze I.S.D. in Southeast Texas when cheerleaders filed suit after the district prevented them from displaying banners emblazoned with Bible verses at high school football games. The district did so to comply with the Supreme Court's *Santa Fe* decision. The matter generated considerable public attention, particularly from those seeking greater accommodation of religion in public schools. They applauded the state district court judge's decision in favor of the cheerleaders. Whether appellate court judges at the state and federal levels would agree remains to be seen.

Clearly the Texas Legislature considered the implications of the *Santa Fe* ruling in crafting the provisions of the Religious Viewpoints Antidiscrimination Act. As noted earlier, RVAA refers to the time before football games, other athletic activities, and pep rallies, as well as to opening announcements for the school day and similar events at which students are to speak publicly, as limited public forums, where students selected in accord with the model policy can speak without discrimination on the basis of religious viewpoints. Unlike the student speaker selection process in *Santa Fe*, the manner of choosing speakers under RVAA is less dependent upon student elections. However, what is central to the thrust of the statute is the characterization of events like football games and pep rallies as limited open forums. The *Santa Fe* litigation suggests that both the Supreme Court and the Fifth Circuit may not view them this way. Time will tell.

Federal courts and the Texas Education Code recognize that students can engage in personal prayer at school and at school-sponsored extracurricular and athletic events separate and apart from school involvement. In *Doe v. Duncanville I.S.D. I*, the trial court pointed out that "Students may voluntarily pray together, provided such prayer is not done with school participation." The judge added, "Athletes may pray before or after games, but again, the activity must not suggest that school officials are sponsoring or participating in the prayer in any manner." The Fifth Circuit affirmed the decision. As noted earlier in the chapter, TEC §25.901 declares that a public school student has an "absolute right" to pray or meditate in school in a nondisruptive manner. Thus, if some or all members of an athletic team as private individuals want to say a prayer prior to the game on their own volition, they may do so. Such prayer is private because it is not school-led, -sponsored, or -encouraged. School employees may be present for custodial purposes, but they may not participate in the prayer.

Teaching Creation-Science

In *Epperson v. Arkansas* (1968), the U.S. Supreme Court had little trouble finding the absence of a secular purpose and neutral effect in a state law prohibiting the teaching of evolution in the public schools. Noted the Court, "The law's effort was confined to an attempt to blot out a particular theory because of its supposed conflict with the Biblical account, literally read." But could the state pass a law prohibiting a teacher from mentioning the biblical view of creation in a lesson plan on the origin of humans? A good case could be made that such a law would have the reverse effect of the Arkansas law—it would discriminate against religion, thus jeopardizing state neutrality with respect to religion, and might interfere as well with the teacher's limited right to freedom of speech in the classroom.

After a number of lower court decisions involving creation-science, the U.S. Supreme Court settled the matter with its 1987 decision in *Edwards v. Aguillard*. The case concerned a challenge to a statute passed by the Louisiana Legislature requiring Louisiana schools to give equal treatment to creation-science. The statute, entitled the Balanced Treatment for Creation-Science and Evolution-Science Act, required that if either evolution or creation-science were taught, the other theory also had to be taught. The law also required each school board to prepare curriculum guides and to make available teaching aids and resource materials on creation-science and prohibited a school board from discriminating against anyone who taught creation-science.

Applying the first of the *Lemon* guidelines, the majority of the Court found that the act's primary purpose was to restructure the science curriculum to conform to a particular religious viewpoint. The Court rejected the state's argument that the statute's purpose was to promote academic freedom. Teachers had ample freedom before the law was enacted to add other scientific theories about the origin of humans to the curriculum. By limiting them to only two views and requiring that both be taught, the Louisiana statute resulted in precisely the opposite of academic freedom.

The decision is important because it adds the U.S. Supreme Court's finality to earlier lower court decisions rejecting the mandatory teaching of creation-science in public schools. But, at the same time, it is important to note that a school district is not confined to teaching only evolution. Justice William J. Brennan, Jr., noted, in a key sentence, "teaching a variety of scientific theories about the origins of humankind to school children might be validly done with the clear secular intent of enhancing the effectiveness of science instruction" (p. 594).

Can the school district add a disclaimer to the teaching of evolution? The Fifth Circuit struck down this disclaimer in a 1999 ruling: "It is hereby recognized by the Tangipahoa Board of Education, that the lesson to be presented, regarding the origin of life and matter, is known as the Scientific Theory of Evolution and should be presented to inform students of the scientific concept and not intended to influence or dissuade the Biblical version of Creation or any other concept." The appeals court found that provision to be unconstitutional because its primary effect was to protect and maintain a particular religious view and because it also amounted to an endorsement of religion. However, the court limited its ruling to this particular disclaimer, noting it was not deciding whether any disclaimer read before the teaching of evolution would amount to an unconstitutional establishment of religion (*Freiler v. Tangipahoa Parish Board of Education*).

Case law in other jurisdictions indicates that courts do not look kindly upon school personnel who take it upon themselves to supplement the science curriculum by inserting their religious views. For example, in *Webster v. New Lenox School District No. 12*, an Illinois social studies teacher claimed a right to teach creation-science in order to balance views in the textbook with which he disagreed (e.g., the world is over four billion years old). The superintendent directed Ray Webster to avoid advocacy of a Christian viewpoint, though he could discuss objectively the historical relationship between church and state when appropriate to the curriculum. The Seventh Circuit upheld the trial court ruling that the teacher did not have a First Amendment right to teach creation-science. The judges noted, "Clearly, the school board had the authority and the responsibility to ensure that Mr. Webster did not stray from the established curriculum by injecting religious advocacy into the classroom" (p. 1007).

In 2010 the Fifth Circuit faced a case involving creation-science from a different perspective. Christina Comer, TEA's Director of Science for the Curriculum Division, contested the termination of her employment after she alerted science teachers to an upcoming presentation critical of teaching creationism in public schools. TEA's reason for the action was the director's alleged failure to follow its policy requiring employees to remain neutral and refrain from expressing opinions on curricular matters that fall within the authority of the State Board of Education (SBOE). Comer argued that the termination violated the establishment clause because the effect of the neutrality policy was to support religion. This is so, she contended, because the policy allows the SBOE to consider creationism as a legitimate part of the science curriculum. The Fifth Circuit rejected the contention, noting that the neutrality policy preserves TEA's limited administrative role in curriculum matters. It is the SBOE that makes decisions about the curriculum. In a footnote, the judges observed that by precluding employees from speaking out, TEA's neutrality policy could be viewed as restricting employee free speech. But the director had not raised a free speech claim, so the judges didn't rule on it (*Comer v. Scott*).

Secular Humanism and Pagan Religion

Some accuse the public schools of fostering an anti-God "religion of secular humanism" by not according religion a greater role in the curriculum. To date, the concept of secular humanism as a religion under the establishment clause has not been accepted by the judiciary. As the U.S. Court of Appeals for the Ninth Circuit has observed, "Both the dictionary definition of religion and the clear weight of caselaw are to the contrary" (*Peloza v. Capistrano Unified School District*).

Parents in the Houston I.S.D. argued in 1972 that the teaching of evolution in the public schools without critical analysis and without the inclusion of other theories in the lesson plan violated the establishment clause because it constituted state promotion of a "religion of secularism." Plaintiffs also asserted that their religious freedoms were compromised because the teaching of evolution constituted a direct attack on their religion. The district court rejected both contentions. District policy did not prohibit discussing the biblical view of creation, and the judge considered classroom materials discussing Darwinian evolution "peripheral to the matter of religion." Nor did the judge find any substantial interference with the right of plaintiffs to exercise their religious beliefs (*Wright v. Houston I.S.D.*). The *Wright* decision is noteworthy because it reconfirms the historic power of the school over the curriculum. The Fifth Circuit noted in affirming the district court's decision, "To require the teaching of every theory of human origin, as alternatively suggested by plaintiffs, would be an unwarranted intrusion into the authority of public school systems to control the academic curriculum" (p. 138).

An issue somewhat related to secular humanism has arisen in actions accusing school officials of unconstitutionally promoting a pagan religion by using an elementary school supplemental reading series called "Impressions." The series consists of some ten thousand literary selections and suggested classroom activities. Parents bringing suit primarily object to thirty-two readings that they contend promote the practice of witchcraft, claiming the readings promote the Wicca belief system. Most of the challenged selections ask children to discuss witches or sorcerers. Some selections also ask students to pretend that they are witches or sorcerers and role-play these characters. The parents argue that the readings and activities constitute impermissible advancement of religion contrary to the establishment clause and also evince hostility to the Christian religion by indoctrinating students in non-Christian values and denigrating Christian symbols and holidays.

In one of the cases, involving a challenge from Illinois parents, the U.S. Court of Appeals for the Seventh Circuit had trouble understanding what religion was being promoted. "[W]e have before us a party claiming that the use of a collection of stories, a very few of which resonate with beliefs held by some people, somewhere, of some religion, has established this religion in a public school. This allegation of some amorphous religion becomes so much speculation as to what some people might think" (*Fleischfresser v. Directors of School District 200*, p. 688). The court went on to find no violation of the *Lemon* guidelines. Nor did the court find the reading program substantially burdened the parents' free exercise rights, noting they remain free to teach their children religion. Further, the court observed that the government has a compelling purpose in using the series to "build and enhance students' reading skills and develop their senses of imagination and creativity." A Florida court of appeals drew from the *Fleischfresser* reasoning in rejecting a similar challenge to the observance of Halloween in an elementary school. The court concluded that Halloween decorations portraying witches, cauldrons, and brooms "make Halloween a fun day for students and serve an educational purpose by enriching their educational background and cultural awareness" (*Guyer v. School Board of Alachua County*, p. 808). Both the Florida Supreme Court and the U.S. Supreme Court refused to hear the *Guyer* case.

Religion in Classrooms, Choir Programs, and Holiday Observances

Teaching about Religion. The U.S. Supreme Court has commented in several decisions that nothing precludes public schools from teaching *about* religion. For example, in the 1963 *Schempp* prayer decision, Supreme Court Justice Tom C. Clark wrote that "one's education is not complete without a study of comparative religion or the history of religion and its relationship to the advancement of civilization. It certainly may be said that the Bible is worthy of study for its literary and historic qualities" (p. 225). Thus, the curriculum need not be sanitized of any mention of religion. In fact, if this were to occur, a strong argument could be made that the school had become hostile, rather than neutral, toward religion. There are strong pedagogical reasons for including religion in the curriculum. Given that we are a religious people, it would be difficult to teach social studies and history classes without reference to religion. Works of literature with religious significance are often read in English classes. Involvement of religion in the curriculum in this manner raises few legal questions as long as it is done objectively as part of an otherwise secular program of study. While the school may not give religious instruction on school premises, the U.S. Supreme Court has upheld release-time programs in which schools have the discretion to dismiss students for off-campus religious instruction (*Zorach v. Clauson,* 1952).

Teaching about religion requires a curriculum that does not favor or denigrate any particular religion or religion in general and teachers who remain neutral. Courses in comparative religion are most likely to fall into the permissible zone. Courses that focus exclusively on the Bible are more vulnerable to constitutional infirmities because the Bible is a religious tract and usually is taught from a distinctly religious perspective. This is particularly true if clergy are the teachers. Thus, it is not surprising that most Bible study courses do not pass constitutional muster.

A particularly insightful decision regarding the use of the Bible as an instructional source is *Herdahl v. Pontotoc County School District,* a 1996 federal district court decision in Mississippi. For fifty years, a Bible committee composed of members of local Protestant churches had sponsored Bible study classes in the district. The committee hired the teachers, and the district allowed them to teach on school district premises. Only instructors who expressed a fundamentalist Christian perspective were selected. While the district did not pay the teachers, it did assert supervisory authority over them and provided funds for books and supplies. After the Mississippi State Department of Education denied accreditation for the class, the committee developed a new curriculum entitled "A Biblical History of the Middle East." However, course content remained the same. It was taught as part of the elementary school curriculum and as a high school elective. The court found the course violated all the *Lemon* tests. It also constituted impermissible governmental endorsement of religion and unconstitutionally coerced students into participating in the program. These latter two standards of scrutiny stem from the U.S. Supreme Court's *Lee v. Weisman* invocation/benediction prayer decision and often are used by federal courts in addition to the *Lemon* tests. "The Bible study program," wrote the judge, "is part of a concerted effort by the religious sponsors of the class, fully condoned by the District, to inculcate students at North Pontotoc into the beliefs and moral code of fundamentalist Christianity—an admirable goal perhaps for some private citizens or for a private religious school, but a forbidden one for the government" (p. 595).

What is helpful about the *Herdahl* decision are the guidelines the judge listed for teaching Bible history in a constitutionally acceptable manner. These include teaching the course objectively as part of a secular program of education; not using the Bible as the only source of historical fact or as if it were actual literal history; requiring other readings from nonbiblical sources; not teaching religious doctrine or a sectarian interpretation of the Bible; and not accepting teachers for the class based in whole or in part on a religious test, profession of faith, or criteria involving particular beliefs about the Bible.

The Texas Legislature enacted a Bible study law in 2007 that appears to track most of these guidelines. TEC §28.011 provides that school districts may offer students in grades nine or above a half-credit elective course on the Bible's Hebrew Scriptures (Old Testament), and an elective course on the New Testament, or an elective course that combines both. If fewer than fifteen students sign up for one of these course, the district doesn't have to offer it. The courses are to address the impact of these books on the literature and history of Western Civilization. The law provides that students may not be required to use a specific translation of the Hebrew Scriptures or New Testament and may opt to use as the basic instructional material a different translation chosen by the school board or the teacher. To assure religious neutrality, the law permits districts to offer similar courses on the books of other religions for both local credit and state elective graduation credit.

Significantly, the statute requires the school district to follow all applicable federal and state law to assure that the courses are neutrally taught and can accommodate diversity of student religious views, traditions, and perspectives. Teachers of these courses must hold a minimum of a high school composite certification in language arts, social studies, or history and, where practical, a minor in religion and must complete staff development training using materials developed by the commissioner of education (TEC §21.459). As noted earlier in the chapter, because teachers are both government employees and role models, it is important that they not give the appearance of endorsing religion in the classroom.

Charter schools have not escaped lawsuits contesting their incorporation of religion in the curriculum. This is particularly true for charter school operators who either once were involved with religious private schools or espouse a philosophy that is closely aligned with religious tenets. A good illustration is a federal lawsuit brought by parents of elementary students against the Vanguard Charter School Academy in Grand Rapids, Michigan, and its educational management operator, National Heritage Academies. Among their claims, the parents alleged that the school taught morality from a religious perspective, permitted the inclusion of material from religious groups in student folders, and allowed a mom's prayer group to meet in a room at the school. The judge dismissed the lawsuit, noting that the school's Moral Focus Curriculum didn't specifically reference religion, material in student folders included announcements from nonreligious groups, and the parent meeting room was out of the presence of students and open to other parent groups (*Daugherty v. Vanguard Charter School Academy*, 2000). What helped the school prevail was its set of guidelines on how to avoid impermissibly advancing religion. The judge pointed out that "By establishing explicit and comprehensive guidelines for Vanguard teachers and administrators to follow, defendants [the charter school operators] have undertaken meaningful steps not only to prevent unconstitutional conduct by teachers, but also to avoid excessive entanglement" (p. 915).

A coalition of seventeen religious and educational organizations has advanced the following six guidelines for teaching about religion in the public school:

1. The school's approach to religion must be academic, not devotional.
2. The school may strive for student awareness of religion but should not press for student acceptance of any one religion.
3. The school may sponsor study about religion but may not sponsor the practice of religion.
4. The school may expose students to a diversity of religious views but may not impose any particular view.
5. The school may educate about all religions but may not promote or denigrate any religion.
6. The school may inform the student about various beliefs but should not seek to confine him or her to any particular belief.

If these guidelines are followed, the potential for a damaging lawsuit will be minimized.

Student Papers and Presentations on Religious Topics. May students give presentations and write papers on religious topics in their classes? Enacted as part of the Religious Viewpoints Antidiscrimination Act (RVAA) in 2007, TEC §25.153 tracks guidelines issued by the U.S. Department of Education as part of the No Child Left Behind Act providing that students may express their beliefs about religion in the form of homework, artwork, and other written and oral assignments free of penalties or rewards based on religious content. Such homework and classroom work must be judged by ordinary academic standards of substance and relevance, and against other legitimate pedagogical concerns identified by the school district.

Student religious expression in the classroom is not without limits. Federal courts have recognized the authority of school districts and teachers to maintain the classroom free of student religious proselytizing. As discussed in Chapter 6, the U.S. Supreme Court ruled in *Hazelwood School District v. Kuhlmeier* that teachers can control what students do in the classroom as long as there is a legitimate pedagogical purpose. Religious proselytizing presentations and papers that do not serve the purposes of the particular lesson being taught pose legitimate reasons to limit student religious expression. Several illustrations from the case law make this point.

In the secondary school context, the 1995 ruling of the U.S. Court of Appeals for the Sixth Circuit in *Settle v. Dickson County School Board* is a leading case. The Sixth Circuit's jurisdiction extends to Michigan, Ohio, Kentucky, and Tennessee. In *Settle*, a ninth grader in a Tennessee school district wanted to write a research paper on the life of Jesus. The teacher refused to approve the topic, contending that the student's strong Christian beliefs could lead to misunderstandings about any negative comments that the teacher might make in grading the paper. She also doubted the student would have to do much new research on the topic, contrary to the purpose of the assignment. The appellate court affirmed the trial court decision that teachers deserve wide latitude in giving assignments. While the judges agreed that students do not shed their constitutional rights in schools, "learning is more vital in the classroom than free speech." The court added, "Papers on the transfiguration of Jesus and similar topics may display more faith than rational analysis in the hands of a young student with strong religious heritage—at least the teacher is entitled to make such a judgment in the classroom."

The same circuit ruled similarly in a Michigan case involving an elementary school student. In this case, a second grader wanted to show, during show-and-tell, a videotape of herself singing a proselytizing religious song during a church service. The teacher had created the show-and-tell program to give each child an opportunity to develop self-esteem through oral presentation. The teacher did not permit the second grader to show the videotape because it would not serve the purposes of show-and-tell. Further, the teacher was concerned about spending considerable time viewing videotapes from other children if she permitted one student to show it. The teacher also was concerned about conveying an impression of religious endorsement if she permitted the student to show the tape. In an unpublished decision, the Sixth Circuit cited the *Kuhlmeier* decision in deciding that the teacher had not converted the classroom into a public forum. The purpose of show-and-tell was not to provide an opportunity for indiscriminate public expression but rather to give students an opportunity to gain experience speaking to the class. A videotape would not accomplish this goal (*DeNooyer v. Livonia Public Schools,* 1993).

The matter has surfaced in lengthy litigation involving Plano I.S.D. Details of that interesting lawsuit are set forth in Chapter 6. As noted there, after a lawsuit was filed, the district modified its policy against allowing elementary students and their parents to discuss or distribute tickets to religious events or hand out candy canes, brownies, and the like with religious messages in classrooms and on campus. The new policy allowed elementary students greater freedom to discuss and distribute these materials on campus thirty minutes before and after school, at recess, and at designated tables, but not in cafeterias and classrooms (the term "classroom" included hallways, gyms, auditoriums, and outdoor facilities) during school hours except for three annual parties designated by the district. For secondary students, the policy permitted wider distribution of religious materials on campus but not in classrooms. The Fifth Circuit upheld the modified policy (*Morgan v. Plano I.S.D.*). The ruling demonstrates once again that the school can control student religious expression in the classroom in the interest of avoiding disruption of the instructional program and the right of students to learn.

But there is a limit to how much control a school can exercise. A case in point is *Pounds v. Katy I.S.D.* In order to raise funds for its art program, an elementary school in the Katy district had students take home an order form from a private company for ordering holiday cards. The order form included the name of the elementary school and the names of the art teachers. If parents ordered the cards, they were to make a check out to the school. The printed cards included the student's own artwork along with a holiday message. Parents had a choice on the order form of selecting one of a number of messages, some secular and some religious (e.g., "Happy Chanukah," "Wishing you a Merry Christmas and Happy New Year," "Happy Kwanzaa/Celebrate Family, Community and Culture"). What triggered the lawsuit was the decision of school officials to black out an option that they believed advanced a particular religion in violation of the First Amendment establishment clause. This option read, "And she shall bring forth a son, and thou

shalt call his name Jesus; for He shall save his people from their sins.
—Matthew 1:21."

The central question was whether the school had sufficient involvement in the art-card program to warrant striking out the specific
religious message in the interest of remaining neutral on the matter of
religion. The federal district court judge ruled that the district did not.
The fact that parents had secular and religious options and made the
choice themselves from the list of messages provided by a private company attenuated the link between the school and religion. For the school
to act as it did constituted impermissible viewpoint discrimination not
justified by seeking to avoid an establishment clause violation.

A related matter involves the posting of religious messages on
school walls, bulletin boards, and the like. How much authority does a
school have to control the content of what students and teachers want
to post? An excellent illustration is a dispute over the decision of school
authorities at Columbine High School not to allow some commemo-
rative tiles to be posted in the school's hallways following the tragic
1999 on-campus shootings that resulted in multiple fatalities. Included
among the rejected tiles were those with religious symbols and messages. Viewing the hallways as a nonpublic forum over which the school
retains control, school authorities disallowed the religious tiles because
they did not want them to foster debate over religion. The U.S. Court
of Appeals for the Tenth Circuit upheld the district's decision, noting
that the school had a legitimate pedagogical purpose in controlling the
content of messages posted on its walls (*Fleming v. Jefferson County
School District R-1*, 2002).

Choir Programs. In the *Doe v. Duncanville I.S.D. II* case discussed
earlier in the chapter, the Fifth Circuit noted that there are legitimate
secular reasons for including religious music in school choir programs.
Forbidding the school choir to have "May the Lord Bless You and Keep
You" as its theme song "would force [the district] to disqualify the
majority of appropriate choral music simply because it is religious."

However, pervasive involvement of religious music in school-
sponsored musical events violates the establishment clause. In 1983
a Texas federal court prohibited a school district from having its high
school song recited or sung at extracurricular activities (*Doe v. Aldine
I.S.D.*). The court found the school song to be essentially a Christian
prayer, noted its pervasive presence at school events and activities, and
observed that school officials frequently led its recitation or singing.
The court also ordered that the posting of the prayer over the entrance
to the school gymnasium be removed.

Holiday Observances. In 2013 the Texas Legislature enacted a statute
intended to restore winter holiday observances in public schools. TEC

§29.920 allows districts to address the history of traditional winter celebrations, and both students and district employees are permitted to offer traditional holiday greetings such as "Merry Christmas," "Happy Hanukkah," and "Happy Holidays." Districts also are allowed to display on school property scenes and symbols associated with traditional winter celebrations, such as a nativity scene, Christmas tree, or menorah, as long as more than one religion is included or one religion and one secular scene/symbol. Given the thrust of this law, it would not be surprising if legal challenges under the establishment clause surface.

The U.S. Supreme Court has had a difficult time determining to what extent religion can be included in government-sponsored holiday observances. For example, the high court allowed a city's inclusion of a Nativity scene as part of an annual city Christmas display (*Lynch v. Donnelly*, 1984). But the Justices were closely divided. Further disagreement among the Justices about the "wall of separation" was apparent in a 1989 decision, in which a slim majority of the Court upheld the display of a menorah together with a Christmas tree at one location but struck down the display of a crèche standing alone at another location (*County of Allegheny v. American Civil Liberties Union*). In 1995 a majority of the Court agreed that the state does not promote religion by allowing the Ku Klux Klan to erect an unattended cross during the Christmas season in a public plaza adjacent to a government building. The Justices, however, were divided on determining at what point government accommodation might amount to unconstitutional endorsement of religion (*Capitol Square Review Board v. Pinette*).

In the public school context, the leading case on holiday observance remains *Florey v. Sioux Falls School District*, a 1980 decision of the United States Court of Appeals for the Eighth Circuit, which has jurisdiction over a number of Midwestern states. *Florey* involved a school policy allowing teachers to observe holidays that have both a religious and secular basis. Among them were Christmas, Easter, Passover, Hanukkah, St. Valentine's Day, St. Patrick's Day, and Halloween. The school policy allowed explanation of the nature of the holidays in an unbiased and objective manner without sectarian indoctrination, together with references to music, art, and literature, and the use of religious symbols. The policy had been developed by a special committee representing various constituencies and faiths in the community. The committee had been set up after complaints about religious favoritism in the schools had arisen. The court concluded that the program passed muster under the Supreme Court's *Lemon* decision.

One of the three judges in the case dissented from the ruling. He maintained that the policy was sectarian in purpose, suggesting that, if the goal were purely instructional, "the observance of the holidays of religions less familiar to most American public school children than either the Christian or Jewish holidays would seem more likely to increase student knowledge and promote religious tolerance" (p. 1324). Given increased religious diversity in many Texas school districts, the dissenting judge's observations have more credence today.

At the same time, there are limits on what teachers can do in observing holiday programs in their classrooms. A good example is the eighth-grade American history teacher in the *Herdahl* case discussed earlier who wanted to balance the secular components of school holidays by showing religious videotapes. He explained that many children believe they are dismissed from school in December because of exams or the pending arrival of Santa Claus and in April because of the Easter Bunny. So he showed videotapes such as *The King Is Born* and *He Is Risen*. The court was not impressed, directing the school district to forbid its teachers from engaging in such obviously sectarian activities (*Herdahl v. Pontotoc County School District*).

Clergy in the Schools

Whether clergy can meet with students on school grounds and under what conditions are matters determined by the school's visitor policy. For example, if the school permits students to invite parents and others from the community to join them for lunch, it cannot be in a position of discriminating against religion by banning invited clergy. At the same time, the school has the authority to set the terms of visitation. TEC §37.102 allows the district to establish rules to protect the welfare of students, and TEC §37.105 allows the district to require identification of all persons and to refuse entry to persons without legitimate business. If any visitors, including clergy, disrupt the learning environment or traumatize students by what they say, the school has the authority, indeed, the responsibility, to take appropriate action.

Seeking a more formal role for clergy in school affairs, the Beaumont I.S.D. instituted a volunteer counseling program in 1996 called "Clergy in the Schools." The program involved only clergy and was separate and apart from a more broadly based school volunteer program encompassing a variety of community groups. Under the Clergy in the Schools program, the district invited members of the local clergy to provide counseling to students during school hours. The clergy, most of whom were Protestant Christians, were cautioned in a district training program not to discuss religion or pray with students, quote religious materials, provide information about church services, identify their church affiliation, or wear distinctive garb. However, some clergy did not observe all of these conditions when they visited with students. Clergy visited each school once or twice during the school year. Prior to the visits, school personnel provided additional training and orientation at a local church, concluding with a prayer. When clergy came to the campus, school officials at each school summoned selected students out of classes and assembled them in another room, where they met with a number of clergy to discuss such matters as violence, peer pressure, racial issues, divorce, harassment, and alcohol and drugs. In addition to religion, clergy were not to discuss sex and abortion. Students were selected to reflect diversity in ethnicity, academic ability, and school deportment. While students could refuse to participate, parents were not notified or asked to give consent. The school principal and counselor attended the sessions. A lawsuit resulted, claiming that the program was an impermissible advancement of religion.

After protracted litigation, the Fifth Circuit sent the matter back to the trial court to determine whether other volunteer programs in the Beaumont schools provided services comparable to the counseling and mentoring by the clergy. If so, then the clergy program would not violate the establishment clause. After remand, the trial judge noted that though the district easily could have integrated the clergy program with nonclergy volunteers, the district had not done so because participating clergy feared it would water down the program. Based on an extensive review, the judge ruled that the absence of comparable nonreligious counseling and mentoring programs for students rendered the Clergy in the Schools program an unconstitutional advancement of religion (*Oxford v. Beaumont I.S.D.*, 2002).

Distribution of Religious Literature

It is impermissible for school personnel or outside organizations to distribute Bibles and other religious material to public school students on school grounds (*Meltzer v. Board of Public Instruction*, 1978). While it is impermissible to allow school personnel and religious officials to distribute religious material, it is permissible to provide a place in a public school where adherents of any faith may deposit religious literature for voluntary student pickup. However, to remain neutral, schools must accommodate requests from any religious denomination, and probably from secular organizations as well, to have materials available for student pickup. It thus may be preferable to have persons from the community wanting to distribute religious and nonreligious literature to students to do so off school grounds.

While school officials and outside groups may not distribute religious literature on campus, such is not the case with students. Student distribution of religious material is within the ambit of the First Amendment free speech clause, subject to reasonable time, place, and manner regulations instituted by the school (e.g., distribution limited to the area outside the cafeteria but not within it).

Wearing Religious Symbols

A clash of interests is evident in the context of the wearing of religious symbols in school. Both students and teachers occasionally want to express their religious beliefs in this fashion. The school, on the other hand, wants to avoid having its staff give the appearance of advancing religion and, in the case of students, to avoid allowing religious symbolism to be a guise for gang activity.

With regard to teachers, Title VII of the 1964 Civil Rights Act prevents discrimination in employment on the basis of race, color, religion, sex, or national origin. Under this law, the school district must accommodate reasonably a teacher's wearing of religious symbols and attire unless it would be undue hardship to do so. In addition to meaning a more than *de minimis* cost to the employer, the term "undue hardship" can encompass a noneconomic burden such as maintaining the appearance of religious neutrality in the public school classroom (e.g., directing a teacher not to wear a large cross that lights up periodically or to display religious materials on the teacher's desk).

As we will see in Chapter 9, Texas public school students have limited personal grooming rights under federal and state law. Thus, the school district can impose restrictive dress codes. However, dress codes cannot be so restrictive that they deny students their First Amendment rights to engage in religiously motivated speech and free exercise of religion. In 1993, a federal district court ruled in favor of Native American students in the Big Sandy I.S.D. who objected to a school rule against wearing long hair as an infringement on their sincere religious beliefs (*Alabama and Coushatta Tribes of Texas v. Big Sandy I.S.D.*). In 1997, students in the New Caney I.S.D. were successful in challenging the application of the district's gang-related apparel rule to the wearing of rosary beads. The school district was concerned that other students might associate the rosaries with a street gang and cause violence. But the federal district court noted that the students had worn their rosary beads outside their shirts for several months without incident. Applying the material disruption/substantial interference test from the *Tinker v. Des Moines* black armband case, the judge found insufficient evidence of actual disruption at New Caney High School to justify infringing on the students' religiously motivated speech (*Chalifoux v. New Caney I.S.D.*). As noted later in this chapter, the Texas Religious Freedom Restoration Act also has been applied in the context of student attire.

Student Religious Groups Meeting on Campus

In 1984, Congress enacted the Equal Access Act (EAA), which gives non-curriculum-related student groups access to public secondary schools during noninstructional time to engage in religious, political, philosophical, or other types of expression. The groups must be student-initiated, voluntary, and student-led. The district and school personnel are prohibited from sponsoring meetings but may attend in a custodial capacity. Further, nonschool persons may not "direct, conduct, control, or regularly attend activities of student groups." The school has the right to bar all nonschool persons or limit the number of times they attend. The law applies only to secondary school campuses in districts receiving federal financial assistance and only if school officials have converted the campus into a "limited open forum" by allowing one or more non-curriculum-related student groups to meet on school premises for expressive purposes (20 U.S.C. §4071(a)). "Noninstructional time" means the time when no instruction is taking place, i.e., before and after school or during a student activities period.

The U.S. Supreme Court ruled in 1990 that the EAA does not violate the Constitution (*Westside Community Schools v. Mergens*). The case involved a Christian club that wanted to use the high school campus before and after school for religious discussion and worship. The school argued that since it allowed only curriculum-related student clubs to use the campus, it did not have to grant access to Bridget Mergens's Christian club. Mergens argued that some of the student clubs were not curriculum-related. She pointed to the chess club, a surfers' group, and a service organization.

The Court interpreted a curriculum-related group to mean one that meets any of the following requirements: (1) the subject matter of the group is taught, e.g., French Club; (2) the subject matter of the group concerns the body of courses as a whole, e.g., student government; (3) participation in the group is required for a course, e.g., band; or (4) participation in the group results in academic credit, e.g., orchestra. Since the chess club, surfers' group, and service organization did not fit into any of these categories, they were non-curriculum-related. Thus, the school had a limited open forum and had to grant the same access to the Christian club as to the other non-curriculum-related clubs, i.e., the right to meet on campus before and after school and access to school bulletin boards, the PA system, and similar facilities to announce its meetings.

The school also had argued that if it allowed the Christian club to use the campus, it would be breaching the wall of separation between church and state. The Court rejected the argument, noting that the EAA does not violate the establishment clause of the First Amendment but rather represents a reasonable accommodation to the free speech and associational rights of public secondary students. In a key passage, the Justices observed that secondary students are sufficiently mature to recognize that the school is not endorsing religion by allowing students themselves to engage in religious communication on campus during noninstructional time.

While the EAA thus allows a student religious group to discuss religion and engage in prayer on campus during noninstructional time if the secondary school maintains a limited public forum, the law specifies that school personnel may only be present at these religious meetings in a *nonparticipatory* capacity. The school may not "influence the form or content of any prayer or other religious activity or require any person to participate in prayer or other religious activity." An interesting situation arose in New York when a student religious group sought to restrict its membership to those of the Christian faith. The U.S. Court of Appeals for the Second Circuit ruled that the school district was justified in requiring the group to have an open admissions policy. However, the group could apply the restriction to its president, vice president, and music coordinator (*Hsu v. Roslyn Union Free School District*).

In Chapter 6 we discussed a federal district court decision that rejected a claim by several members of a student gay rights group that Lubbock school officials violated the First Amendment in refusing to allow them to distribute information about their group at the high school and to meet on campus. The students also argued that the refusal violated the EAA. While recognizing that a limited open forum existed at the high school, the federal judge was not supportive of the students' claim. The judge noted that the act recognizes the need of school officials to maintain order and discipline. Permitting the gay rights group to meet on campus would materially interfere with the school's abstinence-only policy and could invite harassment, safety problems, and lawsuits. Most compelling to this judge was the provision in the EAA stating that nothing in the act limits the authority of school officials to "protect the well-being of students and faculty." If the group were allowed to meet on campus, the discussion of sexual activity could prove detrimental to the physical and emotional well-being of minors. The judge granted the school district's motion to dismiss the lawsuit (*Caudillo v. Lubbock I.S.D.*, 2004). This is the only case in which a gay student organization has been unsuccessful under the Equal Access Act.

It is important to note that the EAA does not limit the First Amendment rights of individual students to come together voluntarily during the school day for religious expression on school grounds, including prayer and the distribution of religious literature, so long as it is done in a nondisruptive manner (*Clark v. Dallas I.S.D.*). It also is important to recall our earlier discussion of the U.S. Supreme Court's *Good News Club* decision permitting religious organizations to meet after school on an elementary school campus under the terms of the school's community use policy.

Texas's Religious Viewpoints Antidiscrimination Act (RVAA) tracks the law in this area and goes beyond it. TEC §25.154 states that students may organize prayer groups, religious clubs, "see you at the pole" gatherings, or other religious gatherings before, during, and after school in a fashion similar to that permitted other noncurricular student activities and groups. No discrimination on the basis of the religious content of student expression is permitted. Religious groups and clubs have access to school facilities and channels of communication to the same extent as other student groups. The school can issue a disclaimer to disassociate itself from these groups and events.

RVAA goes beyond the EAA because it encompasses elementary students as well as secondary students and gives prayer groups, religious clubs, and religious gatherings access to campus during the school day. The dilemma that school administrators face in complying with this provision is that too great an accommodation of student religious groups and activities on campus lends support to the contention that the school is advancing religion. This is most likely to arise in the context of the elementary school, given the impressionable age of these students. Thus, it would not be surprising to hear complaints from parents of elementary students about the presence of Young Life, the Muslim Student Association, or Kids for Wicca at their school during the day. As an alternative, the district simply could declare that its elementary schools (or all schools) are closed to noncurricular student groups and activities. Of course, the school attorney should be consulted before doing so.

Religious Exemptions

In education, the most celebrated free exercise case is *West Virginia State Board of Education v. Barnette*, a 1943 U.S. Supreme Court ruling. There the Court ruled that the school board could not compel Jehovah's Witnesses to salute the flag. The students and their parents objected that in their religion saluting the flag was a violation of a tenet against worshiping a graven image (Exodus 20:4–5). The case is especially important because it asserts that the government may never compel a person to profess a belief.

Writing for the majority, Justice Robert H. Jackson emphasized that the First Amendment was especially designed to protect freedom of spirit and intellect. "If there is any fixed star in our constitutional constellation, it is that no official, high or petty, can prescribe what shall be orthodox in politics, nationalism, religion, or other matters of opinion or force citizens to confess by word or act their faith therein" (p. 642). Jackson added that the ruling was not just confined to those who assert a religious basis for their refusal. "While religion supplies appellees' motive for enduring the discomforts of making the issue in this case, many citizens who do not share these religious views hold such a compulsory rite to infringe constitutional liberty of the individual." Thus a student who refuses to salute the flag for philosophical reasons is entitled to the same exemption as a student who asserts a religious reason for not doing so.

While Justice Jackson was speaking in sweeping terms about the First Amendment, it must be remembered that the decision was announced in the midst of World War II. The excesses of Nazi Germany in promoting nationalism among the youth of that country undoubtedly played a part in the Justice's choice of wording. The West Virginia decision has been confined to the flag-salute context and by no means has been read to allow students and their parents a general First Amendment right to seek exemptions from compulsory school or curriculum requirements (however, as noted in Chapter 1 and below, Texas Education Code §26.010 does give parents the right to request exemptions from school activities to which they object on religious or moral grounds).

Another U.S. Supreme Court decision of great importance is *Wisconsin v. Yoder* (1972), involving the religious objections of the Old Order Amish to compulsory schooling beyond the eighth grade. The Court ruled for the Amish in this instance but cautioned that it would be extremely reluctant to extend the ruling to other religions. To date, no other religion has been given as broad an exemption as the Old Order Amish.

The U.S. Supreme Court has ruled that centrality of faith is not a prerequisite to finding a free exercise violation; sincerity of belief is sufficient (*Employment Division of Oregon Department of Human Resources v. Smith*). The case involved denial of unemployment benefits to a worker who was terminated for using peyote, an illegal hallucinogen, in a Native American religious ceremony. In refusing to overturn the lower court decision against the worker, the high court concluded that religion is not entitled to a special exemption from general laws that are neutrally applied. In the process of deciding the case, the Court made its observation about centrality versus sincerity.

In holding that religion is not entitled to exemptions from general laws that are neutrally applied, the Court in the *Smith* case had to confront the special exemption accorded the Old Order Amish from the compulsory school law in *Wisconsin v. Yoder*. The Court distinguished that ruling by pointing out that *two* rights were involved: the free exercise of religion and the right of parents to control their children's upbringing. The Court termed this a "hybrid" claim. But lower federal courts have not been very supportive of the claim in subsequent cases. For example, in 1998 the Tenth Circuit rejected the assertion of Oklahoma parents that a school district's refusal to permit their homeschooled child to attend school part-time violated both the free exercise of religion and parent rights. Wrote the Tenth Circuit, "Whatever the *Smith* hybrid-rights theory may ultimately mean, we believe that it at least requires a colorable showing of infringement of recognized and specific constitutional rights, rather than the mere invocation of a general right such as the right to control the education of one's child" (*Swanson v. Guthrie I.S.D.*, p. 700).

In 2009 the Fifth Circuit cited *Swanson* in rejecting claims by parents that the University Interscholastic League's (UIL) refusal to extend membership to the Cornerstone Christian Schools, located in San Antonio, intruded on both their free exercise of religion and their right to control their children's upbringing (*Cornerstone Christian Schools v. University Interscholastic League*). The UIL decision was based on its rule excluding private schools that qualify for membership in other athletic organizations. Cornerstone Christian Schools fell into this category. The appellate judges could discern no undue burden on either parental free exercise of religion or due process rights or any combination thereof. The lawsuit, they noted, was more about an asserted right of the student to participate in interscholastic competition than parental rights. As noted in Chapter 2, participation in interscholastic competition is a privilege, not a right.

In reaction to the *Smith* decision, the Texas Legislature enacted the Texas Religious Freedom Restoration Act (TRFRA) in 1999. Codified as Civil Practices and Remedies Code §§110.001–110.012, TRFRA provides that a governmental agency may not "substantially burden a person's free exercise of religion" unless it can establish that the application of burden furthers "a compelling governmental interest" and is the "least restrictive means of furthering that interest." The term "free exercise of religion" is defined to mean an act or refusal to act that is substantially motivated by sincere religious belief. The law does not require that the act or refusal to act must be linked to a central part or requirement of the person's faith, only that it be "sincere." This has the effect of conveying broad support for religiously motivated behavior. At the same time, the burden is heavy on government to justify its actions that substantially burden such behavior. Penalties include injunctive relief, compensatory damages not exceeding $10,000 for each violation, as well as reasonable attorneys' fees, court costs, and other expenses. Only governmental entities, such as the school district itself, can be sued. Individuals cannot be sued in their individual capacities. Further, the law expressly waives sovereign immunity. Punitive damages, however, are not available.

The person claiming to be burdened generally must give sixty days' notice by certified mail, return receipt requested, before filing a lawsuit, thus giving the governmental agency an opportunity to remedy the alleged burden. However, the sixty-day notice is not required if the threat to substantially burden the person's free exercise of religion is imminent and the person did not have knowledge of the government's exercise of authority in time to comply with the notice requirement.

TRFRA was the focus of a 2010 Fifth Circuit ruling involving a Native American elementary school student in the Needville I.S.D. who was restricted from wearing his long hair in two braids down his back. The effort by school officials to accommodate the boy's religion by permitting him to wear his long hair in a bun on the top of his head or as a single braid tucked into the back of his shirt was rejected. The school district's dress code provided that boys' hair was not to cover any part of the ear or touch the top of the back shirt collar in the interest of teaching hygiene, instilling discipline, preventing disruption, avoiding safety hazards, and asserting authority.

The appellate judges agreed with the trial court that the student's religious motivation to wear his hair visibly long was sincere and that the school district's proposed alternatives substantially burdened his belief. While the alternatives the district proposed would still allow the student to wear his hair long when he was not in school, two of the judges pointed out that school is a critical period of time in a child's development and thus preventing him from visibly wearing long hair during the day substantially burdens his religious belief under TRFRA. Undercutting the school district's assertions was its policy permitting girls to wear their hair visibly long (*A.A. v. Needville I.S.D.*).

TRFRA also surfaced in a 2013 federal district court ruling involving Northside I.S.D.'s pilot program requiring students on two campuses to wear Smart ID badges. Smart ID badges look like ordinary picture badges but also carry a battery-operated radio frequency embedded chip that, among other things, enables staff to know the whereabouts of students on campus.

The father of a high school student attending a magnet school where the pilot program was about to begin objected to the tracking badges as violating the family's religious beliefs. The chip in the badge, he and his daughter maintained, was "the mark of the beast." He also argued that wearing the badge with the electrical chip close to the chest posed a health risk. District officials told the parent that his daughter would be allowed to wear the badge without the chip. But the father continued to object, noting that even wearing the badge without the chip conveyed the message that the family supported the program. District officials told the father that his daughter could transfer back to her home campus where only picture badges were required if she refused to wear the tracking badge. She could also hand out literature against the pilot program in compliance with school rules. The father refused to accept these accommodations and sought a preliminary injunction against the tracking program.

The federal judge ruled against the father. The judge first pointed out that the tracking badge requirement is a neutral program applying to all students at the high school where the magnet program was located and thus complies with the U.S. Supreme Court's *Smith* decision. With regard to TRFRA, the judge noted that the student's objection to wearing the badge without the chip was not motivated by sincere religious belief. Further, the district had established a compelling interest in providing security through the tracking badge requirement and had done so in the least restrictive way. Further, the district had provided reasonable ways of accommodating the family objections to the tracking badge. The judge refused to grant a preliminary injunction (*A.H. v. Northside I.S.D.*). Later, the district ended the student ID tracking program, and the family dropped the lawsuit.

The Texas Education Code has several provisions granting exemptions for religious reasons from school-related requirements. As discussed in more detail in Chapter 9, TEC §11.162(c) gives parents the right to opt their children out of a school uniform policy for a bona fide religious or philosophical reason. TEC §26.010 gives parents the right to request an exemption for their child from classroom and other school activities that conflict with a parent's religious or moral beliefs, provided the parent presents a written request and the purpose is not to avoid a test or prevent a child from taking a subject for an entire semester. TEC §25.087 requires school districts to excuse a student from school for religious observances. Excusal includes travel days to and from the observance. TEC §38.001 grants an exemption from immunization requirements for students entering elementary or secondary school upon presentation of an affidavit stating that the applicant "declines immunization for reasons of conscience, including a religious belief." The affidavit must be on a state health department form, be notarized, and be submitted not later than the ninetieth day after notarization. TEC §21.406 provides that a school district may not deny a teacher a salary bonus because a teacher is absent from school for observance of a religious holy day. The law, however, applies only to pay supplements. Thus, a teacher still can be required to supply a substitute or give up regular wages for observing a religious holy day.

As noted earlier, Title VII of the 1964 Civil Rights Act requires employers to make "reasonable accommodation" to the religious practices of employees and job applicants, but not to the point of constituting undue hardship to the employer's business. An ROTC instructor was unsuccessful in asserting that he was the victim of religious discrimination when he was terminated from his position in the Fort Worth school district. As a Seventh Day Adventist, the instructor was unable to work on Friday evening and Saturdays. As much as 40 percent of the instructor's job consisted of extracurricular activities during these times. After he missed a number of activities, including an annual ROTC awards ceremony, he was decertified by the army. The school district subsequently terminated his employment. The court ruled that the district terminated his employment because of the decertification, not his religion. Even if the instructor had established the claim of religious discrimination, the school district could not be liable because it could not accommodate his religious beliefs without undue hardship (*Bynum v. Fort Worth I.S.D.*, 1999).

Similarly, the Houston school district was successful in a challenge by two bus drivers who contested their employment termination after they requested eight days' release time to attend a religious function. The district granted only five days. Fallout over the incident led to their dismissal. The court found that granting more than five days would have constituted undue hardship on the district because of a shortage of drivers (*Favero v. Houston I.S.D.*, 1996).

The U.S. Supreme Court elaborated a bit on accommodating an employee's religious practices in *Ansonia Board of Education v. Philbrook* in 1986. In that case, board policy required the employee to take unpaid leave for a holy day observance after the three days of paid leave for this purpose were used up. The board did allow an additional three paid leave days for personal leave, but these days could not be used for religious purposes. Ronald Philbrook wanted to use the additional personal leave days for religious purposes or, alternatively, to pay the cost of a substitute while still receiving full pay. The school board rejected both proposals. The Court ruled that the board's position was sufficient under the law unless it could be shown that the three days for personal leave could be used for any purpose other than religion, in which case the policy would constitute unlawful religious discrimination.

In 1984 the Texas Commissioner of Education upheld the contract nonrenewal of a teacher who refused to conduct Halloween activities in her fourth-grade classroom because she found Halloween to be synonymous with "anti-Christian, pagan worship" (*King v. Whiteface C.I.S.D.*). The teacher said she would conduct instead autumn art and "food-a-rama" projects. The principal directed her by memo to submit a plan for Halloween observance, but she refused to change her intentions. Later, the principal evaluated her performance as unsatisfactory but noted that he would change the evaluation if she would follow his directive regarding the Halloween program. She refused, and her contract subsequently was nonrenewed. The commissioner noted that the principal had tried to accommodate her religious beliefs by stating in his memorandum that she need not participate in the Halloween activities herself and that the plans could be directed by another teacher or by himself. The teacher did not accept the offer of accommodation. The commissioner held that the school had done all it was required to do under the civil rights laws and that the nonrenewal did not penalize her free exercise rights. "The fact that petitioner has a right to practice her religious beliefs free from school district interference does not mean that she may prohibit her students from engaging in activities she finds morally offensive." He added that "the school district has the right to insist that its employees comply with reasonable directives and cooperate with their superiors, even in matters that would ordinarily be considered relatively minor."

Assistance to Sectarian Private Schools

Many states, particularly in the northeastern part of the country, have long had substantial numbers of children attending private schools. It must be remembered that before there were public schools, education was the province of the private sector. As we noted in Chapter 1, efforts to have all students attend public schools were thwarted by an important U.S. Supreme Court decision, *Pierce v. Society of Sisters* (1925). The Court ruled unanimously that a state law requiring all students to attend public schools would undermine the Fourteenth Amendment property right of private school operators to run schools. The Court also noted that such a law would diminish the Fourteenth Amendment liberty right of the parent to control the upbringing of children. In short, the state could not monopolize the educational process. At the same time, the Court recognized the right of the state "reasonably to regulate" private schools.

Despite the rise of the public school, many states have long sought ways of aiding private schools directly or, more recently, of providing low- and middle-income parents with tuition tax credits or tuition vouchers so that they can enroll their children in private schools. Efforts in these directions have been stimulated by concerns about what some perceive to be a diminished quality of public education. At the moment, about 11 percent of the total U.S. school enrollment attends private schools.

Because most of the private schools are religiously affiliated (over 30 percent of the total are now Roman Catholic), efforts to aid the private sector quickly run into the establishment clause. As noted at the start of the chapter, the U.S. Supreme Court ruled in 1947, in the first major case involving the establishment clause and education, that it is not a breach of the wall of separation between church and state for the government to underwrite the bus transportation costs of pupils attending religious schools. The Court ruled in a 1968 case that a state could loan secular textbooks to religious schools (*Board of Education v. Allen*) and later upheld state-supported standardized testing, diagnostic services, and counseling programs for private schools (*Wolman v. Walter,* 1977). But in 1971, the Court struck down reimbursement to nonpublic schools for teachers' salaries, texts, and instructional materials (*Lemon v. Kurtzman*). In 1973 the Court ruled against state maintenance and repair grants to nonpublic schools (*Committee for Public Education v. Nyquist*).

Then in 1993 the Supreme Court ruled in a narrow 5-4 decision that it is not a violation of the establishment clause for a public school district to pay the costs of a sign language interpreter for a deaf student who attends a private religious school (*Zobrest v. Catalina Foothills School District*). The majority likened the assistance to pupil benefit programs such as bus transportation reimbursement that have only an incidental effect of benefiting religious institutions. In 1997 the Court upheld a government program that permits public-school teachers to deliver remedial education, on religious private-school campuses, to educationally at-risk students under Title I of the Elementary and Secondary Education Act (*Agostini v. Felton*).

The Supreme Court in 2000 continued its trend of being more accommodating to religious private schools by refusing to strike down the loaning of educational materials such as computer hardware and software, library materials, and reference and curricular materials to these institutions under the Education Consolidation and Improvement Act of 1981 (*Mitchell v. Helms*). Chapter 2 of that law permits the federal government to channel funds to state educational agencies and, through them, to local educational agencies for educational purposes. The local educational agency uses the funds to purchase the materials and then loan them to both public and private schools. To reach its decision, the majority used a modified version of the *Lemon* guidelines. As applied to direct aid cases, they now require a secular purpose and a primary effect that assures neutrality by neither advancing nor inhibiting religion. The primary effect inquiry asks in turn whether aid results in governmental indoctrination of religion, defines recipients by reference to religion, or creates excessive entanglement between government and religion. Here, the aid program did not violate these guidelines because the money was provided to both public and private schools and none of the three primary effect criteria was violated.

As noted in Chapter 1, the U.S. Supreme Court ruled 5-4 in 2002 that a publicly funded voucher program does not violate the establishment clause of the First Amendment when parents are given a range of choices in addition to religious private schools (*Zelman v. Simmons-Harris*). This decision, however, said nothing about the application of relevant state constitutional provisions to the question. In the past, the Court has permitted states with stricter anti-establishment provisions to deny indirect forms of aid to religious private schools.

Lacking a long tradition of private education, Texas has not been in the forefront of efforts to aid the nonpublic educational sector, though increasing interest has been expressed in voucher plans. In the last several legislative sessions, bills have been introduced to enact some type of voucher program providing families with state-funded scholarships to send their children to religious and nonreligious private schools. There is little doubt that such a program, if enacted, would be challenged under provisions of the Texas Constitution. As noted at the beginning of the chapter, Article I, §7 of the Texas Constitution states that "No money shall be appropriated, or drawn from the Treasury for the benefit of any sect, or religious society, theological or religious seminary; nor shall property belonging to the State be appropriated for any such purposes." This provision was added in 1896 and represented a victory for public school advocates. Article VII, §5 of the Texas Constitution provides in part that "no law shall ever be enacted appropriating any part of the permanent or available school fund to any other purpose whatever [than support of the public free schools]; nor shall the same, or any part thereof ever be appropriated or used for the support of any sectarian school."

Taken together, these two provisions of the state constitution suggest a stricter adherence to separation of church and state in Texas than under the federal constitution and the constitutions of many states. A review of Texas Attorney General advisory opinions over the years illustrates this point. For example, on several occasions in the 1940s the attorney general cited both clauses of the Texas Constitution in advising that parochial students may not be transported by public school bus (*Att'y. Gen. Op. 0-4220*, 1941; *Att'y. Gen. Op. 0-7128*, 1946). In 1993 the attorney general advised that prekindergarten programs created pursuant to the Texas Education Code must be part of the public schooling system because prekindergarten students are entitled to the benefits of the available school fund. He added, "under Article VII, Section 5, the available school fund can be used only for the support of the public free schools" (*Att'y. Gen. Op. DM-200*). These opinions demonstrate strong endorsement of separating church and state in Texas.

How Texas courts would apply state constitutional provisions to a voucher program channeling public money to parents who then choose from among a variety of public and private religious and nonreligious schools is not known. In the case of higher education, the Texas Attorney General has advised that tuition equalization grants do not violate state constitutional strictures (*Att'y. Gen. Op. M-861*, 1971). The presumption under both state and federal constitutions seems to be that since college students are less impressionable than younger students, this form of indirect aid does not violate strict adherence to separation of church and state.

Individual and general tuition tax credits have been enacted in a few states as a means of providing funding for parents to send their children to private and out-of-district public schools. Unlike individual tax credits, general tuition tax credits enable any entity including corporations to contribute money to a scholarship-dispensing entity and receive a tax credit on income tax due the state. Because tax credits are more likely to be considered private, not government, money, they may be more constitutionally viable than state-funded vouchers. For example, the Arizona Supreme Court upheld that state's tuition tax credit program against a claim that it violated provisions of the Arizona Constitution (*Kotterman v. Killian*).

Later a lawsuit against the program was filed in federal court, challenging the program as a violation of the establishment clause. State taxpayers claimed that Arizona permitted scholarship-dispensing entities to be established by religious organizations to channel funding from tax credits to religious schools. The U.S. Supreme Court dodged deciding the question in 2011, ruling that taxpayers are not sufficiently impacted by the flow of money to these entities to challenge such tuition tax programs (*Arizona Christian School Tuition Organization v. Winn*). Since Texas lacks a state income tax, a similar program in this state would require some artful drafting.

SUMMARY

In this chapter we have reviewed the somewhat stormy relationship between education and religion, a relationship that is still evolving. Both the Texas and U.S. Constitutions make it very clear that public schools are to be neutral regarding religion. Thus, the U.S. Supreme Court has mandated that school-sponsored prayer, even at graduation ceremonies, violates the wall of separation between church and state. At the same time, both constitutions provide strong support for individual freedom of religious belief and exercise. Texas statutes such as the Religious Viewpoints Antidiscrimination Act extend protection to students who want to engage in religious activities on campus. The inherent tensions between avoiding endorsement of religion and accommodating religious activity make decision-making particularly difficult for educators, policy-makers, and judges alike. If there is any consistent line of reasoning running through the case law, it is that public schools must avoid either advancing or inhibiting religion. Teachers and administrators are best advised to fall back on this commonsense rationale when confronted with a complaint, using the cases discussed in this chapter as guidelines. Observing that advice, coupled with keeping a watchful eye on future legal developments likely to emanate from both state and federal courts whose jurisdiction encompasses this state, will go a long way toward avoiding expensive and time-consuming lawsuits.

EIGHT

Student Discipline

PERHAPS THERE IS NO area of school law of more interest to parents and the general public than student discipline. There is a widespread public perception that educators have lost control of students. Many believe that the era of student rights, with its emphasis on freedom of expression and due process, has left educators fearful of litigation and hamstrung in dealing with disruptions in the school setting. There is no doubt that the days when courts automatically affirmed actions of school administrators are long gone. There are legal requirements that must be satisfied. At the same time, the law is designed to empower educators to maintain discipline and an orderly environment. In this chapter, we will examine the legal requirements that apply to student discipline under the U.S. Constitution and Texas statutes.

CONSTITUTIONAL CONCERNS: DUE PROCESS

The starting point for any discussion of the law and student discipline is "due process," a term that is frequently misunderstood. The expression comes from the Fifth and Fourteenth Amendments to the U.S. Constitution, both of which require that the state provide "due process" to an individual prior to taking from that person "life, liberty, or property." There are three key concepts necessary to an understanding of the due process clauses in our Constitution.

First, there must be some action of the state. Generally speaking, actions by private entities do not implicate the due process clause. Thus, a teacher in a private school who is fired without notice or an opportunity for a hearing may rightly complain of a breach of contract or that the school has violated its own policies. But the teacher has no due process case under the Constitution for the simple reason that the private school is not restrained by the Constitution. The same holds true for the private-school student who is expelled without notice or a hearing.

Second, the state must have deprived the individual of "life, liberty, or property." We are not aware of any school in Texas that purports to impose capital punishment. So the educator or student who sues over a violation of due process must assert a "property interest" or a "liberty interest."

Third, the nature of the process due depends on the severity of the deprivation. Due process is a flexible term that fits a wide variety of situations. When the parking meter expires and a fine is imposed, the state has taken action and brought about a deprivation of property. Therefore, some process is due. When the state charges a person with the crime of murder and seeks a life imprisonment or death penalty, the state also is taking action and bringing about a deprivation of life, liberty, and property. Some process is due. But since the second case involves a much greater deprivation than the first, the amount of process due is much greater.

To summarize, an analysis of a due process claim hinges on the answer to three questions: (1) Did the state take action? (2) Did the state deprive the individual of life, liberty, or property? and (3) Did the state provide the process that is due for such a deprivation?

The fundamentals of due process are notice and an opportunity to be heard. However, the degree and specificity of "notice" and the nature of the "opportunity to be heard" vary greatly depending on the situation. The term "due process" is most frequently cited in criminal cases where the stakes are high. Those accused of serious crimes are entitled to a very detailed and specific indictment. They are entitled to see in advance all of the evidence that might be used against them. If any of that evidence was illegally obtained, it will be deemed inadmissible. They are entitled to free legal representation and a full trial before a jury. The case must be proven beyond a reasonable doubt. There are avenues of appeal.

These hallmarks of due process are designed to protect the rights of the innocent, and to require the state to use its power within a legal framework. To what extent should these characteristics of due process be applied in the school setting? Does the constitutional notion of "due process" even apply in a public school? If so, to what extent? Do we want to saddle assistant principals with the same procedural requirements that apply to the district attorney?

Fortunately, we have a Supreme Court case that addresses these issues. In the landmark case of *Goss v. Lopez*, the high court concluded that due process is required before a student can be suspended from school. But since the "deprivation of property" imposed by the state is less harsh than a criminal conviction, the "process" that is "due" is much less burdensome. In *Goss*, the U.S. Supreme Court held that "the total exclusion from the educational process for more than a trivial period . . . is a serious event in the life of the suspended child." The Court continued, "Neither the property interest in educational benefits temporarily denied nor the liberty interest in reputation, which is also implicated, is so insubstantial that suspensions may constitutionally be imposed by any procedure the school chooses, no matter how arbitrary" (Goss v. Lopez). In other words, a deprivation of educational services must involve due process. In Goss, the Court concluded that, because the state provides compulsory schooling, even a short-term suspension deprives the student of a property right and, thus, requires due process. In cases of suspensions of ten days or less, the Court ruled that due process requires school officials to give the student informal notice of the misbehavior and an opportunity to offer an explanation. Such an informal give-and-take is also necessary lest school officials erroneously suspend the wrong student and thereby deprive that student of a protected liberty interest in his or her reputation.

The procedure outlined by the Court requires that "the student be given oral or written notice of the charges against him and, if he denies them, an explanation of the evidence the authorities have and an opportunity to present his side of the story" (p. 581). The interchange can take place minutes after the misconduct has occurred; there need be no time delay. Such a procedure prior to a short-term suspension will, the Court noted, provide a "meaningful hedge against erroneous action. At least the disciplinarian will be alerted to the existence of disputes about facts and arguments about cause and effect. He may then determine himself to summon the accuser, permit cross-examination, and allow the student to present his own witnesses. In more difficult cases, he may permit counsel. In any event, his discretion will be more informed and we think the risk of error substantially reduced" (pp. 583–584).

A 1998 decision from the Fifth Circuit emphasizes that due process must be provided to the student, not the parents. In Meyer v. Austin I.S.D., the principal issued a short-term suspension to five students after personally observing the students wearing clothing that, in the principal's opinion, indicated gang membership. There was some give-and-take between the group of students and the principal, but the students alleged that they were not given the individual opportunity to "tell their side of the story." Several of the parents had extended discussions with the principal, but the students were not present during those discussions. The Fifth Circuit ruled that the case would have to proceed to trial. If any of the students could prove the allegations—that the principal had suspended the student without giving that student an opportunity to tell his or her side of the story—then the principal could be held liable for violating that student's right to due process.

Under a 1984 ruling by the U.S. Court of Appeals for the Fifth Circuit, a student who is suspended over an examination period and receives zeroes on those days is not entitled to anything more than the Goss informal due process procedures (Keough v. Tate County Board of Education). The Fifth Circuit observed that "Goss makes no distinctions between [short-term] suspensions that occur during examination periods and those that do not, and it seems to us, for obvious reasons. In any school year, a number of examinations may take place at various times throughout a given semester which are crucial to a student's performance for the semester" (p. 1080). The court concluded that the informal conversation with the principal was all Chuck Keough was entitled to prior to his short-term suspension. The court hedged a bit, however, noting that the district later allowed Keough to take his tests and, as a result, no harm took place.

Later in this chapter we will discuss the specific due process requirements that apply to various forms of student discipline between the Red River and the Rio Grande.

OTHER CONSTITUTIONAL ISSUES

There are three other constitutional issues worth discussing. Rules developed by schools that impose punishments on students must not (1) be overly broad; (2) infringe on protected activities; and (3) be "void for vagueness."

Overbreadth

A rule is overly broad if it sweeps beyond the area of concern. When determining whether or not a rule is overly broad courts will usually read the rule literally. For example, when Marian the Librarian posts a sign that says "no talking in the library," we know what she means. But if a student were to be suspended for violating the rule, the student might be able to challenge the rule as overly broad. Obviously, some talking in the library is acceptable. The rule, read literally, sweeps too broadly.

This is a good example of a legal concept that some courts will apply with more enthusiasm than others, especially in the school setting. The general disposition of the courts is to defer to the educators in the interpretation of school rules. In 1982 the U.S. Supreme Court in *Board of Education of Rogers, Arkansas v. McCluskey* dealt with a case in which a local school board had expelled a student for drinking. The school rule in question prohibited drug use, and did not mention alcohol. Nevertheless, the Supreme Court ruled for the school district. In a brief unsigned opinion, the Court noted that alcohol can be classified as a drug and concluded that "the District Court and the Court of Appeals plainly erred in replacing the Board's construction of [the rule] with their own notions under the facts of the case." The message was clear—local school boards can interpret their own rules, and courts must defer to those interpretations, within reason.

Protected Areas

School rules that impose punishments must also be limited to actions of students that are the school's business. Moreover, the school rule cannot infringe on the constitutional rights of free speech enjoyed by students. We have a host of colorful cases dealing with student free speech, ranging from black armbands to "Bong Hits 4 Jesus" signs. These cases are discussed in detail in Chapter 6. Here, we will focus on the development of rules and codes of conduct that will pass muster.

As technology has evolved, the cases have changed as well. In the 1960s there were numerous cases involving students publishing and distributing "underground" newspapers. Now, of course, the issue is the use of the Internet. When, if ever, is it permissible for a school to impose rules pertaining to the use of a computer or cell phone at home?

The general rule is that the school must show that it has some legitimate interest in regulating student behavior. Thus, if a student uses his own computer at home on his own time and creates a website or posts messages that school officials find offensive, this alone does not give the school authority to impose discipline. But if the student's activity moves beyond "offensive" to "threatening," the school can assert its interest in maintaining safety by taking disciplinary action. A pair of Pennsylvania cases makes the point.

In the first case, a student created a highly offensive and insulting "Top Ten" list enumerating the personal and professional failings of the school's athletic director. This was done by the student working on his home computer. He never brought the list to school, but he sent it to his friends by e-mail. Someone brought the list to school, and it was widely distributed and posted in the teachers' lounge. The school charged the student with violating its rule against "verbal/written abuse of a staff member" and suspended him from both school and the track team. The federal district court overturned the school's decision. Noting that the student's conduct occurred off campus, the court held that the school had failed to show that the student's actions were materially disruptive to the educational process (*Killion v. Franklin Regional School District*, 2001).

The second Pennsylvania case went the other way, but it was based on more threatening conduct. A student created a website on his home computer that included ugly remarks about his algebra teacher and some school administrators. But the student went well beyond verbally offensive remarks. The website included a picture of a severed head dripping with blood, a picture of the teacher's face that morphed into Adolf Hitler's, and a solicitation of money to hire a hit man to kill the teacher. Knowledge of the student's website eventually spread throughout the school. The teacher who was the primary target of the student became highly upset, to the point that she took a medical leave of absence. The

Supreme Court of Pennsylvania ruled that this conduct was materially disruptive and a substantial invasion of the rights of others. Thus the expulsion of the student was upheld (*J.S., a Minor v. Bethlehem Area School District*, 2002).

Some school districts have developed speech codes to prevent verbal abuse, such as racial and gender harassment, obscenity, and profanity. While cases discussed in Chapter 6, such as *Bethel School District No. 403 v. Fraser*, give school officials considerable authority over student expression, speech codes need to be carefully developed to avoid intruding upon protected rights. A poorly drafted speech code could run aground, as in a 1992 U.S. Supreme Court ruling. In that case, the Court struck down a city ordinance of St. Paul, Minnesota, which outlawed acts that arouse anger or alarm based on race, color, creed, religion, or gender (*R.A.V. v. St. Paul*). The law was judged unconstitutional because it restricted only a certain form of hate speech, and thus was not content-neutral.

The Third Circuit struck down a school district's antiharassment policy in *Saxe v. State College Area School District* (2001). The policy was designed to protect students and staff from harassment based on race, religion, color, national origin, gender, sexual orientation, disability, or other personal characteristics. While that is a worthy goal, the court concluded that the policy was so broadly written that it infringed on free speech. Among other things, the policy prohibited any unwelcome verbal conduct that "offends, denigrates, or belittles" an individual because of any of these characteristics. The policy specifically applied to "unsolicited derogatory remarks, jokes, demeaning comments or behaviors, slurs, mimicking, name calling, graffiti, innuendo, gestures, physical contact, stalking, threatening, bullying, extorting, or the display or circulation of written materials or pictures." The parent who sued the school district over this policy alleged that it could subject his children to disciplinary action for simply speaking out on their beliefs about the harmful effects of homosexuality. The court agreed that the policy swept too broadly into the protected arena of free speech.

On the other hand, the Tenth Circuit approved of a Racial Harassment and Intimidation Policy in *West v. Darby Unified School District* (2000). The Darby policy prohibited any written material "that is racially divisive or creates ill will or hatred." When a student was suspended for drawing a picture of the Confederate flag, he sued, alleging a violation of his right of free speech. The court did not agree. The policy was adopted in response to increasing racial tension. It was narrowly drawn and tied in to potential disruption of school. It included examples of prohibited conduct that specifically mentioned the Confederate flag.

The lesson is simply that educators must walk a fine line in adopting rules that infringe in any way on expressive activities. The *Tinker* standard (see Chapter 6) continues to be the best guideline. Students enjoy free speech even at school, but educators have the authority to quell a disruption that they reasonably can forecast.

Void for Vagueness

A rule must be reasonably clear to be enforceable. A basic element of due process is the concept that a person should have a clear idea of what type of behavior is prohibited. Without such a rule, the state could use its power to punish in an arbitrary way.

Criminal statutes are frequently challenged as "void for vagueness." A Texas case arising out of a school-related party illustrates. Charles Zascavage, a high school wrestling coach, was charged with the criminal offense of "recklessly permitting hazing to occur." The antihazing statute, TEC §37.152, prohibits (1) hazing, (2) soliciting, encouraging, directing, aiding or attempting to aid another in hazing, (3) recklessly permitting hazing to occur, and (4) knowingly failing to report when a person has first-hand knowledge that hazing of a student has occurred or is being planned.

The alleged hazing incident occurred at a party sponsored by the Wrestling Booster Club. The party was held at a private residence. Coach Zascavage was present, as were a number of parents and most of the wrestling team. It was not clear from the record in the case that any of the adults witnessed anything that could be characterized as hazing.

The court held that TEC §37.152(a)(3) was unconstitutionally vague. To pass muster, the court said, a criminal statute must "give a person of ordinary intelligence a reasonable opportunity to know what is prohibited." This section of the statute fell short in that it did not identify any person or class of persons to whom it applied, but instead "simply imposes a duty on every living person in the universe to prevent hazing."

Moreover, the court held that the statute could not be properly applied to the coach in this situation. The court noted that the party was at a private home, was not officially sponsored by the school, was not mandatory for the students, and was attended by a number of parents. Thus the court concluded that the coach did not assume custody or control of the students and so he did not have a legal duty in this situation to prevent hazing (*State v. Zascavage*, 2007).

The Zascavage case arose in a criminal prosecution, and the standards for specificity are more exact in that context than for a code of conduct provision. Nevertheless, rules that leave too much room for interpretation are legally suspect.

CHAPTER 37: AN OVERVIEW

Student discipline in Texas is covered by Chapter 37 of the Texas Education Code, which was originally enacted in 1995 as part of a major overhaul of the Education Code. Most of the key players at the time, from Governor Bush on down, spoke of their strong desire to return to the notion of local control. Decisions should be made in local communities, not Austin. Texas is too diverse to have a one-size-fits-all approach to problems. Let the local people decide.

In many respects, that theme carried the day. But when the legislature got to Chapter 37, Safe Schools, the "local control" concept flew out the window. Chapter 37 gave state law more control over student discipline than ever before. It is interesting to note that the word "may" appears rarely in Chapter 37. "Shall" and "must," however, are frequently present.

A second theme evident in Chapter 37 is the clear desire of the legislature to keep students in school if at all possible. Despite cries for "zero tolerance," the legislature has not made it easier for schools to expel students. On the contrary, the legislature has removed from the list of "expellable offenses" some of the reasons students were expelled in the past. Instead, students who commit these offenses will be placed in disciplinary alternative education programs (DAEPs).

A third theme is the great emphasis on DAEPs. Schools are required to establish DAEPs and are required to place students there in cases of certain misconduct. Students assigned to the DAEP must be separated from the other students. The notion seems to be that if we can keep the disruptive students away from the "good kids," schools will be safer and better. However, DAEPs are not to be viewed as "warehouses" for difficult students. DAEPs are expected to have qualified teachers, strong programs, and structure designed to get students back on track.

The fourth theme evident in Chapter 37 is the interplay between schools and the juvenile justice system. Never before has there been such mandated coordination of schools with law enforcement.

Now let's take a look at some specifics concerning Chapter 37.

Student Code of Conduct

TEC §37.001(a) requires each district to adopt a student code of conduct that will specify standards for student conduct and outline the types of behavior that might get a student in trouble at school. The code of conduct is to be developed with the advice of the district-level committee.

The code of conduct is a familiar concept in school law. It is a basic rule of due process that students can only be punished for misconduct after they are advised that such conduct is prohibited. Most schools discharge this responsibility by distributing a "student handbook" containing all the rules and regulations of the school, including those pertaining to discipline. Most schools require parents and students to sign a receipt indicating that they have received and read the book. The code of conduct must indicate how the district will notify parents of any violations that could lead to suspension from school or the bus, DAEP removal, or expulsion.

A law passed in 2009 requires the code of conduct to specify that four mitigating factors will be taken into account whenever a school orders a suspension, a DAEP or JJAEP (Juvenile Justice Alternative Education Program) removal, or an expulsion. These are (1) self-defense; (2) intent, or lack thereof; (3) the student's disciplinary history; and (4) any disability that substantially impairs the student's capacity to appreciate the wrongfulness of the conduct. Prior to 2009 districts had the discretion to consider these factors or not. Those who chose not to consider these mitigating factors often cited the concept of "zero tolerance." The 2009 amendment moves us away from "zero tolerance." It requires school administrators to exercise some degree of discretion rather than automatically imposing penalties for certain misconduct. Discretion is a good thing, but school administrators must be prepared to explain why different cases are handled differently. Inconsistent enforcement creates problems and accusations of favoritism toward certain students. Most school districts in Texas already require educators to exercise discretion when imposing disciplinary consequences. A typical policy, such as Policy FO (Local) as promulgated by the Texas Association of School Boards, requires that educators take into account the seriousness of the offense, the age of the student, the frequency of misconduct by the student, the student's attitude, and the potential effect of the misconduct on the school environment. That is a far cry from "zero tolerance."

The requirement to take "intent" into account may present some interesting cases involving the possession of items the student is not to have at school, such as drugs, alcohol, and weapons. When caught with such items at school, students often claim that they did not intend to bring the item to school and/or that they did not even know that it was there. In the past, many schools have disregarded intent, holding the student responsible regardless. This is no longer legally defensible, since codes of conduct now require consideration of the student's intent. However, we expect school administrators to make it very clear to students that they will continue to be held accountable for the contents of things that are under the student's control—purses, backpacks, lockers, and automobiles.

A 2006 decision from the Beaumont Court of Appeals provided a preview of how this provision will come into play. A prohibited item (brass knuckles) was found in a student's truck on the school parking lot. The student consented to a search of the vehicle after a drug dog alerted on it. When the knuckles were found, the student explained that they were not his, they belonged to a friend and he was not aware that they were in his vehicle.

The school expelled the student, based in part on the belief of the principal that it did not matter whether the student "knew" what was in his truck—he was responsible for what was there, whether he knew or not. This was the principal's understanding of the school's code of conduct. He understood the code to impose a "zero tolerance" rule whereby a student's knowledge or intention was not relevant.

However, the court noted that the code of conduct required the district to consider the student's intent. The code said that when considering expulsion, the school would take into account the student's "intent or lack of intent." Thus, it was not true that the code required a "zero tolerance" approach with regard to possession of weapons. The district had applied an erroneous legal standard. The student's request for a temporary order to keep him in school pending the outcome of a full trial was granted (*Tarkington I.S.D. v. Ellis*, 2006).

Bullying

The topic of bullying deserves special attention. Intense public interest and media attention led to changes in state law as of 2011. The Texas law on bullying, TEC Section 37.0832, requires schools to adopt policies and procedures designed to attack this age-old problem. In addition, the code of conduct must prohibit bullying. The law defines bullying as written, verbal, or electronic expression or physical conduct occurring on school property, in a school vehicle, or at a school function that (1) has the effect or will have the effect of physically harming a student, damaging a student's property, or placing a student in reasonable fear of harm to person or property; or (2) is sufficiently severe, persistent, and pervasive that the action or threat creates an intimidating, threatening, or abusive educational environment. To be "bullying" the conduct must (1) exploit an imbalance of power between the student and perpetrator; and (2) interfere with a student's education or substantially disrupt the operation of a school.

School boards must adopt policies that (1) prohibit bullying; (2) prohibit retaliation based on good faith reports of bullying; (3) establish procedures for providing notice to parents of victim and bully; (4) establish actions a student should take to obtain assistance and intervention in response to bullying; (5) set out available counseling options for victims, witnesses, and bullies; (6) establish a procedure for reporting and investigating bullying, and determining whether it occurred; (7) prohibit disciplinary measures against a victim on the basis of reasonable self-defense; and (8) require that "discipline for bullying of a student with disabilities comply with applicable requirements under federal law."

These policies must be in the employee and student handbooks, and in the district improvement plan. Procedures for reporting bullying must be posted on the district's website, to the extent practicable.

Districts may transfer a student who has engaged in bullying to (1) another classroom at the campus where the victim was assigned at the time of the bullying; or (2) another campus, in consultation with the parent of the bully. Transfers of a student with a disability who engaged in bullying are subject to TEC §37.004, meaning that the ARD committee (admission, review, and dismissal) must be involved if the transfer amounts to a "change in placement."

The health curriculum must include essential knowledge and skills that include evidence-based practices that will effectively address awareness, prevention, identification, self-defense in response to, and resolution of and intervention in bullying and harassment.

Finally, the law adds bullying prevention as a possible topic for staff development.

Teacher-Initiated Removal

One of the stated purposes of the disciplinary changes incorporated into Chapter 37 was to give classroom teachers more authority. Accordingly, the Texas Education Code spells out three different ways for teachers to remove students from the classroom, at least temporarily. There is teacher removal for assistance; discretionary teacher removal; and mandatory teacher removal. We will examine each in turn.

Teacher removal for assistance is nothing more than a statutory assurance that teachers can do what they have always done—send kids to the principal's office. TEC §37.002 authorizes the teacher to do this "to maintain effective discipline in the classroom." What happens next is up to the principal, who is to "respond by employing appropriate discipline management techniques consistent with the student code of conduct adopted under Section 37.001."

Discretionary teacher removal is authorized for a student:

(1) who has been documented by the teacher to repeatedly interfere with the teacher's ability to communicate effectively with the students in the class or with the ability of the student's classmates to learn; or

(2) whose behavior the teacher determines is so unruly, disruptive, or abusive that it seriously interferes with the teacher's ability to communicate effectively with the students in the class or with the ability of the student's classmates to learn. (TEC §37.002(b))

When the classroom teacher exercises this authority, the principal is required to convene a conference within three class days. The conference should include the parent, the student, and the teacher, but the conference is to go forward whether all parties are present or not, provided that "valid attempts" have been made to require the attendance of all parties. After conducting this conference, the principal can order the student placed in another appropriate classroom, an in-school suspension program, or a DAEP for a period of time consistent with the code of conduct. However, the principal cannot place the student back into the classroom of the teacher who initiated the removal without that teacher's consent. Such a power could be abused if there were no limitation on it. Consider Ms. Downyshanks, who has already turned in her resignation, effective at the end of the year, so that she can attend law school. Such a teacher, armed with a "who gives a flip" attitude along with the power to remove unruly kids and refuse to take them back, could empty out of her classroom all but the most compliant and pleasant children.

To guard against such abuses, the legislature has created PRCs— placement review committees. The primary function of the PRC will be to decide what to do when the principal orders the student back to the classroom of a teacher who refuses to take the student back. The PRC can override the teacher if the PRC decides that placement of the student in that classroom "is the best or only alternative available" (TEC §37.002(c)). PRCs will be composed of three persons. Two PRC members must be teachers, selected to the PRC by the campus faculty. The third member will be a member of the campus professional staff appointed by the principal. If the student is eligible for special education services, the student's ARD committee will usually be involved in these decisions as well.

The third type of teacher-initiated removal, mandatory removal, arises only when the student commits an offense in the classroom that requires removal to a DAEP or expulsion. In that event, the teacher must order the student's removal from class, and the principal must assign the student to a DAEP or seek expulsion. These procedures are described in more detail below.

Teachers will find that their ability to document student behavior and misbehavior in the classroom will be of tremendous significance. The statutory provisions authorizing teachers to remove a student from class will be effectively used only if the teacher is diligent in documenting in-class efforts to bring the student's behavior under control. Teachers must have a set of rules for the class as a whole. The rules should be clearly displayed, reviewed with the students in detail, and consistently enforced. In addition to the general rules, teachers are likely to have to deal with one or more individualized behavior plans. Some children, both in and out of the special education program, will have an individualized BIP (behavior intervention plan) that the classroom teacher will be responsible for implementing.

Suspension

The Education Code contains just one short section dealing with suspension, TEC §37.005. It states that a student may be suspended from school if the student engages in conduct identified in the student code of conduct for which a student may be suspended. In other words, the local school district is authorized to decide what types of offenses should call for a suspension.

Suspension is designed as a short-term disciplinary action. Under TEC §37.005(b), suspension is limited to three days per offense. However, there is no limit on the number of suspensions that might be imposed on a student, provided that each is for a separate incident of misconduct. Thus if a student commits ten separate offenses that call for suspension, the student could be suspended as many as thirty days. While there is no limit on accumulated days of suspension for most students, there are limitations regarding students with disabilities, discussed in more detail in Chapter 3.

Furthermore, it is noteworthy that the law makes no mention of in-school suspension. The three-day limitation in the statute applies to out-of-school suspension. The school district, through its code of conduct, can establish guidelines for in-school suspension assignments.

Removal to a DAEP

The overhaul of the Education Code in 1995 created an alternative to expulsion through "AEPs"—alternative educational programs. Later the term was changed to DAEP—emphasizing that this is an alternative program for students who have committed disciplinary infractions. School districts today may offer a variety of "alternative" educational programs that are available by choice. But the DAEP is not one the student or parent chooses. It is one to which the student is assigned in response to a violation of the code of conduct.

Chapter 37 includes both *mandatory* and *discretionary* placements in the DAEP. Furthermore, the law addresses student misconduct that occurs *at school* as well as *away from school.*

Mandatory Placements. Section 37.006 lists the offenses for which a student must be assigned to a DAEP. Some of these offenses require DAEP placement only if they occur at school, within 300 feet of school property, or at a school-sponsored event. These are: (1) any conduct punishable as a felony; (2) an assault resulting in bodily injury; (3) certain drug offenses; (4) certain alcohol offenses; (5) inhalant offenses; (6) public lewdness; and (7) indecent exposure.

Some of these offenses may lead to expulsion. For example, a school district has the authority to expel a student for certain drug, alcohol, and assaultive offenses. If the school does not expel the student based on such conduct, the school must place the student in a DAEP.

There are other offenses that require DAEP placement regardless of where the behavior occurs. These include (1) false alarm or report involving a public school; (2) terroristic threat involving a public school; (3) the commission of a felony offense under Title 5 of the Texas Penal Code; (4) aggravated robbery; and (5) retaliation against a school employee.

Generally speaking, felonies under Title 5 of the Penal Code involve crimes of violence against a person. The school is authorized to conclude that a student has committed a Title 5 felony if the student has been convicted of such an offense or receives deferred prosecution for such an offense, or if the superintendent or designee "has a reasonable belief" that the student has committed such an offense. If the school acts on the basis of TEC §37.006 based on a "reasonable belief" that the student has committed a Title 5 felony, the student must be placed in DAEP without regard to any conclusion about the dangerousness of the student or the best interests of the school. It is a mandatory placement based on past behavior.

Retaliation claims are governed by Penal Code §36.06. That provision of the Code defines retaliation as any unlawful conduct directed against a public servant or official in retaliation for the public servant's or official's performance of official duties. In other words, the student who vandalizes or assaults a teacher off campus in retaliation for the teacher's performance of job duties must be removed to a DAEP.

A criminal case demonstrates the scope of the definition of "retaliation." A school administrator had seized a red rag from the back pocket of a student, because it violated the dress code. When the student asked that it be returned and the administrator refused, the student threatened to get his gun and shoot him. Though the student later dismissed his own remarks as "playful banter," the juvenile court disagreed and found the student guilty of the criminal offense of retaliation against a public servant by intentionally threatening to harm the administrator (*In the Matter of B.M.*, 1999). Although this took place on campus, the school would have been required to place the student in the DAEP for this conduct even if it had taken place away from school.

Discretionary Placements. In addition to these mandatory DAEP offenses, there are offenses for which a student *may* be placed in DAEP. If a student commits an off-campus felony other than those covered by Title 5, the school district may place the student in DAEP. Again, the school is authorized to conclude that such an offense has been committed on the basis of conviction, deferred prosecution, or the "reasonable belief" of the superintendent or designee. In addition, there must be a determination that the continued presence of the student in the regular classroom threatens the safety of other students or teachers or will be detrimental to the educational process. Furthermore, school districts can send students to DAEPs for reasons other than those listed in state law, provided that the code of conduct advises the students that removal might occur. Most schools inform students that they can be sent to a DAEP for any serious or persistent misconduct.

Title 5 felonies are again discussed in TEC §37.0081. This section overlaps with §37.006 to some extent, but it also applies in other situations. While §37.006 requires DAEP placement if the superintendent has a "reasonable belief" that the student has committed a Title 5 felony, §37.0081 authorizes DAEP placement in additional situations. For example, if the student is merely "arrested for or charged with" a Title 5 felony, the school can act on the basis of §37.0081 without the necessity of a "reasonable belief" finding. However, the school must provide the student a hearing and make a finding that the student's presence in the regular classroom (1) threatens the safety of others; (2) would be detrimental to the educational process; or (3) is not in the best interests of the district's students. Armed with evidence of an arrest, along with a "finding," the school may expel the student and then place the student in a JJAEP (Juvenile Justice Alternative Education Program) or DAEP. The school is authorized to use this process regardless of when or where the student's conduct occurred. It could even be at a time when the student was not enrolled or even residing in the school district. Furthermore, this placement can be for "any period considered necessary by the board or the board's designee." Thus the one-calendar-year limitation discussed below does not apply. However, the school must conduct a "periodic review" at least every 120 days.

Students who are required to register as sex offenders are discussed in an entire subchapter of Chapter 37, beginning at §37.301. If such a student is under court supervision, the student must be placed in the DAEP or JJAEP. If the student is no longer under any form of court supervision, the school district has discretion. It can place the student in the regular classroom or in the DAEP or JJAEP. In any event, the district must review the student's case after each semester spent in the DAEP or JJAEP. In fact, the law sets up a committee to conduct this review. If the student has a disability and is in the special education program, then the student's ARD committee serves as the reviewing body.

It should be obvious that some degree of cooperation between law enforcement and school officials will be needed if these provisions are to be put into effect. Accordingly, law enforcement officials are required to give notice to the superintendent within twenty-four hours after the arrest of a student, or before the next school day, whichever is sooner (Code of Criminal Procedure §15.27). Written notice must follow within seven days and must contain enough information for the superintendent to make a judgment call as to whether or not there is a reasonable belief that the student has engaged in a Title 5 felony offense. The superintendent is entitled to rely on this information from law enforcement in making the call. Thus school officials need not play the role of detective as to off-campus conduct. Instead, they are authorized to rely on the reports received from law enforcement.

State law does not tell us how long a DAEP placement is to last, but it does require the code of conduct to establish guidelines for the length of placement. Moreover, when placing a student in the DAEP the district must issue an order calling for a specific length of placement. But there are three provisions in state law that address long-term DAEP assignments. First, the school must review the student's academic status at intervals not to exceed 120 days (TEC §37.009(e)). If the student is a high school student, this review must include a specific graduation plan for the student. Second, the student can be kept in the DAEP beyond the end of the school year only if the school determines that the student's presence on campus will be dangerous or that the student has engaged in serious or persistent misbehavior (TEC §37.009(c)). Third, the student can be kept in DAEP beyond one year only if, after a review, the district determines that the student is a threat to the safety of others or that extended DAEP placement is in the best interests of the student (TEC §37.009(d)).

Those standards are quite flexible. As one observer has pointed out, keeping a student in the DAEP beyond the end of the school year is not difficult. Consider the case of Jennifer, who was caught smoking in the bathroom her first week of high school. Most codes of conduct will describe smoking as "serious misconduct." Section 37.009(c) tells us that the student can be assigned to DAEP beyond the end of the school year if the board or board's designee determines that the student has engaged in "serious misconduct." While we do not recommend it, it appears that some schools could slap Jennifer into DAEP into the next school year, with appropriate 120-day reviews.

It is even possible to keep the smoker in the DAEP beyond one calendar year. Again, the standards are flexible and school-friendly. It is the district that determines if the student is a threat to others or if the student is better off in the DAEP. If either is the case, the student can be kept in the DAEP beyond a full calendar year.

Procedure Timothy Nevares was among the first students assigned to DAEP after the adoption of the "mandatory placement" provisions in Chapter 37. Nevares was placed in DAEP (then called an AEP) based on off-campus conduct. His suit against the San Marcos C.I.S.D. was followed closely by educators in Texas, since it was the first major court challenge to some of the more controversial aspects of Chapter 37. Though Nevares had some success at the district court level, he struck out before the Fifth Circuit. Nevares had complained of a lack of due process, alleging that the school had tossed him into an inferior program without a proper hearing. But the Fifth Circuit ruled that no process was due, because the student was not deprived of property or liberty. "Timothy Nevares was not denied access to public education, not even temporarily. He was only transferred from one school program to another program with stricter discipline" (*Nevares v. San Marcos C.I.S.D.*, 1997). Since no deprivation occurred, no process of any kind was due. In other words, as far as federal law is concerned, students assigned to DAEP are not entitled to any kind of hearing, not even an informal *Goss v. Lopez*-type hearing. This would appear to close the door to suits alleging a violation of federal due process based on DAEP assignments.

What about the state constitution? That issue arose in *Stafford Municipal School District v. L.P.* (2001). The student argued that the Texas Constitution required some level of due process before a student could be placed into a DAEP. The court disagreed.

Thus we have judicial precedent to establish that there are no due process requirements for placing students in the DAEP under either the U.S. or the Texas Constitution. Just because there are no constitutional requirements, however, does not mean there are no procedural requirements imposed by statute. Section 37.009 of the TEC requires the principal or designee to hold a "conference" not later than the third class day after the student's removal. The conference is supposed to include the principal or designee, the parent, the student, and the teacher, if the student's removal was initiated by the teacher. This conference is the "due process" opportunity for the student. The administrator must advise the student of the reasons for the removal and give the student an opportunity to respond. The conference must take place even if not all parties are in attendance, as long as the principal has made "valid attempts" to require everyone's attendance.

If the student is to be assigned to a DAEP beyond the end of the next grading period, the school is required to give the parents notice and an opportunity to participate in a proceeding before the board or designee. But the law is silent as to the formality of the proceeding.

It appears that the legislature desires disputes over DAEP placement to end within the school district. Whatever decision is made about DAEP placement by the board or designee is "final and may not be appealed." This means that the Texas Education Agency will not hear such an appeal, and neither will the courts. Parents of a student in Wichita Falls did not believe that. But when the appeal was lodged, the commissioner dismissed it for lack of jurisdiction (*Parent v. Wichita Falls I.S.D.*, 2009).

The commissioner knows that he does not have jurisdiction of a DAEP appeal, but state district court judges sometimes think they do. When J.C. was assigned to DAEP for fifteen days in Vidor I.S.D., he filed suit in state district court, seeking a TRO (temporary restraining order).

The court granted it, ordering the district to delay the DAEP assignment until the case could be heard more fully, thirteen days later. V.I.S.D. immediately appealed to the court of appeals, which dissolved the injunction. The Beaumont Court of Appeals noted two problems with what the district court had done. First, it issued a TRO that had the effect of granting to the student all of the relief he sought in the lawsuit. This is contrary to the concept of TROs, which are designed simply to maintain a status quo until a case can be heard. Second, assignments to DAEP are not supposed to be appealed beyond the school board. So the district prevailed here, but at a considerable cost in time, energy, and attorneys' fees. It is ironic that a matter that is supposed to conclude at the school board level can end up in the court of appeals (*In re Vidor I.S.D.*, 2010).

Keep in mind that these decisions from Texas courts of appeals will not prevent suits alleging a violation of federal law. For example, a student with a disability could challenge a DAEP placement on the theory that it violates her federally protected right to free, appropriate public education (FAPE). See Chapter 3 for a discussion. Moreover, a student can challenge DAEP placement based on allegations that the school infringed on protected free speech, or due process. That's what happened in *Hinterlong v. Arlington I.S.D.* (2010). After receiving an anonymous tip, school officials found a small amount of something that smelled like alcohol in a water bottle. The bottle was in the student's car, parked on school property. Following its zero tolerance policy, the district assigned the student to a DAEP. He sued, claiming a violation of due process.

The district prevailed, but it was a close call. The court noted that strict adherence to zero tolerance policies could violate due process standards if they provided for punishment without consideration of the student's intent. In this case, the district gave the student an opportunity to show that he knew nothing about the booze in the bottle—an opportunity the student failed to take advantage of. Thus under these facts, the court reasoned, due process was provided.

As noted above, the legislature moved away from the "zero tolerance" concept in 2009 by requiring school district codes of conduct to take into account intent, self-defense, and other mitigating factors. This may have come just in time, as the *Arlington* case shows that courts might be willing to strike down "zero tolerance."

Life in a DAEP. DAEPs serve students who have gotten into trouble, but they are not intended to be warehouses for kids who are doomed to drop out. In fact, the plan is just the opposite. The plan is to provide a structured avenue for the student's success, including instruction in each foundation curriculum subject, a full seven-hour day, and a ratio of not more than fifteen students to each certified teacher.

It is well known that students assigned to DAEP are more likely to drop out of school than other students. Moreover, research has shown that a disproportionate percentage of students who "serve time" in DAEP later do the same in prison. Consequently, Texas rules about the DAEP emphasize self-discipline, behavior management, safety, parental involvement, and the individual needs of each student. According to a provision of the Texas Administrative Code, the staff is to be trained in positive and proactive strategies for behavior management, including instruction in social skills and problem-solving skills such as anger management and conflict resolution. DAEP procedures must spell out the expectations for the DAEP, including "written contracts between students, parents or guardians, and the DAEP that formalize expectations and establish the students' individual plans for success" (19 TAC §103.1201(j)).

In order to maintain safety, the DAEP students must be separated from other students. Schools can operate a DAEP on campus or off campus, but must ensure separation of DAEP students from the others. In addition, schools must separate elementary school DAEP students from the older DAEP students. Schools can cooperate to set up a DAEP, and many small schools certainly do so.

In keeping with the notion of safety, many school districts require routine searches of students assigned to DAEPs. This practice was approved by a Texas court of appeals in a criminal case arising from the discovery of marijuana in a student's possession at the DAEP. The DAEP required all students to pass through a metal detector, be patted down, empty pockets, and remove their shoes. Marijuana was discovered during one of these routine searches. The student asked the court to suppress the evidence, arguing that the search was illegal. But the court disagreed. The court determined that such searches fell within the category of "administrative searches," which do not require individualized suspicion. Instead, the test is whether the "intrusion involved is no greater than necessary to satisfy the governmental interest underlying the need for the search." The court ruled that the random inspection of students at the DAEP was permissible (*In the Matter of O.E.*, 2003).

The prudent school administrator will put a good deal of thought into the setup of a DAEP. The DAEP should be capable of dealing with any student assigned to it, including students with disabilities. Thus the school will have to think carefully about staffing, equipment, services, and location. The legislature wants to be sure that students in DAEPs are not treated as second-class citizens; thus the law mandates that school districts must allocate the same amount of money for a student in a DAEP that they would have allocated for that student if he or she were assigned to the regular school program (TEC §37.008(g)).

Finally, students who are assigned to a DAEP also must be suspended from extracurricular activities. The students can neither participate in nor attend extracurricular events.

Expulsion

Expulsion is the harshest penalty the school can impose. Thus it is reserved for only the most serious offenses and is available only with students who are at least ten years old. Let's take a look at the grounds and
the procedures required to expel a student from school.

Grounds. Section 37.007 spells out several types of conduct that *require*
expulsion from school. They are:

1. Possession of weapons—firearms, illegal knives, clubs, or any
   other prohibited weapons;
2. Assaultive offenses—aggravated assault, sexual assault, or
   aggravated sexual assault;
3. Arson;
4. Murder, capital murder, criminal attempt to commit murder or
   capital murder;
5. Indecency with a child;
6. Aggravated kidnapping;
7. Aggravated robbery;
8. Manslaughter;
9. Criminally negligent homicide;
10. Continuous sexual abuse of a young child;
11. Drug or alcohol offenses if punishable as a felony; or
12. Retaliatory commission of an expellable offense against a school
    employee.

The first eleven of these reasons for expulsion must occur on school
property or at a school-related function. Retaliation against a school
employee, however, is expellable no matter where it takes place.

Note that the local district has no discretion as to these offenses.
However, there are additional expellable offenses where the district does
have discretion. A student *may* be expelled for drug and alcohol offenses
that are not felonies, simple assaults of school employees or volunteers,
and breach of computer security.

Prior to the 2012–2013 school year, schools could expel students
who engaged in "serious or persistent misbehavior" while attending the
DAEP. The legislature tightened up on this by removing the word "persistent." Thus the law now is that students may be expelled from DAEP
only for "serious misbehavior." Moreover, the district must show that
the misconduct occurred "despite documented behavioral interventions." Furthermore, the definition of "serious" leaves campus administrators with little discretion. The term is defined to include "deliberate violent behavior" along with extortion, coercion, public lewdness,
indecent exposure, criminal mischief, personal hazing, or harassment.

Although expulsion is authorized for these offenses, many students will not be expelled "to the street." Instead, they will be "expelled" from the school's programs (including DAEP) and assigned to a Juvenile Justice Alternative Education Program (JJAEP) or other school program. The 1997 legislature effectively eliminated expulsion "to the street" from the larger counties in Texas, those with a population in excess of 125,000. Students who are expelled due to commission of a *mandatory* expulsion offense likely will be required to attend the JJAEP. Students who are expelled due to the commission of a discretionary offense must be served by their school district. If there were any doubt about legislative intent on this, consider: Students who are expelled are exempt from the compulsory attendance law *unless* they are expelled from a school that is required to have a JJAEP. In effect, this means that students expelled from school in the large counties must continue to attend school (TEC §§25.085 and 25.086).

Procedures. The procedures that must accompany expulsion are more extensive than those involved in suspension or removal to a disciplinary alternative education program. Since the student's "property right" to a public education is being taken, the Fourteenth Amendment requires that the student be afforded an appropriate level of due process. In the *Goss* case, the Court emphasized the informality of what was being required—"less than a fair-minded school principal would impose upon himself in order to avoid unfair suspensions" (p. 583). But the Court stated that, in unusual situations and for suspensions over ten days in length, more formal procedural due process would be necessary. Unfortunately, the Court did not give any examples.

The Education Code does not tell us how much process is due prior to an expulsion. Instead, it merely invokes federal constitutional standards. Section 37.009 provides, "Before a student may be expelled under Section 37.007, the board or the board's designee must provide the student a hearing at which the student is afforded appropriate due process as required by the federal constitution and which the student's parent or guardian is invited, in writing, to attend." State law imposes only two other requirements. First, the student is entitled to be represented at an expulsion hearing by some adult who can give guidance to the student. This individual normally would be the parent or guardian, but can be someone else, as long as it is not a school district employee. Second, if an expulsion is ordered by the board's designee, then it is appealable to the board, and then to the district court of the county in which the school district's administrative office is located.

Most school districts provide a full hearing before expelling a student. The student is given the opportunity to present evidence and witnesses and to question witnesses presented by the school. It is apparent from case law, however, that the right to "question administrators and witnesses" has some limitations. The question often arises, for example, as to the right of an accused student to confront his accusers when some of the accusers are other students. If a student is charged with selling drugs on campus and the only eyewitness is another student, does the school have to produce the witness to testify at the expulsion hearing? What if the witness has legitimate fears of retaliation? Courts consistently have held that the procedures for an expulsion hearing are not as strict as those in a criminal trial. School districts can rely on student or staff witnesses, and even read their written witness statements at an expulsion hearing, without a right to cross-examine by the accused student. Courts have decided that such prerecorded statements—considered "hearsay" and generally inadmissible in court—are admissible in student discipline matters.

In a 1988 case from the U.S. Sixth Circuit Court of Appeals, an Ohio student was expelled for over two months for allegedly selling marijuana. At no time was the student allowed to learn the identity of the two accusing students or to cross-examine them. His attorney was not allowed to cross-examine the principal or the superintendent. Addressing the claim of failure of due process, the court stated:

> In this turbulent, sometimes violent, school atmosphere, it is critically important that we protect the anonymity of students who "blow the whistle." . . . Without the cloak of anonymity, students who witness criminal activity on school property will be much less likely to notify school authorities, and those who do will be faced with ostracism at best and perhaps physical reprisals. (*Newsome v. Batavia Local School District*)

In another case, a student was expelled for striking a coach. The coach did not testify at the student's hearing, but rather submitted a written account of the incident. A Texas federal court ruled that the failure of the coach to testify at the hearing did not amount to a violation of due process. The minimum due process requirements for a long-term expulsion consist of (1) oral and written notice of the charges against the student, (2) an explanation of the evidence, and (3) an opportunity for the student to present his side of the story. The opportunity to cross-examine is not required in this situation. The court held that the burden of cross-examination in a school discipline hearing outweighed any benefit the student might derive from that process in this case (*Johnson v. Humble I.S.D.*, 1992).

Courts have advanced many reasons for denying the right to cross-examine, including (1) the fact that the administrators who investigate the offenses are qualified to determine the truthfulness of student accusers, (2) the fact that, if forced to testify, many students would fail to come forward, and (3) reasons associated with administrative convenience. This question seems relatively settled, with a consistent line of cases dating to the 1970s (for example, *Boykins v. Fairfield Board of Education*, 1974; *Tasby v. Estes*, 1981).

Due process concerns diminish, but do not disappear, when dealing with the student who has admitted guilt. The Fifth Circuit Court of Appeals, which has jurisdiction over Texas, addressed this issue in a case involving a student who admitted possession of marijuana. He contested only the procedures used by the school district during the portion of his hearing where his punishment was determined. He argued that it was unfair for the district to consider evidence of prior misconduct in determining his punishment and that he should have been allowed to confront and cross-examine the three students who reported that he had sold drugs on campus during the preceding three months. The Fifth Circuit disagreed, noting that, once guilt is admitted, there need be only a rational relationship between the punishment and the offense. "We decline to escalate the formality of the suspension process even further by requiring school administrators to provide a fact hearing as to the accuracy of each bit of evidence considered in determining the appropriate length of punishment, a requirement that is not imposed even in criminal cases." The court noted that the statements from the three students were sufficiently detailed to allow the boy to confront the evidence (*Brewer v. Austin I.S.D.*, 1985).

Because of the constitutional dimensions of due process, it would appear that the best policy to follow when students are caught in the act of breaking a school rule and admit guilt is to give them notice of the rule violation and an opportunity in the presence of their parents or a representative to confirm their admission of guilt in writing and to waive formal due process rights. It is essential that coercion, direct or indirect, be absent. Coercion would both invalidate the admission of guilt and create evidence of bias on the part of the school officials. When bias is shown to exist, the constitutionality of the hearing process will be in question.

Are grade-school children entitled to the same due process rights as older students? The answer appears to be yes. Writing in a 1976 case, Supreme Court Justice Harry A. Blackmun pointed out that "constitutional rights do not mature and come into being magically only when one attains the state-defined age of majority. Minors, as well as adults, are protected by the Constitution and possess Constitutional rights" (*Planned Parenthood v. Danforth*, p. 74).

State law specifies that the appeal of a student expulsion is to be heard by the district court by "trial de novo," meaning, essentially, a new trial. However, the expression is misleading. Two courts have now held that the proper standard to be applied is "substantial evidence de novo review" rather than "pure trial de novo" (*Sanchez v. Huntsville I.S.D.*, 1992; *United I.S.D. v. Gonzalez*, 1996). The difference in the two standards is much more than semantic. In a "pure trial de novo" case the school district would bear the burden of proving its expulsion case all over again. In a "substantial evidence de novo review," the court is limited to a review of the record created in the proceedings before the school board. Moreover, the court presumes the findings of the school board are legal and valid and puts the burden on the student to prove that those findings are not supported by substantial evidence. In simple terms, it is much easier for the school district to satisfy the "substantial evidence" test than to start from scratch and prove its case to the satisfaction of a district court judge.

Emergency Actions

School officials encounter emergencies almost daily. Texas law recognizes that there are occasions when a student must be removed from the school due to an emergency. TEC §37.019 authorizes the principal or designee to order the immediate, emergency expulsion of a student if the principal or designee "reasonably believes that action is necessary to protect persons or property from imminent harm." The student is to be given oral notice of the action, with more formal procedures to take place within a reasonable time thereafter.

Emergency removal to a DAEP is also available whenever the principal or designee "reasonably believes the student's behavior is so unruly, disruptive, or abusive that it seriously interferes with a teacher's ability to communicate effectively with the students in a class, with the ability of the student's classmates to learn, or with the operation of the school or a school-sponsored activity." Again, oral notice is all that is required, with appropriate procedures to follow.

Neither emergency placement nor emergency expulsion under §37.019 has a definite time limit. It appears to be a matter of local discretion, but school administrators should keep in mind that these actions clearly are designed to be used only when necessary due to an emergency and should be limited to as short a time as is reasonable. In most instances emergency action should not be viewed as an action to be taken in isolation. In most cases, the conduct of the student that caused an emergency DAEP placement or expulsion also will provide a basis for further disciplinary action. For example, the student who brings a gun to school may be "emergency expelled" as a first step in dealing with the problem. But the second step would be a recommendation for a traditional expulsion, to be preceded by appropriate due process.

Interaction with Law Enforcement

Communication between schools and law enforcement is required in Chapter 37. School districts must notify the juvenile board when students commit an offense that requires placement in DAEP or expulsion.

A copy of the school's order of removal or expulsion must be sent to the authorized officer of the juvenile court (TEC §37.010). Furthermore, the principal of any school—public or private—is required to notify law enforcement officials if the principal has reasonable grounds to believe that a student has engaged in certain types of illegal behavior at school or at a school-related function. The violations required to be reported include drug and weapons offenses.

Texas law also requires local law enforcement officials to give oral notice to the school superintendent when students are arrested or taken into custody in connection with certain offenses, as we discussed above. These include terroristic threats, drug offenses, and weapons offenses. Written notice must follow within seven days. Upon receipt of the written notice, the superintendent must immediately send this information to school employees who need to know and who have "direct supervisory responsibility over the student."

A JJAEP is required in any county with a population in excess of 125,000, with a few specific exceptions authorized by the Education Code. Smaller counties may develop a JJAEP but are not required to do so. JJAEPs serve students who have been expelled and found to have engaged in delinquent conduct. Other students may be admitted to the JJAEP, depending on the agreement between the juvenile board and the school district. The JJAEP program will be a full-fledged educational program, operating seven hours per day, 180 days per year, and focusing on the core curriculum along with self-discipline.

JJAEPs are joint ventures, operated by the school districts in the county along with the juvenile justice board of the county. A 2002 attorney general's opinion clarifies the separation of responsibilities. According to the AG, the county is not responsible for running the JJAEP, but merely for providing funds to the juvenile justice board. The county cannot dictate what discretionary offenses will be subject to JJAEP placement. Instead, this should be negotiated between the school districts and the juvenile justice board and included in their MOU (memorandum of understanding). Further, the school district is not obligated to pay for JJAEP facilities (*Att'y. Gen. Op. JC-0459*, 2002).

One issue not covered by statute concerns the extent to which law enforcement officials can interrogate students at school. Provisions of the Texas Family Code come into play whenever a minor is "taken into custody." Moreover, federal case law (the famous *Miranda* case) requires that suspects be advised of their rights when in custody. These issues get cloudy when school "resource officers" serve the dual function of assisting with school discipline and enforcing criminal law. *In the Matter of D.A.R.* is a case in which the court concluded that a thirteen-year-old student had been "taken into custody" when the school resource officer questioned him at school about possession of a gun. The boy confessed to the crime, but did so before the officer advised him of his rights.

Thus the student's lawyer argued that the confession should be suppressed because it was illegally obtained. The court agreed. The court determined that a reasonable thirteen-year-old in the same situation would have believed that his freedom of movement was significantly restricted. Thus, he was "in custody." The court cited the fact that the armed officer was alone with the student with the door closed and the student was not told that he was free to leave or that he could call an adult to assist him.

There is no doubt, however, about the school's authority to contact law enforcement when a student is suspected of committing a crime. This happened in McKinney I.S.D. on December 3, 2004, after someone had started a fire in the middle school. The assistant principal investigated the matter, and was told that R.J. had done it. She questioned R.J. and he allegedly admitted the act. The assistant principal asked the boy to write and sign a confession. Later, the police arrested R.J. for attempted arson. The school also initiated disciplinary proceedings.

The parents sued the school and the assistant principal over this incident, claiming that the confession was improperly extracted from the student and that the police should not have been involved. The court rejected all claims, strongly supporting the actions of the assistant principal: "The school district has a right to confront R.J. with the allegations against him and to offer him the opportunity to provide his own version of the events without the necessity of first contacting his parents." Furthermore, since the assistant principal had probable cause to believe that the student had committed a crime, police involvement was permissible: "To argue that the police had no right to come and arrest R.J. is simply baseless" (*R.J. v. McKinney I.S.D.*, 2006).

A final provision in Chapter 37 limits the power of a court to order an expelled student back on campus. Here is the typical scenario as it has played out in the past: The student commits an expellable offense and is expelled. The student also is charged with criminal misconduct, is found guilty, and placed on probation. As a condition of probation, the student is ordered right back to the campus from which he was expelled. The law now prohibits a judge from placing an expelled student back in any school program, including a school-operated DAEP, unless the juvenile board and the school board have entered into a memorandum of understanding concerning the juvenile probation department's role in supervising and providing other support services for students in DAEPs (TEC §37.010(c)).

OTHER DISCIPLINARY PRACTICES

State law does not address strategies to be used for routine student discipline. This is a matter largely left to the local school district, its administrators, and its teachers. The most frequently used strategies include verbal reprimand, detention, and revocation of privileges. There are a host of others, including corporal punishment, work assignments, parent conferences, and counseling. The range of alternatives is limited only by the imagination and creativity of the disciplinarian.

Traditionally, teachers and administrators have exercised authority over students on the basis of the common law doctrine of *in loco parentis*, "in place of a parent." According to the theory, as long as educators use the same kind of authority a parent would be likely to use, they enjoy legal protection. However, the notion of *in loco parentis* has had to give way in the face of legal decisions recognizing student rights, such as expression and assembly, within the public school. Due process requirements also have undercut it. However, *in loco parentis* remains a viable concept for routine classroom discipline. This is true particularly where the younger child is concerned.

While no hearing is required legally when using routine disciplinary techniques, it seems wise to inform the student of the infraction and give the student a chance to explain. Doing so will help build respect for the school teacher or official and for the discipline system. It will have the added benefit of helping safeguard the educator from a damage suit under state law when corporal punishment is involved.

Corporal Punishment

Corporal punishment continues to be legal in Texas. It also continues to be one of the few areas where local control truly exists. TEC §37.0011 defines "corporal punishment" as: "the deliberate infliction of physical pain by hitting, paddling, spanking, slapping, or any other physical force used as a means of discipline." Excluded from this definition: (1) "physical pain caused by reasonable physical activities associated with athletic training, competition, or physical education" and (2) "restraint" as authorized by state law.

The law then provides that if the board adopts a code of conduct that permits corporal punishment, a district educator may use corporal punishment unless the parent has previously provided a written, signed statement prohibiting the use of corporal punishment. Parents who wish to prohibit corporal punishment must provide a separate written notice each school year (TEC §37.0011).

In effect, this is an "opt out" provision. Parents who object to the use of corporal punishment can prevent it. However, local boards may choose to do things differently. Many will require parental consent, rather than relying on parental silence as this statute authorizes schools to do.

Some school districts have banned the practice. Others restrict it in various ways. Most districts that continue to permit corporal punishment limit it to situations in which parents have given written consent for its use. In light of the controversial nature of this practice and the always present threat of litigation, this would seem to be a sensible policy.

There was speculation after the 2005 session that the Texas Legislature had inadvertently outlawed the use of corporal punishment by school officials. The concern focused on §151.001 of the Texas Family Code, which states that "only the following persons may use corporal punishment for the reasonable discipline of a child." The statute then lists parents, grandparents, stepparents, and guardians. Conspicuously absent: teachers, coaches, and assistant principals. Did the legislature intend to eliminate the practice of corporal punishment in schools?

The commissioner promptly requested clarification from the attorney general. The attorney general stated that corporal punishment continued to be a viable practice in public schools. The new law was intended to clarify the rights of parents and other family members, and thus to make it clear that reasonable corporal punishment by a person authorized by the statute to administer it is not child abuse (GA-0374, 2005).

There have been efforts to eliminate corporal punishment by judicial decree, but they have not been successful. In 1977, the matter went before the nation's highest court. In the case of *Ingraham v. Wright*, the Court ruled that corporal punishment of public school students (1) did not require any formal due process measures, such as notice and a hearing, and (2) under no circumstances could be considered "cruel and unusual punishment" as that term is used in the Eighth Amendment. Thus, in effect, the Supreme Court (by a 5-4 margin) left the regulation of corporal punishment to state and local officials.

Litigation over the practice continues. The attitude of the federal courts is well illustrated in *Flores v. School Board of DeSoto Parish*, a 2004 decision by the Fifth Circuit. This is a case in which a Louisiana teacher used physical force with a student, but the parties characterized the incident quite differently. The parent said that this was an assault. The teacher said this was corporal punishment—he believed the student was tardy in getting to the detention room where he had been assigned. The court concluded that the allegations amounted to a claim of "excessive force," which could be redressed under the state law of Louisiana. Thus the constitutional claims were dismissed.

This is typical. Federal courts clearly prefer that claims involving corporal punishment should be addressed through the state courts, rather than morphing into constitutional issues for the federal courts to sort out. A 2005 decision by a Texas federal judge is illustrative. In *Causby v. Groveton I.S.D.* (2005), the parents sued the school district and two school employees who had paddled their son. The federal court noted that Texas law, like Louisiana law, offered recourse for the excessive use of force. Thus the claims of constitutional violations were dismissed, and the parents were permitted to refile in state court alleging excessive force by the two employees. The school district was completely dismissed from the case since there was no basis for institutional liability under state or federal law.

Even when suit is filed in state court, parents may run into some procedural obstacles. Teresa Venegas charged an assistant principal in Midland I.S.D. with excessive force on her son. Before filing suit, Ms. Venegas used the district's complaint procedures. The complaint procedures called for three levels of review, the third being before the school board. Ms. Venegas completed the first two levels, but did not take the matter to the school board. Instead, she sued in state court.

The case was dismissed without ever reaching the merits. The court held that the mother was required to "exhaust administrative remedies" prior to filing suit. This meant that she had to take the matter through all three levels of review within the district, including the review by the school board. Since she had not done this, the court concluded that the courts did not have jurisdiction to hear her case. Case dismissed (*Venegas v. Silva*, 2006).

Sometimes teachers who are asked to serve as the "witness" to corporal punishment express concerns over liability. Such a teacher was sued in the case of *Fee v. Herndon* (1990), but the Fifth Circuit held that the teacher who observed the spanking did not have a duty under state law to intervene to stop it. The appeals court noted that the parents could pursue their excessive force lawsuit against the principal in state court and also could argue their negligence theory against the teacher in that forum.

Given these decisions, it seems abundantly clear that public-school children have no recourse in federal court under the due process clause of the Fourteenth Amendment for allegations of abuse of corporal punishment. The fact that prisoners do have such recourse is attributable to the different federal claims they can assert, e.g., cruel and unusual punishment under the Eighth Amendment, and to the fact that they are incarcerated and thus not free to escape the abusive conduct.

While federal causes of action may not be available, state claims are. As discussed in Chapter 10, educators expose themselves to potential personal liability for damages when they paddle children. Even when the practice is authorized by local policy and consented to by the parents, suits can be filed alleging that the paddling was excessive or negligent, thus resulting in bodily injury. Every year there are reported cases in which parents have filed child abuse charges, criminal complaints, complaints to the State Board for Educator Certification, personal suits for damages, or a combination of all of these after an incident of corporal punishment. Whether these actions are successful or not, they are

extremely stressful, and often costly, to the educator who has been accused of wrongdoing. He or she rarely picks up the paddle again.

To lessen the chances of damage suits in state or federal courts,
most schools specify that corporal punishment can be used only under
certain circumstances, by certain people, and in accord with certain procedures. The school administrator or teacher who administers corporal
punishment should be careful and should fully comply with all aspects
of local policy on the subject. See the extensive discussion of this subject in Chapter 10.

While Texas leaves all decisions about corporal punishment to local officials, it does impose statewide restrictions on other practices of
a physical nature. Section 37.0021 of the Texas Education Code absolutely prohibits the use of "seclusion" by public schools. Seclusion is
defined as a technique in which a student is confined in a locked box,
locked closet, or locked room that is designed solely to seclude a person
and whose area is less than fifty square feet. The statute does not completely bar "restraint" or "time out," but requires the commissioner to
develop rules for their proper use. Those rules apply only to students
with disabilities and are discussed in Chapter 3.

Suspension from Extracurricular Activities

Most high school assistant principals can tell you that they spend much
of their time dealing with "the ABCs": Athletics, Band, Cheerleading.
Indeed, disciplinary action that takes Billy off the team or Muffy off
the cheerleading squad can stir up a nest of hornets. However, the law
favors the school district in these disputes.

Let's recall the basics of due process. Pursuant to *Goss*, we know
that a student has property and liberty interests, protected by the Fourteenth Amendment, in attending school. But courts, and the Fifth Circuit in particular, have specifically and repeatedly held that no such
protection attaches to extracurricular activities (*Hardy v. University
Interscholastic League*, 1985; *Walsh v. Louisiana High School Athletic
Association*, 1980). Thus it appears that students can be removed from
extracurricular activities without any formal due process measures.

A case decided by the Texas Supreme Court holds that this is true
even if the student is a world-class athlete competing at the highest levels. Joscelin Yeo was an All-American swimmer and the most decorated
athlete in the history of her home country, Singapore. Yeo transferred
from the University of California to the University of Texas. NCAA
rules required that she sit out a year. This restriction could be waived
by California, but it was not. Evidently, the Californians were miffed
over the student's transfer. The story then got complicated. UT did not
interpret the rule the same way California did, and the West Coast uni-

versity filed complaints with the NCAA. Ultimately, the NCAA sided with California, and informed UT that Yeo could not participate in the national championship swimming competition for 2002.

Yeo obtained an injunction that permitted her to compete, but that did not end the litigation. She then sued UT, alleging that the university had deprived her of the "procedural due process" she was entitled to under the Texas Constitution. This argument was rejected by the Texas Supreme Court. The court noted the ample precedent establishing that there was no constitutionally protected interest at stake with regard to extracurricular activities. The fact that Ms. Yeo was a world-renowned athlete did not change the legal analysis. Her concerns about the injury to her future earning capacity were too speculative, and her "reputation" was not entitled to constitutional protection (*NCAA v. Yeo*, 2005).

Thus, whether you are a third-string soccer player or a world-renowned swimmer, the legal analysis is the same. But what about cheerleaders? Alas, the courts cannot seem to rid themselves of suits over cheerleader tryouts and cheerleader discipline. Let us consider the case of *Flour Bluff I.S.D. v. R.S.* When school officials discovered a cheerleader to be in possession of a prohibited drug at school, they assigned her to thirty-six days in the DAEP, which automatically barred the girl from participating in or attending extracurricular activities. There was no dispute about this, as the student served her time in DAEP at the end of the 2004–2005 school year. The problem arose the next school year when school officials declared that the girl could no longer be a cheerleader. The Cheerleader Constitution, which she and her mother signed, required students to relinquish their positions as cheerleaders if they were ever assigned to DAEP. The student obtained an injunction from a local court placing her back on the cheerleader squad in September 2005. By the time the case reached the court of appeals, the 2005–2006 school year was over, the cheerleader "season" was over, and so the court declared the controversy moot. Nevertheless, the frustrated appellate court delivered a message to the lower court, noting that judges should not "waste [their] valuable time and limited resources on exploring the constitutional implications of whether or not someone gets to be a cheerleader" (*Flour Bluff I.S.D. v. R.S.*, 2006).

In fact, disputes over cheerleaders may now be headed to the Texas Education Agency. A parent in Ennis I.S.D. alleged that the tryouts were biased. The parent took the matter to the commissioner, citing TEC §1.002, which requires schools to "provide equal opportunities" to all. The school district sought dismissal of the case, arguing that the Texas Education Agency does not have jurisdiction in disputes over extracurricular activities. But the commissioner ruled that TEA does have jurisdiction, noting that the statute specifically applies to "services and activities," which is a phrase broad enough to encompass extracurricular activities. Turning to the merits, the commissioner ruled in favor of the school district. Nevertheless, the case opens the door to more such challenges at the Texas Education Agency (*Stokes v. Ennis I.S.D.*, 2007).

Furthermore, in the area of extracurricular activities the school may be able to extend its normal jurisdiction beyond school property. If the proposed sanction is a suspension from extracurricular activities, rather than a suspension from school, the courts are much more likely to support the school district's position. In *Ryan G. v. Navasota I.S.D.* (1999), a student was found to be a "minor in possession of alcohol" away from school during spring break. In accordance with the student handbook, the school suspended the student from the baseball team. The parents appealed this decision to the commissioner, but the commissioner found the rule to be proper. Courts have consistently ruled that participation in athletics and other extracurricular activities is a "privilege" rather than a "right." Therefore, where these activities are concerned, schools have more authority to create and enforce rules, even those that apply off campus.

Courts may be supportive of school officials in these disputes, but a wise educator will remember how important extracurricular activities are to both students and parents. Fairness and good common sense dictate that students should be given some opportunity to defend themselves before being tossed off the team. Rules should be clearly explained, and penalties should be enforced only after notice and an opportunity to respond.

Finally, school officials must be sure not to improperly discriminate in connection with extracurricular activities. For example, as far back as 1974 a court struck down a school district regulation that would have prohibited any married student from participating in extracurricular activities (*Bell v. Lone Oak I.S.D.*). Likewise, extracurricular activities must be open to all races, creeds, and nationalities, and both sexes, although separate teams for boys and girls are acceptable in many sports. And an equal opportunity, accompanied by reasonable accommodations, must be provided for students with disabilities.

SUMMARY

In this chapter we have reviewed the key provisions of Texas laws relating to discipline, as well as the important decisions of state and federal courts that help to shape the contours of the due process required for student discipline decision-making. Keep in mind that an entirely different set of laws comes into play if the student has been identified as having a disability under the IDEA (see Chapter 3). The law pertaining to student discipline, like many other areas of the law, swings like a pendulum from an emphasis on authority to an emphasis on individual liberty. The very early days of school law emphasized the importance of the authority of the schoolteacher and principal. The very concept of *in loco parentis* was designed to recognize that authority to the same degree that the law would recognize a parent's authority.

In the 1960s and 1970s, the pendulum swung toward a greater degree of individual liberty and, thus, restrictions on teachers and principals in imposing their authority. Many predict that the recent heightened concern over school safety will cause courts to defer more readily to school authority figures, even if this means less individual liberty for the students. Perhaps. What is safe to say is that the law will continue to impose some restrictions, both procedural and substantive, on school officials in the area of student discipline. The well-prepared educator must stay abreast of this ever evolving field.

NINE

Privacy Issues: Community, Educators, Students

THE MOST OFTEN QUOTED definition of the "right to privacy" is simply "the right to be left alone." But in our complex and interrelated society, there is often a countervailing right to know. We see this, for example, in the context of employee references and student drug testing. In Texas, the public's "right to know" is evident most clearly in the provisions of the Texas Open Meetings and Public Information Acts.

Our purpose in this chapter is to examine the interplay between privacy and the right to know in the context of Texas public schools. We begin with a discussion of the law of privacy and then look at the Texas Open Meetings and Public Information Acts, educator privacy rights, and student privacy issues. We will also discuss employee lifestyle issues, student records, personal grooming and dress codes, and student searches.

THE LEGAL FRAMEWORK

The U.S. Constitution

The most specific reference to privacy in the U.S. Constitution is found in the Fourth Amendment, which states that "the right of the people to be secure in their persons, houses, papers, and effects, against unreasonable searches and seizures, shall not be violated, and no warrants shall issue but upon probable cause, supported by oath or affirmation, and particularly describing the place to be searched, and the persons or things to be seized." The U.S. Supreme Court has ruled that public school students are entitled to the protections of the Fourth Amendment, which applies to state governments and their political subdivisions through the Fourteenth Amendment. But, at the same time, the Court also has recognized that school officials must have sufficient discretion to maintain order. Thus, as we will see, the standards for a lawful student search by school personnel are less stringent than would be the case if the police were to conduct the search.

Federal courts also have found a right of family and personal privacy inherent in the word *liberty* of the Fourteenth Amendment due process clause ("nor shall any State deprive any person of life, liberty, or property, without due process of law"). In the 1920s, the U.S. Supreme Court construed the word *liberty* to include the right of parents to control the upbringing of their children (*Meyer v. Nebraska,* 1923; *Pierce v. Society of Sisters,* 1925). In 1971, the Court ruled that people have a liberty interest in being free from unwarranted government stigmatization of their reputation (*Wisconsin v. Constantineau*). In 1965, the Court ruled that a state law prohibiting the use of contraceptive devices by married couples violated the zone of personal privacy (*Griswold v. Connecticut*). Later, in a very controversial decision, the Court extended the right to include a woman's choice to have an abortion (*Roe v. Wade,* 1973). The right of privacy in the context of the public school is dependent to some extent on the reasoning expressed in these rulings.

Federal Statutes

The federal privacy law affecting education is the 1974 Family Educational Rights and Privacy Act (FERPA) (20 U.S.C. §1232g, as amended), also known as the Buckley Amendment. FERPA applies to any educational institution receiving federal funds. Thus public, as well as some private, schools and colleges are subject to its provisions. FERPA regulates student recordkeeping activities by giving parents and students access to student records, the right to challenge material contained therein, and the right to restrict disclosure of personally identifiable information. Its provisions are discussed in detail in the section on student rights of privacy later in this chapter.

State Law

The law of torts (civil wrongs committed by one person against another) has had the most to do with privacy. The so-called common law of torts, meaning generally accepted case law as it has developed in Texas and elsewhere, has included the familiar tort of defamation. Defamation through libel or slander traditionally involves the knowing communication of false information to a third party such as to cause the person defamed significant loss (e.g., being fired from a job or suffering a divorce). Other torts related to privacy include trespass and false arrest. A person who can prove in court that he or she has suffered loss because of these torts may recover monetary damages, though as noted in Chapter 10, the immunity provisions in Texas law afford some protection to school districts and school professional personnel.

Aside from these traditional torts, state constitutions, statutes, and case law generally were silent on a personal right of privacy until well into the twentieth century. Industrialization and urban growth, though, have produced an array of privacy threats, ranging from unwarranted noise to newspaper gossip stories and, now, computerized data banks.

By 1960 enough state statutory and case law had developed for commentators to identify the chief components of the evolving common law against personal privacy invasion: (1) intrusion upon a person's seclusion or solitude or into the person's private affairs; (2) public disclosure of embarrassing private facts about a person; (3) publicity that places a person in a false light in the public eye; or (4) appropriation of a person's name or likeness for personal advantage.

Texas courts have recognized these four personal privacy torts but have restricted damage awards to situations where the person bringing suit (the plaintiff) can show: (1) that publicity was given to matters concerning his or her private life; (2) that the publication would be highly offensive to a person of ordinary sensibilities; and (3) that the matter publicized was not of legitimate public concern.

By "publicized," the Texas Supreme Court has indicated that "the matter must be communicated to the public at large, such that the matter becomes one of public knowledge" (*Industrial Foundation of the South v. Texas Industrial Accident Board*, 1976, pp. 683–684). Invasion of personal privacy overlaps somewhat with the traditional tort of defamation and tends to increase the situations in which suits can be brought. Personal privacy torts surface most often in the context of employee references, a topic to be discussed later in the chapter.

THE TEXAS OPEN MEETINGS AND PUBLIC INFORMATION ACTS

The Texas Open Meetings Act (TOMA) and the Texas Public Information Act (TPIA) seem to be in a state of tension with evolving privacy law because they are designed to further public access to government business. Because both are quite detailed, only the major features of each are discussed here.

Texas Open Meetings Act

Chapter 551 of the Texas Government Code requires that meetings of governmental bodies, such as school boards, be open to the public. Section 551.002 of the act states: "Every regular, special, or called meeting of a governmental body shall be open to the public, except as provided by this chapter." Recall from Chapter 1 that TOMA (as well as the Texas Public Information Act) applies to the governing boards of open-enrollment charter schools, as well. All members of a governmental body must complete a training course concerning their responsibilities under TOMA within ninety days of taking the oath of office or taking over the position (Gov't Code §551.005).

For TOMA to apply, five prerequisites must be met: (1) the body must be within the executive or legislative department of the state,

(2) the entity must be under the control of one or more elected or appointed members, (3) the meeting must involve formal action by or deliberation among a quorum (majority) of members, (4) the discussion or action must involve public business or public policy, and (5) the entity must have supervision or control over that public business or public policy.

The law also applies to a committee composed of one or more members of the board of trustees of a school district, comprising less than a quorum of the governing body, if the committee has control over public business or has influence over the governmental body's decisions (*Finlan v. City of Dallas*, 1995). However, a purely advisory committee that can make recommendations but has no supervision or control over public business or policy generally is not subject to TOMA (*City of Austin v. Evans*, 1990; *Roberts v. Wilmer-Hutchins I.S.D.*, 2006).

Meetings and Quorums. A "meeting" under TOMA means a deliberation, or verbal exchange, among a quorum of a governmental body (or between a quorum and another person) during which public business or public policy is discussed or at which formal action is taken. The TOMA definition of "meeting" encompasses staff briefing sessions where board members receive information from or give information to a third party, including employees, as well as engage in questioning. However, a member of a governmental body may leave an open meeting to confer privately with an employee of the governmental body. A private consultation between a member of a governmental body and one of its employees does not constitute a meeting as long as the conversation takes place outside the hearing of a quorum of the other members of the governmental body (*Att'y. Gen. Op. GA-0989*, 2013). The term "meeting" does not include the gathering of a quorum of a governmental body at a social function unrelated to public business, or the attendance by a quorum at a convention, workshop, ceremonial event, or press conference if formal action is not taken and any discussion of public business is incidental to the gathering (Gov't Code §551.001(4)(B)(iv)). In addition, a quorum of a governmental body attending a legislative committee or agency meeting for the purpose of giving testimony is permitted under the Act (Gov't Code §551.0035).

The Texas Supreme Court has ruled that once a quorum is in place, there can be no informal discussion outside of a meeting in which the majority of a public decision-making body is considering a pending issue. "There is either formal consideration of the matter in compliance with the Open Meetings Act or an illegal meeting" (*Acker v. Texas Water Commission*, 1990). The case involved two members (a quorum) of the three-member Texas Water Commission who were overheard in the restroom conversing about an impending application of a water treatment plant.

A quorum generally is required for the board to take action. However, an exception applies if the area has been declared a disaster by the president or governor and a majority of the board members are unable to attend (Gov't Code §418.112). A school board meeting must be held within the boundaries of the school district, unless it is a joint meeting with another district or governmental entity (TEC §26.007(b)).

Notice. Written notice of the date, place, and subject of each meeting must be posted on a bulletin board convenient to the public in the central administration building at least seventy-two hours before the meeting (Gov't Code §§551.041, 551.043). The agenda must be accessible to the public for the full seventy-two hours, even when the building is closed. With few exceptions, the seventy-two-hour requirement must be complied with strictly (*Smith County v. Thornton,* 1987). A governmental body with an Internet website must post meeting notices on its website in addition to the required physical posting. School districts located in a city with a population of 48,000 or more also must post the meeting agenda on their websites (Gov't Code §551.056). A governmental body that makes a good faith effort to comply with this section is not penalized for technical difficulties beyond its control (Gov't Code §551.056(d)).

A 2005 Texas appeals court concluded that a notice is sufficient as long as it makes the public aware of the topic for consideration; the governmental body need not list all the consequences that may flow from discussion of the topic (*Burks v. Yarbrough,* 2005). However, the Texas Supreme Court has ruled that posting notices of meetings with business items indicated in general terms, such as *personnel, litigation,* and *real estate,* violated the TOMA provision regarding posting of agendas (*Cox Enterprises, Inc. v. Board of Trustees of Austin I.S.D.,* 1986). Also inadequate are general phrases such as "City Manager's Report," "Mayor's Update," and "questions . . . regarding city policies or activities" (*Att'y. Gen. Op. GA-0668,* 2008). Notice concerning a land lease complied with TOMA where it specified the parties involved, the type and subject of the agreement, and the size and location of the property (*City of Galveston v. Saint-Paul,* 2008).

A Texas appellate court discussed the notice issue concerning the selection of a principal. Given the special interest of the public in the principalship, posted agendas must specify this position rather than include it within a general "employment of personnel" category. Failure to do so could void the board's selection in a contested case (*Point Isabel I.S.D. v. Hinojosa,* 1990). The Texas Commissioner of Education similarly ruled that an agenda that stated "Recommendation for Proposed Terminations of Instructional Employees" was not sufficient notice concerning the proposed termination of a principal's contract, given the high public interest in the proposed action (*Spaniel v. Fort Worth I.S.D.,* 2010).

On the other hand, TOMA does not create a right for employees to have specific notice of discussion or action pertaining to their own employment. A case in point involved a band instructor in Bridgeport I.S.D. who alleged that board failure to specify in the notice that his particular contract would be discussed in closed session denied him an opportunity to request an open hearing. The Austin Court of Appeals was not persuaded, noting that the purpose of the act is to alert the public to the workings of government, not to provide due process protections to individual employees. The teacher had not demonstrated a special public interest that would require the board to list his specific position as the topic of discussion (*Stockdale v. Meno*, 1993).

A good way to follow the general thrust of TOMA regarding agenda items is to apply the "Joe Citizen" test: Will the average citizen who does not follow school matters as a rule understand the significance of an item on the posted agenda? If not, specificity is lacking. If a member of the public inquires about a subject not on the posted agenda, the governing body may respond with factual information, recite existing policy, or propose to place the item on the agenda for a later meeting. Action taken at a meeting on any item not appearing on the posted agenda may be voided.

A governmental body that recesses a meeting from one day to the next does not have to repost notice as long as the continuation was in good faith and not to circumvent TOMA; however, a three-day continuation does require a second posting (Gov't Code §551.0411). A governmental body that is prevented from convening a meeting due to a catastrophe may follow the two-hour posting requirement for emergency meetings (see below) if it can hold the meeting within seventy-two hours. A meeting held beyond the original seventy-two hours requires reposting (Gov't Code §551.0411).

Emergency Meetings. TOMA allows emergency meetings to be held if two hours' public notice is given stating the nature of the emergency (Gov't Code §551.045). Emergencies are limited by statute to imminent threats to public health and safety or reasonably unforeseeable situations requiring immediate action, e.g., the relocation of large numbers of residents from Louisiana to Texas following Hurricane Katrina (Gov't Code §551.045(b), (e)). The law also allows additional items to be placed on the agenda of a nonemergency meeting after the seventy-two-hour posting deadline if warranted by an emergency or urgent public necessity, as long as the reasons for the additions are noted. In the event of a mass relocation, the governmental body must provide one hour's notice to the news media of an emergency meeting or added agenda item. Special notice of an emergency meeting or emergency agenda item must be provided to the media, if requested, by fax, e-mail, or telephone (Gov't Code §551.047(c)).

Closed Sessions. A closed session is permitted in the following situations:

- to consult privately with an attorney to seek advice about pending or contemplated litigation or a settlement or offer or to discuss a conflict of interest involving the attorney (§551.071);
- to deliberate the purchase, exchange, lease, or value of real property if deliberation in an open meeting would have a detrimental effect on the position of the governmental body in negotiations with a third person (§551.072);
- to deliberate a negotiated contract for a prospective gift or donation to the state or the governmental body if deliberation in an open meeting would have a detrimental effect on the position of the governmental body in negotiations with a third person (§551.073);
- to deliberate the appointment, employment, evaluation, reassignment, duties, discipline, or dismissal of a public officer or employee or to hear a complaint or charge against an officer or employee, unless that officer or employee requests a public hearing (§551.074);
- to deliberate a security audit or the deployment of security personnel or devices (§551.076);
- to deliberate in a case involving discipline of a public-school student or in a hearing involving a complaint or charge brought by one school district employee against another, unless an open hearing is requested in writing by the parent or guardian or by the employee against whom the complaint or charge is brought (§551.082);
- to deliberate a matter regarding a public-school student if personally identifiable information about the student necessarily will be revealed, unless the parent, guardian, or adult student requests in writing an open meeting (§551.0821); and
- to deliberate the standards, guidelines, terms, or conditions the board will follow in a consultation with a representative of an employee group (§551.083).

A closed session is required when a school board discusses academic skills assessment instruments (TEC §39.030(a)). Further, the commissioner has upheld a school board's decision to go into closed session to discuss a grievance concerning cheerleader tryouts. The school board properly closed the meeting in compliance with FERPA to prevent the public disclosure of personally identifiable information about the students (*C.M.G. v. Mercedes I.S.D.*, 2006). As noted above, complaints concerning officers or school employees may be heard in closed session unless the officer or employee complained of chooses otherwise. Note that it is the person complained of—not the person complaining—who gets to decide whether the hearing is in closed session (*Conroy v. Nacogdoches I.S.D.*, 2004).

In a 2010 case, the U.S. Court of Appeals for the Fifth Circuit upheld Texas Association of School Board (TASB) Policy BED (Local), which prohibits the open discussion of specific personnel matters during the public comment portion of a school board meeting. While individuals are free to present general concerns in open session, complaints about a specific matter should be handled through the district's grievance process. The open comment portion of a board meeting is a limited public forum whereby the board may hear general concerns, then direct the speaker to the proper channels for resolution (*Fairchild v. Liberty I.S.D.*, 2010).

Note that a governmental body may admit an officer or employee into a closed session only if that person's participation is necessary to the matter under consideration and the person's interests are not adverse to those of the governmental body. Adhering to this standard, the commissioner determined that the attorneys for the administration and the school board, but not the superintendent, were lawfully allowed into executive session while a grievance was being deliberated (*Walker v. North East I.S.D.*, 2013). Additionally, a board may not hold a "public comment" session during a closed meeting by taking volunteers from the audience to provide input (*Att'y. Gen. Op. GA-0511*, 2007).

The Texas Supreme Court has held that, while board members can express opinions on issues and announce how they intend to vote in closed session, the actual vote or decision must be made in public session. Thus, the board violated the law by conducting a straw vote in closed session and then voting unanimously in open session for the candidate with the most straw votes. The board also violated the law by selecting in closed session a consultant and a search committee composed of nonboard members to screen candidates for the superintendency. Even a discussion of their selection in a closed meeting was prohibited, since consultants are not school employees under §551.074 above. However, the board did not violate the law by deciding in closed session to make public the names and qualifications of candidates for the superintendent's position or discussing the possibility of employing a particular candidate where no vote was taken (*Cox Enterprises, Inc. v. Board of Trustees of Austin I.S.D.*, 1986).

The law requires the presiding officer of a public meeting to announce, after the start of that meeting, the intention to hold a closed session and to identify the reason before doing so. Failure to do so will render actions taken at the meeting voidable (*Rickaway v. Elkhart I.S.D.*, 1995). In a 2006 appeals court case, a city failed to demonstrate that an open discussion concerning the purchase of real property from a school district would have impeded the city's negotiations. At the time of the meeting the city already had the district's resolution and warranty deed for the property; thus the city's vote in closed session to purchase the property was void (*City of Laredo v. Escamilla*, 2006).

The posted agenda need not state that a particular subject will be discussed in closed session (*Att'y. Gen. LO-90-27*). However, the notice requirements regarding specificity are the same for an open or closed meeting. No formal, final action may be taken at a closed session. Matters may be discussed during this time, but formal action must take place in open sessions. Note that a board is not required to deliberate in open session before voting (*Argyle I.S.D. v. Wolf*, 2007). A closed session can be continued from one day to the next as long as the governmental body announces its continuation in open session on both days (*Att'y. Gen. Op. JC-0285*, 2000).

Tape Recordings and Certified Agendas. Governmental bodies must keep a tape recording or minutes of open meetings and make them available to the general public. Video recording also is allowed under the act. For meetings closed to the public, the keeping of a certified agenda or tape recording is mandated except when the closed meeting is for the purpose of receiving legal advice. A certified agenda is a document sworn by the presiding officer to contain a true and correct record of the closed session. A certified agenda must include (1) a statement describing the subject matter of each deliberation, (2) a record of any action taken, and (3) a statement by the presiding officer indicating the date and time at the beginning and end of the closed session. The certified agenda or tape recording is not available to the general public, but is to be kept for a period of at least two years for possible use in legal proceedings involving challenges to closed meetings. The attorney general has advised that individual board members may review the agenda or tape of a closed meeting whether or not they attended the meeting, but may not make additional copies (*Att'y. Gen. LO-98-033; Att'y. Gen. Op. JC-0120*, 1999).

Tape recordings of a closed session may be disclosed only pursuant to a court order issued in a case brought under TOMA. Releasing a certified agenda or tape recording of a closed meeting may result in money damages (Gov't Code §551.146). A federal trial court required a school district to release audiotapes from the closed session of a board meeting where the board allegedly had received testimony and engaged in final deliberations during a woman's level III grievance hearing. The woman was not permitted into the closed session, and her grievance ultimately was denied. Thus the tapes were relevant to the woman's claims; however, confidential information such as employee evaluations and student records can be revealed only to the parties in the lawsuit (*Fairchild v. Liberty I.S.D.*, 2006).

Meetings by Telephone and Videoconference Call. Government Code §§551.125–.127 allow governmental bodies to hold meetings by telephone and videoconference call. The telephone conference call can be arranged only if (1) the meeting is held by an advisory board or (2) an emergency or public necessity exists and the convening of a quorum at one location would be difficult or impossible. Conference call meetings are subject to the TOMA notice requirements. The notice of a public meeting need not state that the meeting will be conducted by telephone. The notice must specify as the location of the meeting the place where meetings of the governmental body usually are held.

The statutory phrase "difficult or impossible" contemplates extraordinary circumstances. Mere inconvenience to board members is insufficient. TOMA does not authorize absent members to participate in a meeting by telephone conference call when a quorum is present at the meeting location (*Att'y. Gen. Op. JC-0352*, 2001). Each portion of the conference call that is required to be open to the public must be audible and tape-recorded. Two-way communication must be provided during the full course of the meeting, and the speakers must be identified prior to speaking.

A videoconference call may be held to enable a member of a governmental body to participate remotely in a meeting. It is defined as a communication in which at least one of the participants communicates through audio and video signals transmitted over a telephone network, data network, or the Internet. A videoconference call is permitted as long as the governmental body establishes one suitable physical space, located in or within a reasonable distance of the jurisdiction of the governmental body, where the presiding officer is physically present. A camera and microphone must be set up for public participation, and a member of the public must be permitted to participate to the same extent as at a regular meeting.

Participants are to be both sufficiently visible and audible that members of the public can observe the demeanor and hear the voice of each participant during the open portion of the meeting. Two-way communication is to be maintained among the locations during the meeting. At a minimum an audio transcription of the meeting must be made. If technical difficulties arise, the meeting must be recessed or adjourned. Note also that a governmental body may consult with an attorney, other than one employed by the body, via telephone or videoconference call in an open or closed meeting (Gov't Code §551.129).

Internet Broadcast. The Act also permits school boards and other governmental bodies to broadcast an open meeting over the Internet (Gov't Code §551.128). To do so, the board must establish an Internet site and provide access to the broadcast. The Internet site must post notice of the meeting within the required timelines under TOMA. The school district also may consult with its attorney through the Internet connection, either publicly or privately, pursuant to TEC §551.129.

Violations. A board's action in violation of TOMA is voidable, but a violation of one item does not affect the validity of other actions taken during the meeting. While an action taken without proper notice may be "voidable," a governmental body may "cure" a prior violation of the Act. An action taken in violation of the Act cannot be ratified to take retroactive effect, but a governmental body can reconsider and reauthorize the action in a subsequent meeting (*City of Galveston v. Saint-Paul*, 2008). Only courts can declare governmental actions void. Any interested party may bring a court action under TOMA. Persons who substantially prevail in a lawsuit are entitled to recover court costs and legal fees.

Criminal Provisions. Government Code §551.143 makes it a criminal offense for members of a governmental body to "knowingly conspire to circumvent [TOMA's requirements] by meeting in numbers less than a quorum for the purpose of secret deliberations." The AG concluded that §551.143 applies to members of a governmental body who secretly discuss a public matter through successive gatherings, even though none of the meetings physically constitutes a quorum at any one time. For example, a member of a governmental body who made successive telephone calls to other members of the body to discuss public business would violate TOMA if the members of the governmental body "knowingly conspired to circumvent TOMA" (*Att'y. Gen. Op. GA-0326*, 2005). Likewise, an e-mail exchange by a quorum of four or more board members about school business would constitute an illegal meeting (*Att'y. Gen. Op. JC-0307*, 2000).

TOMA §551.144 imposes criminal penalties for discussion of public business by a quorum of public officials outside an open meeting. Holding an illegally closed meeting constitutes a misdemeanor punishable by a fine up to $500 or imprisonment in the county jail for up to six months, or both. Knowingly conspiring to deliberate in numbers less than a quorum for the purpose of secret deliberations is subject to the same penalty (Gov't Code §551.143). Claiming ignorance of the law is no excuse (*Tovar v. State*, 1998). However, it is a defense to criminal prosecution that the board member relied on a court order, judicial opinion, attorney general's opinion, or a written opinion by the school district's attorney (Gov't Code §551.144(c)).

A group of city council members challenged the criminal provisions of TOMA, claiming that the prohibition against a quorum of public officials discussing public business outside of an open meeting violated their First Amendment free speech rights. The U.S. Court of Appeals for the Fifth Circuit upheld the TOMA provisions. TOMA is a content-neutral statute that does not prohibit speech based on the viewpoint expressed. Instead, the purpose of the criminal provisions of TOMA is to promote openness in the government's decision-making process. Public officials are free to discuss public business by any number of means as long as they do not knowingly conspire to circumvent TOMA. Moreover, the TOMA provisions are narrowly tailored to serve the significant governmental interests of fostering public trust and discouraging fraud and corruption. The Fifth Circuit found no constitutional right of government officials to discuss public policy among a quorum of their governmental body in private (*Asgeirsson v. Abbott*, 2012).

The legislature in 2013 passed a law providing that a communication among members of a governmental body about public business or policy does not constitute a meeting or deliberation if the communication is in writing and posted to an online message board or similar application that is accessible and searchable by the public. The communication must be posted for at least thirty days and maintained by the governmental body for six years. The governmental body must own or control the message board, and it may have only one. The message board must be prominently displayed on the governmental body's website and not more than "one click away" from the homepage. Only members of the governmental body or authorized staff members may post messages. Governmental bodies may not use the online message board to vote or take other action, and nothing on the board shall be construed as an action of the governmental body (Gov't Code §551.006).

Texas Public Information Act

Formerly known as the Texas Open Records Act and modeled after the federal Freedom of Information Act, the Texas Public Information Act (TPIA) is a companion to the complex open meetings measure. Its provisions are found in Chapter 552 of the Texas Government Code. The TPIA rests on the proposition that "government is the servant and not the master of the people" and thus "each person is entitled, unless otherwise expressly provided by law, at all times to complete information about the affairs of government and the official acts of public officials and employees." The declaration of policy in §552.001 goes on to note that "the people, in delegating authority, do not give their public servants the right to decide what is good for the people to know and what is not good for them to know. The people insist on remaining informed so that they may retain control over the instruments they have created."
The TPIA's declaration of purpose ends by noting that the "provisions of this Act shall be liberally construed" in favor of granting people access to information produced or maintained by a governmental body. Included in the definition of "governmental body" are boards of trustees of school districts. All members of a governmental body must complete a training

course concerning their responsibilities under the TPIA within ninety days of taking the oath of office or taking over the position (Gov't Code §552.012(b)). Note that a school board trustee acting in the trustee's official capacity may access information maintained by the school district without making an official TPIA request (TEC §11.1512(c)). The district may withhold or redact confidential information.

"Public information" is broadly defined to include any information that is written, produced, collected, assembled, or maintained under a law or ordinance or in connection with official business by or for a governmental body, for which the governmental body expends public funds, has a right of access, or owns. The term encompasses information written, produced, collected, assembled, or maintained by an individual officer or employee in that person's official capacity if the information pertains to official business of the governmental body, including any electronic communication created, transmitted, received, or maintained on any device—even the individual's personal device (Gov't Code §552.002). Public information includes any physical material on which information may be recorded, such as a book, paper, letter, document, photograph, map, or drawing, as well as any electronic communication, such as an e-mail, Internet posting, text message, or instant message.

The Act establishes the chief administrative officer or designee of each governmental unit as the officer for public information and requires the officer to display a sign describing the public's rights to inspect and obtain public information, the governmental body's responsibility to produce such information, and the procedures controlling requests and production. The only inquiry to be made of persons requesting information is that they produce proper identification. If a large amount of information is requested, the officer for public information may discuss how the request might be narrowed, but may not inquire as to the purpose for which the information will be used.

If a governmental body believes a certain document should be withheld from the public and there has been no prior determination on the matter, it has ten business days after receiving the request (1) to seek an advisory opinion from the attorney general stating which exceptions apply and (2) to notify the requestor that it has done so (Gov't Code §552.301). Within fifteen business days after receiving the request, the governmental body must submit to the AG (1) written comments stating which exceptions apply and why the information should be withheld, (2) a copy of the request for information, (3) a signed statement or other proof of the date the request was received, and (4) a copy of the information requested, indicating where the exceptions apply (Gov't Code §552.301(e)). The governmental body also must send a copy of its written comments to the requestor not later than the fifteenth business day after receiving the request, redacting the substance of the information requested, i.e., removing the confidential information from the document. Requests, notices, decisions, and other documents required by the TPIA may be submitted electronically to and from the AG's office, as long as the filing is submitted within the specified time period (Gov't Code §552.309).

If the governmental body does not timely request an AG opinion, the information is presumed public and must be released, unless the governmental body can show a compelling reason to withhold the information under an exception to the Act (Gov't Code §552.302). For instance, where the documents are confidential by law and implicate the privacy rights of a third party, as with criminal reports involving the abuse of a child, the documents may be withheld despite an untimely request for an AG opinion (*Doe v. Tarrant County Dist. Attorneys*, 2008). A member of the public also may submit written comments to the AG concerning why information should be withheld or released. That person must send a copy of the written comments to the requestor and to the governmental body, redacting the substance of any information at issue in the copy to the requestor (Gov't Code §552.304).

The AG has forty-five business days after receiving a request to render a decision; however, the AG may extend this time period by an additional ten business days (Gov't Code §552.306). If a governmental body disagrees with a decision of the AG, it has thirty days to challenge the decision in state court. Otherwise it must comply with the AG's ruling (Gov't Code §552.324). If the decision involves a parent's request for records from a school district, only the parent may appeal the court's decision (TEC §26.0085).

Items That Must Be Disclosed. Sections 552.022–552.0225 of the TPIA list several types of information that must be released to the public upon request, unless specifically made confidential by law. Some of the items relevant to education are listed below:

- a completed report, audit, evaluation, or investigation made of, for, or by a governmental body unless dealing with the detection, investigation, or prosecution of a crime under §552.108;
- the name, sex, ethnicity, salary, title, and dates of employment of each employee and officer;
- information in an account, voucher, or contract relating to the receipt or expenditure of public or other funds;
- the name of each official and the final record of voting on all proceedings;
- a policy statement or interpretation that has been adopted or issued by an agency;
- administrative staff manuals and instructions to staff that affect a member of the public;

- information in a bill for attorneys' fees that is not protected by the attorney-client privilege;
- a settlement agreement to which a governmental body is a party; and
- certain investment information.

Personal Information. The law excludes from required public disclosure information deemed confidential by constitutional or statutory provision or by judicial decision (Gov't Code §552.101). Thus, for example, information that would violate someone's personal right of privacy as recognized by Texas law cannot be released. Section 552.102(a) specifically exempts "information in a personnel file, the disclosure of which would constitute a clearly unwarranted invasion of personal privacy." Such information includes an applicant's personal financial history (*Att'y. Gen. ORD-626*, 1994). An evaluation document of a certified administrator or teacher is confidential and cannot be released to the public under TEC §21.355 as incorporated through TPIA §552.101, including a memorandum from a school principal to a teacher directing corrective action (*Abbott v. North East I.S.D.*, 2006). TEC §21.355 also applies to teachers and administrators at open-enrollment charter schools, whether or not certified, except the document may be released to another school where the individual has applied for employment. Section 552.102(a) expressly grants public employees, including teachers or their designated representatives, a general right of access to their own personnel files.

An employee's transcript in a personnel file is exempt from disclosure, except for the degree obtained and the curriculum studied (Gov't Code §552.102(b)). The Texas Supreme Court has ruled that the birth dates of public employees are exempt from disclosure, determining that the employee's privacy interest "substantially outweighs" any public interest in disclosure and noting the risk for potential identity theft (*Texas Comptroller of Public Accounts v. Attorney General of Texas*, 2010). Section 552.147(a-1) makes the Social Security number of an employee of a school district confidential. A district must by policy prohibit the use of an employee's Social Security number as an identifier, other than for tax purposes (TEC §11.1514).

Certain personal information pertaining to current or former employees and officials may be withheld without requesting an AG opinion if the individual timely requests that the information remain confidential, including home addresses, telephone numbers, emergency contact information, and information revealing whether the individual has family members (Gov't Code §552.024). The governmental body must inform the requestor of the nature of the information withheld and provide instructions on how to seek an AG opinion on the matter.

In addition, Section 552.151 permits a governmental body to withhold any information about an officer or employee that would subject an individual to a substantial threat of physical harm if disclosed. For instance, travel information pertaining to the security officers who protect the governor of Texas was deemed confidential (*Texas Dept. of Public Safety v. Cox Texas Newspapers, L.P.*, 2011).

The name of an applicant for a superintendent's position may not be disclosed, though the board must provide notice of the names of finalists at least twenty-one days before the date of the meeting when the selection will be made (Gov't Code §552.126). However, unless specifically exempted by statute from disclosure (as, for example, with candidates for college presidencies and the superintendency), names of applicants for employment must be disclosed (*Att'y. Gen. ORD-585,* 1991).

Except for those assigned to law enforcement officers, the general rule is that cellular car telephone numbers have to be released if the telephones are paid for by public funds, just as they would be for telephones in the school (*Att'y. Gen. ORD-506,* 1988). However, the personal cellular phone numbers and personal pager numbers of government officials are exempt from disclosure (*Att'y. Gen. ORD-670,* 2001). Business e-mail addresses must be released (*Att'y. Gen. OR99-2315,* 1999), as must e-mails between board members on their personal computers, if the e-mails relate to school district business, as discussed earlier. Certain information contained within the e-mails may be withheld if it falls within one of the other exceptions to disclosure under the Act (*Att'y. Gen. OR2003-0951,* 2003).

The AG has listed several items that may be withheld without first requesting an AG opinion, including direct deposit authorization forms; I-9, W-2, and W-4 forms; certified agendas or tape recordings of closed meetings; Texas driver's license or ID card numbers; access device information, such as credit card and debit card numbers; and in most cases the e-mail addresses of members of the public who communicated with the governmental body for a non-business-related purpose (*Att'y. Gen. Op. No. ORD-684,* 2009). A governmental body must notify the requestor in writing when it redacts information pursuant to this determination. Redaction of driver's license and access device information requires notification using a form developed by the AG.

Criminal History Information, Witness Statements, and Investigative Reports. A person's criminal history record is confidential and may be revealed only to that individual and to authorized district personnel (Gov't Code §§411.083(a); 411.0845(d)). The record must be kept separate from the employee's personnel file. School district audit working papers related to a criminal history background check of a public school employee also are exempted from disclosure (Gov't Code §552.116).

The El Paso Court of Appeals has ruled that witness statements obtained during an investigation into alleged sexual improprieties of a police lieutenant did not have to be disclosed. Doing so would amount to a clearly unwarranted invasion of personal privacy against the witnesses and could discourage cooperation in investigations of employee wrongdoing (*Morales v. Ellen*, 1992). However, because citizens have a legitimate public concern with the behavior of a police official that led to his resignation, the lieutenant's statement to investigators did have to be disclosed. The AG has ruled that records and documents resulting from the investigation of sexual harassment allegations against a principal must be released, with the deletion of identities of victims and witnesses but including references to the principal's name, because of the public's interest in sexual harassment in the workplace (*Att'y. Gen. OR2003-5194; Att'y. Gen. OR2003-4773*).

An investigative report compiled by an attorney, however, was ruled exempt in its entirety from disclosure by virtue of the attorney-client privilege under §552.107(1) of the Act (*Harlandale I.S.D. v. Cornyn*, 2000). The name of a student or minor who is the victim of abuse by an educator is not public under the TPIA, even if the name is included in a report to SBEC (TEC §21.006(h); Penal Code §21.12(d)). An "informer privilege" has been added that protects the identity of a student, employee, or former employee who discloses violations of civil, criminal, or regulatory law (Gov't Code §552.135).

Inter- or Intraagency Memoranda. Section 552.111 exempts from disclosure an "interagency or intraagency memorandum or letter that would not be available by law to a party in litigation with the agency." This exception has been the source of litigation that has narrowed its scope. The Austin Court of Appeals has ruled that where the information requested routinely is available in litigation, it must be disclosed (*Texas Dept. of Public Safety v. Gilbreath*, 1992). The practical effect of the ruling was to confine the inter- or intraagency exception to material directly related to agency policy-making.

A Texas court of appeals ruled in 2001 that Arlington I.S.D. had to release to a newspaper the results of its annual school effectiveness survey administered to the staff at each campus. The appeals court concluded that most of the information requested was factual in nature and thus did not fall within the Act's exception for interagency memoranda containing advice, opinions, and recommendations relating to policy-making (*Arlington I.S.D. v. Texas Attorney General*).

The minutes of meetings attended by administrators, teachers, and employee representatives—such as a consultation or campus-based committee—must be disclosed if the committee has the authority to take final action on a matter and did so. If the minutes reflect only deliberation and no final action, they need not be disclosed. However, if the committee serves only in an advisory capacity, the minutes constitute "advice, opinion, or recommendation" and need not be disclosed under §552.111 (*Att'y. Gen. ORD-491*, 1988).

Student Records. The TPIA exempts from disclosure student records at institutions "funded wholly, or in part, by state revenue" (Government Code §552.114). This provision in effect extends the protections of the federal Family Educational Rights and Privacy Act (FERPA) to schools that are state-funded. See the discussion of FERPA later in this chapter.

Other Exempt Items. Other items that are exempted from disclosure include information that if released would give advantage to competitors or bidders, certain economic development information, and certain information relating to a public/private partnership for the development of educational facilities (Gov't Code §§552.104, 552.131, and 552.153). School district security audits and multihazard emergency operations plans are confidential; however, a document that enables a person to verify that the district has complied with the law does have to be released. A Texas appeals court ruled that video images from the security system of a governmental entity are exempt from disclosure if used to protect public property from an act of terrorism or related criminal activity (*Texas Dept. of Public Safety v. Abbott*, 2010). Another Texas appeals court held that a school district was justified in redacting portions of its police handbook and policies under Government Code §552.108 because disclosure would interfere with law enforcement in that it would reveal the department's techniques and limitations (*Texas Appleseed v. Spring Branch I.S.D.*, 2012).

Production of Records. Section 552.221 requires a governmental body "promptly" to produce records for inspection, which is defined as "as soon as possible under the circumstances," "within a reasonable time," or "without delay." If the information is unavailable at the time or cannot be produced within ten business days, the officer for public records must certify that fact in writing and set a reasonable time when the information will be available. A request to provide records is considered fulfilled upon proof that the records were placed in the mail or with a carrier within the required time period. When a governmental body cannot determine the actual date of receipt of a request for public information that was sent through the U.S. mail, the request is presumed to have been received on the third business day after the postmark date (Gov't Code §552.301(a-1)).

If a governmental body is unclear as to what information is sought or if a large amount is requested, it may ask the requestor in writing for a clarification, narrowing, or discussion of the request (Gov't Code §552.222). A requestor has sixty days to respond. On the sixty-first day, the TPIA request is considered withdrawn if the requestor has not responded in writing. When a governmental body requests a clarification under this section, the ten-day timeline for requesting an AG opinion starts over when the governmental body receives the narrowing response (*City of Dallas v. Abbott*, 2010).

A public body may recover the actual cost of reproducing requests exceeding fifty pages, including the cost of materials, labor, and overhead. The charge for requests of fifty or fewer pages must be limited to the charge for each page that is copied without regard to materials, labor, or overhead, unless the records are located in two or more separate buildings or in a remote storage facility. If a request to copy or inspect records will result in a charge of over $40 to produce the information, the governmental body must provide the requestor an itemized statement of estimated charges (Gov't Code §552.2615). Failure to send the statement means that no charges can be assessed. Governmental bodies also may charge for inspection-only requests under certain conditions.

Government Code §552.263 permits a governmental body to require prepayment with a deposit or bond when the cost to produce records will exceed $100 (assuming the governmental body has over fifteen employees). Before fulfilling a request for inspection or production, a district may require a requestor to pay estimated charges, if the requestor has accepted but failed to pay a written, itemized cost estimate within the past 180 days (Gov't Code §552.2661).

A governmental body may set a reasonable limit—not less than thirty-six hours per requestor per fiscal year—on the amount of time personnel must spend producing information for inspection or copying without recovering costs associated with employee time (Gov't Code §552.275). All requests submitted in the name of a minor by any parent or guardian of that minor are treated as coming from a single requestor, collectively.

A requestor must either complete examination of the records no later than the tenth business day after the information is made available or file a request for additional time, or the request is deemed withdrawn (Gov't Code §552.225). While the TPIA limits the time period during which public records may be physically inspected, it does not authorize governmental bodies to deny requests for copies of public records (*Att'y. Gen. ORD-512*, 1988). For information that requires programming or manipulation of data, the governmental body generally has twenty days to provide the requestor a written statement describing the form in which the information is available and explaining the cost and time required to provide the information in the requested form. Within thirty days the requestor must in writing either accept the information as is or agree to the cost and time frame set forth for altering the information, or the request is considered withdrawn (Gov't Code §552.231). Note that the public has no right under the act to use the school's computer to inspect records as an alternative to receiving a computer printout (*Att'y. Gen. ORD-571*, 1990).

Extensive requirements as to the care and disposition of public records are delineated in the Local Government Records Act (Subtitle C, Title 6, of the Local Government Code). The law details when records can be destroyed and who is authorized to destroy them.

EDUCATOR PRIVACY RIGHTS

As we have seen, considerable information about public employees and their work is readily available under the Texas Public Information Act. The zone of employee privacy largely is determined by traditional forms of tort law, such as libel and slander. In Texas, state courts have recognized the tort of personal privacy invasion. A teacher in the Houston I.S.D. tried unsuccessfully to assert this right when school officials sought to videotape her classroom performance. The state appeals court rejected her claim of "involuntary videotaping" and noted that teaching in a public classroom does not fall within the zone of protected privacy, since public school teaching is by its nature open to public view (*Roberts v. Houston I.S.D.*, 1990). However, this does not mean that parents and community representatives have a right to camp out in the class to observe the teacher, as discussed in Chapter 1. Interestingly, some courts, together with the Texas Commissioner of Education, have issued recent decisions to the effect that the classroom is a closed forum and that teachers are engaging in unprotected private speech when they teach. We discussed several of these decisions in Chapter 6.

Lifestyle Issues

Lifestyle behaviors related to marriage and procreation, which have long been recognized as Fourteenth Amendment liberty rights, usually are accorded at least some constitutional protection. In 2003 the U.S. Supreme Court held that private sexual conduct between consenting adults, including homosexuals, is constitutionally protected as a liberty interest (*Lawrence v. Texas*, 2003). In that case, the Supreme Court struck down the Texas law that made same-sex sodomy a crime. The Court stated:

> The case does involve two adults who, with full and mutual consent from each other, engaged in sexual practices common to a homosexual lifestyle. The petitioners are entitled to respect for their private lives. The State cannot demean their existence or control their destiny by making their private sexual conduct a crime. (P. 2484)

In 2013 the U.S. Supreme Court struck down as unconstitutional §3 of the federal Defense of Marriage Act, which excluded a same-sex partner from the definition of "spouse" as used in federal statutes, effectively denying such an individual certain benefits available to persons in "traditional" marriages. In this case, though the woman was lawfully married and lived in a state recognizing same-sex marriages, she was denied the federal estate tax exemption for surviving spouses. The Court held that the provision violated the Fifth Amendment in that the regulation of domestic relations belongs exclusively to the states. Justice Anthony Kennedy stated that New York's granting of marriage equality "is a far-reaching legal acknowledgement of the intimate relationship between two people, a relationship deemed by the State worthy of dignity in the community equal with all other marriages" (*United States v. Windsor*, 2013).

However, as noted in Chapter 4, teachers are considered role models for their students, and lifestyle behaviors on or off campus that endanger students or undermine teaching effectiveness can serve as good cause for termination. The Texas Commissioner of Education has upheld the termination of educators for acts of public lewdness (*Parker v. Dallas I.S.D.*, 1998; *Holland v. Dallas I.S.D.*, 1996). The commissioner also upheld the termination of a principal who admitted having sex with a female security officer on a school picnic prior to the arrival of students and again during the school day while on a trip to buy paint for the school (*Garza v. Edinburg I.S.D.*, 1997).

Clearly, sexual behavior with students falls into the prohibited category. A continuing contract teacher's writing notes to a student, going to the student's house when her parents were not home, and kissing her on the lips constituted good cause for termination on grounds of immorality (*Rabe v. Lewisville I.S.D.*, 1994), and student consent does not get a teacher off the hook (*Molina v. Pasadena I.S.D.*, 1989).

Further, Texas Penal Code §21.12 makes it a crime for primary and secondary school employees to engage in sexual conduct with students enrolled at the school where the employee works, regardless of the student's age. This includes a public school operated by the Texas Youth Commission (*Brookins v. The State of Texas*, 2011). It is an affirmative defense that the student and employee were married at the time of the offense.

Employee Drug Testing

Federal regulations adopted by the Department of Transportation require drug testing of school bus drivers. But when other employees are subjected to testing, legal challenges often surface. The legal issue at stake is the right of privacy, as protected by the Fourth Amendment. Courts consistently have held that when the government requires an individual to submit to a urine test for drugs, it has conducted a "search." As a general rule, searches require some degree of individualized suspicion. Random searches of individuals who are not suspected of wrong-doing usually are illegal, although there are numerous exceptions to that general rule (such as the use of magnetometers in airports and federal courthouses).

The U.S. Supreme Court dealt with the drug testing of government employees in two cases decided in 1989. In *Skinner v. Railway Labor Executives Association*, after a serious accident, the Court approved a drug testing program for railroad employees that called for testing without any requirement of individualized suspicion. In *National Treasury Employees Union v. Von Raab*, the Court approved the practice of the U.S. Customs Service to drug-test employees who seek promotions or transfers to drug interdiction positions that require the employee to carry a firearm.

The Fifth Circuit also decided two cases involving drug testing of school employees in 1998. In the first case, the school district adopted a policy that required any employee who was injured on the job to submit to a urine test or face termination. The Fifth Circuit ruled that, in the absence of a "special need" or individualized suspicion that drug use contributed to the injury, the privacy interests of the employees outweighed the school district's interests in this case and struck down the district's policy (*United Teachers of New Orleans v. Orleans Parish School Board*).

But the Fifth Circuit approved a school district's more carefully constructed policy in *Aubrey v. School Board of Lafayette Parish*. The drug testing applied only to employees who were in "safety sensitive" positions. A school custodian who tested positive challenged the policy. The school considered all of its custodians to be in "safety sensitive" positions because of their access to hazardous chemicals, their interaction with students, and their need to handle dangerous equipment. The custodians were put on notice of the requirements, the method of urine collection was minimally intrusive, and the custodian who tested positive was not terminated but was given the opportunity to attend a substance abuse program. Based on all these factors, the court upheld the district's policy.

Section §81.102(a) of the Texas Health and Safety Code spells out the conditions and requirements for testing persons with AIDS and related disorders. Employers can test employees only when there is a bona fide occupational qualification justifying the testing. Section 81.103 sets forth the conditions for confidentiality of test results.

Personnel Records and Employee References

The law of defamation and privacy invasion is most likely to surface in the education setting in the context of revealing the content of personnel records. The problem for education officials is that other laws—

most notably federal antibias legislation and the state's Public Information Act—often mandate disclosure. Thus, educators sometimes are caught between a "rock and a hard place," where reconciliation is not easily accomplished.

Defamation can be either oral (slander) or written (libel). For defamation to be actionable, several conditions must be met, the most important of which are: (1) the words must meet the definition of defamation, (2) the words must be communicated to a third person, (3) the words must be false, and (4) the communication of the words must have resulted in injury to the person. These conditions suggest some defenses to claims of defamation. For example, if there has been no communication to a third party, there is no viable claim of defamation. Truth is always a defense to a claim of defamation. Mere statements of opinion also are protected as free speech.

In addition, four Texas statutes convey a qualified privilege to employers with respect to employee decision-making. Article 5206 of the Texas Revised Civil Statutes states that "Any written statement of cause of discharge, if true, when made by such agent, company or corporation, shall never be used as the cause for an action for libel, either civil or criminal, against the agent, company or corporation so furnishing same." TEC §22.0511(a) shields school professional employees from liability from damage suits in most situations. The definition of "professional employee" under the statute has been expanded to include a substitute teacher, a teacher employed by a company that contracts with a school district to provide services, and a member of the board of trustees. Section 101.051 of the Civil Practices and Remedies Code does the same for school districts. These laws will be discussed in some detail in Chapter 10. The qualified immunity granted professional employees by TEC §22.0511 requires that the person sued be acting in the scope of his or her public employment. Statutory protection would not otherwise be available. For example, a school employee who released information in his capacity as a Sunday school teacher would have difficulty claiming immunity. The fourth statute was enacted in 1999 as an amendment to the Labor Code. It provides that disclosure by an employer of truthful information regarding a current or former employee is sufficiently important to employment relationships and the public interest to shield the employer from civil liability (Texas Labor Code §103.001).

The U.S. Court of Appeals for the Fifth Circuit cited the qualified privilege provided by TEC §22.0511 (then codified as TEC §21.912(b)) in ruling in 1992 that administrators in the Houston I.S.D. were immune from liability for circulating a memorandum within the district relating to the alleged deficiencies of a substitute teacher (*Jones v. Houston I.S.D.*). A Texas appeals court ruled similarly in a 1991 decision, noting that "a letter of reference written by a professional supervisor of a public school merely expressing his professional *opinion* on an employee's work performance under his supervision is an act within the scope of the employee's duties with the school district and is, consequently, not subject to a libel action by virtue of section 21.912(b) unless such statements are false statements of *fact* or are libelous *per se"* (*Hammond v. Katy I.S.D.*, p. 180).

Probably the best protection against defamation lawsuits in the context of employee references is to secure the employee's permission to release information. An employee who authorizes release of employment information by the former employer limits his or her ability to prevail in a subsequent defamation action. In the *Jones* case above, the substitute teacher had signed a release form and thus was precluded from seeking damages for libel when the memorandum was sent to a prospective employer. In the absence of release forms, many personnel administrators provide only factual information to prospective employers (e.g., the dates of employment and salary). Note that TEC §21.352 specifically authorizes a school district to send a teacher's evaluation and any rebuttal to a new school district where the teacher has applied for employment, at the request of the new school district.

Telephone conversations can present special concerns for administrators. A case in point is *Sitzler v. Babers,* a 1992 decision of the Texas Commissioner of Education. In that case, the teacher filed several grievances in the district prior to resigning. After her resignation, Glenda Sitzler had difficulty securing employment. She contacted her sister, the branch manager of an employment agency, who contacted the principal by telephone for a reference check without revealing her relationship to Ms. Sitzler. The sister learned that the principal could not give a positive reference, in part because of Sitzler's tendency to file grievances. The teacher's cousin, an advocate for the U.S. Small Business Administration, obtained the same information. The commissioner revoked the principal's certificate for penalizing the teacher for exercising her right to file grievances (see Chapter 5).

Public school employees have the right to clear their names if their reputations are stigmatized in the context of contract nonrenewal (*Dennis v. S & S Consolidated Rural High School District,* 1978). However, the stigmatizing has to occur in the context of a loss or a denial of a state-conferred status (here, employment). The U.S. Supreme Court has ruled that stigmatizing by public officials unaccompanied by any loss of status does not trigger a Fourteenth Amendment liberty right violation (*Paul v. Davis,* 1976). Serious stigmatizing, however, might constitute an invasion of personal privacy under state law.

Occasionally, school officials themselves are targets of considerable criticism. Because the law affords great leeway to critics of public officials, school authorities generally will not prevail in defamation suits unless they can establish "actual malice"—that is, that the statements were made with knowledge that they were false or with reckless disregard of their truth or falsity. Thus, an irate Texas football coach was unsuccessful in suing the town newspaper for libel over criticism it printed about his performance (*Johnson v. Southwestern Newspapers Corp.*, 1993). A Utah teacher was no more successful in suing a city and police officer for privacy invasion over the disclosure on a television news program of a prior sexual conviction (*Nilson v. Layton City*, 1995). The constitutional right of privacy does not protect against disclosure of information about unlawful activity, even if it has been expunged from police records. Similarly, an assistant superintendent was unsuccessful in suing a television station over a story in which he was labeled a "racketeer" and "bid-rigger" over a dispute about the bidding process for a health services provider. The court also rejected his claim of intentional infliction of emotional distress (*Beck v. Lone Star Broadcasting Co.*, 1998).

Search of School Computer Files and Pagers

In Chapter 2 we discussed use of computers and the Internet in the nation's classrooms and a school district's ability to enact acceptable use policies to set forth conditions for use of technology at school. In Chapter 6 we discussed First Amendment rights related to computer use. Here we will discuss a teacher's privacy rights in connection with information stored on a school computer or pager.

A Texas court of appeals case sheds light on this issue. In *Voyles v. The State of Texas* (2004), a police sergeant received a tip indicating that a junior high school teacher had exchanged e-mails with a fifteen-year-old girl from London, in which he had solicited sex from the girl and had arranged to meet her. The sergeant then sent the teacher e-mails in which the sergeant described himself as a fifteen-year-old girl. The teacher exchanged numerous e-mails with the sergeant, some of which were sexual in nature. The sergeant then obtained warrants to search the teacher's home and school computers. Child pornography was found on both computers, and the teacher was indicted on felony charges.

The teacher filed a motion asking the court not to consider the evidence found on the computers on the grounds that it was obtained during an unlawful search and seizure in violation of the Fourth and Fourteenth Amendments to the U.S. Constitution. The court held that the evidence obtained from the teacher's school computer was admissible because the teacher had no reasonable expectation of privacy on the workplace computer. The court considered several factors: (1) the computer was owned by the school district and located at the teacher's desk in a classroom computer lab; (2) the computer was available for use by substitute teachers; and (3) the computer was not placed in the classroom for the man's personal or private use but, instead, was placed in the classroom laboratory to allow the man to teach his students about computers. Most employers today make it very clear through accept-able use policies (AUPs) that employees have no expectation of privacy in information stored on work-related computers. Not only may school employees face criminal charges, but courts also have upheld sanctions against them for inappropriate and/or unauthorized use of a school dis-trict's computer system (see *Alejandro v. Robstown I.S.D.*, 2004).

A unanimous U.S. Supreme Court upheld a city's search of an em-ployee's text messages on a pager paid for and provided by the city for work-related purposes. The city's AUP concerning computers, the Inter-net, and e-mail notified employees that they had no expectation of pri-vacy in the use of those devices and that the city had the right to moni-tor all activity without notice. Employees were told that pagers would be treated in the same manner. An employer may conduct a search for a "noninvestigatory, work-related purpose" or for the "investigation of work-related misconduct." Here the search was justified because several employees had exceeded the monthly texting limit and were required to pay overages, prompting the city to conduct a review of its texting limit. Moreover, the search was not excessively intrusive because under the city's policy the officer should have known his actions might be scruti-nized. This case further emphasizes the need for acceptable use policies that clearly define any restrictions and guidelines pertaining to technol-ogy (*City of Ontario v. Quon*, 2010).

Search of File Cabinets

The warrantless search of a file cabinet was upheld after an employee was charged with engaging in a sexual relationship with a student. The court found that the employee had no reasonable expectation of privacy in the file cabinet. The file cabinet was owned by the public school district, school was out for the summer, and employees had been in-structed to take their personal belongings and turn in their keys. The employee had not locked the file cabinet or attempted to keep others from it. Further, the employee handbook plainly stated that employ-ees had no expectation of privacy in their file cabinets. Thus, the war-rantless search was permissible under the Fourth Amendment, and the evidence discovered was admissible in the man's criminal trial for inde-cency with and sexual assault of a child (*Wamsley v. State*, 2008).

STUDENT PRIVACY RIGHTS

Issues of parent and student privacy rights involve both judicial and statutory law and can be separated into several categories. We begin with a general discussion of student personal privacy as it has been ju-dicially developed.

Student Personal Privacy

Courts have recognized that public school students have, to some degree, a constitutionally protected right of privacy. The best-known case is a 1973 ruling by a federal court in Pennsylvania that has gained wide acceptance and has been cited in support of a zone of privacy by the Texas Supreme Court. The case involved the administration of a testing program designed to identify potential drug abusers among eighth-grade students. Through questionnaire responses, the district identified specific behavioral patterns, then assigned potential drug abusers to peer groups for behavioral modification or recommended them for referral to outside specialists.

The court held that the test was an unconstitutional invasion of privacy of the families and students involved. The court noted, "There is probably no more private a relationship, excepting marriage, which the Constitution safeguards than that between parent and child. This court can look upon any invasion of that relationship as a direct violation of one's Constitutional right to privacy" (*Merriken v. Cressman*, p. 918). Particularly troubling was that the parents were not given complete information, those who refused to participate were likely to be scapegoated, and confidentiality could not be assured.

Note that the court in *Merriken* refers to marriage as a constitutionally protected right. The recognition by the U.S. Supreme Court that marriage falls within the ambit of the Fourteenth Amendment liberty provision is one of the main reasons schools no longer can discriminate against married students (*Skinner v. Oklahoma*, 1942; *Loving v. Virginia*, 1967). The prohibition extends to extracurricular activities. As a Texas court of appeals noted in a 1974 decision, it "seems illogical to say that a school district can make a rule punishing a student for entering into a status authorized and sanctioned by the laws of the state" (*Bell v. Lone Oak I.S.D.*).

In a 2013 case from the U.S. Court of Appeals for the Fifth Circuit, the court ruled that a student has no clearly established, constitutionally protected privacy interest in her sexual orientation. The court stated that it has "never held that a person has a constitutionally-protected privacy interest in her sexual orientation, and it certainly has never suggested that such a privacy interest precludes school authorities from discussing with parents matters that relate to the interests of their children." Significantly, the disclosure in that case was only to the student's mother in a meeting called by the softball coaches to discuss concerns over the girl's behavior and compliance with team rules (*Wyatt v. Fletcher*, 2013).

Students may not be disciplined by the school for lifestyle behavior unless school officials can show how the interests of the school are significantly affected. Thus if a physician advises that participation in extracurricular activities by a pregnant student would endanger the health of the student and/or the fetus, the school would be justified in restricting her participation. However, school officials may not isolate unwed mothers from other students, claiming, for instance, that the unwed status indicates a lack of moral character and is potentially harmful to other students. Such isolation is inherently discriminatory because it singles out females for punishment. Both federal and state law prohibit discrimination based on gender unless the school can show a compelling reason. Whenever school officials contemplate such action, they should be prepared for legal challenges.

Student Records

Enacted in 1974, the Family Educational Rights and Privacy Act (FERPA) (20 U.S.C. §1232g, as amended) applies to students in attendance at most educational institutions in the country and gives parents practically unlimited rights of access to personally identifiable information contained in their child's education records. In addition to a student's physical presence on campus and correspondence work, "attendance" also includes participation by "videoconference, satellite, Internet, or other electronic information and telecommunications technologies" (34 C.F.R. §99.3). "Personally identifiable information" includes not only information directly related to the student, but also "indirect identifiers" such as the student's date and place of birth and mother's maiden name (34 C.F.R. §99.3), as well as any information requested by a person who the district suspects knows the student's identity. Biometric records such as fingerprints and handwriting also now fall into this category.

Also known as the Buckley Amendment, FERPA restricts the release of this information to third parties without permission of parents or eligible students. School districts must use "reasonable methods" to verify the identity of persons requesting personally identifiable information to reduce the risk of unauthorized disclosure. Since the Texas Public Information Act incorporates FERPA's provisions, TPIA must be read in harmony with the federal statute. In situations where it is not clear whether requested information should be released to parents or third parties under the provisions of FERPA and the Texas Public Information Act, it is best to request an open records decision from the Texas Attorney General. The basic provisions of FERPA are set forth below.

Parent Rights. At the beginning of the school year or after new student enrollment, school districts must give parents a written explanation of FERPA, including the right to object to the release of directory information (discussed below). The law details certain requirements, including typeface, font size, and specific language that must be included in the notice (TEC §26.013). Further, such notice "shall effectively notify parents of students who have a primary or home language other than English."

Parents exercise the rights conveyed by the law until the student is attending college or is eighteen years of age. Rights under FERPA then transfer to the student. Even then, however, school districts may disclose information to the parents without the student's consent in certain instances, including when: (1) the student is a dependent for federal income tax purposes, (2) knowledge of the information is necessary to protect the student or other person in a health or safety emergency, or (3) a postsecondary student under age twenty-one has committed a disciplinary infraction involving the use or possession of alcohol or a controlled substance. A "parent" includes a natural parent, guardian, or any person acting as a parent in the absence of a parent or guardian. A parent has access to student records even if the parent does not have custody of the child, unless there is a court order to the contrary. See the discussion of child custody issues in the next section.

Parents have a right in most instances to inspect student records and a right to consent to disclosure of personally identifiable information to third persons. They have a right to challenge the accuracy or content of the records and to request that an amendment be added if the records are not accurate or are misleading. Further, a parent is entitled to see most of the internal administrative notes and memoranda pertaining to the conduct record of his child (*Att'y. Gen. ORD-615*, 1993), including, according to a Texas appeals court, internal school documents relating to a bad conduct grade given to the child (*Lett v. Klein I.S.D.*, 1996). Texas parents have significant access to information about their children pursuant to TEC §§26.001–26.012, as discussed in Chapter 2.

Parents also have a right to know what kinds of "directory information" the school assembles about students and to request that it not be released with respect to their children. Directory information generally means information that is not considered harmful or an invasion of privacy if disclosed, such as names, phone numbers, addresses, height, weight, athletic team rosters, and the like. Directory information does not include Social Security numbers or any student number that could be used to gain access to a student's identity. After informing parents of their rights to withhold directory information, a school district thereafter must provide third parties with the requested information if the parents did not object. Thus, if a community group wants a roster of all students in the school, the school must release the information, excluding only the names of students whose parents requested this information not be disclosed. A school must continue to honor any request by a former student to opt out of disclosure of directory information that was made while the student was in attendance.

Education Records. The term "education records" is defined much more broadly than just the information in the student's cumulative folder. Included within the definition are "records, files, documents, and other materials that contain information directly related to the student" maintained by the school or its personnel. In addition, state law provisions give parents access to such information as student attendance records, test scores, counseling records, reports about behavioral patterns, and teaching materials (TEC §§26.004, 26.006). Only a few items are excluded under FERPA's education records definition. Among them are records made by district personnel kept in the sole possession of the person and not revealed to anyone else other than a temporary substitute for the maker of the record (e.g., a substitute teacher). The FERPA regulations specifically exclude from the definition of "education records" grades on peer-graded papers that have not yet been recorded by a teacher. Thus, the practice of students grading each other's papers does not violate FERPA. The term also does not include records pertaining to a former student, unless those records are directly related to the student's attendance while at the school. Records containing only information about the student after graduation (e.g., alumni records) are not protected student records under FERPA.

Disclosure of Records. "School officials" who have a "legitimate educational interest" are among the relatively few persons allowed access to student records by law without the written consent of the parent or eligible student. The district must include in its policies the criteria for determining who has a "legitimate educational interest" in looking at a student's record and must use "reasonable methods," including physical or technological controls, to ensure that only those persons gain access. The term "school officials" now includes contractors, consultants, volunteers, and other persons to whom the school has outsourced services, if the service is one the school typically would perform using its own employees. A school must indicate in its FERPA notice if outside providers may be used and must retain enough control to ensure that only outside persons with a legitimate educational interest actually view the documents.

Access also is provided to school officials in a district to which the student has transferred, as long as the sending district has notified the parent and student that it provides such information. A student's former school may continue to send records to a student's new school—even after enrollment—if the disclosure is related to the student's enrollment or transfer, including supplementing or correcting prior records sent. In addition, school districts, open-enrollment charter schools, and universities are required to participate in an electronic student records system for the transfer of information, including course or grade completion, names of teachers, results of assessment instruments, special education services including IEP, and personal graduation plan (TEC §7.010).

Schools may make limited disclosure to state and local law enforcement personnel to whom criminal activities must be reported under TEC §37.015 and to officials of the Department of Human Services investigating allegations of child abuse or neglect. Law enforcement records created and maintained by campus police for law enforcement purposes are not educational records and thus not subject to FERPA (34 C.F.R. §99.8).

Limited disclosure also may be made to organizations conducting certain evaluative studies, pursuant to strict guidelines set forth in the Act, including a written agreement spelling out the confidentiality requirements (34 C.F.R. §99.31(a)(6)). Any documents provided should be "de-identified" by removing anything that might lead to the discovery of a student's identity, considering other information that might be available to the requestor. A school district may release de-identified student records for educational research by using a "reference code" to match information, as long as the manner of assigning the code is not disclosed and does not reveal the student's identity (34 C.F.R. §99.31(b)(2)). Documents now may be returned to the provider or creator of the record without violating FERPA's prohibition on redisclosure.

When a parent requests a record about the parent's child and information about other children also is contained in the record, personally identifiable information about the other students must be deleted to the extent possible. While parents and eligible students can waive their FERPA rights, as in the case of confidential recommendations for college or employment, the waiver must be a knowing one. That is, the waiver must be completely voluntary and must be made with full knowledge of what is being waived.

Recordkeeping. Records must be kept of every person who requests or obtains access to a particular student's record, except for the student's parents and school district officials. No record need be kept of requests authorized by prior written parental consent and requests for directory information only. An official or agency that "rediscloses" personally identifiable information on behalf of a school district also must maintain a record of that disclosure and make it available to school districts.

Violations. In 2002, the U.S. Supreme Court ruled that there is no private right of action to sue for damages under FERPA. The Court concluded that, unless Congress amends the law, the sole remedy for FERPA violations is to seek the termination of federal funding through the U.S. Department of Education (*Gonzaga University v. Doe*). However, employees who violate the law can face termination. A teacher in the Boyd I.S.D. made a list of forty-two sixth-grade students with "attitude problems," in which she labeled the students as thoughtless, disrespectful, rude, selfish, and uncaring. The teacher gave the list to another teacher to hand over to a juvenile probation officer who had been invited to talk with students about peer pressure, gangs, drugs, and alcohol. That teacher showed her aide, who made a copy. Before long, the list became fodder for the newspapers and television. In the face of parent outrage and community discord, the school district terminated the teacher's contract. The Texas Commissioner of Education noted that the list contained personally identifiable information about the students and that the probation officer was not employed by the district and had no legitimate educational interest in seeing the information. The Fort Worth Court of Appeals upheld the woman's termination (*McGilvray v. Moses*, 1999).

Child Custody Issues

When a divorce case is concluded, the divorce decree usually will name one parent to be the managing conservator (the one with custody) and one parent to be the possessory conservator (the parent with visitation rights), or name both parents as joint managing conservators. Section 153.377 of the Family Code allows a nonparent who is appointed as the possessory conservator the same right of access to medical, dental, psychological, and educational records of the child as the managing conservator, without regard to whether the right is specified in the court order.

Occasionally, school personnel are faced with a request from a divorced parent for a special arrangement involving the child—for example, visitation on the campus. A district should have on file a copy of the divorce settlement and ask the parent with custody to provide a note for the child's file showing the parent's consent to deviate from the court order.

Section 42.003 of the Texas Family Code assesses liability for damages against an individual who assists a person to take or retain possession of a child or to conceal the whereabouts of a child in violation of a court order. This provision protects all persons who have either custody or visitation rights under a court order. Thus, it is especially important for school officials to have all relevant court orders on file for review when disputes about release of the child arise.

Student Dress and Grooming

State law does not give students a right to choose their mode of dress. Thus, the matter of student dress and grooming is left to the discretion of local school districts. Some years ago the Fifth Circuit rejected the contention that public elementary and secondary school students have a constitutionally protected right in personal grooming (*Karr v. Schmidt*, 1972).

While school districts can impose dress and grooming codes, their right to do so is not unlimited. School officials must be careful not to intrude upon the right of symbolic expression upheld by the U.S. Supreme Court in *Tinker v. Des Moines School District* (see Chapter 6). In that case, the Court ruled that students had a constitutional right to wear armbands to school to protest the Vietnam War so long as they did not create material disruption or substantially interfere with the rights of others. Later, the high court ruled that student speech that is indecent, lewd, or profane is not entitled to any constitutional protection (*Bethel School District No. 403 v. Fraser*, 1986). Thus, students who wear shirts with words such as "See Dick drink. See Dick drive. Don't be a Dick" and "Coed Naked Band. Do It To The Rhythm" are unlikely to find much support in court (*Broussard v. School Board of the City of Norfolk*, 1992; *Pyle v. South*, 1995).

Conversely, a student who wears a T-shirt with the words "you can force me to attend school, but you can't force me to learn" may well be engaging in protected speech. Unless the T-shirt proves disruptive or interferes with the rights of others, under the *Tinker* rationale, school officials may not be able to restrict it. In a case from the federal Fourth Circuit Court of Appeals, a student challenged a school district dress code that prevented him from wearing a T-shirt that "depicted three black silhouettes of men holding firearms superimposed on the letters 'NRA' positioned above the phrase 'SHOOTING SPORTS CAMP.'" The dress code prohibited "messages on clothing, jewelry, and personal belongings that relate to . . . weapons." The Fourth Circuit Court determined that the policy likely would be found unconstitutional as overbroad because (1) it prohibited nonviolent and nonthreatening images and messages related to weapons, and (2) there was no evidence that the display of such messages related to weapons would substantially disrupt school operations or interfere with the rights of others (*Newsom v. Albemarle County School Board*, 2003).

The likelihood of substantial disruption was found in a 2009 case from the U.S. Court of Appeals for the Fifth Circuit. The school district implemented a student dress code prohibiting clothing or accessories that had "inappropriate symbolism, especially that which discriminates against other students based on race, religion, or sex." Board policy specifically banned the display of the Confederate flag. Two students who carried purses bearing large images of the Confederate flag challenged the district's policies after they were asked to remove their purses from campus or leave them in the office. The Court upheld the district's policies, based on the school officials' reasonable belief that displays of the Confederate flag would cause substantial disruption of or material interference with school activities. Several incidents of racial hostility already had occurred, including some that involved use of the Confederate flag. The policies were not vague and were rationally related to the legitimate governmental interest in maintaining discipline and order in the public schools (*A.M. v. Cash*, 2009).

In another Fifth Circuit case, *Palmer v. Waxahachie I.S.D.* (2009), the school's dress code prohibited T-shirts displaying any message except for those related to school-sponsored organizations and athletic teams, school "spirit" shirts, and logos smaller than two-by-two inches. The dress code, however, allowed political pins, buttons, bumper stickers, or wristbands, as long as they were not distracting or sexually explicit and did not promote a violation of school rules. Palmer sued when the district refused to allow him to wear shirts with the words "San Diego" and "John Edwards for President '08."

The Fifth Circuit concluded that the school district did not violate the boy's First Amendment free speech rights. Because the dress code was viewpoint- and content-neutral, the court reviewed it under the intermediate scrutiny standard. Under the first prong, the dress code furthered a substantial governmental interest, in that it provided a safer and more orderly learning environment and encouraged professional dress. Second, the governmental interest was not related to the suppression of student expression. Finally, the incidental restriction on free speech was no more than necessary to facilitate the governmental interest, in that students were free to wear what they wanted after school and they were provided with some means of communicating their speech during school. The Fifth Circuit stated: "The district and its administrators— not federal judges—are in a better position to formulate a dress code, and we are understandably hesitant to question their stated justifications" (p. 12). The U.S. Supreme Court declined to hear the appeal.

In *Littlefield v. Forney I.S.D.* (2001), the parents argued that a uniform policy interfered with their right to control their children's upbringing (parent rights are discussed in Chapter 1). But the appeals court rejected the contention, noting that school policy does not violate this right so long as there is a rational relationship between the regulation and the stated governmental interest. Here the uniform policy had such a rational basis in that it fostered education and furthered "the legitimate goals of improving student safety, decreasing socioeconomic tensions, increasing attendance, and reducing drop-out rates."

The Texas Commissioner of Education ruled similarly in 2012, where a parent claimed that the school's dress code violated her fundamental "right to direct the moral and religious training of her child." The commissioner concluded there was no fundamental right to control the dress of her child in the public school, and the district had provided a rational basis for adopting the dress code: "to build self-esteem, bridge socioeconomic differences between students, and encourage positive behavior, thereby promoting school safety and improving the learning environment" (*Parent v. Greenville I.S.D.*, 2012).

As noted in Chapter 1, TEC §11.162(c) allows a parent to seek an opt-out from a uniform requirement based on a bona fide religious or philosophical objection. The commissioner has defined the terms "bona fide," "religious," and "philosophical" in several decisions concerning waivers to the school uniform requirement. A philosophical objection generally is one related to the principles of conduct governing an individual or group. A religious belief is one that is rooted in religion, but need not be based on the official position of a church or other organization. A bona fide belief simply means one that is sincerely held.

The Texas Commissioner of Education set forth the method for analyzing cases involving parental objections to student uniforms as follows. A parent first shall present evidence of a bona fide philosophical or religious belief against school uniforms; then the district may introduce evidence to show the parent's belief is insincere. The board will consider the evidence presented by both the parent and the district and make a determination concerning the sincerity of the parent's belief. For example, in a 2012 case the commissioner upheld a school district's decision to deny a parent's request to opt her children out of the school's uniform policy. The record showed that her children wore uniforms in other settings, e.g., one child was on a drill team. Thus, the board correctly had concluded that her objections were not "bona fide" (*Parent v. Crandall I.S.D.*, 2012).

While parents may be allowed to opt their children out of a school uniform policy based on religious or philosophical objections, parents may not opt them out of a school dress code. What is the difference between a uniform policy and a dress code? In *Parent v. Greenville I.S.D.* the school district's dress code policy required the wearing of red, white, and black solid shirts and khaki or black solid shorts, pants, and skirts, while restricting the color of outerwear, belts, socks, and shoes. Because a number of clothing styles and color options remained available to the students, the commissioner found it unlikely that an outside observer "would conclude that the students were wearing distinctive dress that would identify them as members of a particular group." Thus the district had merely established a dress code, which was not subject to the opt-out provisions of TEC §11.162.

Can school districts have dress codes that discriminate on the basis of gender? This matter has been extensively litigated in Texas. In a decision styled *Barber v. Colorado I.S.D.* (1995), the Texas Supreme Court ruled that the Equal Rights Amendment in the Texas Constitution, Article I, §3a, does not restrict school districts from having grooming codes that treat male dress differently from female dress. The court upheld the district's policy restricting boys from having long hair or wearing earrings, including students age eighteen and older.

Likewise, the Texas Supreme Court has held that a hair length regulation against boys wearing hair below the shirt collar did not violate the state civil rights law that prohibits discrimination by public officials against persons on the basis of race, religion, sex, or national origin (Texas Civil Practices and Remedies Code §106.001(a)). Noting that courts should not be in the business of deciding matters of student grooming, the court held that, like the Equal Rights Amendment, the law was not intended to be applied to school dress and grooming codes (*Bastrop I.S.D. v. Toungate*, 1997). However, as noted in Chapter 7, sometimes sincere religious belief will justify an exemption from a dress code policy. The two cases discussed in this context in that chapter involved Native American students who objected to hair length restrictions.

Students have been equally unsuccessful in claiming that sex-based grooming requirements are a form of illegal sex discrimination under either the Fourteenth Amendment or Title IX. While at one time schools receiving federal funds were not allowed to have different grooming codes for males and females under Title IX regulations, the regulations have been revoked, and the Office of Civil Rights no longer pursues dress code complaints.

STUDENT SEARCH AND SEIZURE

The law involving student search and seizure has developed rapidly, and we address it in several categories, beginning with a discussion of the basic principles laid down by the U.S. Supreme Court in the seminal *New Jersey v. T.L.O.* decision.

Standards for Student Searches

The U.S. Supreme Court first ruled in 1985 that the Fourth and Fourteenth Amendments, protecting persons from unreasonable searches and seizures, apply to public school students. The Court in *New Jersey v. T.L.O.* rejected arguments that school officials have the same authority to search that parents do (the *in loco parentis* theory). However, given the school's need to preserve order, the full protections of the Constitution do not apply. Thus, the Court specifically held that neither a warrant nor probable cause is required. To conduct a lawful search of a student, a school official must (1) establish reasonable cause for believing that the student is violating or has violated a school rule or a law and (2) ensure that the search is reasonable in scope in light of the age and sex of the student and the nature of the offense.

Using these standards, the Court upheld the pocketbook searches of T.L.O., who was reported to the principal to be smoking in the restroom in violation of school rules. When she denied it, the principal searched her purse and found both cigarettes and a package of rolling papers (the first search). The presence of the rolling papers justified searching further (the second search). The principal found marijuana and a list of names suggesting drug dealing. The student then was turned over to the police and subsequently adjudged a juvenile delinquent. Both searches were justified because there was reasonable cause to conduct them and because they were not excessively intrusive.

"Reasonable cause" is a lesser standard than the probable cause standard for the issuing of warrants as stated in the Fourth Amendment, but requires more than a hunch that wrongdoing might be involved. Searching a truant student who is seen hanging around the school bleachers where illicit activity occasionally takes place, or searching a student who tries to hide a bulging calculator behind his back, falls into the "hunch" category (*Matter of Pima County Juvenile Action*, 1987; *In re William G.*, 1985). Generally, as in the *New Jersey v. T.L.O.* decision, "reasonable cause" means that there exist some articulable grounds to conduct the search. Texas appeals courts have ruled that an anonymous tip ordinarily does not rise to the level of reasonable suspicion necessary to justify a search absent corroborating evidence of criminal activity, a violation of school rules, or possession of a weapon (*In re A.T.H.*, 2003; *In re K.C.B.*, 2004). In a 2007 case out of Austin, reasonable cause to search was found where the informant was known and provided information directly to the assistant principal; the tip was specific as to the suspect, location, and time of day; and the accused behaved suspiciously (*In the Matter of B.R.P.*). In determining whether a search is justified at its inception, a court must balance the diminished rights of students in the school setting with the governmental interest in protecting students from harm.

The Fifth Circuit upheld the search of a student's book bag and his person after his younger brother brought to school a controversial picture that the older boy had drawn. The older boy admitted drawing the picture, which depicted violence against school employees and students and contained obscenities and racial epithets. The search revealed a box cutter; notebooks containing references to death, drugs, sex, and gang symbols; and a fake ID. He was arrested and spent four nights in jail, enrolled in an alternative school, and ultimately dropped out of school. The court concluded that the search was reasonable in scope and reasonable at its inception, given the school's interest in ensuring the safety and welfare of its students (*Porter v. Ascension Parish School Board*, 2004). The school had reason to believe the search would turn up evidence of the violation of a school rule or policy.

A 2008 appeals court case considered the reasonableness of the scope of a search, i.e., whether the search was excessively intrusive, under the *T.L.O.* guidelines. In that case, the assistant principal saw two boys in an off-limits area of campus. One student acted nervous and began grabbing his waistband. The assistant principal smelled marijuana on his breath and hands. The assistant principal asked the boy to raise his shirt, whereupon the man put his thumbs between the waistband of the boy's baggy pants and the gym shorts he was wearing underneath. The assistant principal felt an "awkward ball" that turned out to be a plastic bag of marijuana. The court upheld the search, concluding that it was reasonably related in scope to the circumstances that justified the search and was not excessively intrusive. The waistband was a common place to hide drugs. The search was neither a strip search nor "near strip search." The boy was not required to remove his clothing, and the assistant principal did not see or touch a private area of the student's body (*In re A.H.A.*, 2008).

What happens when a student refuses to comply with a request to conduct a search? We believe that the lower standard of *T.L.O.* moots the need for student consent in routine searches. Having said that, we also believe that it would work to the school district's advantage to turn the search over to the parents or to the police where the student refuses to consent and the search would be particularly intrusive. Falling into this category would be searches of the student's locked car and searches of the student's person requiring the removal of clothing. Involving the police has the advantage of helping maintain a chain of custody of confiscated items and diverting potential litigation from the district.

When conducting student searches, can a police officer follow the reasonable cause standard of *New Jersey v. T.L.O.* or does the more stringent probable cause standard apply? This was the issue in a case involving an initial pat-down followed by a pocket search of a high school student by a security officer assigned to the school by the Richardson Police Department. A parking lot attendant notified the principal that three students were smoking in a car. The principal directed the students to come to the office. She noticed one of the students "messing with" the pockets of his cargo shorts. Fearing he might have a concealed weapon, she asked the police officer to intervene when the student refused to empty his pockets. The officer conducted a pat-down, then discovered a bag of marijuana. The student later tried to suppress the use of the evidence in a juvenile proceeding. The court of appeals ruled that the search was both reasonable and not excessively intrusive under the circumstances; thus the evidence could be used at trial. The appeals judges opted to follow the reasoning of courts outside of Texas that when school officials initiate the search or police involvement is minimal, the reasonable cause standard from *T.L.O.* applies. However, if the search had been initiated by the police officer or done by school officials at the request of the officer, then the more stringent probable cause standard would apply (*Russell v. State*, 2002).

The fact that a search is conducted off campus during a field trip does not alter the *T.L.O.* standards, according to a decision of a New York federal district court. The case involved the search of student hotel rooms after the school principal smelled marijuana smoke in the hallway. Both students and their parents had signed pledges that the students would not use drugs or alcohol during the field trip, and the students were warned that room checks might be conducted. The principal found marijuana in one student's room and alcohol in another. The students argued that *T.L.O.* applies only to on-campus searches and that the higher probable cause, not reasonable cause, standard should apply to searches conducted off campus. The court disagreed. "Where, however, a field-trip is part of a school activity, organized at school, and administered completely by school employees, *T.L.O.* clearly applies" (*Rhodes v. Guarricino,* 1999).

While the *T.L.O.* case provides guidance concerning the search of students, it does *not* say anything about searches of lockers and desks; cell phones; use of sniffer dogs; strip searches; student drug testing; and the use of magnetometers, metal detectors, and Breathalyzers. We take up each of these types of searches in the following sections.

Strip Searches

The most intrusive search, of course, is the strip search. In June of 2009 the U.S. Supreme Court struck down the strip search of a thirteen-year-old middle school girl who was suspected of possessing naproxen and prescription-strength ibuprofen at school. On the morning of the search, a male student gave the assistant principal a white pill identified as prescription-strength ibuprofen, which the boy claimed he had been given by another student. A search of that student produced a blue pill later identified as over-the-counter naproxen, four white pills identified as prescription-strength ibuprofen, and a razor blade. The girl claimed that Savana Redding had given her the pills. The girl also had a day planner belonging to Savana Redding in her possession, which contained knives and other contraband.

The assistant principal then called Savana Redding into his office. She admitted the planner was hers but denied knowledge of the contraband and the pills and further denied giving pills to other students. She agreed to a search of her belongings. A search of her backpack produced nothing. The assistant principal then asked an administrative assistant and the school nurse, both female, to search the girl's clothing. They asked her to remove her jacket, socks, and shoes, and again found nothing. Then they directed Savana to remove her clothing except for her underwear, then "pull out" the elastic band on her bra and underpants. Again nothing was found. Savana sued the school district and administrators involved in the search, and the case made its way to the U.S. Supreme Court.

Analyzing the case under the *T.L.O.* standards outlined above, the Supreme Court ruled that the strip search violated the girl's Fourth Amendment rights. School policy prohibited the nonmedical use, possession, or sale of any drug on campus, including prescription and over-the-counter medication, without prior permission. Given all the facts, the Court determined that the school had reasonable grounds to suspect that Savana Redding had violated school rules by bringing prohibited drugs to school without permission. Thus, the district satisfied the first prong under *T.L.O.*, because the search was justified at its inception. The question at hand was whether the scope of the search was reasonable in light of the age and sex of the student and the nature of the offense.

While the Court approved as reasonable the initial search of Savana's backpack and outer clothing for drugs, the subsequent strip search violated her Fourth Amendment rights. The Court found that the level of suspicion did not match the degree of intrusion. When the search of Savana's backpack and outer clothing failed to turn up additional drugs, the search should have stopped there. The drugs in question were common pain relievers, which would harm students only in large quantities. The assistant principal had no reason to suspect that large numbers of pills were being circulated or that any individual student was receiving an excessive number of pills. Thus, there was no indication of danger to other students. Further, there was no reason to suspect that Savana was hiding pills in her underwear. While upholding the *T.L.O.* guidelines, the Court added that a strip search requires either a reasonable suspicion of danger or a suspicion that underwear has been used for hiding evidence of wrongdoing before a search exposing "intimate parts" is permitted. The Court, however, found that the constitutional right was not clearly established at the time of the search; thus, the school administrators were entitled to qualified immunity on the claims against them. The case was remanded to the Ninth Circuit to discern the liability of the school district (*Safford Unified School Dist. #1 v. Redding*). Many commentators advise that school officials should leave strip searches to parents or the police except in circumstances of imminent harm.

Use of Magnetometers, Metal Detectors, and Breathalyzers

Under the *T.L.O.* guidelines discussed above, individualized suspicion is required in conducting pocket and purse searches of students. While the Supreme Court in *T.L.O.* did not rule on the general student search, it stated in a footnote that "exceptions to the requirement of individualized suspicion are generally appropriate only where other safeguards are available to assure that the individual's reasonable expectation of privacy is not subject to the discretion of school officials." The law involving the use of magnetometers through which all students pass as they enter school and the use of handheld metal detectors has developed rapidly.

An "administrative search" in which all students are searched as part of the school's daily routine (as opposed to an individualized search of a particular student) generally is upheld as reasonable "when the intrusion involved is no greater than necessary to satisfy the governmental interest underlying the need for the search." Texas appeals courts have upheld administrative searches of students upon entering alternative schools where they have been placed for disciplinary reasons. In a 2009 case out of San Antonio, a district required students to remove their shoes, socks, and belt and submit to a pat-down (*In the Matter of P.P.*). A 2003 Austin case considered a similar policy, but in addition the students were required to empty their pockets and walk through a metal detector (*In the Matter of O.E.*). In both cases, the search was found not excessively intrusive in light of the district's need to maintain discipline and safety. Also in both cases the students and parents were notified of the search policy and thus had a diminished expectation of privacy.

While decisions involving magnetometers usually uphold their use based on the limited intrusion on student privacy and on the grounds that school officials cite for conducting the search, there are exceptions. For example, an Illinois appeals court granted a student's right to suppress evidence when the student was forced to go through the magnetometer after he turned to leave. Upon being notified that he would have no choice but to submit to the search, the student raised his shirt to reveal the handle of a semiautomatic pistol. The court concluded that the search was not justified at its inception since the officer who instructed the student to go through the magnetometer was acting only on a hunch. Further, in stopping the student from leaving of his own free will, the police officer effectively had "seized" the student in violation of the Fourth Amendment restriction on unreasonable searches and seizures (*People v. Parker*, 1996).

A federal district court in Oregon upheld the use of a Breathalyzer by police to ferret out alcohol users among students embarking on a field trip. The school bus had just left at 5 A.M. from the school when one student became ill and another appeared to be passed out. School officials turned the bus around and drove to the police station, where Breathalyzer tests were administered to all students. One student argued that the Breathalyzer test was illegal. While not addressing the generalized nature of the search, the court found that the Breathalyzer test administered by police and school officials to the student who had filed the lawsuit was based on probable cause, did not require a warrant, and was reasonable (*Juran v. Independence Oregon Central School District 13J*, 1995).

To many commentators, the use of Breathalyzers is similar to employing metal detectors. Clearly a Breathalyzer search is more likely to be upheld if it is amply justified and balances student personal privacy rights with the interests of the school in ensuring a safe school environment.

Locker and Desk Searches

Searches of lockers and desks are considered permissible upon reasonable cause to believe that they contain illegal items or for periodic inspection purposes—for example, a search for overdue library books or spoiled food at the end of the semester. Thus a Texas court of appeals had no difficulty in concluding in a 1998 case that an assistant principal had cause to search a student's locker after she had left a student alone in the office for a few minutes, only to discover a short time after that the assistant principal's purse was missing (*Shoemaker v. State*). The student had a record of thefts and was the only one in the office prior to the theft.

Since lockers and desks are jointly held property, the school may limit student expectation of privacy. In the *Shoemaker* decision, the court noted that the school had a policy that warned students that their lockers could be opened at any time. If board policy permits general searches, students should be notified through the student code of conduct. Students also should be put on notice that any illicit items "in plain view" will be confiscated and may subject the student to disciplinary measures. Commentators in this area of the law advise school personnel against conducting general "fishing expeditions" not undertaken for health and safety reasons. General searches have always been frowned upon. Indeed, the Fourth Amendment was added to the Bill of Rights to prevent government officials from carrying out blanket searches as the British had done during colonial times.

A Texas appeals court upheld the search of a junior high school student's locker as both justified at its inception and reasonable in scope. The search initially was justified based on a tip that the student was "high" and the assistant principal's observations that the student's eyes were red and pupils dilated. After a pat-down and search of the student's notebook by campus security officers produced nothing, the assistant principal directed the officers to search the student's locker for drugs. As they opened the student's locker he admitted that he had brass knuckles, a prohibited weapon, which were then found by the campus security officers. The student claimed the search was illegal and attempted to exclude the evidence from his criminal trial. The court concluded that the locker search was reasonably related in scope to the circumstances justifying the initial search and was not excessively intrusive. The assistant principal had reasonable grounds to suspect that a search of the student's locker would produce evidence that the student had violated school rules. The court noted that the student had no legitimate expectation of privacy in his locker, as the student code of conduct specifically stated that lockers were owned by the school and were subject to search. Any contraband found in a locker search, even if not related to the initial purpose of the search, can be confiscated and used against the student in a disciplinary hearing if school policy states that students have no privacy rights in their lockers (*In the Matter of S.M.C.*, 2011).

Search of Cell Phones and Electronic Communications

The search of a cell phone confiscated or found at school should be treated the same as any student search. A search of a student's cell phone must be justified at its inception and reasonable in scope. Absent reasonable grounds to believe the search will prove that the student is in violation of the law or school rules, school administrators may not search the phone. Thus in a Pennsylvania federal case, school officials were not justified in calling nine other students listed in the directory of a phone that had been confiscated to determine if those students, too, were violating the school's cell phone use policy (*Klump v. Nazareth Area School District*, 2006). In an unpublished decision, a Texas court of appeals has ruled that an individual has no reasonable expectation of privacy in information stored in a cell phone that the individual has loaned to a student. Thus the court denied a woman's motion in her criminal trial to suppress evidence of sexually explicit text messages obtained after her phone was confiscated when the student was caught texting in class (*Young v. State*, 2010).

A federal trial court in Minnesota denied qualified immunity to school officials who demanded that a twelve-year-old student provide her e-mail and Facebook user names and passwords or face detention after they learned from other students the girl had used profanity and discussed sexually explicit topics in her electronic communications. The court allowed the case to proceed to determine whether the school officials had conducted an unreasonable search in violation of the Fourth Amendment when they accessed the nonpublic areas of her online postings that were within her exclusive possession or only available to her friends. The court noted that the misbehavior did not involve illegal acts or violations of school policy; thus it was difficult to determine whether there was any legitimate interest at stake in the school search (*R.S. v. Minnewaska Area School Dist.*, 2012).

Use of Sniffer Dogs to Conduct Searches

The U.S. Court of Appeals for the Fifth Circuit has ruled that the use of sniffer dogs generally to inspect lockers and automobiles on school property is not a "search." However, if the dog's alert on a car or locker is used as a basis for "reasonable suspicion" to conduct a search, then the dog must be sufficiently reliable to detect such contraband at the time the sniff occurs (*Horton v. Goose Creek I.S.D.*, 1982).

A Texas appeals court in 2010 upheld a school district's use of sniffer dogs to conduct a sweep of classrooms for drugs while students were not in the room. The students were instructed to leave all their belongings behind and wait outside. After the dog alerted to a girl's backpack, a search by school officials revealed marijuana. The court concluded that the minimally intrusive search and seizure of property did not violate the girl's Fourth Amendment rights but instead served the legitimate governmental interest of protecting student health and safety in light of the reported drug problem among students at school. The appeals court noted that the U.S. Supreme Court has not required an individualized suspicion of wrongdoing in efforts to combat student drug use in the public schools (*In the Matter of D.H.*, 2010).

As discussed earlier, turning some searches over to the police can make it easier to secure a criminal prosecution. Doing so also may work to the advantage of the school district. A case in point is *Jennings v. Joshua I.S.D.*, a decision of the Fifth Circuit in 1989. In *Jennings*, sniffer dogs alerted school officials to the presence of forbidden substances in a car in the school parking lot during a general sweep. The student's father had directed his daughter not to permit a search. When he was contacted, the father also refused to consent, whereupon the school officials turned the matter over to the police. A search warrant was obtained, but nothing illegal surfaced when the car was searched. The father later filed a civil rights lawsuit against the school district, school officials, the dog handling company, the police officer, and the city. The Fifth Circuit upheld dismissal of the lawsuit against the school district and school officials. Because the matter was turned over to the police when the father refused to unlock the car, school officials "cannot be liable for any constitutional violation that followed."

Student Drug Testing

In June 1995 the U.S. Supreme Court revisited the student search and seizure area, this time in the context of drug testing. By a 6-3 margin the Court upheld a school district drug-testing policy for students participating in interscholastic sports (*Vernonia School District v. Acton*). In the face of a serious drug problem among student athletes, the district implemented the testing program in 1989. Only those students involved in interscholastic sports were tested and then only after a consent form had been signed. Those taking medication provided a copy of the prescription or a doctor's authorization. Testing was done at the beginning of the season and then randomly on a weekly basis thereafter. Adult monitors of the same sex accompanied students to the locker room. Male students produced a sample at a urinal with their backs to the monitor; female students produced a sample in an enclosed stall. The samples were checked for temperature and tampering, then turned over to the testing agency. Testing results were made available only to selected school personnel and were 99.94 percent accurate.

Penalties were limited. If the first test was positive, a second test was administered. If the second test also was positive, the student was given a choice of participating in a six-week assistance program that included weekly urinalysis or being dropped from athletics for the remainder of the current season and the next athletic season. Second and third offenses resulted in longer suspension from athletics. Testing results were not used for internal school disciplinary measures and were not turned over to the police.

With these features, the Vernonia drug-testing policy passed constitutional muster as a reasonable search under the Fourth Amendment, even though it lacked individualized suspicion. The Court based its ruling on three factors. First, students have a diminished right of privacy in public schools, particularly in the context of athletics. Justice Antonin Scalia pointed out that students who volunteer for athletics willingly subject themselves to a greater amount of regulation than other students. Second, the Vernonia drug-testing procedures adequately protected student privacy. And third, the Court noted the strong interest of the school district in deterring drug use among athletes. The Court decided the constitutionality of the Vernonia policy only and cautioned against assuming that suspicionless drug testing in other contexts would pass constitutional muster.

The U.S. Supreme Court ruled in 2002 that the general drug-testing policy approved in *Vernonia School District v. Acton* can be extended beyond the context of competitive athletics to students participating in nonathletic competitive extracurricular activities such as choir, band, academic teams, and National Honor Society (*Board of Education v. Earls*). A student challenged the policy as a violation of her Fourth Amendment rights, claiming no demonstrable drug problem existed among participants in extracurricular activities that would justify a suspicionless general search. In a 5-4 ruling, the Court upheld the policy, noting that students have limited privacy rights in public schooling in general and even more restricted rights in extracurricular activities. Further, the school has a strong interest in preventing illegal drug use among students, and there is a potential for injury to drug-impaired participants in extracurricular events.

Moreover, the collection procedures were virtually identical to those used in *Vernonia* (e.g., urine sample given behind a closed stall door), and the ultimate sanction for a positive test was only suspension from extracurricular participation. The results were not turned over to law enforcement, and there were no disciplinary or academic penalties. Thus, Justice Clarence Thomas wrote, the policy was a "reasonable means of furthering the School District's important interest in preventing and deterring drug use among its school children."

Note that the Court did not endorse a general drug-testing program for all students. In supplying the fifth vote for the majority, Justice Stephen Breyer noted in his concurring opinion that the testing program had limited impact on student privacy rights because it involved only extracurricular activities and not the entire student body. Further, the conscientious objector could refuse testing and thus forfeit participation in the extracurricular activity, a penalty that "is less severe than expulsion from the school." It seems reasonably clear that Justice Breyer, and perhaps others in the majority, would not endorse a general drug-testing program for all students, absent a compelling reason for one. Thus a U.S. district court's 2001 decision against a general drug-testing program involving all students in the Lockney I.S.D. as unjustified by exigent circumstances remains good law (*Tannahill v. Lockney I.S.D.*).

The parents in one Texas case based their drug-testing challenge on an alleged violation of the state constitution. In *Marble Falls I.S.D. v. Shell* (2003), the district required mandatory drug testing of all junior and senior high school students who participated in extracurricular activities. The district tested the students twice a year for alcohol, barbiturates, cocaine, and steroids, and additional random testing was implemented throughout the year. Students could choose whether to submit urine, hair, or saliva samples for testing. Test results were confidential and were used only to determine eligibility for participation in extracurricular activities. The Texas appeals court upheld the district's drug-testing policy, based on the *Vernonia* and *Earls* decisions. First, the court found that the policy did not violate the students' religious freedom guaranteed by Article I, Section 6 of the Texas Constitution. The students in question occasionally consumed wine during religious observances of their Jewish faith; thus their father feared that participating in their religion could disqualify them from extracurricular activities at school. However, the court noted that the right to the free exercise of religion does not relieve an individual from complying with laws that are neutral with respect to religion. The policy applied equally to all junior and senior high school students who participated in extracurricular activities. Although some religious groups could have been adversely affected by the policy, it was neutral with respect to religion as written and applied.

Further, the policy did not violate the students' due process rights guaranteed by Article I, Section 19 of the Texas Constitution. The three objectives of the policy were: (1) to provide a deterrent to drug use for students who participated in extracurricular activities, (2) to provide a drug education program for students who tested positive or were at risk for drug use, and (3) to ensure the health and safety of students who participated in extracurricular activities. The court found that the policy's stated objectives were legitimate and that the drug-testing procedures were rationally related to achieving those objectives. Finally, the policy did not violate the students' privacy rights guaranteed by Article I, Section 9, because the policy was found "minimally intrusive," in that the students could provide a urine, hair, or saliva sample; the purpose for which the test results could be used was limited; and test results were confidential.

Texas students who participate in UIL athletic competitions must agree to submit to random testing for illegal steroids, and parents must sign an acknowledgment form (TEC §33.091). Initial positive test results must be confirmed through a subsequent test using a sample obtained at the same time as the original sample. Testing must be performed by a certified lab, and results are provided only to the student, parents, and necessary school officials, unless otherwise required by court order. A student receiving a positive test result or refusing to submit to testing will incur a period of ineligibility for UIL athletic competition. A student is not penalized for use of a prescription steroid.

SUMMARY

While the right of privacy has evolved slowly, so, too, has the public's right to know what its government is doing. The latter certainly is evident from the continual refinement of the Texas Open Meetings and Public Information Acts. At the same time, the Family Educational Rights and Privacy Act protects against disclosure of personally identifiable information about students and their families, as well as gives parents access to student records. The Fourth Amendment to the U.S. Constitution has provided some degree of protection for students in the context of searches and seizures, and courts have found a personal right of privacy for both students and teachers in the word *liberty* of the Fourteenth Amendment. But these rights are limited. Courts in recent years have recognized the responsibility of school officials to maintain an ordered and safe educational environment and have not been sympathetic to student claims of invasion of personal privacy in the context of dress codes, locker searches, interscholastic sports drug testing, and use of metal detectors. At the same time, excessive control and monitoring not only risk lawsuits but also send out a message that public schools are not open, friendly places. As always, caution, legal advice, and common sense are the best guides when privacy-related issues surface.

TEN

Legal Liability

"CAN I BE SUED?" This is the question educators ask lawyers more than any other. The answer is always "yes." In America, anyone can sue anyone over anything at any time. The more relevant question is: "Can I be held liable?" The answer to that question turns on a host of factors. Are we talking personal injury or constitutional claim? State or federal court? Liability of the school district or the individual? In this chapter, we will examine how these factors come into play in a variety of situations.

IDENTIFYING AREAS OF LEGAL LIABILITY

Basically, legal liability can be separated into two distinct categories. The first, criminal law, involves crimes against the state.

In this chapter, we are more concerned with the second category of legal liability, claims arising under civil law. Most civil cases involve a lawsuit brought by one person against another, usually seeking monetary damages. We already have looked briefly at contract violations related to employment. The focus of our concern in this chapter is the law of torts, that is, civil wrongs against another that cause the injured party to go to court seeking compensation from the wrongdoer for damages. There are many kinds of torts, among them defamation, negligence, assault, and invasion of privacy. Negligence, which involves the failure to use reasonable care to avoid causing harm to someone, is the most common in the educational setting. All of these we classify as state torts.

Federal torts involve the infringement of a person's recognized constitutional or federal statutory rights. Each will be discussed in turn.

STATE TORTS

School District Immunity

The starting point in analyzing claims asserting the liability of a school district under state law is the general legal principle of sovereign immunity, by which governmental entities, such as school districts, are immune from liability. To hold a school district liable under state law, the plaintiff must point to some specific statute that authorizes the courts to impose liability.

The statute most frequently cited is the Texas Tort Claims Act, which spells out the circumstances under which a governmental entity in Texas can be held liable for a personal injury. The Act permits injured parties to recover from most governmental entities damages caused by the negligent acts of employees arising from the operation of motor vehicles or from some condition of public property—for example, an unsafe stairwell. But with regard to school districts and community colleges, liability can be imposed only when the injury arises from the negligent use or operation of a motor vehicle operated by a school officer or employee within the scope of employment. Hence, unless motor vehicles are involved, a school district is shielded by Texas law from tort liability.

A 1978 Texas Supreme Court case makes this clear. In *Barr v. Bernhard,* a student was severely injured when a calf he was tending in conjunction with a voc-ag course bumped a pole supporting the roof of a barn, causing the roof to collapse upon him. The barn was part of a seventy-three-acre facility maintained by the Kerrville I.S.D. The parents of Mark Bernhard sued the school district for negligence, claiming the barn was in disrepair and improperly supervised. The Texas Supreme Court dismissed this part of his suit, stating that "the law is well settled in this state that an independent school district is an agency of the state and, while exercising governmental functions, is not answerable for its negligence in a suit sounding in tort" (p. 846).

Note that the court referred to the school district "exercising governmental functions." Tort cases involving governmental entities have long turned on the distinction between the entity's "governmental functions" and its "proprietary functions." The general rule was that the entity was liable for negligence in carrying out proprietary functions, but immune from liability when performing governmental functions. Fortunately for the taxpayers of Texas, our courts consistently have ruled that virtually everything a school does is classified as a governmental function. This theory was put to the test in *Fowler v. Tyler I.S.D.,* a state court of appeals decision in 2007 involving a slip and fall on bleachers during a high school football playoff game. Tyler I.S.D. did not have a team in the game—it made its facility available for a rental fee so that the two teams could play at a neutral site. Even though it was not a Tyler I.S.D. event, and the district charged a fee, the court still held that Tyler I.S.D. was acting in a "governmental" capacity and was entitled to sovereign immunity.

In 1987, the Texas Supreme Court had another occasion to consider the extent of school district liability under the Tort Claims Act. Celeste Adeline Hopkins, a student in the Spring I.S.D., allegedly was left unsupervised and sustained head injuries after being pushed into a stack of chairs in a room at the school. At the end of the day, the child rode on the school bus to a day-care center, and during the ride she suffered severe convulsions. In the subsequent lawsuit, the mother argued that the school district could not claim the defense of governmental immunity, because the child's injuries were aggravated when she had seizures on the bus and the district personnel failed to provide adequate medical care. Thus, the mother argued that the injuries arose from the "use or operation of a motor vehicle."

The Texas Supreme Court rejected the argument. The court observed that previous cases had denied liability for injuries that occur on a bus unless they also are caused by the negligent use or operation of the bus. The court concluded, "Applying the common and ordinary meaning of the words 'operation' or 'use,' Celeste Adeline's injury could not have arisen from the use of a motor vehicle as contemplated by the statute" (*Hopkins v. Spring I.S.D.*).

There are numerous cases involving all manner of fact situations in which Texas courts have adjudicated disputes involving governmental immunity of school districts and the motor vehicle exception in the Tort Claims Act. As noted in the *Hopkins* case, even when a school vehicle is involved, the school district may be immune from liability.

Consider, for example, the case of *LeLeaux v. Hamshire-Fannett I.S.D.* (1990). The student in that case jumped up into the rear door frame of the bus and hit her head, causing injury. Her suit against the school district failed, largely because the bus was parked and the motor was turned off when the student injured herself.

The case of *Simon v. Blanco I.S.D.* (2011) presents another situation in which a student was injured on the bus, but not due to the negligent operation of the bus. Therefore, the district was entitled to immunity from liability. The plaintiff alleged that he was assaulted by fellow students while riding the school bus. He alleged that the bus driver was negligent in allowing students to stand on the bus, failing to stop the bus immediately when the assault occurred, and failing to get immediate medical help for the student. The court, however, classified all of those allegations as addressing negligent supervision of students. There was no allegation of negligent operation of the bus itself. Thus the injury occurred on the bus, but was not caused by its negligent operation. No liability.

Sometimes what looks like a motor vehicle is not. In 1989, the San Antonio Court of Appeals issued a significant decision in the case of *Naranjo v. Southwest I.S.D.* The school district was not liable for injuries suffered by a student who was repairing an immobilized car in an auto mechanics class. For liability to attach for the negligent operation or use of a motor vehicle, the vehicle must be used for transporting persons: "[A] teaching tool or teaching equipment, as was this immobilized Ford, is not such a 'motor vehicle.'" Other decisions have excluded from the definition a motorized forklift and a boat having a motor. However, the mechanical wheelchair ramp affixed to a school bus was considered a part of the bus, such that negligent use of it, which led to a student's injury, waived the district's sovereign immunity (*El Paso I.S.D. v. Apodaca*, 2009).

Even when a school district is liable, there are limitations on the extent of that liability. In 1983 the Texas Supreme Court recognized the liability of districts in conjunction with the operation of a school bus in *Madisonville I.S.D. v. Kyle*, but reversed the lower court with respect to the extent of liability. The high court pointed out that, under the Tort Claims Act, school district liability is limited to $100,000 per person and $300,000 per occurrence for losses arising from bodily injury. Property damage losses are limited to a maximum of $100,000. The case involved the death of a child who had disembarked from a school bus and was struck by a car when crossing the street. The court limited district liability to $100,000. These limits remain in the statute, now at Civil Practices and Remedies Code §101.023.

As another protection of the public trough, the courts have ruled that school bus drivers are not to be held to the same high standard of care that applies to commercial bus or taxi drivers. The standard of care required of a bus driver is that required of the general public and not that of drivers for common carriers (*Estate of Lindburg v. Mount Pleasant I.S.D.*, 1987).

The same test applies when a school contracts with a private company to transport students. In *Durham Transportation, Inc. v. Valero* (1995), the school district contracted with Durham to provide bus service. Again, the issue of "standard of care" arose, and again the court ruled that the lower, ordinary negligence standard should apply. The court distinguished Durham's services from those of a commercial carrier based on the fact that the commercial carrier makes its services available to the public at large. Here, Durham transported only schoolchildren pursuant to a contract with the school district.

Very often the outcome of a case turns on the court's characterization of what happened. Two cases with similar fact situations illustrate this. In Elgin I.S.D., a small child fell asleep on the bus on the way to school in the morning. Upon arrival at school, the driver and bus monitor, not noticing the child sleeping, locked up the bus with the child trapped inside. The little girl stayed there until 3 P.M., when school was over. The mother sued, alleging negligence. This case was more about negligent supervision than negligent operation of the bus. Nevertheless, the court found a way to impose liability on the school, holding that the act of locking up the bus was a "use" of the motor vehicle sufficient to impose liability (*Elgin I.S.D. v. R.N.*, 2006).

The second case involved a wheelchair-bound, nonverbal four-year-old who was picked up in the morning by the bus driver. Rather than going to the elementary school, the driver went to the bus barn, parked the bus with the girl on board, and left her there for two hours. Upon returning to the bus, the driver took the girl home, and said nothing about the mishap to the mother. When the mother discovered what happened, she took the little girl to the hospital, where the child was treated for heat exhaustion. The court concluded that the school was not liable. The bus driver simply forgot about the little girl. This was negligent supervision, not the negligent use or operation of a motor vehicle (*Breckenridge I.S.D. v. Valdez*, 2006).

Some of the cases involving student injuries present bizarre fact situations that lead to novel legal arguments. For example, Michael Bigler hurt his arm during his agriculture science class as the class constructed a fence around the gymnasium. The student was operating an auger that was attached to and powered by a tractor. Both the auger and tractor were owned by the superintendent. The teacher of the class was supervising the activity, and in fact, sitting in the tractor's seat. Michael sued the district after he got his jacket tangled up in the auger and twisted his arm, causing injury. But was this negligence in the use or operation of a motor vehicle by a school employee? The court held that it was. The tractor qualified as a "motor vehicle," and it provided the power to the auger. Thus, the court reasoned, without the tractor there would have been no injury. Although the teacher was not "driving" the tractor, he was "operating" the tractor to provide the power to run the auger (*Lipan I.S.D. v. Bigler*, 2006).

Then there is *Vidor I.S.D. v. Bentsen* (2005). Levi Bentsen, a student in Vidor, was injured when a school employee used a rope attached to his truck to move a concrete picnic table. The student became entangled in the rope while it was attached to the truck and was dragged. This was similar to the *Lipan* case, in that the argument focused on the cause of the student's injuries—was it the rope or the truck? The court held that the rope alone would not have hurt the boy. It was when the truck was put in motion that the student got hurt. The court held that the student had alleged sufficient facts to survive the district's motion to dismiss.

Note that the severity of the injury is not a factor in the legal analysis of these cases. Whether the student sprains an ankle or dies, the analysis turns on the factors spelled out in the Tort Claims Act. Leonel Morales was tragically killed by a motor vehicle as he and the other members of the Luling High School cross-country team were gathered on the shoulder of a two-lane highway after a warm-up run. The driver of the vehicle claimed that he moved onto the shoulder of the road to avoid the coach's vehicle, which was parked on the opposite shoulder with its hazard lights flashing. Thus the driver of the vehicle that killed the student was not a school employee, but in the suit, the mother alleged that it was the coach's negligent use of his vehicle and its hazard lights that caused the accident. The court disagreed. The court concluded that the location of the coach's truck "did no more than furnish a condition that made the injury possible." It did not cause the accident, and thus the district was immune from liability (*Morales v. Barnett*, 2007).

An employee of Education Service Center (ESC) Region II in Corpus Christi was traveling on ESC-related business when she allegedly caused an accident that caused injuries to two people in another car. The plaintiffs sued the ESC employee and the ESC, but did not provide the advance notice that is required by the Tort Claims Act. The court dismissed the suit for lack of jurisdiction, thus effectively confirming that ESCs are "governmental units" covered by the Tort Claims Act (*Education Service Center Region II v. Marikudi*, 2010).

The University Interscholastic League (UIL) is also entitled to governmental immunity. So ruled the Austin Court of Appeals in *University Interscholastic League v. Southwest Officials Association, Inc.* (2010). This suit challenged UIL rules that required referees at interscholastic competitions to be registered with, and pay dues to, the UIL. Noting that the UIL is a part of the University of Texas, established by Texas Education Code Section 33.083, the court concluded that the UIL is a unit of government, entitled to sovereign immunity.

New theories of liability keep crashing against the firm bulwark of the Texas Tort Claims Act. In the Denton I.S.D. a teacher sued the district over medical problems related to mold in the school building. Mold-related suits have had notable success in the private sector, but when the defendant is the local public school district, such claims are likely to fail. The teacher in Denton alleged that the district was guilty of intentional nuisance and intentional pollution. But the court concluded that these were tort claims and did not in any way involve a motor vehicle. Case dismissed (*Foster v. Denton I.S.D.*, 2002).

The general rule is that sovereign immunity can be waived only by the Texas Legislature. However, the school district can also voluntarily waive its immunity by initiating a suit that seeks damages. This is the lesson of *Carroll I.S.D. v. J&A Construction Services Group* (2006). The school board approved J&A as program manager for a bond program, conditioned on formal approval of a contract. J&A began working for the district, but delayed presenting a contract to the board for over six months. Meanwhile, four new board members took office. A few months later, the board rejected J&A's proposed contract and denied its request for payment for work done so far.

The district then initiated the legal proceedings, seeking a declaration from the court that it owed the company nothing. The district also sought to recover money damages, attorneys' fees, interest, and costs. J&A countersued for breach of contract, at which point the district amended its original suit, dropping all claims for money and leaving only the request for a declaratory judgment. As to the countersuit, the district asserted sovereign immunity.

The court held that the district had waived its own immunity by filing suit in the first place. Previously, the Texas Supreme Court had held that by filing suit seeking damages, a governmental entity waives immunity for any claim that is "incident to, connected with, arises out of, or is germane to the suit or controversy that it brings." The district then pointed to its amendment of the suit, and the fact that it was no longer seeking any damages. But the court held this was too late: "when an entity has waived its immunity by asserting a claim, withdrawing that claim does not defeat the trial court's jurisdiction."

Although governmental immunity has its critics, thus far the legislature has not seen fit to impose further burdens of liability upon public schools. In effect, Texas law places the risk upon the individual family rather than the school district. One way school districts help families to meet this burden is by providing inexpensive insurance, which families may purchase to protect against the costs of injuries at school. Texas Education Code Section 33.085 authorizes school districts to purchase insurance for students engaged in athletics or other school-sponsored activities.

Sovereign Immunity and Contract Cases

Does the notion of sovereign immunity apply when the school district enters into a contract with a private entity? Section 271.151 of the Local Government Code addresses this issue. The statute makes it clear that governmental entities, including school districts, can be sued and can be held liable for breach of contract, if the contract was entered into after the effective date of the statute, September 1, 2005. The statute continues to limit the damages that can be recovered in such a suit. The law authorizes recovery of the balance owed by the school district on a contract, but does not permit recovery of "consequential" or "exemplary" damages. Nor can the plaintiff in such a suit recover attorneys' fees unless the contract expressly says so and specifically references the statute (Texas Local Government Code §§271.151 et seq.).

Not all contracts will open the door to liability. The contract must satisfy the standards of the Local Government Code. The Texas Supreme Court identified the five essential elements of such a contract in *City of Houston v. Williams* (2011). The court held that a contract was "subject to this subchapter" when it (1) was in writing; (2) stated the essential terms of the agreement; (3) provided for goods or services; (4) to the local governmental entity; and (5) was executed on behalf of the local governmental entity.

The court then held that city ordinances concerning overtime pay and other benefits for firefighters created a "unilateral contract" that satisfied all five elements. The firefighters had sued the city in an effort to enforce the ordinances, and the city asserted governmental immunity. But the state's highest court held that the city had waived its immunity be adopting ordinances that, taken together, created a unilateral contract.

Qualified Immunity for Public School Professional Employees

Since school districts are shielded from liability in Texas, injured parties are apt to sue school employees. What protection do school administrators and teachers have? Let us return to *Barr v. Bernhard,* for there school officials also were sued. Attorneys for Bernhard claimed that school employees were negligent in maintaining the ag barn and in supervising its use. No school professional had been present when the structure collapsed. Once again, the suit was unsuccessful because of a provision of the Texas Education Code that provides professional school employees with what is called "qualified immunity" from tort liability. The specific provision, now found at TEC §22.0511, provides in part that a professional employee of a school district is not "personally liable for any act that is incident to or within the scope of the duties of the employee's position of employment and that involves the exercise of judgment or discretion on the part of the employee." The majority on the court observed that this statute (then codified at TEC §21.912(b)) goes on to list use of excessive force in student discipline and negligence resulting in injury to a student as exceptions, but the majority tied the negligence clause in with student discipline. Thus, the Texas Supreme Court determined that the only exception to immunity for professional employees under the statute relates to the use of excessive force in disciplining students or being negligent in disciplining students so as to cause an injury. Since Mark Bernhard was not being disciplined when the injury occurred, school employees were not liable. The dissenters disagreed, reading the negligence clause as referring to any negligent action resulting in student injury, not just negligence in disciplining students.

Thus, unlike the situation in many states where school employees are legally liable when students are injured at school, school professionals in Texas are shielded by law from such liability. Those who have damage claims against school districts and school professionals have little recourse but to shoulder the costs themselves.

Only "professional employees" are covered by TEC §22.0511, but the statute has an expansive definition of the term. It includes superintendents, principals, teachers, substitute teachers, supervisors, social workers, counselors, nurses, teacher's aides, student teachers, DPS-certified bus drivers, school board members, teachers employed by a third party that contracts with the school district, and anyone else whose employment requires certification and an exercise of discretion.

Yet another provision in the Code protects volunteers. Section 22.053 provides that "direct service volunteers" in the district enjoy the same immunity from civil liability that professional employees have under TEC §22.0511. However, volunteers can be liable for intentional misconduct or gross negligence.

The immunity statute also applies to all employees and volunteers working for a regional Education Service Center (ESC) (TEC §8.006). This statute came into play when the director of ESC 19's Head Start program was sued for defamation. The ESC had terminated the employment of a number of people who worked for the Center in the Head Start program. The director of the program gave an interview to a local TV station and then was sued for defamation by some of the former employees. But the court ruled that the qualified immunity statute applied. Giving an interview to the media about a local story was within the scope of the director's employment and involved the use of judgment or discretion (*Enriquez v. Khouri*, 2000).

Keep in mind that some school employees remain potentially liable for student injuries. Cafeteria and maintenance workers, for example, are not "professional employees" and thus enjoy no special protection. However, many school districts now have broad insurance policies protecting all paid employees.

Furthermore, those who do enjoy the protection of the statute must remember that the immunity, though broad, is not absolute. To be protected, professional employees must be acting in the scope of their duties, must be exercising judgment or discretion, and must not be using excessive force in disciplining students or have been sufficiently negligent in disciplining students to cause bodily injury. Statutory immunity is weakest when force is used in student discipline, a topic explored in detail below.

The final limitation of the qualified immunity defense under state law is that it does not apply to the operation, use, or maintenance of motor vehicles. So suppose a school bus driver is negligent while operating the bus. Can the school and the driver each be held liable? Yes—they can *each* be liable, but it would not be accurate to say that they can *both* be liable. In its 2003 session, the Texas Legislature imposed a new "tort reform" statute that requires the person filing suit to choose only one defendant. If the injured party sues a governmental unit, such as a school district, the plaintiff has thus made "an irrevocable election" that "immediately and forever bars any suit or recovery by the plaintiff against any individual employee of the governmental unit regarding the same subject matter." It works the other way as well. If the suit is filed against a school employee, there can be no suit against the school district (Civil Practices and Remedies Code §101.106). Likewise, any settlement of a claim against one possible defendant rules out any recovery against other potential defendants.

This provision came before the Texas Supreme Court in *Mission*

C.I.S.D. v. Garcia (2008). Ms. Garcia sued both the district and the superintendent, alleging intentional infliction of emotional distress, intentional misrepresentation, fraud, and defamation in connection with the termination of her employment. These are all considered common law tort actions and are thus subject to the election of remedies provision. Citing that provision, the district argued that it was entitled to be dismissed from the suit, because Garcia had also sued the superintendent. The court agreed. Moreover, because she sued the district, the superintendent was entitled to a dismissal as well. Thus failure to choose one defendant enabled both defendants to get out of the case. One part of her lawsuit remained alive. The suit also alleged that the district violated the Texas Commission on Human Rights Act. Noting that the TCHRA provides for governmental liability, the court allowed that part of the case to proceed. All other allegations and causes of action were dismissed.

Even when an employee is held liable in a court of law for damages, state law imposes limits on the amount of damages. Section 108.002 of the Civil Practices and Remedies Code limits the damages that can be assessed against a governmental employee to $100,000, so long as the employee was acting within the scope of employment and is covered by insurance or an indemnity arrangement. This provision appears to be designed to guarantee that governmental employees will be covered by insurance up to $100,000 so that injured parties will have a "deep pocket" from which to recover.

The notion of qualified immunity for school professionals is well established in Texas law. Courts have had numerous opportunities since *Barr v. Bernhard* to reconsider the matter but have continued to uphold the doctrine. For example, in *Hopkins v. Spring I.S.D.*, discussed above in connection with district immunity, the Texas Supreme Court also took another look at qualified individual immunity under the Education Code. The plaintiff asked the court to overrule *Barr v. Bernhard* and hold that school district personnel can be held liable for their negligent acts that result in serious bodily injury to students. A majority of the court declined to do so, stating that any waiver of governmental immunity is a matter to be addressed by the legislature. Three justices dissented.

A review of the case law shows that Texas state courts generally interpret the qualified immunity statute liberally in favor of protecting school professionals, who must oversee the activities of numerous students on a daily basis. For example, in *Schumate v. Thompson*, a 1979 court of appeals case, the court dismissed a suit against a teacher for personal injuries in a playground incident. The teacher, an employee of Cypress-Fairbanks School District, instructed her aide, a mentally handicapped person, to take the class outside to play. The aide directed a student to high-jump a stick held by herself and a classmate. The injury occurred when the student fell. A similar decision was reached in a 1980 court of appeals case, *Wagner v. Alvarado I.S.D. Wagner* involved a damage suit against the school district and several of its employees over injuries sustained when a student fell while carrying a jar full of acid from one physics lab to another. The physics teacher was one of the employees sued. The court upheld dismissal of the suit against both the school and the professional employees, citing the immunity of each under Texas law.

In *Stout v. Grand Prairie I.S.D.* (1988), the injured student attacked the constitutionality of the qualified immunity statute. The student alleged that such a statute deprived injured parties of any recourse, while providing no public benefit whatsoever. The statute, it was argued, benefited teachers only, but not the general public. The court rejected that argument, noting that "if competent people are discouraged from entering the teaching profession because of potential tort liability, the public education system will be adversely affected." Thus the statute served a public purpose and was constitutional.

The qualified immunity doctrine was applied to a case with a tragic outcome that began when a student in the Cypress-Fairbanks School District was suspected of selling drugs on campus. School administrators investigated the matter, sent the student home with her parents, and gave notice of proposed expulsion. Alone at home, the girl committed suicide. The parents subsequently sued two assistant principals and the principal, alleging that their improper handling of the matter caused the distraught young girl to kill herself. The court of appeals granted summary judgment for the school administrators, citing the qualified immunity statute once again (*Fowler v. Szostek*, 1995).

The matter of qualified immunity came back to the Texas Supreme Court in *Downing v. Brown* (1996). In that case, a student alleged that she was injured by her fellow students and asserted that the teacher's negligence in maintaining classroom discipline was a cause of the injury. The court of appeals rejected the teacher's qualified immunity defense because the teacher allegedly had failed to post a set of classroom rules, as she was required to do. The court of appeals ruled that this moved the case out of the arena of "discretion" into mere "ministerial acts." Recall that one element of the qualified immunity defense is that the teacher was exercising judgment or discretion. The Texas Supreme Court, however, reversed the court of appeals with the observation that "In our view, maintaining classroom discipline involves personal deliberation, decision and judgment." Thus the teacher was exercising discretion and was entitled to qualified immunity.

While most of the reported cases deal with physical injuries of some sort, the professional employee's qualified immunity applies to suits alleging slander as well. When a newspaper reported that one high school baseball coach had accused a rival coach of violating University Interscholastic League (UIL) rules, the accused coach sued, alleging slander, defamation, and intentional infliction of emotional distress. The federal court dismissed all these claims, citing the qualified immunity statute (*Anderson v. Blankenship*, 1992). Similar decisions are discussed in Chapter 6.

In a 2003 decision, a superintendent was sued for sending a letter to a builder assuring him that a planned subdivision was in his school district. A couple bought a home in the subdivision in reliance on the builder's assurances as to which school district the lot was located in. When it turned out that the home was not in the desired district, the couple sued the builder, and the builder sued the school superintendent. Once again, qualified immunity came to the rescue. The superintendent was acting within the scope of his employment when he issued his letter. The fact that he turned out to be mistaken was legally irrelevant (*Choctaw Properties L.L.C. v. Aledo I.S.D.*).

School employees are not always acting "within the scope of employment." When they step outside that protective bubble, they stand to lose their qualified immunity. A good example of this is the 1981 Houston Court of Appeals case of *O'Haver v. Blair*. The case involved a teacher at Madison High School in San Antonio who struck a student in the course of trying to halt use of the school's football field on a Sunday afternoon in October. The teacher, Tommy Blair, was attending a coaches' meeting at the high school. When the coaches learned that a group of people were using the football field, they attempted to get them to leave. Coach Blair pushed Shaun O'Haver, whereupon O'Haver started pushing back. The two began to struggle, and Coach Blair struck O'Haver in the mouth, knocking out two of his teeth and loosening several others. The appeals court held that it was not clear that Coach Blair had fulfilled all the elements necessary to claim immunity under the statute. Specifically, the court questioned whether Coach Blair was acting in the scope of his duties when the incident occurred, whether he was employing judgment or discretion, and whether he was not in fact disciplining the student. Noting the rulings in *Barr v. Bernhard*, *Schumate v. Thompson*, and *Wagner v. Alvarado I.S.D.*, the court pointed out that "the distinctions between these cases and the present case are obvious. In the case at bar there is no dispute that a teacher struck a student with his fist with enough force to knock out teeth" (p. 469).

It should be clear from *O'Haver v. Blair* that the immunity conferred upon Texas public school professional employees by the qualified immunity statute is not automatic. Furthermore, protection from civil liability is weakest when hands-on discipline is involved.

More recently a teacher in Schulenburg I.S.D. made a creative argument to convince the court that she was entitled to immunity after she deliberately teased a student over his failed romance with a girl. The teacher went so far as to create a fake newspaper article in which the student was accused of "stalking." Suit was filed against the teacher for intentional infliction of emotional distress, negligence, and slander. But the teacher persuaded the court that she was entitled to immunity. She was acting "within the scope of employment" by attempting to build a good rapport with the student by using good-natured teasing and humor (*Kobza v. Kutac*, 2003). This case is an excellent illustration of the qualified immunity teachers in Texas enjoy, and its limitations. Both the school district and the State Board for Educator Certification (SBEC) took disciplinary action against the teacher in this case for violating the Educator's Code of Ethics. In fact, the plaintiff in the lawsuit relied on those findings in an effort to show that the teacher went beyond "the scope of employment." But the argument did not work. The court concluded that violating the Code of Ethics does not necessarily mean that a teacher has stepped outside of the "scope of employment." Furthermore, the fact that the teacher exercised poor judgment was not enough to expose the teacher to liability. Indeed, almost all of the cases under §22.0511 involve poor judgment by a teacher.

For example, there is the case of the kindergarten teacher who brought her electric frying pan to school to make doughnuts. This was an effort to teach the letter "D." Unfortunately, one of the little ones stepped on the cord, which toppled over the skillet and spilled hot grease on the student. The lawyer representing the student made the interesting argument that since the activity was fun, it could not be instructional. Therefore, the argument went, the teacher should not be immunized from liability. The court rejected that argument, noting that "fun" and "education" are not mutually exclusive. Some report that this lesson has not sunk in at all levels of education (*Chesshir v. Sharp*, 2000).

Not every case has gone in favor of the educator, however. One court focused on the requirement that the teacher's immunity applies only when the teacher is exercising "judgment." In *Myers v. Doe*, the court concluded that no judgment call was involved. The case involved allegations of repeated sexual assaults by a male student against a female student. After the first incident, the school imposed some rules designed to prevent recurrence. Among other things, the elevator where the first assault occurred was to be locked. Second, both students were to be escorted at all times. Third, if either student were tardy to class, it was to be reported to the office. The parents of the girl alleged that these policies were announced but not implemented. They also alleged that the boy assaulted the girl two more times. Based on this record, the court was not convinced that school employees were using "judgment or discretion," as the statute requires. In effect, the court drew a distinction between developing a policy and implementing a policy. Judgment or discretion may be involved in the development, but not necessarily in the implementation. Take the issue of locking the elevator, for example.

Deciding to do so is a "judgment" call. Once the decision is made that the elevator always must be locked, there is no more room for "judgment or discretion." Therefore, the court refused to dismiss the case prior to a full trial (*Myers v. Doe*, 2001).

Besides §22.0511, there are other statutes designed to provide a measure of immunity to public school employees in various situations. TEC §22.052 provides civil immunity from damages or injuries resulting from the administration of medication to students if the school district has adopted a policy on the subject, the school has received a written request from the parent or guardian, and the medication appears to be in the original container and to be properly labeled. However, the statute does not provide immunity "from civil liability for injuries resulting from gross negligence."

TEC §37.016 provides that a school employee is not liable in civil damages for reporting to a school administrator or governmental authority, in the exercise of professional judgment within the scope of duties, a student whom the person suspects of using, passing, or selling on school property marijuana, a dangerous drug, an abusable glue or aerosol paint, a chemical inhalant, or an alcoholic beverage. Again, the critical point is that the report must be made within the scope of duties.

What about the duty to report child abuse? As discussed in more detail below, Texas does have a statute that requires all persons who have cause to believe that a child has been abused or neglected to report the situation to appropriate authorities. Failure to make such a report when required is a criminal offense. But does it also create personal liability in a civil suit? Apparently not for teachers. The Texas Supreme Court dealt with the general contours of tort liability under the child abuse reporting statute in *Perry v. S.N.* (1998). The court held that the statute does not establish "a duty and standard of conduct in tort." The court's analysis was limited to what the lawyers call "negligence per se"—the theory that violation of the statute is automatic evidence of tortious liability. The court in *Perry* left open the possibility that there was a "common law" duty to report abuse that would lead to liability. But three years later, a federal court in Texas held that the "common law" duty, if it existed at all, would be "discretionary" with teachers, thus keeping them in the zone of qualified immunity under Texas Education Code §22.0511. "Assuming such a cause exists," the court ruled, "Section 22.051 [now 22.0511] would provide [the teacher] immunity against it" (*Doe v. S & S C.I.S.D.*). The Fifth Circuit affirmed this decision.

Besides statutory immunity, educators also can assert the doctrine of "official immunity." In fact, official immunity may apply when the statutory immunity created by the Education Code does not. A case in point is *Moore v. Willis I.S.D.* A coach punished a student by requiring him to perform one hundred "up and down" exercises. The parent sued the coach, asserting that the student suffered physical injuries. Since the coach was charged with excessive force or negligence in disciplining the student, the statutory immunity set out in TEC §22.0511 was unavailable. However, the court ruled that the coach was entitled to "official immunity." This protection applies to governmental employees who are performing discretionary duties in good faith. The court concluded that the coach was acting in good faith, even if the purpose of the punishment was to inflict a certain amount of pain. The Fifth Circuit affirmed the trial court's decision and specifically rejected any liability under the U.S. Constitution (*Moore v. Willis I.S.D.*).

Does "official immunity" protect negligent bus drivers? According to *Los Fresnos C.I.S.D. v. Southworth* (2005), it does not. The plaintiffs claimed that they were injured when the bus "veered off the road and rolled onto its right side in a plowed field." This sounds like a straightforward negligence case, but the school district argued that the bus driver was entitled to official immunity. She was within the scope of her employment, and no one questioned her "good faith," so the case turned on the issue of "discretion." Citing earlier decisions, the court concluded that driving a bus is "ministerial" rather than discretionary. A function is considered "ministerial if the law prescribes and defines the duties to be performed with such precision and certainty that nothing is left to the discretion of the actor." According to the court, "ministerial functions" would include such things as "the driving of a bus along a given route on a certain day, at a specified time, and in accordance with the law and the driving rules and regulations promulgated by the policy-decision makers." Thus the driver was not immune from liability. We expect the judges on the court have never had to drive a school bus full of hyperactive adolescents. We think there is a lot of "discretion" left to the beleaguered bus driver, but the law sees it otherwise.

Those who contemplate suits versus schools or school employees also must take into account statutes designed to protect the public from defending frivolous suits. Section 11.161 of the Education Code authorizes a court to require the payment of court costs and attorneys' fees by a person who files a frivolous suit against a school district or school officer. A similar provision applies to suits versus school employees (TEC §22.055).

There are also procedural hurdles for those who would sue a school employee. A person must give ninety days' written notice of an intent to file suit against a professional employee of a school district. If the suit ultimately is filed but dismissed due to the application of the immunity provisions set out in the Texas Education Code, the plaintiff is liable for the attorneys' fees and court costs incurred by the professional employee (TEC §§22.0513 and 22.0517). This is exactly what happened in *Ward v. Theret* (2009). The salacious backstory behind this case involved photographs of students in their cheerleader costumes in various provocative and suggestive poses, while handling phallus-shaped objects. Not surprisingly, a made-for-TV movie ensued: *Fab Five: The Texas Cheerleader Scandal.* The teacher/cheerleading sponsor sued the principal for wrongful termination and defamation, but all of her claims arose from actions taken by the principal in the scope of her employment. The principal was entitled to dismissal of the case and the recovery of $14,000 in fees.

Even with all that protection, suits will be filed and legal costs will be incurred. Consequently, state law authorizes school districts to purchase insurance policies protecting the district and its employees against legal claims (Tex. Civ. Prac. & Rem. Code §101.027). Also, the legislature has authorized school districts to pay actual damages awarded against employees if the damages result from an act or omission of the employee in the course and scope of employment and arise from a cause of action for negligence. The statute further authorizes a district to pay the court costs and attorneys' fees awarded against such an employee. Also, the district may provide legal counsel to represent the employee. Payments are limited to $100,000 per person or $300,000 per occurrence in the case of personal injury or death or $100,000 per occurrence of property damage. Since these authorizations are all limited to causes of action for negligence, and school employees have extensive protection from such suits, they may not come into play very often, at least with regard to actual damages. However, the legal defense provision will apply, and will be appreciated, even when the suit lacks merit.

There are some exceptions to the grant of authority. A district may not pay damages awarded against an employee that arise from official misconduct, a willful or wrongful act or omission, or gross negligence (Tex. Civ. Prac. & Rem. Code §§102.001–102.004).

Since we can anticipate that lawsuits will continue to be brought against school districts and school professionals, and since we cannot be sure that Texas professional employees will always be so well protected in the future, the best advice is to observe school policies and rules carefully and to be sure to act within the ethical standards of one's profession in carrying out assigned duties. When all else fails, good common sense usually offers excellent protection.

The Special Case of Corporal Punishment and Physical Force

As noted in the chapter on student discipline, the U.S. Supreme Court has ruled that no due process is necessary prior to the imposition of corporal punishment (*Ingraham v. Wright*, 1977). Since that ruling, the courts have been reluctant to become involved in corporal punishment cases on constitutional grounds, as illustrated by the decisions discussed in Chapter 8.

Despite these rulings, it makes good sense to comply with minimal due process procedures, given the limited protection from damage suits that public school professionals enjoy under Texas law where student discipline is involved. Recall that the relevant provision in the Texas Education Code states that professional employees are not personally liable for their acts as employees "except in circumstances in which a professional employee uses excessive force in the discipline of students or negligence resulting in bodily injury to students." The best way to avoid falling into the "excessive force" or "negligence" categories of TEC §22.0511 is to follow school policy scrupulously.

Can parents prohibit the use of corporal punishment? In Texas they can do so by exercising their statutory right, on behalf of their child, to "opt out" of corporal punishment by giving written notice to the district each year. We discuss this statute (TEC § 37.0011) in Chapter 8. Prior to the enactment of that statute, however, there was no such right. A federal district court ruling, which the U.S. Supreme Court subsequently affirmed, held that a school district is not legally required to defer to the parents' wishes (*Baker v. Owen*, 1975). The court ruled that the interest of the school in maintaining an orderly environment outweighs the liberty rights of parents to control their children's upbringing. That decision was a long time ago and has now been superseded by the Texas statute. On top of that, good common sense should guide the prudent school administrator to administer corporal punishment only with parental approval.

Those professional educators who serve as the campus "designated hitter" should also be aware that a flagrant abuse of the educator's right to use hands-on discipline may constitute a criminal offense as an assault as well as a civil wrong (tort). Thus, not only might professional employees find themselves involved in a civil suit for money damages in such a situation, but they might also be subject to criminal prosecution and/or child abuse investigations. Texas Penal Code §22.04 states in part that

> (a) A person commits an offense if he intentionally, knowingly, recklessly, or with criminal negligence by act or intentionally, knowingly, or recklessly by omission causes to a child, elderly individual, or disabled individual:
> (1) serious bodily injury;
> (2) serious mental deficiency impairment, or injury; or
> (3) bodily injury.

Another section of the Penal Code, §9.62, does recognize that educators may use force, "but not deadly force," with regard to students under their charge "when and to the degree the actor reasonably believes the force is necessary to further the special purpose or to maintain discipline in a group." However, the Court of Appeals for Texarkana has ruled that the use of force "must be that which the teacher *reasonably* believes necessary (1) to enforce compliance with a *proper* command issued for the purpose of controlling, training, or educating the child, or (2) to punish the child for prohibited conduct; and in either case, the force or physical contact must be reasonable and not disproportionate to the activity or the offense" (*Hogenson v. Williams*, 1976, p. 460, emphasis added). The court specifically stated that "we do not accept the proposition that a teacher may use physical violence against a child merely because the child is unable or fails to perform, either academically or athletically, at a desired level of ability, even though the teacher considers such violence to be 'instruction and encouragement.'" The case involved a football coach at Terrell Middle School in Denison, Texas, who used physical force on a student during a practice session of the seventh-grade football team, causing injury. The coach claimed that he was trying to "fire up" the student and instill spirit in him. Based on the broadened definition of assault given by the court of appeals, the case was sent back to the trial court for a new trial. The coach had been exonerated on the basis of §9.62 at the first trial. It should be emphasized that the qualified immunity from damage suits conveyed by TEC §22.0511 would not immunize an employee in the event of a challenge under criminal law.

A 1994 decision indicates that courts will continue to protect school employees who use some degree of physical force in handling students. In *Doria v. Stulting* the student alleged he was physically injured by his teacher when the teacher physically escorted the student out of the classroom. The departure from the classroom was occasioned by student misbehavior, and the teacher was taking the student to the vice principal's office for the imposition of disciplinary consequences. Thus it would appear to be a use of force in the context of discipline. Nevertheless, the court ruled that the teacher was entitled to immunity under the qualified immunity statute. The court observed that the term "discipline" normally refers to punishment. The court reasoned that the teacher was not disciplining the student—the teacher was acting "to protect the school learning process from disruption by a wrongdoer by physically removing the wrongdoer to the public official designated by rule, regulation, or law to impose the necessary and proper 'discipline-punishment'—the vice principal." Since the teacher was not disciplining the student, the teacher could not be held liable even if the student were injured in the process.

Cases alleging a negligent "failure to discipline" have so far been unsuccessful. When a student assaulted another student during class and broke the jaw of the second student, the second student sued the teacher and principal. The allegation was that these professional employees knew or should have known that the assaulting student was a delinquent with a propensity for violence. The school employees were charged with negligent failure to discipline the student who committed the assault. Once again, the courts protected the school employees from liability. The court ruled that the qualified immunity statute applied in this context (*Pulido v. Dennis*).

So it is reasonably clear that personal liability for student injuries under state law can be applied to the professional school employee only for the excessive or negligent use of physical punishment as discipline. However, this is not limited to paddling. Such is the lesson of *Diggs v. Bales* (1984), a case in which the court offered some important commentary about the liability of professional employees for injuries resulting from student discipline. Both trial and appeals courts decided in favor of the Plano school district and its employee in a suit involving a student who was struck in the eye by an object allegedly shot at him by another student. The appeals court observed that liability of professional employees is restricted to situations involving student discipline, and here discipline was not an issue. However, the court also observed that *direct* use of force need not be necessary for an actionable case to arise. As an example, the court noted that, if a teacher's assignment for students to run laps around an athletic field is the proximate cause of a student injury, the teacher may be liable despite the qualified immunity statute.

What about threats of force? In *Spacek v. Charles* (1996), two coaches threatened to hang or shoot a fourteen-year-old student if his grades did not improve. To illustrate what might happen, one coach reached for an extension cord, and the other placed a starter pistol to the student's head after placing him in a headlock. The student sued, and the coaches mounted a "we were just kidding" defense, asking the court to toss the case out on the basis of qualified immunity. The Houston Court of Appeals declined to do so, stating that there was enough evidence of possible excessive force that the case would have to be decided after a full trial.

Finally, in a related matter, the Texas Commissioner of Education revoked the certificate of a teacher who injured a child by striking the student with a wooden paddle. The teacher was indicted and later pled guilty to a reduced charge of assault. The commissioner observed that while the teacher's action might have constituted corporal punishment and been excused under Penal Code §9.62, "the fact that respondent was indicted and pled guilty to assault leads this decision maker to conclude that the actions were not legally excusable." The incident underscores the need to be especially careful when using corporal punishment, given the legal consequences under state law (*Texas Education Agency v. Darthard*, 1991).

In an effort to provide more protection for classroom teachers, the Texas Legislature has amended TEC §22.0512 to state that a professional employee of a school district may not be subject to "disciplinary proceedings" for the employee's use of force against a student to the extent force is justified under §9.62 of the Penal Code. The term "disciplinary proceedings" is defined in the law to include nonrenewal, suspension, or termination of the employee, or SBEC proceedings to enforce the Educator's Code of Ethics. It does not bar a civil suit against the teacher, but we expect to see teachers arguing that the statute does reflect legislative intent to shield from negative consequences teachers who find it necessary to use physical force. In *Peters v. Dallas I.S.D.* (2013) the commissioner noted that this statute gives "a high level of protection for a teacher" to the extent that "if a parent could lawfully use force, a teacher could lawfully use force." Despite that sweeping language, the commissioner held that the teacher's use of force in this case would not be viewed as necessary by a reasonable teacher. The teacher's termination was upheld.

The Paul D. Coverdell Teacher Protection Act is a federal law along the same lines. It is also designed to protect teachers who find it necessary to use some degree of force with students. The Act was invoked in a case at the Prestonwood Christian Academy after an aide informed the parents of a kindergarten girl that the teacher was mistreating their daughter. The parents sued the school and the teacher. The teacher successfully asserted her immunity under the Coverdell Act. The Act expressly applies to both public and private schools in states that receive federal funds. The court noted that Texas receives federal funds for education and thus the teacher had proven that she was entitled to the Act's protections. The Act applies if (1) a teacher is acting within the scope of employment; (2) the actions of the teacher comply with the law and were taken in an effort to control, discipline, suspend, or expel a student, or to maintain order in the school; (3) the teacher was properly licensed, certified, or authorized; and (4) the harm was not caused willfully, with gross negligence, reckless misconduct, criminal misconduct, or conscious flagrant indifference to the rights or safety of the individual who was harmed. In her testimony, the aide stated that she did not believe the teacher intended to hurt the child. Therefore, in the absence of any evidence of intentional wrongdoing, the Act applied and the case was dismissed (*Morrone v. Prestonwood Christian Academy*, 2007).

Law and the School Counselor

School counselors often ask if they have special protection under state or federal law from legal liability. Specifically, they are concerned about the degree of confidentiality they and their student clients are entitled to. Do they have to reveal the substance of confidential conversations to parents upon request? If they fail to do so, are they likely to be sued? Do counselors have to testify about a confidential conversation in court?

Regarding disclosures to parents, the Texas Education Code contains strong language that requires disclosure of materials upon request. Section 26.004 tells us that a parent is entitled to access to "all written records of a school district concerning the parent's child," including counseling records and psychological records. Section 26.001 describes parents as "partners with educators, administrators, and school district boards of trustees in their children's education." With that in mind, it would seem that a counselor would have to disclose any notes or other records that have been made in connection with counseling sessions with the student.

What, then, about the notion of the confidential counselor-patient relationship? In a 2002 opinion, Attorney General John Cornyn sorted out the various state and federal laws pertaining to confidentiality and ruled that counseling records could be withheld from a parent only under very limited circumstances. First, the records would have to be maintained by a "licensed professional counselor" (LPC) as opposed to a person certified as a school counselor. Second, the records would have to meet the federal definition of "sole possession records" under the Family Educational Rights and Privacy Act (FERPA), meaning that they are not disclosed to any other person. Third, the LPC would have to determine that release of the records would be harmful to the student's physical, mental, or emotional health (*Att'y. Gen. Op. JC-0538*, 2002).

This is somewhat ironic, since state law does not require counselors to have parental consent to meet with children in certain situations. Section 32.004 of the Texas Family Code permits a minor to meet with a counselor without parental consent if the counseling concerns suicide prevention; chemical addiction or dependency; or sexual, physical, or emotional abuse.

Regarding disclosure of confidential information to people other than the student's parents, the relevant law is FERPA, which is discussed in detail in Chapter 9. The issue that arises most often with counselors concerns the disclosure of information to other school personnel. Can the counselor share information about a student with other members of the staff? Under FERPA, such disclosures are permitted. FERPA requires parental consent for the disclosure of confidential information, subject to several exceptions. One of those exceptions permits school officials to release confidential information to other school officials who have "a legitimate educational interest" in the student and in the information. This provision is designed to facilitate the sharing of relevant information by school officials. This provision applies to the records of a counselor just as it does to the records of a teacher. If there is a legitimate educational reason why information pertaining to a particular student, or records concerning that student, should be shared with other school officials, the counselor can do so.

Counselors often are concerned about the scope of other laws that appear to require a higher degree of confidentiality. However, those laws defer to FERPA. For example, the Texas Health and Safety Code requires that counseling records be kept confidential, but allows an exception if the disclosure is "to a governmental agency if the disclosure is required or authorized by law" (Health and Safety Code §611.004(a)). Since FERPA authorizes the disclosure of information to other school officials with a legitimate educational interest, then such a disclosure is permissible under the Health and Safety Code as well.

Likewise, the statutes pertaining to the licensed professional counselor (LPC) do not appear to restrict intraschool disclosures. The regulations governing LPCs permit disclosure of records if such disclosure is permitted by the Health and Safety Code or any other state or federal statute or rules.

This is not to suggest that counselors should be careless or thoughtless about the disclosure of information. The point is that the school counselor does stand in a different position than the counselor's private counterpart, at least insofar as intraschool disclosures are concerned. Furthermore, the school counselor, like any counselor, can be sued for *not* disclosing information in certain situations. The case of *Tarasoff v. Regents of the University of California* (1976) best illustrates the point. In that case a distraught student met with a counselor employed by the university. The student told the counselor of his desire to kill his ex-girlfriend. Two months later, he did just that. The young woman's parents sued the psychologist and the university for the failure to warn of this threat. The Supreme Court of California held that the special nature of the relationship between a psychologist and a patient created a legal duty to use reasonable care to protect third parties from serious bodily injury or death.

Texas law appears to acknowledge such a duty as well. The Texas Health and Safety Code, referred to above, provides that confidentiality does not extend to disclosure of information "to medical or law enforcement personnel if the professional determines that there is a probability of imminent physical injury by the patient to the patient or others or there is a probability of immediate mental or emotional injury to the patient" (Health and Safety Code §611.004(b)).

However, the Texas Supreme Court has ruled that there is no duty requiring a mental health professional to warn a known victim or the victim's family of a patient's threat (*Thapar v. Zezulka*). Thus it appears under current state law that "mental health professionals" such as LPCs have a limited duty to speak up when there is the probability of imminent physical injury, but that the duty is to notify medical and/or law enforcement personnel rather than the potential victim.

School counselors frequently are involved in the report of suspected child abuse. Any person who has cause to believe that a child may be the victim of abuse or neglect is required to report it, but certain "professionals" must make the report within forty-eight hours. The term "professional" in the Texas Family Code encompasses any person who is licensed or certified by the state, or who works for a facility licensed, certified, or operated by the state, who in the normal course of duties has direct contact with children (Texas Family Code §261.101). Clearly this includes certified educators and counselors in public schools.

Child abuse reporting statutes represent one of the few areas where the law criminalizes inaction. It is the failure to report that can lead to criminal liability. Reporting suspected abuse, even when no abuse has in fact occurred, cannot lead to personal liability as long as the person reporting was acting in good faith (Texas Family Code §261.106). As discussed above, courts in Texas have ruled that the fact of criminal liability for a failure to report does not automatically lead to civil liability.

What about the wrongful disclosure of confidential information— can this lead to liability? Under the federal statute governing student records, the answer is no. As discussed in more detail in Chapter 9, the U.S. Supreme Court has ruled that there is no "private right of action" for violations of FERPA. That is, an individual cannot sue in court for damages or injunctive relief because the school district has violated FERPA. The only remedy available to the aggrieved under that statute is to have the federal funds of the institution withheld.

FEDERAL CIVIL RIGHTS LIABILITY

Much of the previous discussion of qualified immunity under state law should be tempered by the fact of potential liability under federal law. Lawyers are a creative and persistent lot. When state law avenues are closed, a good lawyer will explore the possibility of framing the suit to fit federal law. So let us now turn to an examination of liability under federal law.

School administrators are aware that many of the federal lawsuits filed against school districts and their employees are referred to as "§1983" suits. While other federal statutes protect more specific rights, the federal statute codified as §1983 of volume 42 of the United States Code (hence, 42 U.S.C. §1983) provides a broad basis for litigation in federal court. Section 1983 was enacted shortly after the Civil War (1871) and was designed to protect the civil rights of citizens. It reads as follows: "Every person who, under color of any statute, ordinance, regulation, custom, or usage, of any State or Territory, subjects, or causes to be subjected, any citizen of the United States or other person within the jurisdiction thereof to the deprivation of any rights, privileges, or immunities secured by the Constitution and laws, shall be liable to the party injured in an action at law, suit in equity, or other proper proceeding for redress."

In essence, §1983 grants the litigant the right to hold liable every person who has deprived the litigant of rights protected by the U.S. Constitution or by federal law, when that person has done so acting under color of state law. Section 1983 does not reach purely private conduct, because such conduct is not taken "under color of state law" as is required. Liability attaches under §1983 only to a person who carries a "badge of authority" of a state or local government.

A §1983 suit thus basically involves a charge of an abuse of governmental authority that deprives someone (e.g., a student, a teacher) of federally protected rights. The rights at stake can range from a student's Fourth Amendment right to be free from an unreasonable search to an employee's First Amendment right to speak out as a citizen on matters of public concern. While §1983 speaks of holding "every person" liable, the scope of liability under the statute is not unlimited. The federal courts apply different tests to determine the liability of the government itself, as opposed to the personal liability of officers and employees of the government. That difference is the subject of the following section.

Governmental Liability

Section 1983 speaks of "every person." Is a city a "person"? Is a school district a "person"? In 1978, the U.S. Supreme Court held the term "person" in Section 1983 includes governmental entities such as cities and school districts (*Monell v. New York City Department of Social Services*). With that single decision, overturning prior cases, the Court ushered in a new era of spirited federal civil rights litigation.

There is, however, a critical limitation upon governmental liability. As the Court explained in *Monell*, a government is not liable merely because a governmental employee commits a wrong that deprives someone of his or her federal rights. That sort of liability is referred to in the law as *respondeat superior*, a Latin term meaning, roughly, "make the boss pay for it." It is *respondeat superior* that allows the injured party to sue the deep-pocket brewery when a shallow-pocket driver runs over the plaintiff with the beer delivery truck. Such is not the case with civil rights liability.

Under *Monell*, the governmental entity can be held liable *only* if the wrong is committed pursuant to either an official policy of the government or a "custom," even though the custom has not received formal approval through the governmental body's official decision-making channels. Thus, the entity may be held liable only when the injury is inflicted by a government's "lawmakers or by those whose edicts or acts may fairly be said to represent official policy."

The theory behind the *Monell* case is that the taxpayers should not be held liable merely because they have employed a wrongdoer. They should be held liable only if the wrong is attributable to the policy or custom of the governmental entity itself. For example, the parent of a special education student sued the Harris County Department of Education after her son choked on some food and died at the school. Tragic though the facts were, the Fifth Circuit summarily rejected the lawsuit, noting that there was no evidence that any school policy or custom was the actual cause of the student's death (*Lewis v. Igwe*, 2007).

The general rule is that employees who are constrained by policies that they do not have the authority to create or ignore are not "policy-makers" for the district. Thus the district can distance itself from the wrongful actions of those employees. Therefore, in the typical school district situation, it is very difficult to make the school district liable for the acts of principals, central office personnel, or even the superin-tendent. All of those officials make decisions that are constrained by policies not of their making; their decisions are subject to review by the school board; the school board has retained the authority to measure the official's conduct for conformance with board policy. The mere fact that the school board fails to investigate the basis for a principal's or superintendent's decision does not create liability for the district. Only when the board hears the matter and approves of the handling of it does the school district expose itself to potential liability.

Two decisions from the Fifth Circuit illustrate how these principles have been applied in the context of Texas education. Both cases involved the superintendent, the highest ranking school employee. In both cases the school district itself escaped liability.

The first case was brought by an employee who challenged his trans-fer from one position to another. The superintendent made the final call on the transfer, and the employee never appealed the superintendent's decision to the school board. Thus there was action by the superinten-dent, but no action by the school board. Can the school district be held liable? No. The court ruled that "Texas law is clear that final policy-making authority in an independent school district, such as DISD, rests with the district's board of trustees. . . . Nothing in the Texas Education Code purports to give the Superintendent any policymaking author-ity or the power to make rules or regulations, whether as to teacher or teacher/coach transfers or otherwise" (*Jett v. Dallas I.S.D.*, 1993).

The *Jett* case established the rule that in Texas, the school board alone enjoys "final policymaking authority," but that was in the con-text of the reassignment of an employee. Would the same rule hold in the case of a hiring decision? Consider the fact that the Education Code requires both superintendents and school boards to play a role in the hir-ing of professional staff. The superintendent recommends, and the board hires. The board cannot hire a person until that person is recommended by the superintendent. Does that mean that the superintendent is also a "policymaker"?

That was the issue presented by the second case, *Barrow v. Green-ville I.S.D.* (2007). This is a case in which a teacher claimed that she was denied promotion to an administrative position because she would not take her children out of a private school and enroll them in the public school. Among other claims, the teacher asserted that this violated her constitutional right as a parent to direct the upbringing of her children.

According to the teacher it was the superintendent and other administrators who informed her that she would not be recommended as long as her children attended private school. Thus the superintendent did not recommend her, and so the board never considered her for the job.

The trial court dismissed the constitutional claims against the district, but allowed certain other claims to go forward. Ultimately a jury ruled against the superintendent, but in favor of the district. The teacher appealed the decision, seeking to hold the district liable.

The Fifth Circuit ruled for the district, and in so doing, reaffirmed the basic principle that only the school board is a "policymaker" under Texas law. Liability of the district, as a governmental entity, attaches only when the wrongful act can be attributed to a "policymaker." The court concluded that Texas law made the board the "final policymaking authority," even in hiring decisions where the superintendent plays a crucial role.

It is clear, then, that the school district can be liable under Section 1983 only when the school board itself violates an individual's rights. Violations by teachers or administrators cannot be attributed to the school district, since they do not have "final policymaking authority" as that term has been defined in the controlling cases.

When the governing board takes official action, the "policymakers" have spoken. Thus the district can be liable for decisions made by the school board that violate a person's federally protected rights. A case involving a city contract illustrates. Oscar Renda Contracting was the low bidder on a project for the City of Lubbock. However, the city hired another firm. The Renda company sued, claiming that Lubbock had rejected it in retaliation for the fact that Renda had previously sued another city in Texas for violating its First Amendment rights. The Fifth Circuit held that these allegations presented a valid cause of action for First Amendment retaliation, and thus the case should not be dismissed (*Oscar Renda Contracting, Inc. v. City of Lubbock*, 2006).

Individual Liability

In a suit that seeks to impose liability on an individual, the plaintiff faces an additional obstacle—the defense of qualified immunity. This defense is not available to the school district. Governmental entities cannot avoid liability by claiming that they were acting in good faith (*Owen v. City of Independence*, 1980). If it is determined that a person's rights were violated pursuant to a policy or custom of the entity, includ-

404 EDUCATOR'S GUIDE TO TEXAS SCHOOL LAW

ing the acts of those identified by the court as being final governmental policy-makers, the entity itself is liable. The "But we meant well" defense does not work for the school district.

The law is different, however, for individuals who are sued in their individual capacities. Individual employees can escape personal liability by asserting and proving the defense of qualified immunity. The heart of the defense is this: "government officials performing discretionary functions generally are shielded from liability for civil damages insofar as their conduct does not violate clearly established statutory or constitutional rights of which a reasonable person would have known" (*Harlow v. Fitzgerald*). The Court declared that the judge may determine whether the law in question was clearly established at the time the employee acted. If the law at that time was not clearly established, an official cannot reasonably be expected to anticipate subsequent legal developments and cannot fairly be said to "know" that the law forbade conduct not previously identified as unlawful. If the law was clearly established, the immunity defense should fail, since a reasonably competent public official should know the law governing his or her conduct.

The theory behind this is great. In effect, this is a "knew or should have known" standard. For example, the right of students to refuse to salute the American flag has been "clearly established" since the 1943 Supreme Court case of *West Virginia State Board of Education v. Barnette*. Every school administrator should be aware of this. Suppose, then, that Patty Principal, acting in complete good faith as well as total ignorance of the *Barnette* case, were to suspend a student for refusing to salute the flag. The "qualified immunity" defense would not rescue Patty from personal liability. If it did, we would be rewarding ignorance among our educational leaders. Thus, school teachers and administrators are expected to have a basic understanding of what the law requires. In practice, however, the matter gets a lot murkier. Most cases are not as neat and clean as the flag-salute hypothetical.

An illustration of the application of the qualified immunity provision comes in the Supreme Court case of *Safford Unified School Dist. #1 v. Redding*. This case, discussed in more detail in Chapter 9, held that the strip search of a thirteen-year-old girl was a violation of the girl's constitutional rights under the Fourth Amendment. Eight of nine Justices agreed on that point, with Justice Thomas as the lone holdout. But seven of the nine, including Thomas, turned around and held that the assistant principal who ordered the search, Mr. Wilson, should not be held personally liable. Justices Stevens and Ginsburg dissented, but the other seven took the assistant principal off the hook.

At the time of Mr. Wilson's actions, it was "clearly established" that searches of students by school officials implicated the Fourth Amendment. It was clearly established that the search had to be "justified at its inception" and "reasonable in its scope." It was clearly established that the intrusiveness of the search would be measured "in light of the age and sex of the student and the nature of the infraction." So . . . was it "clearly established" that a strip search of a thirteen-year-old girl in pursuit of a few painkillers was unconstitutional? Seven of nine justices said "no."

The Court bolstered this conclusion by noting the wide spectrum of opinions of federal district court judges on the issue of strip searches. Some courts upheld strip searches of students suspected of concealing drugs (e.g., *Williams v. Ellington*, 1991). One case granted qualified immunity to a teacher and a police officer who conducted a group strip search of a fifth-grade class looking for $26 (*Thomas v. Roberts*, 2003). Justice Souter noted that "these differences of opinion from our own are substantial enough to require immunity for the school officials in this case."

Moreover, the Justices did not doubt Mr. Wilson's motives or his character: "In so holding [referring to the Court's conclusion that the search was unconstitutional], we mean to cast no ill reflection on the assistant principal, for the record raises no doubt that his motive throughout was to eliminate drugs from his school and protect students." The Court sympathized with what it perceived to be Mr. Wilson's overreaction: "Parents are known to overreact to protect their children from danger, and a school official with responsibility for safety may tend to do the same."

Morgan v. Swanson (2011) is a very important *en banc* Fifth Circuit case involving individual liability under federal law. *En banc* means that all the judges assigned to the circuit participate in deciding the case. This is just the latest ruling in long-running, and still pending, litigation over the distribution of religiously oriented materials in the elementary school setting in Plano I.S.D. The plaintiffs alleged that their children were not permitted to distribute gifts to their classmates at a holiday party because the gifts included religious messages. The plaintiffs alleged that this was a clear-cut case of viewpoint discrimination because the children were allowed to distribute all manner of gifts, but not anything that expressed a religious message. The suit was filed against the district, but also against two elementary school principals.

The principals sought qualified immunity. They argued that they did not violate clearly established law. Taking the allegations as true, which the court was required to do at this pretrial stage of the proceedings, the federal district court denied the request for qualified immunity. The panel of the Fifth Circuit affirmed that decision, holding that the principals could be held personally liable for damages.

The appellate court then granted an *en banc* review to this case, thus vacating the panel's decision. After considering numerous briefs and spirited oral argument, the full Fifth Circuit granted qualified immunity to the two principals, thus dismissing them from the case.

The key, according to the majority opinion, was that the law pertaining to the distribution of religious materials in school settings was not "clearly established." The court wrote: "When educators encounter student religious speech in schools, they must balance broad constitutional imperatives from three areas of First Amendment jurisprudence: the Supreme Court's school-speech precedents, the general prohibition on viewpoint discrimination, and the murky waters of the Establishment Clause. . . . The many cases and the large body of literature on this set of issues demonstrate a 'lack of adequate guidance,' which is why no federal court of appeals has ever denied qualified immunity to an educator in this area. We decline the plaintiffs' request to become the first."

The court held that the students had the constitutional right to distribute their religious materials in the school setting, and that the district had engaged in unconstitutional viewpoint discrimination. However, due to the murkiness of the law, the individual principals would not face personal liability. The "clearly established law" test is designed to ensure basic fairness. School administrators should not face personal liability based strictly on second-guessing by a court. They should be liable only if the law was so well and clearly established at the time that any decent administrator would have known what to do.

The defense of qualified immunity does not always work. Let us offer four cases to demonstrate that teachers, principals, superintendents, and school board members are all potentially liable. While teachers generally are not as knowledgeable of school law as are administrators, the courts expect classroom teachers to have a basic understanding of key concepts. Thus the defense of qualified immunity failed in the case of *Jefferson v. Ysleta I.S.D.* (1987). The facts alleged are unfortunate to say the least. Allegedly, a teacher tied a second grader named Jardine to a chair, using a jump rope and securing her by the waist and legs. During the first day Jardine was tied to the chair for the entire school day, except for the lunch hour. On the second day she was tied to the chair for protracted periods. While tied, Jardine was denied access to the bathroom. This treatment allegedly was not intended as punishment but, rather, as "an instructional technique." Jardine claimed damages, including humiliation, mental anguish, and an impaired ability to study productively.

The teacher raised the defense of qualified immunity, but the Fifth Circuit rejected that defense. The court stated that, in determining what a reasonable teacher should know, it is not necessary to point to a court case that is factually identical with the case in question. It suffices that a reasonable teacher be aware of general, well-developed principles. The court declared that a competent teacher should have known that to tie a second-grade student to a chair for an entire school day and for a substantial portion of a second day, as an educational exercise with no suggested justification, was constitutionally impermissible. The court concluded that a young student has a constitutional right not to be lashed to a chair through the school day and denied, among other things, the basic liberty of access to the bathroom when needed. The court found Jardine's constitutional right in the Fifth and Fourteenth Amendment rights to substantive due process, specifically her right to be free from bodily restraint.

The second case, involving a principal, is *Santamaria v. Dallas I.S.D.* (2006). This case involved allegations of racial discrimination in the assignment of students to particular classes in a D.I.S.D. elementary school. The court, after a full trial, found that the principal violated the equal protection clause of the Fourteenth Amendment and could be held liable personally. The court dismissed all claims against the district, the board of trustees, and the superintendent. It was the principal who had the power to assign students to classes. The court characterized the classroom assignments as "the result of intentional discrimination based on race or national origin." This not only violated D.I.S.D. policy, it violated the Constitution. Moreover, the qualified immunity defense did not work. The court observed that the law prohibiting segregation was clearly established, and that no reasonable school official could have believed that the actions of the principal were lawful.

In the third case, the Fifth Circuit rejected the qualified immunity defense of a superintendent in *Barrow v. Greenville I.S.D.*, discussed above. Recall that the teacher applied for a job as an assistant principal, but was told by the superintendent that she would not be considered for the job unless she took her children out of the private school they attended and put them in public school. The woman refused to comply with this request and was not considered for the job. She sued the superintendent in his individual capacity, and the superintendent asserted that he was entitled to qualified immunity. The Fifth Circuit rejected the superintendent's argument. The court cited earlier decisions that had established that public school employees have a constitutionally protected right to place their own children in private schools. The court held that a reasonable school administrator should have known that the school's practice violated the constitutional rights of the teacher.

This case is a good illustration of how slippery the notion of qualified immunity can be. Prior cases that established the right of public school employees to send their children to private schools had dealt with lower-level employees, such as a secretary. The superintendent in Greenville I.S.D. could have done a thorough review of case law on the subject without finding a single case in which such a policy was applied to administrators. As a general rule, courts have permitted the school district, as an employer, to impose certain conditions on the higher-level staff. So the superintendent's belief that the law on this subject was not "clearly established" was understandable. Nevertheless, the court held that the law was clearly established, and the superintendent should have known of it.

Qualified immunity was also denied in *Juarez v. Aguilar* (2011). The suit was filed by the chief financial officer in Brownsville I.S.D., alleging that board members retaliated against him for exercising his First Amendment rights by reporting alleged criminal activity to law enforcement authorities. The board members sought dismissal of the suit due to qualified immunity. At that stage of the proceedings, the court was required to assume that the allegations in the suit were true. That being the case, the court refused to dismiss the board members from the case. The plaintiff had alleged facts which, if proven true, would show that he suffered an adverse personnel action (nonrenewal of contract) because of his exercise of constitutional rights.

Qualified immunity certainly is no guarantee against individual liability. It is significant that the issue is not what the particular defendant knew about the law but, rather, whether there has been a violation of a well-settled right of which a *reasonable* person would have known. Public school employees frequently are exhorted to keep abreast of the law. That is good advice.

Furthermore, although this immunity is often referred to as a "good faith" immunity, the good motives of the defendant are not dispositive of the outcome. The test is not whether the educator meant well—it is whether the educator violated rules that are so clearly established that he or she should have known better. It is not a subjective test, but an objective one.

The defense, however, is of value to individuals who are sued. It is often said that the individual is not required to predict the future course of the law, and that is true. The individual school employee or trustee is entitled to escape any personal liability for damages if at the time of the action there was no well-settled principle of law to the contrary of which a reasonable person would have known.

When qualified immunity is asserted, the specific factual context will be important. For example, in *Wyatt v. Fletcher* (2013) two coaches were sued personally for allegedly disclosing to a parent that her daughter was a lesbian. The disclosure of this piece of information came in the context of a discussion with the mother about behavioral problems and concerns the coaches had, which led to their decision to suspend the girl from the softball team. The Fifth Circuit held that a right to privacy regarding one's sexual orientation was not "clearly established"—at least not where the disclosure was to the mother of a minor student in the context of a conference concerning disciplinary issues.

Personal Injuries and the Constitution

A person who sues the local school district or school official over a personal injury faces yet another problem that a typical plaintiff who falls down in a grocery store does not encounter. The person who sues under

§1983 must establish that he or she has suffered an injury that deprives the individual of federally protected rights.

State law is, by tradition and long-standing practice, the protector of broken arms and dented fenders. Until recently, suits involving §1983 concerned injured rights rather than injured bodies. Section 1983 suits generally involved deprivation of due process, freedom of speech, equal protection, or the right of privacy. Of late, however, attorneys have attempted to convert garden-variety personal injury suits into matters of constitutional law. And there has been some success. However, such suits must establish (1) that a constitutional right is involved; and (2) that the actions of school officials exceeded mere negligence.

Frequently the constitutional right cited is the right to work or attend school in a safe environment. But in a 1992 case the U.S. Supreme Court seemed to cool on the idea of city liability for injured workers, particularly in those cases where state law provides a remedy. In *Collins v. City of Harker Heights* (1992), the Court was faced with a case in which a widow alleged that her husband's death while working for the city was evidence of the city's violation of his right "to be free from unreasonable risks of harm." The widow alleged that the city showed deliberate indifference toward its employees in failing to train them for certain dangerous work assignments.

The Court rejected the notion that the Constitution imposes on local governments any affirmative duty to provide a safe and secure working environment. The Court indicated that the government takes on such a duty only when it has taken steps to deprive an individual of normal personal liberties. So the government does have a duty to protect the safety of prisoners and involuntarily committed mental patients. But city workers—and school employees—are there by choice and cannot use the Constitution to hold the government responsible for failing to provide a safe working environment.

What about children? Can the school be liable under federal law if it fails to provide a safe environment for students? This argument has not had much success in the public school context. The Supreme Court has ruled that the state takes on the duty to protect an individual whenever the state takes affirmative acts to restrain that person's freedom to act on his or her own behalf, through "incarceration, institutionalization, or other similar restraint of personal liberty" (*DeShaney v. Winnebago County Department of Social Services*, 1989). Thus the state clearly owes some duty of protection to prisoners and involuntarily committed mental patients.

State law requires students to attend school. Does this amount to a deprivation of normal personal liberties serious enough to warrant a constitutional right to a safe school environment? The pronouncement of the Fifth Circuit on that issue came in the case of *Walton v. Alexander*. The case involved a sexual assault of a student at the Mississippi

School for the Deaf by another student. The injured student alleged that the school had a duty to protect him from injuries inflicted by other students. Therefore, the argument went, the school and the superintendent were liable under Section 1983. The Fifth Circuit, sitting *en banc*, rejected that argument:

> But far more important for our purposes today, the record also reflects that Walton attended the school through his own free will (or that of his parents) without any coercion by the state. Although Walton's freedom was curtailed, it was he who voluntarily subjected himself to the rules and supervision of the School officials. Walton's willful relinquishment of a small fraction of liberty simply is not comparable to that measure of almost total deprivation experienced by a prisoner or involuntarily committed mental patient.

The court concluded that compulsory attendance laws do not create a duty to protect one student from another. The key discussion was contained in a footnote in which the court overruled one of its earlier cases:

> Prior to *DeShaney*, in *Lopez v. Houston Indep. Sch. Dist.*, [cite omitted], we found that a school bus driver was entrusted with the care of students attending school under the state's compulsory education statute. . . . Clearly, this is not the type of restraint on personal liberty nor the type of affirmative act by the state intended by *DeShaney*. To the extent the holding in *Lopez* is directly contrary to our holding today, as well as the holding in *DeShaney*, we overrule it.

Bear in mind that Walton was a student at a residential school, the Mississippi School for the Deaf. If the state has no legal duty to protect a child in that setting, it surely has no duty to protect a child in a regular public school, when the child goes home to her parents every night. Indeed, the dissenting opinion in the *Walton* case drew a stark picture:

> Following this decision, parents should be aware when the school bus doors close that if their child is sexually or physically assaulted, the driver of the bus has no constitutional duty to intervene, stop the assault, summon assistance, or attend to any injuries that may have been sustained. Under the majority's reasoning, he may with full knowledge of the assault be totally indifferent to it.

The *Walton* case is a good illustration of a situation where moral duties and legal duties do not coincide. The indifferent bus driver described by the dissent violates his moral duty, but not his legal duty. His actions lead to moral consequences, not legal judgments.

Despite the clarity of the *Walton* decision, the issue keeps coming up. In 2012, a frustrated Fifth Circuit, sitting *en banc*, noted its own "decades of binding precedent" regarding any "special relationship" that would create liability for the school district based on the wrongful acts of third parties. This was a case where a little girl was allegedly sexually assaulted by a man who was allowed to take her out of school during the day, even though he was not authorized by the parents to do so. The court held that there was no "special relationship" and therefore, no liability for the school (*Doe v. Covington County School District*).

If there is, then, no general duty to protect students while they are at school, does federal law provide any recourse for personal injuries? Yes, it does. But the plaintiff must prove (1) the deprivation of a federally protected right (2) for which the district itself should be accountable and (3) which involves a degree of culpability that exceeds mere negligence. These factors all come together in cases where a student is sexually molested or abused and school officials knowingly turn the other way.

A Federally Protected Right. The issue first arose in the context of Texas education in *Doe v. Taylor I.S.D.* (1994). The suit was based on a sexual relationship between a teacher/coach and a minor student. Rather than seeking redress under state law for assault or negligence of some sort, the student alleged that her constitutional rights had been violated. The student alleged that the Constitution protects her from physical sexual abuse at the hands of her teachers. The Fifth Circuit agreed with that argument, citing the "right to bodily integrity" as a constitutionally protected right. This opened the door to potential liability for the school district.

The District Itself Is Responsible. If a teacher molests or sexually abuses a student, the student's right to bodily integrity has been violated, but the basic rules of Section 1983 litigation continue to apply. That means that to hold the school district liable for the injury, the plaintiff must prove something beyond a poor hiring decision. There must be proof that someone who had the power to stop the abuse knew what was going on. A case from Conroe I.S.D. illustrates. A student in Conroe had a sexual relationship with her volleyball coach that lasted several years. Rumors about this reached an assistant principal in 1998. The assistant principal questioned the coach, but she denied any wrongdoing. The assistant principal cautioned the coach to maintain professional standards in her relationships with students. The student finally came forward with the truth in 2002, and one year later sued the school district, the assistant principal, and the coach.

The decision in this case does not tell us what happened with the suit against the coach, who had already pled guilty to sexual assault of a child. The issue before the court was the liability of the assistant principal and the school district. The court concluded that neither was legally responsible for what happened to the student. To impose liability on the district under Title IX, the student had to prove that a school employee with supervisory power over the coach had actual knowledge of the situation and responded with "deliberate indifference." The evidence fell short. The assistant principal had "supervisory responsibility," but he did not have actual knowledge of sexual misconduct. And his response to the rumors he heard could not be characterized as "deliberate indifference." The student alleged that the coach's mother, who was also a teacher in the district, had knowledge of the affair. But the court observed that as a teacher, the mother did not have "supervisory responsibility" over her daughter. Thus both the district and the assistant principal were dismissed from the case (*King v. Conroe I.S.D.*, 2005). This case is not reported in the official legal reports and does not serve as precedent. However, the decision is illustrative of some key points.

More Than Negligence. As noted in the Conroe case, the plaintiff also bears the burden of proving a level of culpability that exceeds negligence. "Deliberate indifference" is the standard as enunciated by the U.S. Supreme Court in *Daniels v. Williams* (1986). In *Daniels*, the plaintiff sued a deputy sheriff, alleging that, while an inmate, the plaintiff had slipped on a pillow negligently left on a stairway by the deputy. Plaintiff claimed that the alleged negligence deprived him of a liberty interest without due process in violation of the Fourteenth Amendment. The Supreme Court concluded, "To hold that injury caused by such conduct is a deprivation within the meaning of the Fourteenth Amendment would trivialize the centuries old principle of due process of law." Thus garden-variety negligence claims are not sufficient to impose §1983 liability. Instead, the injured party must establish "deliberate indifference" on the part of the defendant. This is difficult to prove.

Thus the door to liability is open, but not very wide. Plaintiffs who sue a school district under federal law for sexual misconduct by school employees face an uphill battle. A case in point is a 1993 Fifth Circuit decision involving an Ysleta I.S.D. teacher who was accused of sexually molesting a first grader. School officials had conducted a cursory investigation after two previous reports of the teacher's improper contact with students, such as letting them sit on his lap and putting his arm around their waists. Following the investigation, the school board decided to transfer the teacher to a different school rather than terminate the teacher's contract, as was customary in the district when instances of child abuse arose. The molestation occurred after the transfer. The parents of the student sued the school district in federal court, alleging that by not terminating the teacher, the district was deliberately indifferent to the student's welfare. The Fifth Circuit ruled that the district's transfer action constituted official policy under 42 U.S.C. §1983. The appeals court viewed the transfer decision to be "not only negligent but also inconsistent with the district's handling of other cases of suspected sexual abuse." However, because the board had not ignored the previous allegations but had ordered an investigation, the board was not deliberately indifferent to the welfare of its students when it made the transfer decision. Making a poor judgment call in matters of this nature may be viewed as negligent, but it is difficult to characterize such judgments as "deliberate indifference." On the other hand, doing nothing in the face of known facts could be construed as deliberate indifference, which could lead to liability (*Gonzalez v. Ysleta I.S.D.*).

Cases involving student injuries, of course, do not always revolve around sexual misconduct. In *Leffall v. Dallas I.S.D.* (1994), a student was shot and killed by random gunfire at a school-sponsored dance. The Fifth Circuit absolved the Dallas I.S.D. of any potential liability due to two critical factors. First, the death was not caused by a school official, but rather by the wrongful act of a third party who was not acting "under a badge of authority." In so holding, the court rejected the theory that the school district had a legal duty to protect students from other students, thus anticipating its later *en banc* decision in the *Walton* case. Second, the most that could be said of school officials in this case is that they were negligent, and that simply is not sufficient to impose liability under §1983.

A more mundane example of this arose in *Myers v. Troup I.S.D.* (1995), in which a football player allegedly was injured due to the negligence of school officials. The student asserted that school officials sent him back into the game five minutes after he was knocked unconscious, and that the school was negligent in doing so, particularly since the school had no medical personnel on the sidelines. The federal district court, citing its desire not to trivialize the Fourteenth Amendment, said: "Plaintiff's claims are grounded in negligence; they do not raise a constitutional question." Thus the case was dismissed from federal court.

Indeed, there are many cases that present disturbing fact situations that fall short of the "deliberate indifference" standard. One such case involved the death of a student after training activities for the basketball team. Perhaps school staff could have responded faster or more effectively when the girl collapsed, but there was no evidence of anyone's deliberate indifference (*Livingston v. DeSoto I.S.D.*, 2006). Likewise, when a first-grade boy was sexually abused by other students in the bathroom, none of the school staff could be described as deliberately indifferent (*A. v. Laredo I.S.D.*, 2007).

A New Theory. While it appears well settled that courts will not impose liability against a school district based on allegations of a "special relationship" between school and child, there is an emerging second theory that administrators should be aware of. This is the so-called "state-created danger" theory of liability. The idea is that if the state takes affirmative action to create a dangerous situation, to make a dangerous situation worse, or to leave an individual more vulnerable to existing dangers than he or she otherwise would have been, the state should be held liable for the individual's injuries even though the injury actually was inflicted by a private actor.

Some circuit courts recognize this theory of liability, while others do not. Our Fifth Circuit has danced around the issue. The confusion started in a case that arose from a tragedy well remembered by most readers of this book—the collapse of the Texas A&M Aggie Bonfire in 1999. The plaintiffs in the Bonfire case sought to impose liability for the deaths and injuries of numerous students on the university and some of its officials. The Fifth Circuit at first recognized the "state-created danger" theory as a valid basis for the lawsuit (*Breen v. Texas A&M University*, 2007). In fact, the court looked back at its 2003 ruling in the same case (*Scanlan v. Texas A&M University*) and declared that the theory was recognized then.

However, just three months after its 2007 decision, the Fifth Circuit simply announced that it was withdrawing and deleting the state-created danger section of its decision. To say that this left us all confused is an understatement. But in subsequent cases, the Fifth Circuit has continued to refuse to explicitly accept or reject the theory. The ruling in *Doe v. Covington*, discussed above, is typical. There, the court said that the allegations in the case "would not support such a theory."

What is clear, however, is that plaintiffs will continue to pursue liability under this theory until a court definitively rejects it. Thus school administrators must be aware of potential lawsuits and potential liability if a plaintiff can prove that the defendants (1) used their authority to create a dangerous environment for the plaintiff and (2) acted with deliberate indifference to the plight of the plaintiff.

Liability under Federal Statutory Law

Section 1983 is available to redress violations of the U.S. Constitution. If the suit alleges a violation of federal statutory law, a different analysis may apply. While liability of Texas school districts under each and every federal law is beyond the scope of this book, we will address the area that has generated the most litigation, which is sexual harassment, under Title IX.

The leading precedent on that issue comes from the U.S. Supreme Court itself, in a case arising in Texas. In *Gebser v. Lago Vista I.S.D.* (1998), a student sued the school district pursuant to Title IX, the federal statute that prohibits discrimination based on sex in institutions that receive federal financial assistance. The case involved a teacher-student sexual relationship, which school administrators did not know about at first. When they did find out about it, they took swift action to terminate the teacher's employment. Can the school district be held liable under these circumstances? The Supreme Court said no. The Court ruled that the student would have to prove that someone with the authority to correct the problem had actual knowledge of the teacher's misconduct and responded in a way that could be characterized as "deliberately indifferent." In effect, this imposes liability on the district itself based on the same standard that *Doe v. Taylor I.S.D.* applies to individual administrators.

The Supreme Court imposed similar standards, as well, when the harassment was from student to student. *Davis v. Monroe County Board of Education* (1999) arose from a fifth-grade classroom. The parent of a female student alleged that a fifth-grade student sexually harassed her daughter, that this went on for a long time, that school officials knew of it, and that they failed to stop it or otherwise respond appropriately. The Supreme Court, in a 5-4 decision, ruled that it was possible to impose liability on the school district in such a situation. The Court emphasized that the liability attaches not because one student harasses another, but rather, only if the school district wrongfully ignores it. Again, the student would have to prove that school officials were deliberately indifferent to known incidents of sexual harassment that effectively denied the student equal access to an educational program or activity. Furthermore, the harassment would have to be severe, pervasive, and "objectively offensive."

School district liability for violation of federal statutory law is not limited to sexual harassment cases. In 2003, the Supreme Court held that local governmental units could be held liable under the Federal False Claims Act. This was an attention-getter. The Act allows civil suits to recover federal funds obtained fraudulently. Penalties range up to $10,000 plus three times the amount of damages suffered by the federal government. When sued under this act, Cook County (Illinois) asserted that a county was not the type of entity that could be sued under this statute. The Supreme Court already had decided that states were not subject to suit under the Act. However, Cook County lost the argument. The Court held that counties and other units of local government can be sued and held liable under the Act (*Cook County v. United States ex rel. Chandler*, 2003). Thus a local school district that fraudulently obtains a federal grant could face penalties.

The Federal False Claims Act is in effect a whistleblower statute, permitting the person who exposes fraud to recover damages. But the plaintiff must be the "original source" of the information. Thus Mr. Fried lost his case against the West I.S.D., alleging fraud in the employment of retired educators for one day in order to qualify them for some Social

Security benefits. This practice was widely known and reported on before Mr. Fried blew the whistle, and thus he was not entitled to recovery (*United States ex rel. Fried v. West I.S.D.*).

SUMMARY

Texas public school educators have no immunity from violations of criminal law. However, insofar as civil damage suits are concerned, educators are shielded by state law from tort suits as long as they are acting in the scope of their duties and are exercising discretion. Only in disciplinary matters or in the operation, use, or maintenance of a motor vehicle are school professionals vulnerable to damage suits. All school officials should have a basic understanding of the notion of confidentiality of student records, but this is perhaps most important for the school counselor. School districts, under Texas law, are immune from tort suits except in matters involving motor vehicles.

There is an increase in cases brought under federal law, but plaintiffs carry a heavy burden of proof in those cases. Moreover, if they seek to impose liability on individuals, they must overcome the qualified immunity defense.

How to Find and
Read a Court Case

MOST LIBRARIES HAVE at least one of the three sets of volumes (called "reporters") containing the decisions of the U.S. Supreme Court. The official set, *United States Reports*, is printed by the U.S. Government Printing Office. The two commercial sets, *Supreme Court Reporter* and *Lawyers' Edition*, augment their coverage of Supreme Court decisions by adding headnotes, digests, and other material of importance to practicing attorneys and legal researchers. Both the official set and the *Supreme Court Reporter* are cited in the Index of Cases of this book, with the latter confined to recent cases that are not yet available in the official reporter.

The published decisions of the lower federal courts are usually available at larger libraries, including those at public and private universities and, of course, at law schools. The decisions of the federal courts of appeals can be found in the *Federal Reporter*. Federal district court decisions are printed in the *Federal Supplement*. The *Federal Appendix* includes judicial opinions of the U.S. courts of appeals that are not selected for official publication in the *Federal Reporter*. These "unpublished" decisions have lesser value as legal precedent but are considered "persuasive" authority.

The appellate decisions of Texas courts, along with the courts of several other states, can be found in the *Southwestern Reporter*, a set of volumes that is generally available in larger libraries. There also are regional reporters for the court decisions of other states.

Specific cases can be easily located once one knows how the citation system operates. Both federal and state cases are cited the same way. The citing pattern consists of the name of the case, the volume number, the name of the volume, page, and date—in that order. Thus, the U.S. Supreme Court decision *Tinker v. Des Moines School District*, the so-called black armband case, is cited 393 U.S. 503 (1969). This means that in volume 393 of the *United States Reports* the reader will find the case beginning on page 503. The two commercial reporters containing the decisions of the U.S. Supreme Court are abbreviated "S.Ct." for *Supreme Court Reporter* and "L.Ed." for *Lawyers' Edition*. The *Tinker* case citations to these volumes are 89 S.Ct. 733 and 21 L.Ed. 2d 731, respectively.

Recent federal courts of appeals decisions are cited as "F.3d," meaning they are printed in volumes of the *Federal Reporter* (3d series), while recent decisions of the federal district courts are cited as "F. Supp. 2d" for *Federal Supplement* (2d series). Cases reported in the *Federal Appendix* are often noted as "Fed. Appx." Recent Texas appellate court decisions are to be found in the *Southwestern Reporter* (3d series), abbreviated "S.W.3d" in citations.

In a case citation, the name appearing on the left is that of the initiator of the suit, or plaintiff, and the name on the right is that of the defendant. The adversarial character of our legal system is clearly evidenced by the "v." or "vs." appearing between the names, abbreviations for *versus*. Frequently, the order of the names will reverse on appeal, since, if the plaintiff wins in the trial court, the defendant (or now appellant) is the initiator of the appellate review action in this situation. In this event, the plaintiff becomes the appellee.

Once a case is located in a reporter, the reader will first be confronted with a brief syllabus of the opinion and a series of short headnotes. The latter are for the benefit of the legal researcher, as they call attention to important points of law reflected in the decision. Following the headnotes is the actual opinion of the court. And following the majority opinion may be one or more concurring and/or dissenting opinions. The concurring and dissenting opinions have no immediate value aside from setting forth the views of a particular judge or a group of judges. It is often said, however, that today's dissent may become tomorrow's majority opinion, so these should not be completely ignored.

Opinions are sometimes very readable and sometimes not. Much depends on the importance of the case, its complexity, and the judge's (or law clerk's) writing style. The lay reader will quickly see how influential precedent is in judicial decision-making, for judges repeatedly cite other cases, statutes, and secondary sources, such as law review articles and legal encyclopedias, to back up their points. The law is anchored by precedent; this keeps it from "lurching after the passing day's fancy," as one federal judge put it. Consistency and stability over time are the hallmarks of a sound legal system. Generally, lower court decisions tend to be shorter than those of higher courts—some recent opinions of the U.S. Supreme Court run over a hundred pages. The lay reader quickly develops the knack of skimming over the opinion first to see how it is laid out. Often, only a few pages or paragraphs will reflect the essence of the case—what the decision is and why the court decides it this way.

Readers should be aware that the law is never static. It is constantly growing and changing. Thus, the opinion one reads today may eventually be overturned on appeal to a higher court. Those skilled in legal research are well aware of the transitory nature of case law and will utilize techniques of legal research to track a case through the judiciary to determine its continuing validity and its influence on other courts. Fortunately, the development of computerized legal retrieval systems, such as Lexis and Westlaw, has made this job and the task of legal research in general much easier.

Lexis and Westlaw are the two primary subscription-based online research services for legal professionals in the United States. Lexis is part of Lexis-Nexis, an online database of content from legal documents and other printed sources such as magazines and newspapers. Westlaw is the online component of the West legal publishing company, a division of Thomson Reuters. Both services give subscribers unique access to case law, statutes, constitutions, administrative opinions, and other sources of state and federal law, all of which are electronically linked and searchable in a vast online library.

Cases on Lexis and Westlaw are organized in a format similar to cases in a reporter: The reader will first see the case title and citation, followed by a series of headnotes, then the opinion and any concurrences or dissents. In addition to the official reporter's citation, Lexis and Westlaw have their own systems of citing cases. In some instances a case will be retrievable on Westlaw or Lexis although it was never published in an official reporter. You will know when you have encountered one of these "unpublished" cases because only the Westlaw or Lexis citation is available. As with the appellate decisions found in the *Federal Appendix*, these cases are considered to have inferior legal value. Note that, just as in a reporter, the case headnotes are provided by the online publisher for the benefit of the legal researcher and are not issued or endorsed by a court of law.

In addition to Lexis and Westlaw, many websites containing legal materials can be accessed without a subscription. For example, Findlaw .com is a reliable source for state and federal case law, constitutions, and statutes. See Appendix C for additional sources.

Perhaps the greatest advantage of a computerized legal retrieval system is that the researcher can follow electronic links to research the history of a case or point of law. Thus, you can learn instantly whether a case is still good law, or whether it has been overturned or cited positively or negatively by another court. Lexis and Westlaw headnotes are also interactive; subscribers may click on highlighted text, which will lead to additional cases, or other resources, regarding the same topic.

One final word of advice. Do not be afraid to ask for help. Your time is too valuable to be spent wandering around a legal reference section or attempting to master the intricacies of a computerized legal retrieval system. You can speak to a librarian at the reference desk of a law library, or call a Westlaw or Lexis reference attorney if you subscribe to one of these services. If you are particularly shy or inclined toward doing it yourself, one handy paperback worth purchasing is Morris L. Cohen and Kent Olson's *Legal Research in a Nutshell.* The most recent edition includes instruction on how to access and use major online databases. Both Lexis and Westlaw also provide online tutorials for subscribers. Additional sources are listed in Appendix C.

Glossary of Legal Terminology

THE WORDS AND DEFINITIONS below are intended to help the lay reader better understand this guide, case reports, and other materials on school law. Only a few of the many terms related to law are included; for a more extensive list, consult Bryan A. Garner, ed., *Black's Law Dictionary, 4th Pocket Edition* (see Appendix C).

Amicus curiae: "Friend of the court"; a person or organization allowed to appear in a lawsuit, usually to file arguments in the form of a brief supporting one side or the other, even though not a party to the dispute.

Appellant: See *Plaintiff.*

Appellee: See *Defendant.*

Attorneys' fees: Refers to the practice of according the winning party's costs to the losing party in a civil case. The 1976 Civil Rights Attorneys' Fees Awards Act gives courts this power in civil rights suits.

Back pay: Lost wages that must be paid to employees who have been illegally discharged or laid off.

Cause of action: Facts sufficient to support a valid lawsuit.

Certiorari: A writ issued by a court asking the lower court to submit the record in a case, thus indicating the willingness of the higher court to entertain the appeal; "cert." for short.

Civil case: Every lawsuit other than a criminal proceeding. Most civil cases involve a lawsuit brought by one person against another and usually concern money damages.

Civil liberties: Fundamental individual freedoms that are constitutionally protected. Provisions listed in the Bill of Rights to the U.S. Constitution, such as freedom of speech and religious exercise, are considered civil liberties.

Civil rights: Rights that provide access to the legal system and equitable treatment before the law. Civil rights can be provided by a constitution or action of a legislative body. Thus, one is entitled to freedom from discrimination based on race, color, religion, sex, or national origin in public and private employment by provisions of Title VII of the 1964 Civil Rights Act.

Class action: A lawsuit brought by one person on behalf of himself or herself and all other persons in the same situation.

Code: A collection of laws. The Texas Education Code is a grouping of state statutes affecting education.

Common law: Law that develops by custom and is given expression through court rulings. Many student and teacher rights have developed this way, as has the tort of personal privacy invasion. Many common law principles have been incorporated into legislative enactments (statutes).

Compensatory damages: Damages that relate to the actual loss suffered by a plaintiff, as opposed to punitive damages.

Complaint: The first main paper filed in a civil lawsuit in federal court. It includes, among other things, a statement of the wrong or harm supposedly done to the plaintiff by the defendant and a request for specific help from the court. The defendant responds to the complaint by filing an "answer." The equivalent term in state court is "original petition."

Contract: An agreement that affects the legal relationship between two or more persons. To be a contract, an agreement must involve persons legally capable of making binding agreements, at least one promise, consideration (i.e., something of value promised or given), and a reasonable amount of agreement between the persons as to what the contract means.

Criminal case: A case involving crimes against the laws of the state; unlike in civil cases, the state is the prosecuting party.

De facto: "In fact, actual"; a situation that exists in fact, whether or not it is lawful. De facto segregation is that which exists regardless of the law or the actions of civil authorities (see also *De jure*).

Defamation: Impugning a person's character or injuring a person's reputation by false or malicious statements. This includes both libel and slander (see these terms).

Defendant (appellee): The person against whom a legal action is brought. This legal action may be civil or criminal. At the appeal stage, the party against whom an appeal is taken is known as the appellee. Usually, the appellee is the winner in the lower court.

De jure: "Of right"; legitimate; lawful, whether or not in actual fact. De jure segregation is that which is sanctioned by law (see also *De facto*).

De minimis: "Trivial, small, unimportant."

Dictum: See *Obiter dictum.*

Disclaimer: The refusal to accept certain types of responsibility. For example, a college catalog may disclaim any responsibility for guaranteeing that the courses contained therein will actually be offered, since courses, programs, and instructors are likely to change without notice.

Eminent domain: The power of states and local governments to take private property for public use. The power may be exercised for a public purpose only and requires fair compensation to the property owner.

En banc: The hearing of a case by an appellate court in which the full complement of judges rather than a small panel presides.

Expunge: Blot out. For example, a court order requesting that a student's record be expunged of any references to disciplinary action during such and such a time period means that the references are to be "wiped off the books."

Fiduciary: A relationship between persons in which one person acts for another in a position of trust. Some courts hold private schools to a fiduciary relationship with students and may intervene if the school has not acted fairly, as, for example, in expelling a student.

Forum: A place for communication. In the context of the First Amendment to the U.S. Constitution, a *public forum* means a place where First Amendment rights are almost unlimited in their scope, a *limited public forum* allows government some restriction over speakers and content of expression, and a *closed forum* refers to government property traditionally not open to public communication.

Grievance: An employee complaint concerning wages, hours, or conditions of work, i.e., literally anything connected with employment. A grievance system consists of steps by which an individual employee or a group of employees seeks a solution to a complaint. First, the grievance is brought to the attention of the employee's immediate superior. If no satisfactory adjustment is made, the employee may continue to appeal to higher levels. While virtually all collective bargaining contracts contain a grievance system, such systems are also increasingly part of organizational life whether or not a union is present, since they afford the means to channel and resolve disputes.

Hearing: An oral proceeding before a court or quasi-judicial tribunal.

Holding: The rule of law set forth in a case to answer the issues presented to the court.

Informed consent: A person's agreement to allow something to happen (such as surgery) that is based on a full disclosure of facts needed to make the decision intelligently. Certain types of student searches are best carried out with informed consent of the student being searched or the parents.

Infra: Later in the article or book. For example, *infra,* p. 235, means to turn to that page, which is further on. Opposite of *supra.*

Injunction: A court order requiring someone to do something or to refrain from taking some action.

In loco parentis: "In place of a parent"; acting as a parent with respect to the care, supervision, and discipline of a child. The development of student rights law has curtailed the common law *in loco parentis* powers of public school officials.

Ipso facto: "By the fact itself"; by the mere fact that.

Jurisdiction: Right of a court to hear a case; also the geographic area within which a court has the right and power to operate. Original jurisdiction means that the court will be the first to hear the case; appellate jurisdiction means that the court reviews cases on appeal from lower court rulings.

Jurisprudence: Philosophy of the law; the rationale for one's legal position.

Justiciable: Proper for a court to decide. For example, a justiciable controversy is a real dispute that a court may handle.

Law: Basic rules of order. Constitutional law reflects the basic principles by which government operates. Statutory law consists of laws passed by legislatures and recorded in public documents. Administrative laws are the decisions of administrative agencies, for example, a State Board of Education ruling. Case law consists of the pronouncements of courts.

Libel: Written defamation; published false and malicious written statements that injure a person's reputation.

Litigation: A lawsuit or series of lawsuits.

Mandamus: A court order commanding some official duty to be performed.

Mediation: The involvement of a neutral third party to facilitate agreement.

Moot: Abstract; for the sake of argument; not a real case involving a real dispute.

Negligence: A tort or civil wrong that involves failure to exercise reasonable care when one has a duty to do so and as a result someone or something is harmed. Different degrees of negligence trigger different legal penalties.

Obiter dictum: A digression from the central focus of a discussion to consider unrelated points; often shortened to *dictum.*

Parens patriae: The historical right of all governments to take care of persons under their jurisdiction, particularly minors and incapacitated persons. Thus, states have acted *parens patriae* in establishing public schooling systems for the benefit of all people within their borders.

Per curiam: An unsigned decision and opinion of a court, as distinguished from one signed by a judge.

Petitioner: The one bringing an action; similar to *plaintiff.* Opposite of *respondent.*

Plaintiff (appellant): The person who brings a lawsuit against another person. At the appeal stage, the person bringing the appeal is called the "appellant" and is usually the one losing in the lower court action.

Plenary: Complete or full in all respects.

Police power: The traditional power of governments to establish criminal laws and to enforce them.

Precedent: A court decision on a question of law that gives authority or direction on how to decide a similar question of law in a later case with similar facts. Ruling by precedent is usually conveyed through the term *stare decisis.*

Prima facie: Clear on the face of it; presumably, a fact that will be considered to be true unless disproved by contrary evidence. For example, a prima facie case is one that will win unless the other side comes forward with evidence to dispute it.

Punitive damages: Money awarded to a person by a court that is over and above the damages actually sustained. Punitive damages are designed to serve as a deterrent to similar acts in the future.

Quasi-judicial: Refers to the case-deciding function of an administrative agency. Thus, a school board is a quasi-judicial body when it holds a formal hearing on a teacher dismissal case.

Remand: To send back; for example, a higher court may send a case back to the lower court, asking that certain action be taken.

Res judicata: "A thing decided." Thus, if a court decides the case, the matter is settled and no new lawsuit can be brought on the same subject by the same parties.

Respondent: The party responding to an action; similar to *defendant.* The opposite of *petitioner.*

Right to work: The term used to apply to laws that ban union-security agreements, such as the union shop, by rendering it illegal to make employment conditional on membership or nonmembership in a labor organization. Unions are particularly opposed to these state laws because they allow "free riders"—those who share in the collective benefit but pay nothing for it.

Sectarian: Of or relating to religion or a religious sect.

Secular: Of or relating to worldly concerns; opposite of *sectarian.*

Slander: Oral defamation; the speaking of false and malicious words that injure another person's reputation, business, or property rights.

Sovereign immunity: The government's freedom from being sued for money damages without its consent. At present, Texas school districts enjoy a kind of sovereign immunity from most damage suits involving torts under state laws, for example, negligence.

Standing: A person's right to bring a lawsuit because he or she is directly affected by the issues raised.

Stare decisis: "Let the decision stand"; a legal rule that, when a court has decided a case by applying a legal principle to a set of facts, the court should stick by that principle and apply it to all later cases with clearly similar facts unless there is a good, strong reason not to. This rule helps promote fairness and reliability in judicial decision-making and is inherent in the American legal system (see also *Precedent*).

State action concept: For the Fourteenth Amendment of the U.S. Constitution to apply to a given situation, there must be some involvement by a state or one of its political subdivisions. A public school falls into the latter category. Wholly private action is not covered by the Fourteenth Amendment. Thus, private schools and colleges, like corporate organizations and private clubs, are not subject to its strictures.

Statute: A law enacted by a legislative body.

Summary judgment: A decision for one side in a lawsuit rendered on the pleadings and before the trial begins.

Supra: Earlier in an article or book. For example, *supra*, p. 11, means to turn to that page, which appeared earlier. Opposite of *infra*.

Tort: A civil wrong done by one person to another. For an act to be a tort, there must be a legal duty owed by one person to another, a breach of that duty, and harm done as a direct result of the action. Examples of torts are negligence, battery, and libel. Texas school districts are immune under state law from most nonconstitutional tort damage suits, but they are not immune from damage claims resulting from the deprivation of a constitutional or federal statutory right. Texas public school professional employees also enjoy substantial immunity from nonconstitutional tort damage suits.

Trial: A process occurring in a court in which opposing parties present evidence, subject to cross-examination and rebuttal, pertaining to the matter in dispute.

Trial de novo: A completely new trial ordered by a judge or appeals court.

Ultra vires: Going beyond the specifically delegated authority to act; for example, a school board that is by law restricted from punishing students for behavior occurring wholly off campus acts *ultra vires* in punishing a student for behavior observed at a private weekend party.

Waiver: The means by which a person voluntarily gives up a right or benefit. To be valid, waivers have to be worded very carefully. Thus, in a case where a parent is asked to sign a waiver absolving the school or teacher from liability in the event of an accident to his or her child on a field trip, the waiver must make it clear what the parent is giving up, for example, the right to sue *even if* the school or teacher is negligent. Some courts have ruled that, even if parents sign such a knowing waiver, the child may recover damages in his or her own right. The services of an attorney are best secured in drawing up waivers.

Reference Sources

THE FOLLOWING MATERIALS will provide more information about topics discussed in this volume. Some are designed for the lay reader, while others require a trip to the library and the assistance of a librarian.

TRADITIONAL/PRINT RESOURCES

Cohen, Morris L., and Kent Olson. *Legal Research in a Nutshell*, 11th ed. Eagan, Minn.: Thomson West, 2013. Excellent paperback for the layperson who wishes to learn how to use a law library or computerized legal research system. Order from the West website at http://www.west.thomson.com.

Garner, Bryan A., ed. *Black's Law Dictionary, 4th Pocket Edition*. Eagan, Minn.: Thomson West, 2011. This is the condensed, paperback edition of the well-known, comprehensive *Black's Law Dictionary*. It is an excellent simplified resource for school district personnel who work with legal materials and attorneys. Order from West (see Cohen and Olson entry).

Kemerer, Frank R., and John A. Crain. *The Texas Documentation Handbook*, 5th ed. (2011). The handbook provides a detailed discussion of the mechanics of effective documentation for employee appraisal, nonrenewal, and termination. Included are sample forms, including a series of focused observation instruments for targeted classroom data-gathering. Available from the publisher of the *Texas School Administrators' Legal Digest* (see this reference below).

Ogonosky, Andrea. *The Response to Intervention Handbook*. Austin, Tex.: Park Place Publications, 2008. *Response to Intervention for Secondary School Administrators*. Austin, Tex.: Park Place Publications, 2009. *Response to Intervention Documentation Handbook*. Austin, Tex.: Park Place Publications, 2011. In these step-by-step guides, an educational consultant and school psychologist shows educators how to implement RtI in a three-tier process that is time- and cost-efficient. Available from the publisher of the *Texas School Administrators' Legal Digest* (see this reference below).

Texas Digest 2d.* Eagan, Minn.: Thomson West. A multivolume reference source on Texas federal and state case law. Look up "Schools
and School Districts" in the appropriate volume; consult pocket
parts at the rear of the volume for recent cases. Available at larger
libraries.

Texas Register. A weekly state publication containing information
about various facets of state government, including announcements
of administrative rules, attorney general opinions, executive orders
of the governor, bills introduced into the legislature, and other information of value to the public. Available at larger libraries, the
Register is also posted online on the website of the Texas Secretary
of State, at http://www.sos.state.tx.us/texreg/index.shtml.

Texas School Administrators' Legal Digest. This monthly legal periodical features articles written by leading Texas attorneys and commentators, as well as summaries of court rulings, commissioner's
decisions, special education hearings, and attorney general opinions
affecting Texas education. The *Legal Digest* also offers a series of law
charts and DVDs that describe legal requirements in complex areas.
For information contact *Texas School Administrators' Legal Digest*
staff by phone at 512-478-2113 or e-mail at info@legaldigest.com,
or visit the *Legal Digest* website at http://www.legaldigest.com.

Texas School Law Bulletin. Eagan, Minn.: Thomson West, latest edition. This large paperback is a Texas Education Agency–sponsored
collection of Texas statutes directly affecting education. Published
biennially. About half of the book is devoted to the Texas Education Code. It is the single best print source for statutory information short of visiting a law library. Many schools make the *Bulletin*
routinely available to principals; it also is a standard feature of most
school law courses taught in the state. Its chief limitation is that it
does not contain administrative rules, decisions by administrative
agencies, or court rulings. One should be cautious about relying
on the wording of statutes alone, since they are subject to interpretation by administrative agencies and courts. Available from
the Publications Distribution Office, Texas Education Agency; call
512-463-9744 or e-mail pubsdist@tea.state.tx.com.

Vernon's Texas Statutes and Codes Annotated* (Education Vols. 1–4).
Eagan, Minn.: Thomson West. This multivolume source contains
the provisions of the Texas Education Code and supplements them
with interpretive case law, attorney general opinions, and legal
commentary. Be sure to consult the pocket parts for recent developments; available at larger libraries.

Walsh, Jim. *The Common Sense Guide to Special Education Law,*
2d Ed. Austin, Tex.: Park Place Publications, 2012. A brief and accessible guide to conformity with the law, aimed at educators and
administrators who deal with the day-to-day reality of serving stu-

dents with special needs. Available from the publisher of the *Texas School Administrators' Legal Digest.*

* These volumes can also be accessed and searched online through Westlaw.

ONLINE RESOURCES

Family Policy Compliance Office:
http://www.ed.gov/policy/gen/guid/fpco/index.html

FERPA Online Library:
http://www.ed.gov/policy/gen/guid/fpco/ferpa/library/index.html

Findlaw:
http://www.findlaw.com
A free online searchable database of state and federal law, including cases, constitutions, and statutes.

National School Boards Association:
http://www.nsba.org/
Material regarding school governance, board policy, and other issues relevant to public school boards. Click on "School Law" to subscribe to "Legal Clips," a free weekly e-mail newsletter with summaries of recent cases and other developments in education.

No Child Left Behind:
http://www.ed.gov/nclb/landing.jhtml

Office of the Attorney General:
http://www.oag.state.tx.us/
Links to the most recent versions of the state *Open Meetings Act Handbook* and *Public Information Act Handbook.* Also includes Attorney General's *Nepotism Laws Handbook* and 2012 *Texas Ethics, Gifts and Honorarium Laws Made Easy.*

Special Ed Connection:
http://www.specialedconnection.com
Subscription-based service for special education case law, regulations, statutes, and more operated by LRP Publications.

Special Education Rules and Regulations in Texas:
http://www.tea.state.tx.us/index2.aspx?id=2147497444

State Bar of Texas School Law Section:
http://www.schoollawsection.org

State Board for Educator Certification:
http://www.tea.state.tx.us/index4.aspx?id=3461

Teacher Retirement System:
http://www.trs.state.tx.us/

Texas Administrative Code:
http://info.sos.state.tx.us/pls/pub/readtac$ext.viewtac
Link to the most current Texas regulations, including Title 19, Education.

Texas Association of School Boards:
http://www.tasb.org

Texas Commissioner Hearing Decisions:
http://ritter.tea.state.tx.us/commissioner/

Texas Constitution:
http://www.constitution.legis.state.tx.us/

Texas Legislature Online:
http://www.legis.state.tx.us/

Texas Special Education Due Process Hearing Decisions:
http://www.tea.state.tx.us/index2.aspx?id=6728

Texas State Library and Archive Commission Local Schedule SD:
http://www.tsl.state.tx.us/slrm/recordspubs/sd.html
Retention schedule for records of public school districts.

Texas Statutes, including Texas Education Code:
http://www.statutes.legis.state.tx.us/
This site contains links to current Texas statutes and a free search engine, enabling the user to search across all Texas statutes or in one specific code.

United States Court of Appeals for the Fifth Circuit:
http://www.ca5.uscourts.gov/

United States Department of Education IDEA site:
http://idea.ed.gov/

United States Department of Education Office of Special Education Programs (OSEP):
http://www.ed.gov/about/offices/list/osers/osep/index.html
Links to guidance, publications, and policy documents.

United States Supreme Court:
http://www.supremecourtus.gov/
Official site of the U.S. Supreme Court, this site includes full-text opinions, transcripts of oral arguments (beginning with October 2006, made available on the same day as oral argument; past transcripts archived from 2000), and other court-related information.

Also see www.scotusblog.com for news, information, and commentary related to the Court.

University Interscholastic League:
http://www.uiltexas.org/
UIL constitution, contest rules, and booster club policy.

Index of Cases

Index of Topics